A GUIDE TO CARE OF THE ELDERLY

(55 Contributors from UK, India, USA, Singapore and Australia)

EDITORS:

Dr R B Shukla MD, FRCPI
Consultant Physician
Department of Medicine for the Elderly
North Manchester General Hospital
Central Drive
Crumpsall
Manchester
M8 6RL
Tel: 0161-720-2789

and

Dr D Brooks MD, FRCGP, D.obst., DRCOG
General Practitioner
Peterloo Medical Centre
133 Manchester Old Road
Middleton
Manchester
M24 4DZ
Tel: 0161-643-5005

आयुषायुःकृतां जीवायुष्मान् जीव मा मृथाः
प्राणेनात्मन्वतां जीव मा मृत्योरुदगा वशम् ा

Die not, O men, live on to a ripe old age,
Live with a heroic spirit
Equipped with strong will-power
and submit not to the fear of death. — *Atharva Veda (19-27-8)*

D1333379

London: HMSO

ISBN 0 11 701830 9

AGED
HEALTH SERVICES FOR THE AGED
GERIATRICS
COMMUNITY CARE

WT 100
HU 300.

Published by HMSO and available from:

HMSO Publications Centre
(Mail, fax and telephone orders only)
PO Box 276, London SW8 5DT
Telephone orders 0171 873 9090
General enquiries 0171 873 0011
(queuing system in operation for both numbers)
Fax orders 0171 873 8200

HMSO Bookshops
49 High Holborn, London WC1V 6HB
(counter service only)
0171 873 0011 Fax 0171 831 1326
68–69 Bull Street, Birmingham B4 6AD
0121 236 9696 Fax 0121 236 9699
33 Wine Street, Bristol BS1 2BQ
0117 9264306 Fax 0117 9294515
9–21 Princess Street, Manchester M60 8AS
0161 834 7201 Fax 0161 833 0634
16 Arthur Street, Belfast BT1 4GD
01232 238451 Fax 01232 235401
71 Lothian Road, Edinburgh EH3 9AZ
0131 228 4181 Fax 0131 229 2734
The HMSO Oriel Bookshop
The Friary, Cardiff CF1 4AA
01222 395548 Fax 01222 384347

HMSO's Accredited Agents
(see Yellow Pages)

and through good booksellers

Chapter List and Contributors

© Raghu B Shukla/David Brooks 1995
Applications for reproduction should be made to the editors
First published 1996

ISBN 0 11 701830 9

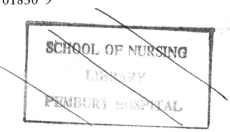

Contents

Section A: Foundations of Elderly Care

Section B: Common Medical Problems in the Elderly

Chapter 11
Multi-disciplinary
Management of Falls in
the Elderly

Dr Douglas MacMahon
Consultant Physician with special responsibility
   for the elderly
Barncoose Hospital
Redruth
Cornwall TR15 3ER

Chapter 12
Dyspnoea

Dr Martin Connolly
Senior Lecturer in Geriatrics
Barnes Hospital
Kingsway
Cheadle
Stockport SK8 2NY

Chapter 13
Psychology of Ageing

Dr E Stirling
Consultant Psychologist
Tayside Clinical Psychology Department
Royal Dundee Liff Hospital
Dundee DD2 5NF
Scotland

Chapter 14
Sexuality in the Elderly

Dr Ivor L Felstein
Senior Hospital Medical Officer
Department of Medicine for the Elderly
Bolton General Hospital
Minerva Road
Farnworth
Bolton BL4 0JR

Chapter 15
Nutrition in the Elderly

Dr A K Banerjee
Consultant Physician
Department of Medicine for the Elderly
Bolton General Hospital
Minerva Road
Farnworth
Bolton BL4 0JR

Chapter 16
Dental Care of the
Elderly

Professor R Yemm, Dr J R Drummond & Dr
   J P Newton
Department of Dental Prosthetics & Gerontology
University of Dundee
Park Place
Dundee DD1 4HN
Scotland

Section C: Some Important Specific Diseases

Section D: Development and the Wider Picture

*This book is dedicated
to our parents*

A Guide to Care of the Elderly

Editors:

Dr R B Shukla MD, FRCPI
Consultant Physician
Department of Medicine for the Elderly
North Manchester General Hospital
Crumpsall
Manchester
M8 6RL
Tel: 0161-720-2789

Dr David Brooks MD, FRCGP, D.obst, DRCOG
General Practitioner
Peterloo Medical Centre
133 Manchester Old Road
Middleton
Manchester
M24 4DZ
Tel: 0161-643-5005

Preface

The ever-increasing number of elderly people is a real challenge to those of us who are engaged in caring for them. Indeed, their care will form the bulk of medical care in the decades ahead. This book has been composed with this in mind. However, when a new book emerges, usually three questions are asked: what is the book all about? why this book?, and what is its readership?

The Book Itself

Although this is not meant to be a text book of Geriatric Medicine, great care has been taken to include important and wider aspects of the care of elderly patients. The book has 39 chapters and it is divided into four sections. Where possible, each chapter starts with an objective setting and ends with Practical Points.

Section A. As more than 90 per cent of elderly people live in the community, this section emphasises the community aspect of elderly care. The introductory chapter provides an overview of the care of the elderly in this country. The section also deals with all-important background information about elderly people, ie, demography and age-related changes in various systems.

Section B. This section deals with the important general medical problems which are usually dealt with by a multi-disciplinary team. Arguably this is the most important section and hence is the main body of the book.

Section C. The management of some specific diseases in elderly people need special expertise. Only selected topics have been included under this section.

Section D. New ideas in the management of patients, research and audit are catalysts for improving medical care. This innovative section contains articles which fulfill these requirements.

Why This Book?

In the new National Health Service, collaboration between hospitals and the community is going to be at the heart of services for the elderly. This is exemplified by the amalgamation of Health Authorities and Family Health Services Authorities. We, therefore, feel that there is a need for a book like ours, which is edited jointly by a Consultant Geriatrician and a General Practitioner. We have tried to include several topics which have received scant or no attention in the available texts on the subject. The contributors are well known in their area of expertise and most of them have had their work published before. To reflect the widest possible views and experiences, contributors have been drawn, apart from a few from overseas, from the length and breadth of the United Kingdom – from Dundee to Southampton and Cardiff to Cambridge – and besides doctors, they represent other relevant disciplines such as the Law and the Social Services. At any rate, we sincerely hope that this book will prove to be a useful addition to the existing texts.

Readership

There is a new and well-defined readership – Senior House Officers and General Practitioner Trainees. In the United Kingdom, the bulk of the care of the elderly is provided and/or supervised by General Practitioners. At any one time in this country there are about 1,000 General Practitioner Trainees in post and 2,000 Senior House Officers preparing for a career in general practice. There is, therefore, a large and continuing need for a concise book which achieves a synthesis between the general characteristics of ageing and specific health care problems in the aged. This is what this book aims to provide. As many doctors often sit the Diploma in Geriatric Medicine (approximately 200 candidates sit annually), it will be found useful for that examination too. Of course, other hospital doctors and General Practitioners and indeed all those connected with care of the elderly, including Senior Nurses, will benefit from this book.

We thus hope that this book, which has taken well over 5 years to develop, will particularly help Senior House Officers and young General Practitioners in dealing with the challenges of looking after elderly patients. It is also our wish that other doctors concerned with the care of the elderly patients will find this book useful.

We have been assisted by many people in the development and production of this book.

We are very grateful to Professor Peter Millard, Professor of Geriatric Medicine, St George's Medical School, London and Dr Arup Banerjee, Consultant Physician in the Department of Medicine for the Elderly, Bolton General Hospital, for their help and encouragement at all stages of this book's development. Help, when needed at a critical stage, came from Professor David Metcalfe, Professor (Emeritus) of General Practice, University of Manchester and Sir Michael Drury, Professor (Emeritus) of General Practice, University of Birmingham and Chairman, Age Concern England. We are also grateful to Professor Raymond Tallis, Professor of Geriatric Medicine, University of Manchester and Professor Grimley Evans, Professor of Geriatric Medicine, University of Oxford, for their helpful suggestions during the earlier stages of the book's development.

We also thank our colleagues for their support and continuing encouragements during the preparation of this book and to Dr T M Pathrose for his help with proof reading.

We thank the Examinations Department, Royal College of Physicians of London, for providing us with details of the Diploma in Geriatric Medicine examination.

We, of course, thank all the contributors as, without their contributions, this book would not have seen the light of day.

We are grateful to our respective secretaries Lisa Churchman and Lynne Coyne, for their unflinching secretarial assistance.

Finally, our sincere thanks to the Publishers, HMSO Books, and their Publishing Officer, Mr Chris Stone, who has been extremely helpful and supportive during the publication of this book.

Manchester, England   R B SHUKLA
January 1996   D BROOKS

Section A

Foundations of Elderly Care

Chapter 1

Introduction

Professor Sir Michael Drury, OBE, FRCP, FRCGP, FRACGP
Chairman, Age Concern, England
Astral House
1268 London Road
London
SW16 4ER

Biosketch:

Prof. Drury is Emeritus Professor of General Practice, The University of Birmingham, past President RCGP, past member GMC, SCOPME, CSM etc. His research interests are in Therapeutics and the Organisation of Practice. Author of seven books on Drug Therapy, General Practice, Practice Management and the training of Practice Nurses, Practice Managers and Receptionists. He has research papers on all these topics. He is currently Chairman of Age Concern, England and is involved with four other charities.

Introduction

The illnesses of older people typically present with multiple problems and a complex interrelationship between social and medical issues. Medical students and young doctors learning how to manage ill health in older people tend to concentrate upon diseases and, whilst such knowledge is very important, there is no group of patients for whom a holistic attitude to care is more necessary. This chapter takes a wide view of some of the issues facing doctors in the care of the older person. It will paint upon a broad canvas to convey some of the changes occurring in society and some of the changes in attitudes that are required of carers. It will show that care of the older person is not the prerequisite of Geriatric Medicine, however much we have to learn from their special expertise, but is something in which every doctor must be proficient.

The increased number of older people is now a well recognised fact. The number in all age groups will increase over the next forty years and there will then be more than 12 million people over the age of 65. In 1950 the number of centenarians receiving a telegram from the Queen was just a few hundred, this year there will be more than 4,000 recipients. It is not that the life span of humans has changed. This has altered little over thousands of years, but the number living into older age has increased steadily. Centenarians were identified in Roman times and the health problems besetting older people have changed very little over the centuries. Hippocrates in 400 BC wrote that *old men suffer from difficulty in breathing, catarrh accompanied by coughing, strangury, difficult micturition, pain at the joints*" and so on and most observers would regard this as quite an accurate description of disease in the elderly today. The facts are that the proportion of people living into this area of problems has increased. The change in the population is not due to people living longer but because less people die prematurely. It is, therefore, a success story and should be recognised as such. The fact that more of our work is involved with this age group should be a source of great and increasing satisfaction and not a problem to be regretted. In the Middle Ages men became of age at 15 but very few lived to experience the joy of seeing their grandchildren born and grow into a new generation.

The implications of these changes upon the pattern of life of all of us are not so well recognised. There will, of course, be more dependent people in the community in proportion to independent wage earners. This means that old patterns of work, old systems of housing and attitudes to age have to alter. The skills and experience of older people will have to be used. Currently most men retire at the age of 65 and women five years earlier. The pension is geared to this, benefits such as cheap travel and reduced entry charges tend to apply from this age, few are able to work on beyond this time and those who do are sometimes seen as workaholics. In the future undoubtedly people who are able to work longer will be encouraged to do so and this will require changed attitudes and changes in systems such as taxation. Some will be paid work and some voluntary, but it is likely to be to the benefit of society and the individuals and, therefore, to be encouraged. There will also, of course, be a need for more health care. Already approximately half of all the hospital facilities are used by people over the age of 65. One third of all the resources of primary care and one quarter of all prescriptions written are consumed by pensioners. The proportions of people with chronic disease and multiple pathology and, therefore, the highest consumers from the resources will increase as the years go by. While this can be viewed with foreboding, it can also be seen as a great opportunity to think and act differently; to utilise resources not previously put to use; to devise different styles of life; and to set about adding value to the third of life regarded as 'old age'.

One challenge will be to mobilise the skills and experience of older people themselves in a way that both contributes to the well-being of them and society and minimises preventable morbidity. This requires a change in attitude to ageing and a recognition that older people need change, work, stimulation, excitement and even risk to get the best out of life.

Most elderly people are healthy in both body and mind and lead independent unsupported lives. Many 90 year old people fall into this category and can rightly be described as the biologically elite. Not all are, but how do we work to maximise this number? Out of 10,000 people over the age of 65, currently 9,928 are to be found living in their own homes or in homely settings. But out of 10,000 people who have reached the age of 90, more than half will be in institutions: half of them in hospital and the remainder in private or local authority care.

There has been a huge increase in private residential and nursing homes subsidised by the public purse. The cost has risen from £10 million in 1979 to more than £1,000 million in 1989.

Attitudes to Older People

There is little doubt that elders were valued more by previous generations than is the case today. The term geriatric was coined by I L Nascher[1] in an article in the New York Medical Journal in 1909. In this article he argued that there was a special branch of medicine with different anatomical features, physiological functions, diseases and treatment needed. He suggested the name for it and a period of special training. This was an important advance at the time, but more recently the term 'geriatric' has become a pejorative word of abuse, associated with very negative concepts of senility and loss of independence. To take this further, M K Thompson[2] described how the aged are seen as avid consumers, not so much of material goods but of social and institutional services, and it is true that societies' model of older people is generally negative and disparaging. Yet in studies looking at what are usually regarded as the normal characteristics associated with ageing, such as increased levels of neurosis, neglect of personal hygiene, increased drug taking and negative view of life, young students have shown even higher scores in every category than older people.

The Attitudes of Older People

It is often held that the process of ageing leads to negative values in older people themselves, but even if this is partially true it is undoubtedly exaggerated by the way in which attitudinal studies have been designed. Bennett and Ebrahim[3] pointed out that a study of the current health attitudes of older people will show a preoccupation with bowel habits and worry about insomnia. With the middle aged group, there will be found increased anxiety with indigestion and the need to take medication for this, whereas the young are more convinced of the need to take high fibre diets and vitamin supplements in order to remain healthy. What is almost certain is that these attitudes reflect the cultural norms different groups grew up with and therefore, carried into

older age. In twenty years time indigestion will be the preoccupation of the elderly and in forty years dietary supplements. These do not represent a change in beliefs as one grows older but part of the baggage we carry through life. Cross sectional studies may throw up a lot of similar behavioural characteristics associated with an age group which can be contrasted with other ages but following a cohort through a longer period of time, is likely to paint a truer picture.

The lives of younger people are thought most commonly to be associated with gain. The acquisition of partners, children, increasing income, job status and a widening range of choice of leisure activities, holidays and travel are characteristics sought after by most people in their twenties and thirties and are seen as gains. From the age of 60 onwards loss is seen as the predominant characteristic: a loss of status either as the bread winner for a family or as the carer upon whom a family is dependant; loss of a partner and friends; loss of health leading to less mobility; and independance and thus the ability to control one's own environment; and loss of intellectual and mental stimulation. There is, of course, some truth in these stereotypes but lives are seldom all one thing or another. All ages have their losses and gains. Young people may feel and regret the loss of support and protection from parents and schools and the loss of innocence. Increasing income is often accompanied by increased debt as aspirations outrun resources. Older people may feel the gain derived from having to compete less, having more time to think and look back on life's achievements and more time to spend on personal relationships and may find that resources meet aspirations better. Many older people also find it much easier and comfortable to talk openly about, and prepare for, death.

It is valuable here to recognise the importance that reminiscence and recall have to older people, particularly those with handicaps such as hearing or speech difficulties, depression or dementia and for persons from different countries and cultures. Reminiscence preserves the cultural heritage, encourages feelings of self-worth, can alter carer's understanding and assists the process of life review. Training in reminiscence work[4] can be a valuable skill for carers.

Ageing

An important component of successful ageing is to be found in the capacity of the individual to adapt, – adaptation to changes in bodily function, to relationships and to changes in expectations and resources. This ability very much depends upon a positive attitude to this period of life amongst older people and those who care for them. It is important here to recognise the heterogeneity of the individuals within the group known as 'older people'. We have to avoid placing older people within the sterotype selected by the doctor or nurse especially for those people who are cared for in institutions. Doing this can be particularly demeaning and de-personalising and the use of collective nouns, such as 'the aged' or 'the elderly' should be avoided wherever possible, in the same way as we are now taught to avoid classifying people as 'asthmatics' or 'hypertensives' and to think of, and refer to, individuals with asthma or with hypertension. It is not just a matter of semantics. Categorising leads us into the sin of ageism as we can be lead insidiously into racism.

An older person may not be able to carry out all the activities required for daily independent life, but those that can be achieved should be assiduously maintained and for those that cannot be mastered, but which are among the priorities of the individual, adaptation should be sought. We are familiar with the concepts of bringing the bath or the hairdresser to those who cannot visit them unaided. We are less open to ideas of bringing the pub, the shop or the entertainment to the hospital or the nursing home. These concepts have to be tempered by the realisation that for some people the 'rocking chair' syndrome will suit best.

Care in the Community

Care of the older person constitutes the best example of the absolute need for a seamless medical and social service. The problems of older people are usually multiple, both medical and social and these are interdependent on each other. The difficulties posed by this pattern of need were the driving force behind the NHS and Community Care Act of 1990[5]. This seeks to promote the development of services within the home, to provide practical support for carers, to make assessment a key feature and to do all this in a mixed economy of public and private services.

Many of the changes in society over the past half century have been detrimental to older people. In the first half of the century there was a relative excess of younger females largely due to the high mortality of the Boer and first world war. This, combined with the limited range of work opportunities for women outside the home, allowed grandparents to remain within the family circle to the mutual benefit of all. A higher standard of living began to disturb this interdependence, aided by increased mobility and less sex discrimination in the work place. Women were needed to work at a wide range of tasks during the second world war and this pointed the way towards more equal opportunities in peace time.

Patterns of shopping have changed to suit the two car family of the second half of the century. Those without personal transport now find shopping more difficult than it was in the past. As local shops and smaller service outlets have become less older people have lost some of the social contacts these made possible and, as smaller shops have disappeared, short distance public transport to those remaining has become more scarce. Some health care has become less accessible with the advent of large group practices serving 10 to 20 thousand people. Lessening in home visits by Health Staff and the disappearance of Cottage Hospitals and inner city General Hospitals has not helped in this respect. The high cost of providing any service within the home, from receiving a visit from the chiropodist to having an electrician out to attend to faulty equipment, has increased the sense of isolation of some people. There have, of course, been many gains to offset against these losses. The almost universal possession of the telephone and home entertainment equipment helps to keep the old in touch with family and friends. The design of new shopping malls with seats, plentiful toilets and refreshment areas has made shopping easier for some once they get there. However, on the whole these benefit the active and relatively independent whilst the disadvantages fall most heavily on the frail and relatively immobile.

Support Networks

All of us, when we become ill, are dependent upon others. With a short term illness our needs are small particularly when we are young and otherwise vigorous. With chronic illnesses our needs become more complex and when our problems are both multiple and a mixture of social and medical, as is usually the case with older people, the support network required is very complex. It will involve formal and informal carers and can vary greatly between individuals. The diseases people suffer from may be similar but the support networks are very individual and idiosyncratic. If management plans for older people fail to take note of these and use them they are usually doomed to failure. It must be recognised that older people do not necessarily have family support. A high proportion have no families. In 1978, 30% of people in Great Britain aged over 75 had never had any children and 7.5% had outlived their children. In 1987, 61% of women over 80 living at home lived alone[6].

In the front line of most care of older people are families, friends and neighbours. The needs of carers now attract more attention and there is an organisation concerned with their interests[7] but most still have little training or support. Many feel unable to ask for help and others do not wish to be regarded as carers and think of their role as wife, neighbour or friend. Some help with very intimate tasks and carry out skilled nursing, bathing and lifting tasks. The work can be very demanding and stressful but equally rewarding. Within these groups there is often a high level of anxiety and this can reach a pitch where it is very destructive. Helping the carer with this will help the patient and containment of the level of anxiety to a tolerable level can be the most important factor in enabling someone to remain in their own home. Much anxiety is a product of ignorance and can be lessened by good communication. This does not often necessitate spending a lot of time on lengthy and complicated explanation. Indeed a surfeit of information can make the recipients feel they are drowning. It is a nice judgement to get this right, but most importantly the need can be met by being accessible so that carers feel they have 'permission' to discuss whatever troubles them. Very often they will not feel the need to bang on a door that is open.

Some anxiety is a product of guilt. The carer will frequently feel he, or she, is not doing as much as could be done or, even more commonly, has not done enough in the past. They may express this feeling by becoming hostile, irritable or violent. It is a response sometimes found within doctors and nurses who become frustrated by their apparent inability to help. It should be recognised.

At other times the anxiety is worsened because the relatives are unable to accept the lowered standard of care that has to be accepted in the balance between need and resources. This may not be what everyone has been used to but with chronic disability it may be inevitable and carers may require help to come to terms with it. In similar mode a family's anxieties may be heightened by the difficulty they have in accepting risk. In many situations risk is present. It may be risk associated with a level of solitude, but the risk may be a worthwhile trade off for allowing a patient to remain in their own home.

There are virtually always complex psychodynamics in the relationship between an older person with problems and carers. Many may originate from the difference in expectations of carer and patient, the varied cultural backgrounds of each or the effects of experiences in life upon present behaviour. Doctors need to recognise these. In this context the role of voluntary organisations can be very helpful. These largely consist of people who have a particular investment in the problem by virtue of having already met it in relation to a family member or friend. They often come from similar peer groups and may be age specific, such as Age Concern or Help the Aged or concentrate upon special problems such as bereavement, Alzheimer's disease, Parkinson's disease or stroke. They have a fund of experience because they specialise within that area and have gained long term experience in common problems and ways to help. They are usually sharply focused because they know well what the priorities of people are and they are able to be much more flexible and adaptable than formal systems of care which are by nature more bureaucratic. The support of such an organisation may be the most valuable resource for families and patients.

Teamwork

It will be apparent now to the reader that a feature of care of the older person is the requirement for teamwork, as the range of skills, attitudes and knowledge required is so varied. Not every problem needs this approach but most do and so it is incumbent upon the doctor to learn the requirements for good teamwork. An understanding of the role and training of others, shared and explicit goals, defined responsibility and good communication systems are needed wherever care is carried out. Very often it is easy to forget the most important member of the team, the patient, and not to take on board their wishes, likes and dislikes and to fail to communicate adequately with this person who is the sole object of the work. Without a good knowledge of the practical working requirements of shared care and teamwork it is too easy for responsibility to become blurred leading to poor care. As with any sort of relationship, from parenthood to leisure pursuits, it has to be worked at and team building is an important element.

Thus all doctors involved with clinical work in any field need to be skilled in the care of older people, need to develop positive attitudes, to be able to utilise the whole range of social and medical resources and need to be able to work as a team member. None of this means that the skills of the specialist Geriatrician are not a key resource. Indeed, Departments of Medicine for the Elderly up and down the country have been in the fore-front of providing rehabilitation services and opportunities for acute therapeutic interventions in elderly patients. Generalists, however, have to be constantly aware of their limitations and recognising when appropriate referral is required is a crucial factor in good management. Every patient needs a doctor who has had a wide and general training and who has acquired breadth of outlook. Equally all need to have access to specialist skills when required. This is particularly important when new ways of handling old problems, often involving high technology medicine, enter the field. Furthermore, older people have an equal need and indeed right to have access to specialist advice. The high technology medicine should not be denied to them on the grounds of age alone. Finally, it is worth considering the impact of UK Health Services reforms and also our membership of the European Union (EC) on the overall care of the patients. So far as NHS reforms are concerned – apart from existing reforms – Family Health Service Authorities are merging with District Health Authorities.

These joint 'Commissioning Authorities' will identify local health needs and plan services as necessary. Clearly, how this will work out remains to be seen. On the EU level, on the other hand, the impact of EU directives on our services will be little. This is so because the health-systems are highly country-specific (ie dependent on complex inter-relationships of a country's social security structures, educational and finance systems, as well as historical and cultural factors) and hence they cannot be uniformly harmonised[8]. It seems that, in coming years, the member States, including the United Kingdom, will retain their basic health care priorities but will function within strategic guidelines on specific initiatives emanating from Brussels.

Introduction

Practical Points

1. The increasing number of older people is now a well-recognised fact.

2. Many elderly patients have multiple pathologies and have polypharmacy.

3. There is unusual presentation of diseases in many elderly patients.

4. The diagnosis and treatment in this age-group should be instituted without delay to prevent unnecessary mortality and morbidity.

5. A holistic approach – consideration of physical, mental, social and age-related changes – to care is essential.

6. Care of elderly patients requires team-work, but the overlapping of care should be avoided.

7. Elderly patients deserve and should receive a high standard of care, both in the hospital and in the community. High-technology medicine should not be denied to them on the ground of age alone.

8. Helping the carers should be part and parcel of overall care of elderly patients.

9. The efforts of Royal Colleges, voluntary organisations and the British Geriatric Society, from time to time, to improve the care of elderly patients, should be welcomed.

References

1. Nascher IL (1909) *Geriatrics*, New York Medical Journal, 358–359.

2. Thompson MK (1984) *The care of the elderly in general practice*, Churchill Livingstone, London.

3. Bennett GJ & Ebrahim S (1992) *Health of the elderly*, Edward Arnold, London.

4. Gibson F (1994) *Reminiscence and recall*, ACE Books, London.

5. *National Health Service and Community Care Act 1990*, HMSO, London.

6. ANON (1991) *An Aging Population*, Family Policy Studies Centre, Fact Sheet 2, London.

7. Carers National Association, 20/25 Glasshouse Yard, London EC1A 4JS.

8. Berman PC (1994) *The European Union and healthcare*, Journal — Irish College of Physicians & Surgeons, 23, 263–266.

Chapter 2

Demographic Characteristics

Dr Yolande Coombes
Lecturer in Health Promotion
Health Promotion Sciences Unit
Department of Public Health and Policy
London School of Hygiene and Tropical Medicine
Keppel Street
London
WC1E 7HT

Dr Alex Kalache
Head, Public Health Implications of Ageing Programme
London School of Hygiene & Tropical Medicine
University of London
Keppel Street
London
WC1E 7HT

Biosketch:

Yolande Coombes BA (Hons), PhD, is a lecturer in Health Promotion in the Health Promotion Sciences Unit at the London School of Hygiene & Tropical Medicine. She is the organiser of the MSc in Health Promotion Sciences. Her background is in Medical Geography and her research interests include Ageing, the New Public Health, Models of Behaviour Change, and AIDS.

Alex Kalache MD, PhD, is a senior research fellow in the Health Promotion Sciences Unit at the London School of Hygiene & Tropical Medicine (LSHTM). He came to England from Brazil in 1975 for training in Public Health Medicine. In 1984 he joined the LSHTM to set up a programme on the Epidemiology of Ageing in association with the WHO Global Programme on the Health of the Elderly of which he has recently been appointed the head.

Introduction

The main purpose of this chapter is to highlight the key demographic characteristics of Britain's elderly population. The chapter begins by looking at the increases in the elderly population, and projections for the coming decades; it then goes on to examine the main factors influencing the proportion of elderly people both in terms of fluctuations in fertility rates and increases in life expectancy reflecting declines in mortality rates. This is followed by a discussion highlighting some of the special groups within the elderly population such as ethnic minorities, childless individuals, and widows, demonstrating the impact these groups have on the demography of the elderly as a function of their special needs. Finally, the chapter concludes by examining ageing-related demographic perspectives and ways in which we can influence a healthy active life expectancy for the elderly population.

Increases in the Elderly Population

Population ageing is a recent phenomenon which has been achieved through declines in mortality and fertility rates. In Britain, this process called demographic transition, had started by the middle of the 19th Century. Gradually the proportion of the population aged over 65 increased; in 1901 it was only 4.7% of the total population, in 1991 the proportion had risen to 16% – a total of 9 million people over the age of 65 years. This is expected to increase to 11 million or 18.1% of the population by the year 2021. As women retire at the age of 60, five years before men, the proportion of retired elderly people in 1991 was 18.7% or 10.3 million people. Table 1 shows the absolute number of elderly and proportion of elderly in the population 1961–1991 and projections for the years 2001–2021.

Proportion in Different Age Groups

Since the turn of the century both the total number and the proportion of elderly people in the population have more than trebled. Recent trends and projected figures (table 1) show that the number of elderly people is increasing at a fast rate. More importantly, as table 1 shows, the fastest growing segment of the elderly are those aged over 85 – the frail elderly, who need more care and thus more resources.

Table 1

Numbers (millions) and Proportion of Elderly Population in United Kingdom 1961–1991, Estimates for 2001–2021

	65+	(%)	75+	(%)	85+	(%)
1961	6.2	11.7	2.2	2.5	0.3	0.6
1971	7.3	13.1	2.5	4.6	0.4	0.8
1981	8.1	14.8	3.1	5.7	0.6	1.1
1991	9.0	16.0	3.9	7.0	0.8	1.5
2001	9.2	15.6	4.4	7.4	1.2	1.9
2011	9.8	16.2	4.5	7.5	1.3	2.2
2021	11.0	18.1	4.9	8.1	1.4	2.3

Source: Central Statistical Office (1994), Annual Abstract of Statistics. No 130. London. HMSO.

Thus for the foreseeable future the most important demographic change to occur in Britain is the 'ageing' of the elderly population. OPCS estimates, show the proportion of elderly who are aged over 85 increasing by just over one third by 2001, and 65% by 2021. However, if death rates in old age continue to decline more rapidly than in recent years (as emerging data seem to suggest) the proportion of very elderly people may be even higher.

Table 2 shows the projected changes in the population 1989–2026 in England and Wales. In parallel to the substantial increases in the elderly age groups the table shows reductions in the proportion of young adults. This has implications for the population dependency ratio.

Distribution of the Population by Sex

Figure 1 shows the numbers of men and women in 5 year age groups from age 60. The data is from the 1991 census. There are increasingly more women than men in all old age categories as the population ages. Out of the population of pensionable age only one third are male, reflecting the fact that there is a large cohort of women in the age group 60–65, in which men are not yet retired. Mortality rates in older age are lower for women than men. As a result there are almost two women for every man in the 75–84 age groups; the ratio increases to 4 to 1 among those aged over 85. The demographic characteristics have many social and health implications, particularly in relation to numbers of frail women in very old age living alone, as the risk of widowhood is much higher for females than males, both because they live longer and because they tend to marry men older than themselves.

Table 2

Projected Change in Population 1989–2026, England and Wales

Age Group	1989 (millions)	2026	Absolute Change	Percentage Change
0–4	3.3	3.4	0.1	3
5–14	6.1	6.7	0.6	10
15–24	7.7	6.7	–1.0	–13
25–44	14.6	13.9	–0.7	– 5
45–64	10.9	13.6	2.7	25
65–74	4.5	5.5	1.0	23
75–84	2.8	3.7	0.9	33
85+	0.8	1.3	0.5	66
All Ages	50.6	54.8	4.2	8

Source: OPCS Monitor PP2 91/1

Figure 1

UK Population Pyramid for age 60 and above, 1991

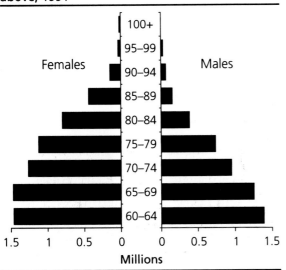

Source: OPCS. 1991 Census

Future trends regarding the male-female ratios in old age are set to change, with an increase in the relative numbers of old men in all age groups. This is partly due to the replacement of cohorts which, for specific historical reasons, (eg World Wars), were particularly female dominated. A second reason comes from the fact that the sex differentials in mortality have begun to narrow, and women are losing their advantage.

Geographical Variations

The census data for 1991 shows that the proportions of elderly living within England, Scotland and Wales follow similar patterns. But within each country there are marked regional variations. Broadly speaking, there are two distinct geographical locations where higher than average proportions of elderly live in England: the coastal areas, particularly in the south and south-west (desirable as post-retirement places to live), and inner city areas in the north and north-west (reflecting migration of younger people leaving their elders behind). Wales and Scotland have high proportions of elderly living in rural and often remote country areas. Future geographical variations in the elderly population are predicted to change from the present pattern. For example, new towns such as Milton Keynes or Telford, which currently have a high middle-aged population, will age significantly as this cohort moves into retirement. Many of the areas with large elderly populations, for example coastal towns such as Worthing or Hastings, have relatively stable elderly populations as there are fewer middle aged people. However, these populations may receive new cohorts of elderly who migrate to coastal towns on retirement.

International Comparisons

Presently, two thirds of the World's elderly population live in developing countries. This is largely a consequence of the much larger populations in countries in Asia, Latin America and Africa. Apart from those countries in sub-Saharan Africa, most developing countries are well into the process of demographic transition, fast moving from high mortality and high fertility to low mortality and fertility and hence a rapidly ageing population. The World's elderly population is increasing at a rate of 2.5% per year which is faster than the total population growth rate of 1.7%. In 1990 just under 10% (1/2 a billion) of the World's population were over 60 years old,

Figure 2

Deaths From all Causes by Sex and Age in England and Wales, 1991

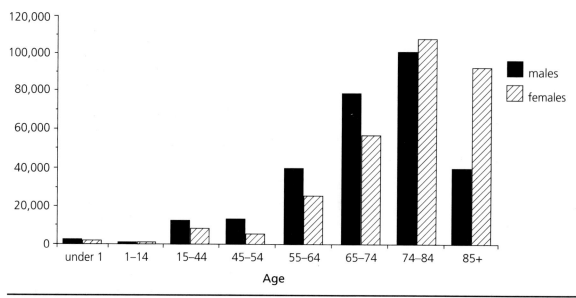

Source: OPCS Monitor DH2 92/2

and this figure is expected to have tripled by the year 2030 to 1.4 billion.

The United Kingdom is typical of many countries in Europe, where fertility rates are below the natural replacement level, and mortality continues to decline. Within Europe the countries of Scandinavia and Western Europe have the highest proportions of elderly people. In terms of Life Expectancy at Birth, England and Wales are very similar to most other European countries at around 72; however, life expectancy at age 65 is higher in all other countries of Europe except for those from Central and Eastern Europe. This is

Table 3

Elderly Persons Aged over 65 as a Percentage of Total Population (1991)

Belgium	16.3	Italy	15.2
Denmark	15.3	Luxembourg	15.5
France	14.5	Netherlands	14.4
Germany	15.9	Portugal	11.9
Greece	14.2	Romania	10.1
Hungary	12.3	Sweden	18.1
Ireland	10.1	UK	16.3

Source: World Bank. 1993 World Development Report. Oxford. Oxford University Press.

because death rates in the elderly population have not declined as fast in the UK as they have in most other European countries. Table 3 shows the proportion of elderly (aged over 65) for selected countries in Europe.

Mortality Rates

Disease patterns change as countries experience the process of demographic transition – the so called epidemiological transition. At the final stage of the demographic transition, the leading causes of death are typically chronic degenerative diseases. The leading cause of death in developed countries is ischaemic heart disease which claims 2.4 million deaths per year, closely followed by malignant neoplasms – 2.3 million deaths per year. Completion of the demographic transition is also characterised by a concentration of mortality in later life.

Figure 2 shows deaths from all causes in England and Wales for 1991. The percentage of deaths in most Western European countries is over 75% for those aged 65 years and over 50% for those aged 75 years and above.

Male mortality rates are higher in all age groups except for 'older' elderly and this reflects

A GUIDE TO THE CARE OF THE ELDERLY

Figure 3

Main Causes of Death, 1991

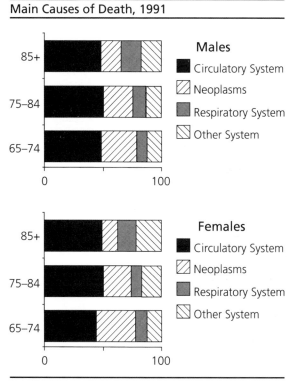

Males
- ■ Circulatory System
- ▨ Neoplasms
- ▦ Respiratory System
- ◩ Other System

Females
- ■ Circulatory System
- ▨ Neoplasms
- ▦ Respiratory System
- ◩ Other System

Source: OPCS Monitor DH2 92/2

the unequal gender distribution of the elderly population. In England in 1990, 33% of female deaths occurred in those aged over 85.

The continued decline in mortality rates will play the most significant role in the population ageing process in the coming decades in the United Kingdom. Most developed countries are showing a decline in mortality rates for all age groups, although many of the Eastern European countries are showing an upward trend in male mortality. There has been a marked decline in British death rates among older age groups in recent years, but they still remain higher than most other OECD countries. In Japan, where life expectancy is now the highest in the world, mortality rates have decreased most dramatically resulting in more rapid population ageing, thus demonstrating how much can be achieved in a relatively short period of time.

Figure 3 shows the main causes of death in elderly males and females. The patterns for both males and females are similar. Circulatory diseases account for almost half of male deaths in

the age groups shown, and half for women in the two upper age groups. Diseases of the respiratory system increase with age, yet mortality from cancer drops signficantly in both men and women as age increases. Cancer is responsible for almost half the deaths in women aged 55–64, but only 11% in those aged 85+. However, it must be noted that death certificates are recorded less accurately for older people, and this may have an effect on the cause of death statistics. There are considerably more male than female deaths in the younger age groups and twice as many female to male deaths in the 85+ age group.

Life Expectancy

In Britain life expectancy at birth (LEB) has increased considerably throughout the last century – by about 30 years since 1900. In addition, life expectancy amongst older age groups has shown some increases, particularly among women. At the age of 60 years, male life expectancy has increased by approximately 4 years since 1900, and females by 7 years. Similarly, at the age of 70 years male life expectancy has increased by 2 years and female by almost 5 years. Life expectancy at age 60 is continuing to rise and by the year 2001 it should have risen by approximately one further year for both men and women.

Figure 4 shows life expectancy at birth and at age 65 for selected countries. As would be expected, life expectancy for men is lower on average than for women at age 65 and at birth. In relative terms the UK used to have one of the lowest mortality rates in the world, however now there are many other countries with better life expectancies at birth and age 65. For example developing countries such as Uruguay and Sri Lanka have a higher life expectancy at age 65 for men than England and Wales. This is largely due to the cumulation of risk factors for chronic diseases which is associated with the urban/post industrial lifestyle more common here than in the developing world.

Although life expectancy for elderly people continues to increase, it is often associated with a poor quality of life in terms of health. For example mortality rates from stroke are declining yet the incidence of stroke seems to be on the increase, suggesting that people may be living longer but with a potential risk of increased disability.

Figure 4

Life Expectancy in Selected Countries at Birth and Age 65, 1985

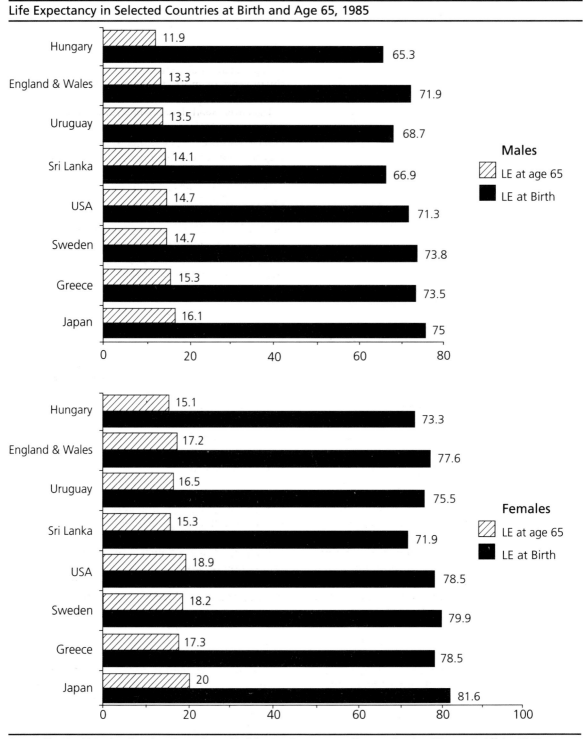

Source: The World Ageing Situation: Strategies and Policies, UN Department of International and Economic Affairs, 1985.

A GUIDE TO THE CARE OF THE ELDERLY

Figure 5

Aged Dependency Ratios in the UK, 1990–2030

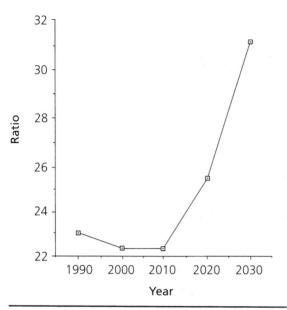

Source: OECD 'Ageing Populations: The Social Policy Implications', Paris 1988.

Fertility Rates and Dependency Ratios

In addition to declines in mortality having an effect on the demography of the elderly population, declines in fertility rates will further increase the proportion of elderly people in the population. In the UK the crude birth rate (births per 1000 of the population) has declined from 18.2 in the period 1960–1965 to 12.3 in the period 1990–1995. As was shown in table 2, the younger cohorts in the population are increasing at a much lower rate, and young adults are actually decreasing in proportion. This change in the structure of the population due to declines in fertility will have a large impact on dependency ratios.

Traditionally, dependency ratios have been defined as the population aged over 65 years and under 15 years as a percentage of the population aged 16–64 years (the population of working age). At the beginning of this century dependency ratios were still high due to the large numbers of children who had to be supported. However as fertility rates have declined and the population has aged, the dependency ratio is now increasing

due to the large numbers of elderly people who need to be supported. An important part of the dependency ratio is that children are dependent for 15 years before moving on to become independent. Elderly people are moving from being independent to dependent and may be so for thirty years or more (twice the length of time that children are dependent).

Recently, aged dependency ratios have been calculated which calculate the ratio between the elderly and the economically active population. Figure 5 shows the aged dependency ratios and projections for the UK from 1990 to 2030.

Although the aged dependency ratio will decrease slightly over the next decade due to the large cohort of people in the 44–64 age group presently, it will rise very steeply as this cohort becomes elderly. By the year 2030, for every three people of working age in the population there will be one elderly person to support.

Special Groups

The elderly are not an homogenous group, as with all sectors of society they have different characteristics and different subgroups. This section of the chapter looks at some of the key subgroups within the elderly population and their special characteristics.

Residential Status

As people age the proportion of people living alone increases. Approximately 15% of men aged 65–69 and 30% of women in the same age group live alone. However, 45% of men and 60% of women aged over 85 live alone. At all ages the proportion of women living alone is greater than that of men, partly because of the difference in life expectancies. There is also a cohort of women who never married, who were born in the early 1900s and did not marry due to the huge loss of male lives in World War I. The elderly who live alone in the older (85+) age groups are a particularly vulnerable group, because they are more likely to be in need of care and help with activities of daily living, as they become increasingly frail.

Table 4 shows the living arrangements of the elderly population from 1962 to 1989. The table shows a clear trend towards more elderly people living alone or living with their spouse only, compared to thirty years ago when people were more likely to live in extended familes. Other contributory factors to more people living alone include the increase in separation and divorce over the last few decades. In addition there are a number of childless couples who have no immediate family to care for them.

Table 4

Living Arrangements of People Aged 65 and Over, 1962–1989

%	1962	1976	1980	1985	1989
Lived Alone	22	30	34	36	36
Lived With Spouse Only	33	44	45	45	46
Lived With Others	44	27	21	19	18
All Persons Aged 65 Years And over	100	100	100	100	100

Source: Central Health Monitoring Unit Epidemiological Overview Series. The Health of Elderly People. HMSO. 1992.

Marital Status

Figure 6 shows the marital status of the population aged over 65 at the time of the 1991 census.

The pie charts clearly show that more women are either widowed, divorced or single compared to men and are thus more likely to live alone. More elderly men are married, this is partly due to the fact that most elderly men are in the 'younger' older age groups and are thus more likely to still be married. In addition women tend to be younger than their husbands but have an increased life expectancy, therefore they are more likely to be widowed.

Women

Women are a special group amongst the elderly population. In any society, one of the poorest groups are the elderly and amongst them, elderly women are particularly disadvantaged. This is often due to having had a low socio-economic status or having been dependent on their spouse

Figure 6

Marital Status of Population Aged 65+, 1991

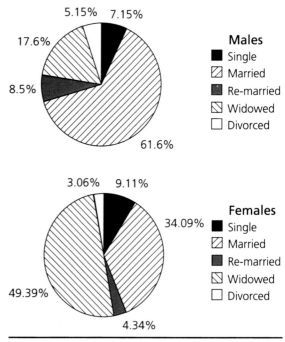

Source: OPCS 1991 Census.

for income and support and not having contributed to pension schemes on an individual basis. In addition women are a special group because they make up the majority of the very old. As previously mentioned this is due to having an increased life expectancy, lower mortality, and because there is presently a large cohort of elderly women compared to elderly men because of the large numbers of men who died in World Wars I and II. As we have seen elderly women are more likely to be widowed, and to be living alone, and thus as a group will have special needs.

Women often perform the main care functions within the family, as life expectancy increases it is not unusual to find retired elderly women caring for their elderly parents. Performing the tasks of a principle carer can be very demanding, particularly at a time when the carer is also moving more towards being dependent on others.

Ethnic Minorities and Migrants

Although Britain does not have a large elderly ethnic minority population at the present time, this will increase over the coming decades as the present cohorts of middle aged ethnic minority populations age. Elderly ethnic minority people are less likely to speak English, and are less likely to be aware of services and benefits available to them. At present 13% of all ethnic minorities are aged over 65 for men or aged over 60 for women.

Other problems encountered by ethnic minorities and migrants is that they are often ageing in an alien environment. Within the country, elderly people who migrate to another area on retirement also face similar problems, including being separated from their family, who would have been the principle carers of their elderly relatives. In the year before the census 6% of the elderly population had moved compared to 9.8% of the population as a whole, so elderly people are in fact a more stable population.

Conclusions

In many ways the elderly population are similar to the population as a whole, for example in terms of social class they follow a similar distribution to that of the total population. However, in other ways they have distinct differences, for example there are concentrations of elderly people in certain geographical locations, there are less ethnic minorities, and there are many more female elderly than male elderly people.

The most important demographic characteristics of the elderly are that they are the fastest growing segment of the population, and that amongst the elderly the segment containing those aged over 75, is increasing the fastest. Mortality is now concentrated in later life, as is morbidity. Even though life expectancy at all ages including those in later life is increasing, it is a longer life with increasing disability. In addition, the very elderly people are more likely to be living alone, and as they are no longer part of the workforce, are more likely to be economically disadvantaged.

Demographic Characteristics

Practical Points

1. **Demographic Transition:** The elderly are an important and growing sector of the population. Those aged 85+ form the fastest growing sector, and they are the most dependent elderly, in need of more care, services and resources to support them.

2. **Social Processes:** Elderly people are more likely to live alone, particularly as they get older. A large number of the elderly are widowed or single (especially women). They are more likely to be in need of financial support. Migration on retirement is contributing to elderly people being separated from their families.

3. **Dependency:** The proportion of dependent elderly people is increasing, and as the population of working age is declining, mechanisms to maintain economic support and care need to be put into place or resources will have to be diverted from other groups in society in order to care for the growing elderly population.

4. **Chronic Diseases:** Chronic degenerative diseases as opposed to infectious diseases are more prevalent in old age. Efforts to reduce the incidence and prevalence of these diseases are needed as well as evaluation of appropriate and cost effective care.

5. **Healthy Ageing:** Mortality and morbidity are now concentrated in later life. There is a need to promote health throughout life – healthy children become healthy adults and healthy elderly people. The aim is to increase life expectancy whilst maintaining healthy, disability free years.

References

1. OPCS Monitor DH2/92

2. Grundy E. (yr?) *Demographic trends and their implications*, in: S Ebrahim, J George (eds), Health Care of older women, Oxford University Press, Oxford.

3. Suzman R, Kinsella K & Myers GC (1991) *Demography of older populations in developed countries*, in: Oxford Textbook of Geriatric Medicine, Oxford University Press, Oxford.

4. The World Bank (1994) *Averting the Old Age Crisis*, Policy Research Report, Oxford University Press, Oxford.

5. Lopez A & Cliquet RL (1984) *Demographic trends in the European Region: health and social implications*, WHO, Geneva.

6. OPCS (1992) *1991 Census*. HMSO, London.

7. OPCS (1990) *Labour Force Survey 1987–89*, HMSO.

Chapter 3

The Ageing Process

Peter H. Millard, MD, PhD, FRCP
Eleanor Peel Professor of Geriatric Medicine
St George's Hospital Medical School
London
SW17 0RE

Biosketch:

Professor Peter Henry Millard is the Eleanor Peel Professor of Geriatric Medicine, Division of Geriatric Medicine, St. George's Hospital Medical School, Cranmer Terrace, London SW17 0RE, and a visiting professor to the Mathematics Department at the University of Ulster and Ex-President of The British Geriatrics Society. His research interests are related to the development of rehabilitation services for older people, the impact of personal belongings in long term care, and the modelling of hospital services.

Introduction

Ageing is a progressive, generalised, impairment of function resulting in a loss of the adaptive response to stress and a growing risk of age related disease. Ageing leads to progressive loss of capacity to survive environmental pressures. In each species there is a specific chronological loss of function during the lifespan of an organism; the chronological age is the actual time since birth, whereas the biological age is the impression of the extent of change due to the ageing process in a particular individual – some seem to age quicker than others. Senile is a term which is frequently reasoned to mean old and stupid. It is often used as an insult, partly based on the misconception that old must mean daft, but ageing *per se* does not indicate disease, for old age and disease are not synonymous.

Geriatric Medicine is the branch of medicine or social science dealing with the management of illness in frail, and older people. Gerontology is the scientific study of old age and of the process of ageing. Experimental work in gerontology depends on the hypothesis that 'Ageing is a biological process involving a rate or rates and where there is a rate it can generally be altered'.

To understand ageing it is important to grasp the difference between apoptosis, biomorphis and senescence. Apoptosis is a continually cycling process of renewal and death, eg red blood cells live and die in 120 days and crypt villi cells are constantly lost and replaced every two to three days. Biomorphis is a process of biological change that occurs continually from conception to death, eg bone remodelling. Senescence is the process of deterioration in structure and function, resulting in decreased viability and increased vulnerability to external and internal insults, ultimately ending in death, eg – loss of dentition in wild animals. Apoptosis is preplanned cell death; biomorphis continues as the animal ages; and senescence is the downward decline at the end of life.

Age Changes vs. Age Differences

An age change is a process of change occurring progressively with the chronological passage of time in all members of a species, ie 'ageing', eg everybody's skin gets thinner, more transparent, and less elastic with age. An age difference is simply a difference observed when directly comparing individuals of different ages, eg the use of walking aids increases with age; and skin differences occur, though these may not be purely due to the ageing process as the difference in individuals may reflect sunlight or steroids. Age changes are demonstrated by longitudinal studies whereas age differences are observed in cross-sectional studies.

Longitudinal studies involve taking a cohort of individuals and following them through time. The problems with longitudinal studies are time, especially when dealing with long-lived species, expense, emigration, interference with lifestyle of subject, changes in technology of tests and the impossibility of taking into account all of the variables that will affect somebody's life. Cross-sectional studies involve a comparison of individuals of different ages from within one population evaluated at the same point in time. The problems with cross-sectional studies are comparing different generations (different social upbringing, education, diets etc) and past life histories, which may be completely incomparable, and the fact that immigration may have occurred.

Longevity, Life-span, Life Expectancy

Longevity, life-span and life expectancy are terms with different meanings. The lifespan is the length of life of individuals or groups of individuals. It is the period of time between birth and death and as such it can be directly measured only after death. Lifespan is influenced by the environment and therefore may be altered, in contrast longevity is specific to the species.

Life-expectancy is a mathematical prediction of the number of years of life remaining to each person of a specified age. It is calculated from observed age-specific death rates and takes into account the environment and possible future technological advances. The major past cause of changing life expectation is change in childhood death rate; future change depends on controlling death from cancer or ischaemic heart disease.

Longevity is the *theoretical* maximum time that a cohort of a species could hope to survive to under ideal conditions. Consequently it has intrinsic genetically determined components. For each species it is a fixed value which may be estimated and is specific to the species. Only a few individuals reach the species longevity due to the influence of environmental factors.

'Squaring the Rectangle'

Survival curves yield a graphical representation of population survival with age. In populations which do not age (eg sea anemones) death of individuals occurs randomly from causes that would kill at any age. In such populations, if the rate of mortality is constant, the number of survivors falls logarithmically with age. Medawar used the illustration of self-reproducing teacups: there would always be some old teacups but most would be young.

A logarithmic survival curve is characteristic of populations in which individuals, while potentially able to age, live under such severe conditions of life that few live long enough to become old, eg wild birds, although potentially able to live up to 20 years and show characteristics of ageing, normally die within six months due to predation and environmental conditions. In contrast, when in captivity, they show a normal survival pattern. In populations which do age, the survival curve becomes much more rectangular. Figure 1 shows the population changes in the United Kingdom for the cohort aged 0–5 born in the years preceding the 1841, 1881, 1931 and 1951 census.

Notice that with improvements in lifestyle, sanitation, food and public health, the curve undergoes rectangularization, particularly as a result of decreased infant mortality. As the factors that cause early death are controlled the shape of the survival curve changes. The ideal curve 'squaring the rectangle of survival' is described by Fries and Crapo[1,2].

The change in the pattern of survival in figure 1 is interesting. The 1841 cohort had a seemingly constant risk of death, whereas the 1881 cohort had an increased death rate in the early years. Notice that death before the age of 20 increased between 1841 and 1881. Between 1881 and 1931 the change in life expectation was mainly due to a decline in infant mortality rates. To live to be old, one must not die young: increased standard of living, improvements in public health (immunisation, antibiotics), improvements in sanitation, and improved diet were the major factors. The figure clearly shows that death rates declined between 1881 and 1931 in the second, third, fourth and fifth decades. I think that a major cause of decline in childhood death rate may have been the abolition of corn laws in 1842 for this, coupled with metal ships, allowed for the importation of cheap American food. In all

Figure 1

Squaring the rectangle: population survival in the UK since 1841

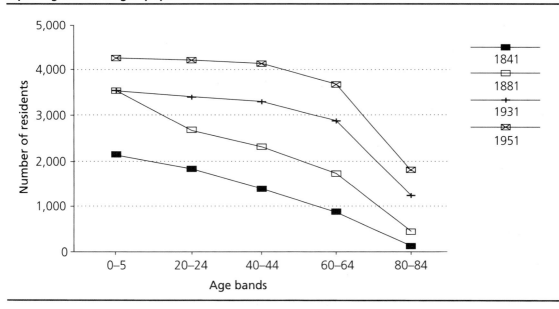

countries that control water, sewage, sanitation and food supply this process of rectangularization takes place. In many third world countries this process still needs to take place.

The pattern of survival may be considered in terms of 'death strikes' that hit a population at certain times. These death strikes are related to the species and their lifestyle, and may be altered or removed, causing 'squaring of the rectangle' of survival. Infant mortality is decreased by adequate nutrition and other health and hygiene measures. In contrast, mortality in older age groups will be changed by an attack on those factors that lead to arterial, degenerative and malignant diseases.

Aspects of Ageing

Only since the beginning of this century has the life expectancy of babies at birth exceeded 50 years in developed countries. The problems associated with an ageing society are, therefore, new and of increasing importance. There are two ways of looking at the ageing process. The traditional approach identifies three phases: childhood, associated with growth and development; the adult state, characterised by homeostasis and old age; and senescence, characterised by a loss of homeostasis and deterioration. Ageing cannot be considered as being independent from growth – biomorphic ageing begins at conception and is inseparable from development.

Strehler, an American gerontologist, proposed in 1962 that any physiological phenomenon must meet four criteria before it can be unequivocally stated to be a component of the overall ageing process[3]. It must be Universal, Intrinsic, Progressive and Deleterious.

Universal: the process must be identifiable in all members of a species, but may affect individuals to a different extent, eg, baldness – all humans lose a proportion of viable hair follicles as they age.

Intrinsic: the changes are restricted to those which are of endogenous origin, because it is the intrinsic response to the external stimulus rather than the stimulus itself which is age related, eg, many of the changes found with ageing in the skin may be seen in an accelerated form in subjects exposed to high doses of ultraviolet radiation. The term 'photoageing' has been given to this phenomenon but it cannot be regarded as a true age change, being the result of exogenous factors.

Progressive: implies that the age change develops progressively with increasing age. It is important not to confuse this with conditions which have a higher incidence above a certain age but which develop rapidly. Most ageing processes start in utero and continue until death.

Deleterious: finally it must be deleterious, as an ageing process is (eventually) harmful to the organism. Some observed changes are simply a progression of changes which were beneficial to the organism during the period of growth and development, eg: cross-linkage of collagen first allows growth, then gives strength and finally leads to rigidity.

Strehler's criteria are useful for distinguishing between ageing and disease. The difference is summarised in the table below.

Ageing	Disease
Universal	Affects individuals
Intrinsic	Intrinsic or extrinsic
Progressive	Progressive, but may be halted or reversed
Deleterious	Deleterious, but may be arrested or cured

Why do we Age?

There are three views. First, ageing is the inevitable price the organism pays for complexity. Over time, 'wear and tear' results in the decline of function and eventually death. Second, in the adaptive evolutionary view ageing is selectively advantageous to the species. It is a programmed event that prevents overcrowding and competition for resources. Third, in a non-adaptive evolutionary view, either ageing occurs because the powers of natural selection decline with age or because genes, which earlier in life were beneficial, later prove harmful. Probably, ageing is an inevitable consequence of complexity, and we age because we live in a complex structure, that has to reproduce to survive.

The Disposable Soma Theory

Professor Tom Kirkwood developed the disposable soma theory of ageing[4]. Biologically an organism is essentially an entity that transforms energy into progeny. To do this the body can be considered to have two parts, the germ cells and the soma (rest of the body). Energy taken in is balanced between foraging, feeding, somatic maintenance vs reproduction. When a soma dies, the energy invested in it is wasted, so too small an investment in the soma leads to death before reproduction and too great an investment in the soma leads to waste/inefficiency. Since no soma can survive indefinitely because of the continual hazard of accidental death, the most efficient soma will invest less energy than is needed for indefinite survival. There is no point in investing vast quantities of energy into a soma which, although potentially able to survive for a long time, will not do so due to predation and environmental hazards. Such an organism would gain a selective advantage by investing more of its energy into rapid and prolific reproduction, and less into somatic maintenance.

Theories of Ageing

The many theories of ageing can be broken down into theories at a level of the whole organism and theories at the level of the cell[5].

Theories at Level of Whole Organism
Wear and Tear

In the wear and tear theory, ageing is perceived to be due to the gradual wearing out of non-replaceable body constituents – a form of use atrophy, eg African elephants die when their teeth wear out because they become unable to feed.

Accumulation

In the accumulation theory, ageing is considered to be due to the accumulation of waste products within the body, eg intercellular accumulation of myocardial collagen thus decreasing mechanical efficiency of heart.

Exhaustion

Theories associated with exhaustion consider that ageing is due to the exhaustion of some irreplaceable vital substance that may be related to 'rate of living'.

Neuroendocrine Changes

In neuroendocrine theories, ageing is considered to be due to changes in hormone levels which results in homeostatic decline.

Immunological

In immunological theories, ageing is due to a declining ability to mount a normal immune response, along with an increase in autoimmunity. The evidence for decreasing immunity is that older people are more susceptible to infections and conditions such as primary tuberculosis reappear. However, there is increasing evidence that the decline in immune function reported to occur in old age is due to sub-clinical malnutrition.

Decline in Control of Proliferative Homeostasis

This theory considers that ageing is due to a loss of control of cell proliferation, resulting in a mixture of hyperplasia and atrophy, eg proliferation of osteocyte and chondrocytes in osteoarthritis.

Luck

There is no point being programmed to live for 100 years if you get run over by a bus!

Theories at Level of the Cell
Random Error

The random error theory considers that errors occur at the level of DNA as a result of either mutations or macromolecular damage. This causes degeneration of the genetic material.

Error Catastrophe

In the error catastrophe theory errors occur at the level of transcription or translation and involve the insertion of an incorrect amino acid into a protein chain. If the protein is one involved with protein synthesis or DNA repair (eg an enzyme) then a cascade of defective proteins would result and the cell would rapidly die.

Hayflick Phenomenon

Leonard Hayflick demonstrated that tissue cultures of fibroblasts underwent a set number of divisions before dying. The number of potential divisions was related to the maximum lifespan of the species and from this he suggested that there was a cellular clock controlling the rate of ageing.

The Free Radical Theory

In the free radical theory more free radicals are produced with age which cause damage by reacting with nucleic acids, lipids and proteins. This theory supports the concept of the body 'rusting'.

Ageing as a By-product of Flux of Reducing Sugars

In certain circumstances post translational reactions between proteins and reducing sugars can cause features of ageing, eg premature ageing in diabetes mellitus.

Cross-Linkage Theory

As we age, the collagen sub-structure changes to allow growth, development and ageing. Increasing rigidity is achieved by intra and inter molecular cross-linkage between collagen molecules and collagen strands. Thus ageing is associated with changes in bone strength – that is why the child has a 'green-stick' fracture while the aged person has a 'brittle' fracture. Cross linkage between macromolecules causes a decline in their activity.

Programmed Theory

If ageing is pre-programmed it has to be controlled by genes.

The Genetics of Ageing

The precise role of genes is not clear but it is certain that they are involved in the ageing process. Genes are involved in ageing because longevity is species specific: children of long-lived parents are more likely themselves to live for longer and twin studies imply a genetic influence on lifespan. Probably only a few genes are responsible for determining longevity. The evidence for this is that several disorders of known genetic origin, eg, Down's Syndrome, carry with them features of premature ageing. Also, viral infection may confer immortality on a cell line, and since viruses only carry a small amount of genetic material this suggests that immortality may be due to few genes. Finally, the genetic make-up of man and chimpanzee are 99% similar, yet this small change has resulted in a large change in longevity, from 40 to a 100 years. Probably only a handful of genes programme for longevity so it

is possible (in the realms of science fiction) that genetic manipulation may eventually influence ageing.

Experimental Gerontology

The object of age research is the identification of the cause of disease, the introduction of measures to prevent and treat disease and the prevention of premature death. Much work has been done, particularly with rats, into trying to extend lifespan.

The classic experiments of McCay showed that a diet deficient in calories but adequate in all other respects increased the observed maximum lifespan of mice by 50% but at a cost. It delayed puberty and the prepubertal animals were more susceptible to infections resulting in the death of 50% of animals soon after being weaned. Moderate exercise may increase lifespan eg rats swimming for 15 minutes each day showed a 20% increase in lifespan. Sexually active rats have been shown to live longer than abstainers. It is not known whether this is related to testosterone, exercise, or to the fact that life was worth living!

Ethoxyquin, an antioxidant seemed to increase lifespan, but the evidence is confusing since the rats ate less. Rats injected with Gerovital – procainamide, lived longer than a control (saline) group, however, both groups however lived less than the average species lifespan. Studies with Drosophila (the fruit fly) have shown that a lower temperature increases lifespan. Finally overcrowding of animals decreases lifespan.

Long Lived Populations

Three remote communities have received considerable scientific attention in recent years because of claims that their populations live to extreme old age. These are Vilcabamba in the Andes of Ecuador, the Abkhazians in USSR and the Hunzas on the China/Pakistan borders.

Vilcabamba is in a crescent of isolated inaccessible valleys 1,500 m above sea level. It is near the equator with constant temperature (18°C), rainfall, humidity, and the day length equals night length. Due to its isolation, there is a lot of inbreeding producing a population with the following features: fair, hairy skin, 5'5" tall, very little obesity and thick calves which are considered by some to be a muscle pump '2nd heart'. The children are physically immature – male puberty is at 15 and female puberty is at 18 – but women continue reproducing into their fifties and men far beyond. It is a male orientated society with a very severe life, but despite heavy drinking and smoking there is no cancer, heart disease or diabetes. There is a high infant mortality rate with only fit individuals surviving. The elderly however have a large social role and remain active, lucid and retain their memories well. Support for the important role of nutrition is shown by the fact that their diet is low calorie and generally vegetable in nature.

The Hunzas and Abkhasians, although not well studied, appear to have similar features. The problem, however, is the validity of the records in such isolated communities. Localised populations even within England show a slight increase in their aged population, eg, Cornwall, Cumbria and East Anglia.

Sociology – The Theory of Old Age

The idea of a healthy old age is a modern phenomenon as it is only recently that a significant number of people enter old age. In the next Century the total world population will grow by 37.5%, but the over 60's will grow by 60.5%. This disproportionate number of elderly people changes the financial demands on the community for the taxes of the working population are used to pay for the pensions and services of the elderly. In less developed countries, the population over 60 is growing rapidly and has still to reach its peak. This may become a major problem due to the lack of social structure in these nations to support them.

Population pyramids can be used to follow changes in the population structure. Initially there is the traditional pyramid shape with a high number of young and few people reaching old age. Progressively there has been a shift to a 'barrel-shape' with an increasing number of middle and old aged, a decrease in the infant mortality rate and a decrease in the number of births, slowing the population growth. Finally as the number of children being born decreases it reaches an inverted pyramid with an increasingly elderly population. The changing demographic structure of the United Kingdom between 1901 and 2031 is shown in Figure 2. Notice the change from the pyramidal structure of 1901 to the barrel shape of 2031.

Demographic and Social Aspects of Ageing

In the UK and throughout the world there is an awareness of a 'demographic time bomb' or 'rising tide' of the increasing number of older people. Due to a reduction in mortality and a decrease in fertility, population 'pyramids' have transformed themselves into barrel shapes. In the UK this is particularly noticeable because of the decline in the numbers of the 17–24 age group relative to those aged over 65. This process is a modern one; in 1901 there were 2 million 65+, by 1951 the number had increased to 5 million 65+; today there are 9 million 65+ (16% of total population). Remember that elderly people are not a homogenous group and they can change in composition over time (eg more older old 85+). While old age is not synonymous with ill health and dependency, increasing age is connected with frailty.

Two studies (OPCS disability survey and the General Household survey) illustrate this: aged 65–69 only 5% cannot walk down the road unaided but aged 85+ 47% cannot do so; 70% of disabled adults are aged over 60; 75% of the most severely disabled are aged over 60[6].

Life expectancy for both men and women has increased marginally over the last 20 years but the disability free life expectancy has dropped: for men from 83% in 1976 to 82% in 1985; for women from 81% in 1976 to 79% in 1985. The interaction between the frail older population and the general public is considerable: 75% of the 6 million carers in Britain are caring for an older person.

Male and female differences in cohort survival in 1841, 1901 and 1951 are shown in figures 3, 4 and 5. In 1841 there was little difference in male/female survival, but by 1901 there is a marked difference: part of this was due to the First World War, part was due to improved midwifery and hygiene at child-birth. In 1951 the demographers forecast a marked difference in male/female survival after the age of 60. This forecast for life expectancy is based on the current death rates for men. Hopefully, the reality will be different and eventually male female survival will be similar.

Residential and nursing home care is connected to levels of physical dependency, the availability of social support, and the availability of places. Higher levels of dependency can be accommodated in the community if the individual is not isolated. The numbers of people in residential,

Figure 2

Actual and predicted demography of the United Kingdom 1901 to 2031

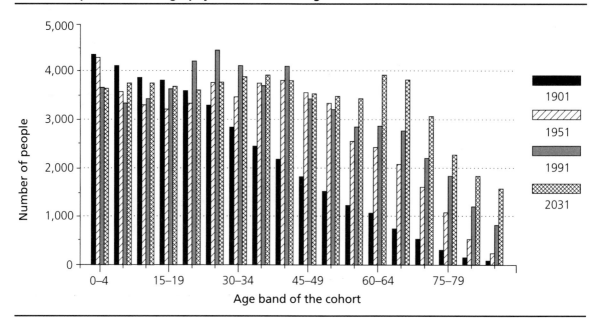

Figure 3

Male and female differences in cohort survival of cohort born in 1841

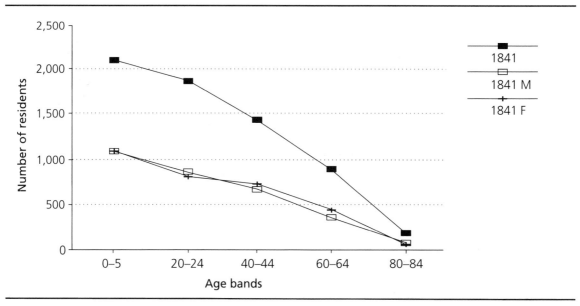

Figure 4

Male and female differences in cohort survival of cohort born in 1901

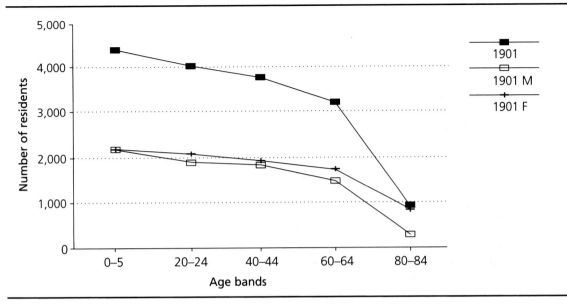

Figure 5

Estimated differences in cohort survival of the 1951 under fives

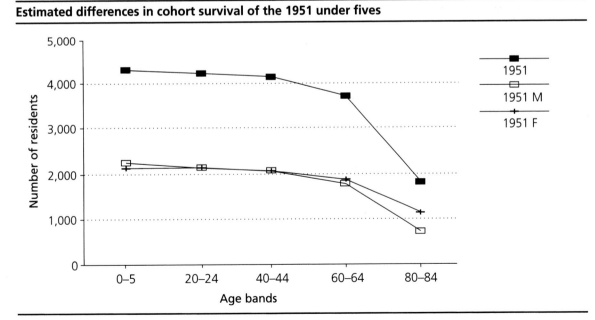

nursing and geriatric hospital beds has risen from 250,000 in 1970 to 500,000 in 1990 (the numbers in nursing homes from 20,000 to 125,000).

Sociological Theories of Old Age

Role Theory (Talcott Parsons)

The role theory is primarily a descriptive theory about personal adjustment to old age, thus little in-depth sociological theory, more psychology. Men are seen to need to adjust to the demoralisation and loss of self-esteem following retirement from work. Some individuals are seen as lacking 'new scripts' for increased leisure opportunities. The theory stresses the need for 'role flexibility' – ie new hobbies and interests. It has been criticised for ignoring women and being too functionalist.

Disengagement Theory (Neugarten)

The disengagement theory based on a longitudinal study in Kansas City, saw retirement as consisting of a mutual withdrawal of older people from society for the benefit of society; premised on the idea that individual's 'ego-energy' became redirected to personal pre-occupations, eg hobbies and family. This meant that younger people could step into their shoes. Women did not disengage until they were widowed. Disengagement was seen as a universal phenomenon, but is it just a rationalization of existing power inequalities? Criticisms are based on the functionalist approach and the theory is contradicted by empirical evidence which suggests older people often want to be more involved in society.

Structural Dependency Theory (Townsend, Walker)

Based on the idea that old people are deliberately made dependent by a society based on economically powerful groups who run government. Legally defined retirement ages and low state pensions push older workers out of the workforce and into poverty. Creation of the idea of old people as an economic burden and the need to control expenditure on them adds to the feeling of dependency. Abolition of SERPS (State Earnings Related Pension Scheme) as too costly, and low rates of increase for the state pension increases the gap between rich and poor. This affects older single women (85+) particularly, for nearly half are on income support.

The theory sees continuation of class-based inequalities continuing into old age. Exclusion from society through poverty is compounded by physical dependency which further makes older people powerless. Structured dependency sees the institutionalisation of older people in hospitals and homes as the double exercise of power against the old – through not having alternatives and through not having a say. The theory has been criticised for being too pessimistic and not acknowledging the well off older person (WOOPIE).

Psychology of Old Age

(See Chapter on Psychology of Ageing)

The psychology of old age may be divided into 3 areas of change: in cognition; in character and temperament (personality); and in adjustment. Cognition changes reflect a decline in ability to acquire new intelligence but a sustained ability to apply existing knowledge (ie, wisdom is maintained, wit declines). Ageing has little effect on the size of working memory, but it does impair the transfer of information from the short term to long term store. New information may therefore have to be presented more slowly and be repeated. The loss of existing knowledge (eg how to dress) is a pathological change and not an ageing one.

Character and temperament changes include personality changes, most typically a decrease in neuroticism and an increase in introversion. As we age we adjust. Elderly people have to come to terms with what they are and their changing role in life. Individuals respond in different ways. The disengagement theory implies that elderly people are removed from most of their social roles along with society withdrawing from them. There is also a loss of social conformity and a decreased desire for social respect. Structured dependency occurs, because society causes the elderly to assume a dependent role through retirement and pensions. Some elderly people are quite content to accept these changes, others try to deny that they are occurring or may even become depressive as a result of them. Many people, however, use the extra time that they have to take up additional activities and interests and have a fulfilling old age.

Practical Points

The ageing of a population reflects the control of causes of premature death. The disposable soma theory sees ageing as a biological necessity. As we age we have to adjust. Life style factors such as exercise, nutrition and stress, influence the rate of ageing in individuals. Each person's rate of ageing is genetically predetermined; with luck, all of us will reach our biological maximum. Clinically, it is important to understand the difference between ageing and disease. Strehler's concepts of universality, intrinsicality, progressiveness and deleteriousness are useful. Ageing changes occur gradually, so if any change occurs suddenly, *a priori*, it is not due to disease. More subtle changes like hypothyroidism and osteomalacia creep on slowly and the physician may miss these. It is a good practice to search for a treatable cause. Always bear in mind that if a one hundred and ten year old human is 'biologically elite' then that is the goal for which humanity should strive.

Acknowledgements

I thank my consultant and academic colleagues whose contribution to our course notes contributed to the content of this chapter. Two Bsc students, Raelene Groom and Justin Baseley rewrote the notes to make them user friendly. Copies of the notes can be obtained from my secretary Mrs Elizabeth Mosby whose help in the completion of this manuscript was invaluable. Data for the graphs was compiled from the Registrar General's Statistical Returns.

References

1. Fries JF & Crapo LM (1981) *Vitality and aging.* W H Freeman & Co, San Francisco.

2. Fries J (1993) *Compression of morbidity 1993: life span, disability and health costs.* in: Vellas B, Albarede JL, Garry PJ, (eds) Facts and Research in Gerontology. Paris: Serdi, 183–190.

3. Strehler BL (1962) *Time, cells, and aging.* Academic Press, New York.

4. Kirkwood TBL (1992) *Biological origins of ageing,* in: Grimley Evans J, Franklin Williams T, (eds) Oxford Textbook of Geriatric Medicine. Oxford University Press, Oxford, 35–40.

5. Rudd AG & Millard PH (1988) *What is ageing?* Baillière's Clinical Obstetrics and Gynaecology, 2 (2), 241–259.

6. Tinker A, McCreadie C, Wright F & Salvage AV (1994) *The care of frail elderly people in the United Kingdom.* HMSO, London.

Further Reading

Finch CE & Schneider EL (1985) *Handbook of the biology of aging. Second edition,* Van Rostrand Reinhold Company, New York.

Chapter 4

Retirement

Professor M R P Hall MA, BMBCH, FRCP (Lond & Edin)
Professor Emeritus of Geriatric Medicine
University of Southampton
Peartree Cottage
Emery Down
Lyndhurst
Hampshire
SO43 7FH

Biosketch:

Michael Hall read medicine at Oxford qualifying in 1952. After holding various junior medical appointments at the Radcliffe Infirmary, Oxford, he was appointed as the first Consultant Physician/Geriatrician at the Newcastle General Hospital in 1962 where he established an integrated service for the medical care of the elderly. In 1970 he was appointed Foundation Professor of Geriatric Medicine at the new Medical School at Southampton University and became Emeritus on his retirement in 1987. Currently, he chairs Age Concern Hampshire, is Vice-Chairman of the Brendoncare Foundation and a Governor of Research into Ageing, as well as being involved with other charities concerned with older people. His interests are cricket, fly fishing, gardening and golf.

Introduction

"Grow old along with me, the best is yet to be."—(Robert Browning)

It is perhaps appropriate that this chapter is written by a retired person for at least I can write from some personal experience. In addition, I have for many years been involved in pre-retirement education, initially as a member of the Medical Committee of the Pre-retirement Association, and more recently as Vice Chairman of the Southampton Branch Pre-retirement Association.

Preparation for Retirement

If one is going to live for as long a time after retirement as one spends at school it is clearly important to give some thought as to what one is going to do with all this 'spare time'! Retirement is a time when one can explore new avenues of knowledge and gain new experience in the subject of one's choice, 'the years still unexplored'. It is an advantage if one has ensured a firm base before retirement from which to launch one's activities. Retirement, therefore, needs to be planned. Some years ago I asked an eminent German Professor of Social Gerontology at what age she felt pre-retirement education should begin? Her reply was 'In the Primary School'. In other words, she felt that one couldn't start too early. There is sense in this view, for education should be continuous. Professor Alistair Heron (1961) enumerates six indispensable bases for a satisfactory retirement[1]:

1. Good physical and mental health.
2. An income substantially above subsistence level.
3. Suitable accommodation.
4. One or more absorbing hobbies.
5. Congenial friends and neighbours.
6. An adequate philosophy of life.

How many elderly at the present time achieve this base? But what is more important, how many will achieve this in the future? Much lip service is paid to the importance of preparing for retirement but how many people actually attend a course which is designed to do this. Pre-retirement Education is a 'hard sell', for retirement is a modern phenomenon. The work ethic still tends to be dominant in people's lives and little thought is given to what may happen when work is over. Consequently, retirement can become an eventless interregnum between work and death. Some businesses and organisations have recognised that a problem does exist and encourage their workers to participate in pre-retirement courses such as those run by the WEA, either by organising a course within the organisation or giving people time off to attend a course. Others have gone further, adopting various methods of smoothing the transition from work to retirement viz:

1. Graduated retirement, whereby the employee reduces his contact with his work by one day a week per year in the preceding 5 years prior to his retiral. Hence if his retiral age is 65 years and he works a 5-day week then he/she will work a 4-day week from 60–61 yrs, a 3-day week from 61–62 yrs, etc until he/she retires at 65 yrs.
2. The establishment of ex-employees groups/clubs, whereby the retired person maintains contact with their previous occupation and other ex-colleagues. This contact can vary from social gatherings or activities, to more personal services such as home visits to colleagues who are handicapped or have become older and frailer, thereby creating a self-help group.

The creation and responsibility for such pre- and post-retirement planning and activity should form part of the personnel function of the employer. However, not all employers give priority to such activity, while others do not have a sufficiently large workforce to justify the creation of a specific organisation. Moreover, research has shown that most workers welcome retirement and miss nothing when they retire, except perhaps money. Disengagement from work is not a concomitant to retirement. It may involve engagement in other activities. Not all retired people are alike, they do not all want to remain engaged in 'work', though plenty of opportunity exists for those who want to continue working even if that 'work' is 'voluntary' and thereby unpaid. There are 170,000 registered charities in the UK ranging from large organisations like 'Age Concern' or 'Save the Children', employing professional staff, to small local 'self-help' groups. Almost all will welcome help; for volunteers are in short supply. The Abbeyfield Society, one of the organisations for which I work, has 12,000 volunteers and could use many more! The opportunities that exist for continuing interesting occupation are therefore considerable.

1. Physical and Mental Health

The cross National Survey of populations in Denmark, Great Britain, and the United States of America in the 1960's showed that contrary to many people's preconceived notions, health improved after retirement in those subjects studied[2]. This is perhaps not surprising since many people may force themselves to work as retirement looms knowing that they only have a limited time left in work. Having stopped work their stress level falls and their health improves.

However, this survey took place 30 years ago. The new contractual arrangements for general practitioners that were introduced on 1 April 1990 lay particular emphasis on health promotion and screening procedures. As a result health checks are now necessary on all newly registered patients; patients not seen within 3 years; and patients aged 75 yrs and over. In addition, health promotion clinics are a regular feature of the practice schedule. A scheme of target payments has been introduced to encourage higher levels of cover with regard to cervical cytology and childhood immunisation. Influenza immunisation is positively encouraged, particularly for the elderly and other groups at risk.

The emphasis on health promotion should mean that people will be fitter at the time of their retirement and will remain so during their retirement. Some evidence to support this concept comes from Japan where Tatara and his colleagues (1991) have shown that strong health service programmes that start in middle age decrease the demand for inpatient care of the elderly[3]. It may also be a reason why life expectancy has increased so dramatically in Japan, rising from 67.8 yrs at birth to 80.9 yrs in women, and 63.6 yrs to 75.2 yrs in men during the 20 yrs period 1955 to 1986. The figures for the same period in England and Wales were 73.1 to 77.7 and 67.5 to 71.9 respectively. That such improvement is not just due to mortality in the first year of life is shown by the fact that Japanese life expectancy at 65 yrs has risen from 14.1 yrs to 19.3 yrs in women and 11.8 to 13.4 years in men.

2. An Income Substantially Above Subsistence Level

One of the major complaints that people have when they retire is shortage of money. In 1986 two thirds of pensioners had incomes of less than 140% of income support level (House of Commons Paper 378–11). The Family Expenditure Survey 1988 reported that 53% of elderly households had incomes of less than £100/week, while only 18% had incomes of more than £200/week. Moreover, elderly household incomes were lower in the over 75's. So much for income, what about capital? Financial Research Services (1988) reported that 62% had less than £2,000 while only 18% had over £10,000. There is no doubt therefore that a lot of people have little income and capital. To what is one entitled?

Your rights – each year Age Concern (England) publish 'A guide to money benefits for older people' with this title. It used to cost 50p but the 1995–96 edition costs £3.25. This booklet has 120 pages and spells out in simple language one's entitlement. It is pointless to attempt to reproduce all the details contained in this very informative book in a short chapter such as this. The reader is advised to buy a copy. A few basic points are worth making:

1. In order to qualify for a State Retirement Pension you must be of pensionable age (60 for women and 65 for men) and fulfil the National Insurance (NI) contribution conditions.
2. The pension may consist of a Basic Pension plus an Additional Pension (based on contributions after April 1975). If drawing the pension is deferred then an extra pension may be received. These are all taxable.
3. Additional benefits such as Income Support, Housing Benefit and Community Charge Benefit may also be claimed depending on the person's income and savings. Many people entitled to claim these benefits fail to do so. They are not taxable.
4. The Basic Pension is paid at the same rate to all people who have fulfilled the conditions. It is index linked and the rate varies from year to year.
5. The Additional Pension, paid under the State Earnings-Related Pension Scheme (SERPS) started on 6 April 1978 and is based on earnings on which contributions have been paid since then.
6. The Graduated Pension scheme existed from April 1961 to April 1975 and was based on graduated contributions paid from earnings. If these were paid a Graduated Pension can be received even if the individual is not qualified to receive a Basic Pension.

7. There is also a non-contributory Retirement Pension for people over the age of 80 who have no Retirement Pension. There is a residential qualification for this pension of 10 years or more in any 20 year period after the 60th birthday. It is taxable.

8. People with disabilities and their Carers may be eligible for additional benefits. These include **Attendance Allowance** (Two Rates) which can be claimed after the day and/or night conditions have been fulfilled for six months. This period may be waived in the case of people who are terminally ill. It is not affected by income or savings and does not depend on NI contributions. It is not taxable but has to be claimed by the person requiring help, who will be assessed by a visiting doctor. **Invalid Care Allowance** can be claimed by a carer who is over 16 and under pension age and spends a minimum of 35 hours a week looking after someone in receipt of attendance allowance. It is taxable. **Mobility Allowance** can be claimed by people who cannot walk or can only walk with great difficulty. Claims however must be made before the 66th birthday and the allowance will be paid until the age of 80 as long as the qualifying conditions are fulfilled. It can be paid to people at home or in hospital or other institution. It is not taxable.

9. Monetary help may be obtainable for a variety of other things such as fuel, house insulation, repairs to property, paying for residential or nursing home care and health costs not provided free by the NHS.

10. Travel concessions are available on rail, underground, bus services and some airlines to pensioners.

While some of these pensions are available to all retired people, who have reached retirement age and are qualified, others are means tested. If savings are more than £8,000 then Income Support cannot be obtained. If savings are less than £3,000 and total income is less than your applicable amount, (ie Personal allowance and any entitled Premium) then Income Support benefit is obtainable. Between £3,000 and £8,000 every £250 counts as £1 a week extra income. The applicable amount is considered as being equal to subsistence level. In order to achieve an income considerably above this one must plan to save and the most effective way to do this is to join an occupational pension scheme. If this is not possible, take out an insurance policy. If one is going to do this one needs to start early in life, as the cost will then be lower. Also, if one thinks ahead it is possible now to anticipate needs that might arise in old age as a result of ill-health by purchasing insurance against the possibility of requiring long-term care.

Pensions

Retirement age is at present 65 years for men and 60 years for women. But in May 1990 the European Court of Justice ruled that men and women should be able to draw pensions from the same age (Barber v Guardian Royal Exchange). A consultation document on retirement is due to be published shortly. Currently many companies are trying to pre-empt whatever happens by raising the retirement age for women to 65 years. On the other hand the Labour Party's Charter for pensioners would give men the right to draw the State pension at the age of 60 years.

Under the Social Security Act 1990 pension funds will have to guarantee minimum annual increases – limited price indexation (LPI). The Occupational Pensions Advisory Service (Opas) was set up as a charity in 1982 and recently received a grant for the first time. Opas works with local Citizens Advice Bureaux to help pensioners with queries. A pension ombudsman was appointed in April 1990 who deals with tricky cases that Opas has not resolved. The pension scheme registry once established will be very useful in helping pensioners who have changed their jobs several times during their working life to trace the amounts and claim their dues.

3. Suitable Accommodation

This means different things to different people. Not only is the location important but so is the design. I bought my house 20 years ago with retirement in mind. The ground floor has no steps and sufficient rooms and facilities to enable my wife and I not to have to go upstairs if we become frail and disabled. But we have a large garden useful at present as a hobby and productive of fruit and vegetables. We are also some distance from shops (½ mile) and public transport is non-existent. But there is an excellent village community of which we are a part. So far it has been a good choice but it is one that would not suit everyone and there are some obvious potential snags. However, we are very fortunate, what about the rest of the elderly?

In 1986, of dwellings where the head of the household was over 70 years, 49% were owner occupied, 37% were rented from the Local Authority and 24% from another source (Social Trends 1989). However, many of the owner occupied houses were of old construction so that a third were in an unsatisfactory or poor condition and many lacked basic amenities. Since most elderly wish to continue to live in their own homes or at least remain in their own communities, a local and national policy to enable them to do this is needed. Various schemes are available to elderly owner occupiers but tenants, particularly in the private sector, are often less well served.

Home Improvement Grants are available as indicated in the previous section. All are means tested but 100% grants are made to those below a certain income level and for adaptations to disabled people. Grants or discretionary loans for small but essential repairs can be made, up to a total of £1,000 from the Social Fund of the LA to people on Income Support. Many elderly have difficulty in applying for these grants and dealing with the builders.

Housing Agency Services have developed in recent years to help elderly with some of these problems. The service has three basic components – design service; grant administration and financial advice; and construction supervision. The best known initiatives in this field are those provided by the Anchor Housing Trust and 'Care and Repair'. The National Home Improvement Council through its Neighbourhood Revitalisation Services has also developed 25 area based agencies in older housing areas.

Home Equity Transfer is a scheme which enables elderly owner occupiers to release the equity stored in their homes as cash income. This is usually done through a bank or insurance company, but risks are involved and interest rates and house prices are unpredictable. On retirement the decision has to be taken whether to move. Government policy is for people to remain in their own homes for as long as possible, if they so wish. However, many people decide to move out of the family home on the grounds that it is too big for them. In the case of Local Authority (LA) housing stock this decision is often welcomed by the housing department, for it may free

a larger house for a young family, as well as enabling them to upgrade the house. A dwelling suitable for an elderly person is offered in exchange. This could be in warden supervised sheltered housing or in housing linked to a call system or in another type of small dwelling.

In the case of owner occupiers, sale of the family home will enable them to buy a smaller dwelling which may have been specially designed for ease of running and may be linked to other facilities relating to either leisure and/or care. The decision to move is one that should be taken only after careful consideration. Moving is a potential hazard to the elderly and any move should be so planned as to avoid the need for a future move. The problem of housing in retirement has been researched and reviewed by Williams (1990)[4].

4. One or more Absorbing Hobbies

It has been suggested that one needs at least three hobbies and one of these you should be able to do after the age of 90 years! There is no doubt that retirement is a time of great opportunity. It is possible to teach 'old dogs' new tricks. Work done 20 years ago in the University of Queensland showed that the elderly could learn and teach German to 'A' level standard, even though previously they had never learned a foreign language. Similarly, they were able to learn to play a recorder and tour with an orchestra. The choice of hobby, activity or pastime is obviously an individual one, but it is important. The literature on this subject is vast and has been very well reviewed by Jean Macheath (1984)[5]. Further education of all elderly and those who are in any way involved with them is essential if people are going to be able to continue their individual development. It must be remembered though that 'Our tastes greatly alter. The lad does not care for the child's rattle and the old man does not care for the young man's whore', as Dr Johnson once remarked. Old age therefore, is a time during which it should be possible to do more and more of the things that one wants to, and those which are purposive are likely to be of the greatest value in promoting self esteem.

5. Congenial Friends and Neighbours

This means making the effort to keep in contact with friends and trying to be a good neighbour yourself. Cumming and Henry (1961) suggested that retirement is a period of disengagement from life[6]. With ageing some degree of ego reduction takes place. It is important therefore to maintain one's self esteem and keep up one's morale. Keeping socially active with one's friends and neighbours may be a very good way of maintaining morale. It is possible too, that involvement with friends and neighbours in clubs, pubs, and other social activities encourages reminiscence as a means of promoting interest and engagement. Ageing and reminiscence processes have been excellently described by Coleman (1986)[7].

6. An Adequate Philosophy of Life

This is again, very much a personal matter and the point which caused Heron[1] the most trouble to explain. One must have a purpose, something which one has to do: and also something that one enjoys doing, that has no objective other than pleasure. An example of this is the answer given by a 96 year old Northumbrian farmer. When asked by a young reporter to what did he attribute his long life, he replied, *"I put my boots on every morning"*. In other words he had a purpose, which required him to put on his boots, even if it was only to enjoy himself.

Retirement

Practical Points

1. More and more people are living to reach retirement and this number will increase in the future.

2. People will need to plan for a longer period of retirement, perhaps 20 to 30 years.

3. Preparation and planning are needed to make the most of the opportunities presented. This should start as early as possible, even in the primary school.

4. Requirements for a satisfactory retirement include good physical and mental health, an income substantially above subsistence level, suitable accommodation, absorbing hobbies, congenial friends and neighbours and an adequate philosophy of life.

5. The transition from work to retirement needs to be designed.

References

1. Heron A (1961) *Preparation for retirement; solving new problems*, National Council for Social Service, London.

2. Shanas E, Townsend P, Wedderburn D et al (1968). *Old people in three industrial societies*, Routledge, Keegan, Paul, London.

3. Tatara, Kozo, Shinsho, Funiaki, Susuki, Masatake et al (1991) *Relation between use of health check-ups starting in middle age and demand for inpatient care by elderly people in Japan*, Br Med J, 302, 615–618.

4. Williams G (1990) *The experience of housing in retirement*. Gower Publishing, Aldershot.

5. Macheath J A (1984) *Activity, health and fitness in Old Age*. Croom Helm/St Martins, New York.

6. Cumming E & Henry W (1961) *Growing old: the processes of disengagement*, Basic Books, New York.

7. Coleman PG (1986) *Ageing and reminiscence processes. Social and clinical implications*, John Wiley & Sons, Chichester.

8. Age Concern England (1995) *Your Rights*.

9. Heron 38

10. House of Commons

11. Social Trends (1989)

Chapter 5

Community Care for Elderly People

Dr P J Elton, MBChB, MSC, FFPHM
Director of Public Health,
Wigan and Bolton Health Authority
43 Churchgate
Bolton
BL1 1JF

Fran McCabe, SRN, Health Visitor, BA, MSC Geriatric Medicine
Assistant Director
Social Services Department
PO Box 536
Manchester Town Hall Extension
Manchester
M60 2LA

Biosketch:

Dr Elton has been a Consultant in Public Health Medicine for 12 years, including 7 years as Director of Community Health Services in North Manchester. His research responsibilities at Tameside, Glossop and Oldham have included contributing to Community Care plans. He has recently joined as Director of Public Health at Wigan & Bolton Health Authority.

Fran McCabe SRN, Health Visitor, BA, MSC Geriatric Medicine
Currently: Assistant Director of Community Care (Provision) in Manchester Social Services. Worked over 30 years in the field of health and social care in Coventry, Birmingham, London, Leicester and Manchester; in the health services, voluntary sector and in research as well as Social Services.

Community Care

'*Community care means providing the services and support which people who are affected by problems of ageing, mental illness, mental handicap or physical or sensory disability need to be able to live as independently as possible in their own homes or in homely settings in the community*'. This is the opening statement of the British Government's 1989 White Paper, 'Caring for People'[1]. It represents the kernel of the strategy to provide for an increasing need.

The immediate challenge arises from the dramatic increase in the very elderly.

The rise in those aged over 85 is particularly significant as the prevalence of disability increases rapidly with age (table 2)[4].

It is possible to grade disability by severity. A combination of the disability scores of the areas mentioned in Table 2 gives a measure of disability. Only amongst the most severe, do a majority live in communal establishments. It is probable that for most of the disabled, except for the least severe, some assistance in daily living is required. It is amongst the most disabled that the increase with age is most striking (table 3)[4].

Table 1

The Present and Projected Population of the Elderly in England and Wales 1991 Census Population[2] and Mid 1991 Projections[3]

	(Thousands)		
	65–74	75–84	85+
1991[2]	4,505	2,776	763
2001[3]	4,311	2,922	1,087
2011[3]	4,814	2,936	1,304
2021[3]	5,704	3,495	1,459
2031[3]	6,453	4,136	1,934

Even if the age-specific prevalence rate of disability declines[5], there is likely to be a substantial increase in disability associated with the growing number of very elderly in the next few years.

In April 1993, the major new piece of legislation, 'Caring for People', came into force and largely determined the way in which elderly people will be cared for by services.

Fuelled by the escalating costs of private residential care, which has increased from £10m in 1979 to over £1,000m in May 1989, disquiet

Table 2

Estimates of Prevalance of Disability among Elderly in Great Britain by type of Disability (rate per thousand)

Type of Disability	Minimum Definition	Aged 60–74	Aged over 75
Locomotion	Cannot walk 400 yards without stopping or severe discomfort	198	496
Reaching & Stretching	Has difficulty putting one arm behind back to put jacket on	54	149
Dexterity	Has difficulty using a pair of scissors	78	199
Seeing	Has difficulty seeing to read ordinary newspaper print	56	262
Hearing	Difficulty following a conversation against background noise	110	328
Personal Care	Has difficulty getting in and out of bed	99	313
Continence	Loses control of bladder occasionally or uses a device to control bowels or bladder	42	147
Communication	Other people have some difficulty understanding him/her or has some difficulty understanding what other people say or what they mean	42	140
Behaviour	Difficult to stir or has feelings of aggressiveness	40	152
Intellectual Impairment	At least one problem eg cannot write a short letter	40	109

A GUIDE TO THE CARE OF THE ELDERLY

Table 3

Estimates of Prevalence of Disability among Elderly in Great Britian by Severity (rate per thousand)

	Aged 60–74	Aged over 75
Least Severe	51	70
Intermediate Severity	209	516
Most Severe	4	45
	264	631

about the standards of care in both private and local authority homes; and the fact that elderly people generally do not want to go into residential care, the legislation recognises that they may prefer to remain at home with adequate support when their health and social conditions deteriorate.

A key objective of the legislation is 'to promote the development of domiciliary, day and respite services to enable people to live in their own homes'[6]. To do this, funds which were administered through the Department of Social Security (DSS) are being progressively transferred to the Local Authority. Until the implementation of the legislation, the decision as to whether a person should receive financial support for residential or nursing home care was decided upon by adjudication officers at the DSS. No professional assessment was necessarily required and indeed did not take place[7]. Under the new legislation, professional assessment is the responsibility of the Social Services Departments and is a pre-requisite for financial support.

In order to ensure that elderly people do have a choice and an opportunity to stay at home, in the future, emphasis is on a needs led approach to assessment. The White Paper stated:

'The objective of assessment is to determine the best available way to help the individual. Assessment should focus positively on what the individual can and cannot do, and could be expected to achieve, taking account of his or her personal and social relationships. Assessments should not focus only on the user's suitability for a particular existing service. The aim should be first to review the possibility of enabling the individual to continue to live at home even if this means arranging a move to different accommodation within the local community, and if that possibility does not exist, to consider whether residential or nursing home care would be appropriate.'

This approach has implications for early assessment. People with health and social problems frequently present themselves to the general practitioners who are in an ideal position to carry out an assessment, allowing the possibility of addressing remediable problems, which are often neglected, or referring on as appropriate. It is important not to dismiss a person's difficulties as a natural concomitant of old age. Depressive illness may be overlooked because both the person and the professional feel that it is natural to be sad when many of their contemporaries have died and yet the majority will respond to treatment[8]. Other problems may be considered trivial but ill-fitting dentures, for example, can severely restrict a person's diet[9]. Some conditions such as urinary incontinence may be wrongly thought to be intractable when this is clearly not so[10]. It is important to provide help to people with hearing, vision and chiropodial problems which are common, remediable and increase disability. (See chapter 9, Role of General Practitioners in The Care of The Elderly).

The screening of people over 75 years of age provide a particular opportunity to identify social care needs. The way in which referrals will be received by Social Services changed with the new legislation. In many instances, especially where a continuing social care need is likely, referral will be for a social care assessment rather than an assessment for a particular service. The Community Care legislation sees the Local Authority having the responsibility for ensuring an assessment will be carried out and by transferring finances from the DSS to Social Services. The Social Services can provide some of the services themselves, but 85% of the funds transferred from the DSS must be spent in the independent sector[11].

Furthermore, the Local Authority are required to produce and publish criteria for people who are priorities for their services. Information is, therefore, required from the person or agency referring so that the degree of their priority for help can be ascertained and an appropriate assessment be made. Thus referrals in many cases need to be made for an assessment of social need, rather than for a particular service.

The White Paper stated that help should be targeted upon those in greatest need. As such, the future will see the home help service moving towards focusing its help on people with the greatest disability, rather than providing domestic help to elderly people who have minimal levels of disability and can otherwise manage everyday tasks.

The legislation has had major implications for a greater collaborative approach between Health and Social Services. Elderly people who need community care often have multiple pathologies combined with social care needs requiring the *assessment* skills of both Health and Social Services personnel. The distinction between health and social care needs is frequently arbitrary and interdisciplinary assessments are often necessary.

In a Social Services Inspectorate Report[12] where practices in local areas were surveyed, the evidence indicates that 'agencies have developed a common language for defining service requirements and a common understanding of who controlled the resource, but there was no such common language covering the effective communication of users' social care needs'. Progressively, it is likely that at the policy level, formal arrangements for interagency assessment, based on agreed criteria and procedural document, will develop. In the meantime, practices are likely to develop out of good local relationships between Health and Social Services' personnel which involves clients and their carers in developing appropriate services.

Community care requires collaboration around the *provision of services* and other help for elderly people. At a minimum, visiting workers should complete a record kept by the elderly person so that other services know who else has visited. In other instances one service may do an assessment whilst another service can provide the necessary care, eg chiropodists may assess that a person requires only simple foot care which the district nurse, who is for other reasons regularly visiting, will undertake. Even when they have major disabilities, elderly people generally wish to stay at home but are faced by a lack of choice and inflexibility of services, often operating predominantly 9–5 and only offering a limited service. There is also an overlap in service provision, perhaps most evident at the level of practical support at home. A number of projects have tried to co-ordinate care at this level, avoiding duplication and providing a more comprehensive service. The Darlington Community Care Project, for instance, combined the role of a home help and a nursing auxiliary[13].

The wishes of the elderly and their carers may be complex. In relation to housing, the elderly

may wish to stay in the same accommodation with or without adaptations or move to other accommodation, but in a specified location. If there is a desire to move, it may be for a different type of housing, eg without stairs, sheltered housing, residential or nursing home. For those who wish to enter a residential or nursing home in another Local Authority, for example, to move nearer to family or friends, the new legislation allows a Local Authority to fund a place for one of its residents in another area. At present 12% of people over 65 in communal establishments never receive a visit and 47% have a visitor less than once a week[14].

A significant proportion of people with disabilities feel that they could be helped by an item of equipment or adaptation which they do not have (table 4)[14].

Screening of locomotor disability has been found to identify many low cost pieces of equipment that would help older people in everyday living[15].

Another outcome of a needs led approach to elderly people's problems is that help outside the home may be identified, such as day care or respite care. Day care encompasses a large range of activities: a therapeutic intervention or specialist assessment or rehabilitation approach that may be undertaken in day hospitals; a mix of social, educational and therapeutic activities that can be undertaken in Local Authority and voluntary day centres.

For many elderly, a social club or a peripatetic day centre which is available on only certain day(s) of the week may be more appropriate. Advancing age should not preclude people taking holidays although they may need some support in order to be able to go.

Even amongst the most disabled, only a small minority of people receive respite care. The legislation allows funds to be used to support people in the community which had previously been reserved for residential care. Moreover, even for residential care, the easy option for private homes is to keep their beds full with long-term residents rather than people coming in for respite care unless there is appropriate compensation.

Respite and relief care also supports carers. Data shows that there are about 6 million carers, 8% of whom carry out the main responsibility for looking after someone who is elderly or physically or mentally disabled[16]. A key objective of the White Paper was to 'ensure that service

Table 4

Equipments and Adaptations that Disabled Adults in Private Households did not have but which they thought would help them

Disability	Equipment	% of people with disability without any equipment who thought that equipment would help	% of people with disability who had one type of that equipment but thought more of that type of equipment would help
Locomotion	Mobility equipment	7	5
Locomotion	Home adaptation	43	39
Reaching and Stretching	Small equipment or gadget	30	33
Dexterity	Small equipment or gadget	32	33
Seeing	Vision equipment	13	13
Hearing	Hearing aid or other aids to hearing, eg telephone adaptor	33	39
Personal Care	Special furniture	16	31
Personal Care	Home adaptation	41	43
Continence	Incontinence aid	17	14

providers make practical support for carers a high priority'. Consistently, research and experience has indicated that carers need information and advice about caring, recognition from professional carers, practical help, regular respite and emotional support and psychological insight. Respite can be in the form of someone coming to the home to allow a chance for the carer to carry out some other aspect of their life (epitomised in the Crossroads Care Attendant Schemes), day care, short term arranged care in residential, nursing home or hospital, or schemes such as day fostering. There are many examples of local initiatives that support carers of elderly people, including those with dementia, but they all tend to be small scale and are often associated with voluntary activity[17]. In the future, work with carers, and supporting and voluntary activities, is likely to feature more in meeting community care needs of elderly people.

The wishes of the elderly person are not only important in their own right but also allow that person to retain the maximum independence that they seek. Consideration to detail is necessary, ranging from provision of equipments to help cooking or the offer of accommodation which does not require the elderly person to cross a main road to reach the shops or the church. Involvement may be in the form of one-off help or an input from a range of agencies that will reduce the handicap of impairments and disability in elderly people, and ultimately reduce their need for community care services.

The early findings on community care do indicate that there are real assessments of people's needs which may still lead to residential or nursing home care, but there is an increasing ability to provide alternative care at home[18]. Other benefits that are being realised are the involvement of users and carers in the assessment process, the legal rights of users to have choice in their care and the closer working relationship between Health and Social Services in many parts of the country. There are undoubted difficulties, such as some delay in discharging some patients from hospital, but the legislation does present a continuing challenge to provide a more responsive service.

Community Care for Elderly People

Practical Points

1. 'Caring for People' came into force in April 1993. It recognises that people may prefer to remain in their own homes rather than enter residential care.

2. A key objective is the promotion and development of domiciliary, day and respite services to enable people to stay in their own homes.

3. Assessment will be based on what people can and cannot do and can be expected to achieve.

4. The general practitioner is ideally placed to carry out early assessment.

5. Practical support for carers will have a high priority. This involves information, advice, recognition, practical help, regular respite and emotional support and psychological insight.

References

1. Secretaries of State for Health, Social Security, Wales & Social Security, Wales & Scotland (1989) *Caring for People*, HMSO, London (Cmnd 849).

2. SASPAC (1994) Local Research Centre, London.

3. OPCS (1993) OPCS Monitor PP2 93/1, OPCS.

4. Martin J, Meltzer H & Elliot D (1988) *The prevalence of disability among adults*, HMSO, London.

5. Schneider EL & Guralnik JM (1987) *The compression of morbidity: a dream which may come true, someday*, Gerontologica Perspecta, 1, 8–14.

6. *Community Care in the Next Decade and Beyond*. Policy Guidance, HMSO, London 1990.

7. Hepple J, Bowler I & Bowman CE (1989) *A Survey of Private Nursing Home Residents in Weston-Super-Mare*, Age and Ageing, 18, 61–63.

8. Baldwin B (1988) *Late life depression? Undertreated?* Br Med J, 296, 519.

9. Heath MR (1972) *Dietary selection by elderly persons, related to dental state.* Brit Dent J, 132, 145–148.

10. Vetter NJ, Jones DA & Victor CR (1971) *Urinary incontinence in the elderly at home.* Lancet, 2, 1275–1277.

11. Department of Health (1994) *Community Care – Special Transitional Grant. Independent Sector expenditure in 1993/94.* March 1994. LASSL(94)3.

12. Social Services Inspectorate (1991) *Assessment systems and Community Care.* Department of Health and Social Security, Lancashire.

13. Challis D, Darton R, Johnson L, Stone M, Traske K & Wall B (1989) *The Darlington Community Care Project, supporting frail elderly people at home.* Personal Social Services Unit, University of Kent.

14. Martin J, White A & Meltzer H (1988) *Disabled adults: services, transport and employment.* HMSO, London.

15. Hart D, Bowling A, Ellis M, & Silman A (1990) *Locomotor disability in very elderly people: value of a programme for screening and provision of aids for daily living.* Br Med J, 301, 216–20.

16. Haffenden S (1991) *Getting it right for Carers, Setting up Services for Carers, Guide for Practitioners.* Department of Health, Social Services Inspectorate.

17. Hills D (1991) *Carer support in the community. Evaluation of the Department of Health initiative: 'Demonstration Districts for Informal Carers'.* 1986–1989, Department of Health, Social Services Inspectorate.

18. Social Services Inspectorate, Department of Health (1993) *Caring for People. Progress Review: North of England Region.* Sept. 1993.

Chapter 6

The Accommodation Needs of the Elderly

Wally Harbert OBE, AAPSW
Executive Director, Planning and Development
Help the Aged
St James's Walk
London
EC1R 0BE

Biosketch:

Wally Harbert is Director of Planning and Development for Help the Aged. He trained as a psychiatric social worker and is a former Director of Social Services. He has written four books on the management of social services and undertaken assignments in Europe for the United Nations, the World Health Organisation and the European Union. He has served on several government committees. He was President of the Association of Directors of Social Services in 1978/9 and was awarded an OBE in 1984. He lives in Bath with his wife who works as a tourist guide.

Introduction

Perceptions about the needs of elderly people and how they should be met are changing rapidly. Just as advances in medicine and medical knowledge are transforming health care so a changing appreciation of the social needs of elderly people is stimulating significant adjustments to the way in which social care is provided. Furthermore, a change in distribution of wealth and income is placing power in the hands of increasing numbers of elderly people who, having benefited from the rewards of a consumer society, demand a style of provision and a quality of services far in advance of that provided in former years.

The mechanics for determining which needs will be met and the methods of meeting them has largely been a matter for professional carers and statutory services to determine. Now the consumer is a force to be reckoned with and there is a multiplicity of providers competing with one another. Pressures on Social Services, Housing and Health Authority budgets have prompted new thinking about the way in which services are offered. Hospitals are no longer regarded as suitable places for the long term care of elderly people and the development in the early 1980s of Social Security funding for people in private nursing homes had the effect of switching long term nursing care from public hospitals to the private sector, releasing Health Service funds for acute care.

The provision of appropriate accommodation for elderly people requires a government strategy and long-term investment. Government policy in the United Kingdom has placed reliance on the private market. Large numbers of elderly people have insufficient capital to meet their accommodation needs by purchase and the supply of rented accommodation is dwindling. However, Government money has been available to pay for elderly people to enter residential homes; as a consequence many of them continue to be badly housed and others are offered inappropriate residential care.

Care at Home

The care and accommodation needs of elderly people are inextricably interwoven; those who are fit can live non-restricted lives in any location and if they need assistance at a time of crisis, they may receive help from various medical, nursing and other services. The onset of physical frailty will make it desirable to live near relatives or in close proximity to public transport and other amenities. Special adaptations may be required to ensure that a dwelling is suitable for someone with reduced mobility.

Most elderly people wish to remain living in familiar surroundings close to friends. Often their dwellings can be adapted to meet their individual needs. This may take the form of a ramp to facilitate wheelchair access, a stair lift, the provision of a downstairs toilet and shower, grab rails in the bathroom or even a hoist to lift a disabled person in and out of bed. Local Authority Social Services departments are responsible for assessing need and in some instances funds can be attracted from housing departments or from charitable sources. However, there is often a long waiting list both for assessment and the provision of assistance. The elderly person may be required to make a financial contribution towards costs.

Many people are worried about what may happen if they have a fall while they are alone at home and unable to summon help. Community alarms have been designed to enable people to call for help even if they cannot reach a telephone. The alarm consists of a normal telephone with an attachment that enables direct contact to be made with a control centre. A special feature is a pendant which can be worn round the neck; if the elderly person is unable to reach the telephone, by pressing the pendant, he or she can trigger the dialling mechanism and two way speech can take place with the control centre even if the telephone is in another room.

The control centre is able to contact emergency services or arrange whatever other help is necessary. The apparatus is becoming more sophisticated every year and it is now possible to attach devices which act as a smoke detector, a burglar alarm and even provide a signal in the event that the temperature falls to the extent that there is a danger of hypothermia.

Some elderly people live in dwellings that are too expensive for them to maintain. A number of organisations provide re-mortgaging facilities enabling elderly people to release the capital tied up in their homes to meet the cost of repairs or to provide a steady income. However, some of these schemes have severe drawbacks and no commitment should be entered into without independent expert advice.

Sheltered Housing

Many elderly people want to live independently but with the added security that someone familiar near by can be called upon for assistance in the event of an emergency; they may also prefer to live in well designed, purpose-built accommodation that is easy to clean and maintain. Sheltered housing schemes are designed to meet these needs, although the facilities they provide vary enormously. They range from luxury apartments and bungalows to self-contained flats, bed-sitting rooms and rooms with shared facilities.

The distinguishing feature of sheltered housing is the presence of a manager or warden. With the development of community alarm systems, some schemes have become semi-sheltered housing, dispensing with a warden and linking residents to a control centre. This means that they are outside the normal definition of sheltered housing.

Wardens are selected for their knowledge and experience of the kinds of problems encountered by elderly people. They can be regarded as good neighbours who offer advice, summon help when required and maintain regular contact with residents. Residents are encouraged to be as independent as possible and they make use of the range of services available to other elderly people in the community. For example, they choose their own general practitioner and can request assistance from a community nurse or home help.

In recent years, sheltered housing has been developed by housing associations and by private developers. Some housing associations provide leasehold arrangements whereby an elderly person with capital from the sale of a house, but who cannot afford the purchase price of a sheltered unit, can pay 70% of the price and the same proportion is received back when the property is re-sold; rent is paid on the remaining 30%.

The annual charges levied by private companies for the services of a warden, for building maintenance, for the upkeep of gardens and for cleaning common areas, can increase dramatically and purchasers are therefore advised to satisfy themselves that their resources are sufficient to meet likely increases.

There is no doubt that the potential of sheltered housing to provide high quality accommodation and care for elderly people has been neglected, not only in the United Kingdom, but in many other western countries. Both the buildings and the staff have been ill-equipped to respond to the needs of people when they become frail and there is pressure to transfer elderly people to residential homes when they need more care than can be offered on the basis of good neighbourliness by a warden working from nine to five, five days a week.

Very Sheltered (or Extra Care) Housing

The concept of very sheltered or extra care housing has been developed to enable frail people to continue living in independent accommodation. Such schemes mostly include a communal kitchen and dining room so that at least the main meal of the day can be provided. Other features include specially designed bathrooms and toilets for disabled people, a plentiful supply of hand rails, a medical room and sick bay. Twenty-four hour staffing arrangements are similar to those of an elderly persons home but residents have more independence, better private facilities and the dignity of their own front door. They can entertain friends and relatives in their own accommodation, choose which meals to eat in the dining room and use the communal lounges as and when they please. It has been shown that extremely frail and infirm elderly people can be offered high quality care in domestic scale accommodation so that admission to a conventional residential care home or nursing home is avoided.

Very sheltered housing is undoubtedly the pattern of future care arrangements for the majority of elderly people who can no longer be cared for in their own homes. Although private residential homes have increased rapidly in recent years, local authorities and housing associations have been turning to very sheltered housing schemes and some are examining ways of converting existing residential homes to very sheltered housing. Several other countries are moving in this direction – Denmark and the Netherlands are no longer building traditional elderly persons homes and Sweden is replacing them by very sheltered housing and improved domiciliary care. A nursing home in Denmark has been converted to the principles of very sheltered housing[1].

Residential Care

Traditionally, decisions about the admission of an elderly person to long term nursing or residential care have been made by professional carers with little regard to the long term impact of admission on the personality of the elderly person. Institutional care has been seen as a beneficial way of responding to needs, as a means of surrounding the elderly person with care and control. Yet we know that even with highly motivated staff, routines in institutions tend to take on a grey uniformity for residents who are dependent on staff for fulfilling their basic human requirements. Because of the imbalance of power between users and providers it is easy for residents to opt out rather than assert their individuality and independence. Residential care can create a stigma, segregation and over-dependence leading to a loss of emotional vitality and of personal dignity.

The Association of Directors of Social Services and the British Geriatric Society have argued that a thorough medical examination should be undertaken prior to an elderly person being admitted to residential care. This helps to identify medical conditions that require treatment and sometimes the need for admission to a home can be avoided. Regular medical examinations and carefully devised care plans are required for each resident.

All available research shows that elderly people prefer to remain living in their own homes with appropriate practical help and services provided for them. Until recently they have been offered little choice between 6 or 7 hours a week of home care with occasional visits by the community nurse and 168 hours a week in an institution. The market was so constructed that a Social Services department could not provide services costing £50 per week to keep an elderly person at home and, as a consequence, the income support system provided £160 per week for, what amounted to, their second choice – institutional care. The report of Sir Roy Griffiths (1988) and the subsequent Health Service and Community Care Act of 1990 were designed to bring this fragmentary and destructive policy to an end[2]. Since April 1993 the Government has permitted expenditure previously made available exclusively for residential care, to be used to support elderly people in their own homes.

The availability of residential services on a large and expanding scale has mitigated against the development of adequate domiciliary services. Large numbers of elderly people have been admitted to residential care with no adequate assessment of their needs and there has been little use of intensive domiciliary care as a means of assessing need so that the least disruptive form of care is offered to elderly people.

While studies of the aspirations of elderly people around the world show that overwhelmingly they wish to remain in their own homes, investigations in institutions reveal that large numbers of residents do not need to be in them. A study by Ovenstone and Bean (1981)[3] found that nearly half the residents in Local Authority elderly persons homes were inappropriately placed; another study by Brocklehurst et al (1978)[4] produced the figure of 28%. Plant (1977)[5] found that nearly a third of elderly people on waiting lists for residential homes in 8 London boroughs were considered by social workers to be capable of managing in sheltered housing. Professionals in several countries, including Czechoslovakia and Germany complain that expensive hospital beds are occupied because cheaper and more satisfactory alternatives are not available. In England the government has blandly stated 'there are elderly people in hospitals who do not need to be there'[6].

Too often elderly people accept residential care because there is a paucity of alternatives. Indeed many elderly people accept it because during the course of their lifetime they have cared for a dependent relative and are aware of the limited assistance offered to carers by State services; they may enter residential care, not from active choice, but because they do not wish to be a burden on their relatives. Only such an explanation accounts for the fact that so many people apparently choose to live in a single room dominated by a bed; why others, after eighty years of family life apparently choose to share a bedroom with strangers; why as they become frail and incontinent they find themselves in accommodation where the toilet is less accessible; why, just as personal relationships are becoming more important they must entertain family and friends in a room designed for one or in a communal setting; and why their possessions, accumulated over a lifetime must be relinquished save for what can be fitted into a wardrobe and two drawers.

The combination of public and private expenditure on services for elderly people in western countries is considerable. But funds have tended to be allocated inefficiently between various forms of care and occupational groups. Nurses who work both in institutions and in the community, while lamenting the paucity of community services, continue to press for more

institutions[7]. As a result services for the elderly
people do not represent good value for money,
elderly people receive a poor service and informal
carers suffer, indeed, the literature of social care
contains considerable evidence about the burdens
carried by informal carers.

Until existing expenditure is rearranged to provide better value for money it is difficult to face
politicians with the need for more expenditure.
There is every reason to believe that elderly
people and their families will become more
articulate in future and press for services that
more effectively meet their needs.

Professional carers must listen to the views of
elderly people and their carers and press for a
redistribution of public expenditure in ways that
meet articulated needs.

The Accommodation Needs of the Elderly

Practical Points

1. Increasingly 'consumerism' is playing a part in perceptions of the wants/needs of elderly people and how they should be met. Expectations are now greater.

2. Most elderly people wish to remain at home. Community alarms enable a call for help to be made even if a telephone cannot be reached after an emergency.

3. Re-mortgaging facilities can help with the ever increasing expenses of staying at home.

4. Sheltered housing schemes range from luxury apartments and bungalows to self contained flats and rooms with shared facilities. The distinguishing feature is the presence of a manager or warden. Its potential has been neglected.

5. Extra care housing usually contains a communal kitchen and dining room, specially designed bathrooms and toilets and plenty of hand rails. Twenty-four hour staffing arrangements are similar to an elderly persons home. There is however, more independence and privacy.

6. Residential care can create a stigma, segregation and over-dependence leading to loss of vitality and dignity. Most old people do not want this and too many residential homes contain people who need not be there. Admission should be accompanied by regular medical and social assessment and a care plan.

References

1. Wagner L (1989) *A proposed model of care for the elderly*, International Nursing Review, 36(2), 50–54.

2. Griffiths R (1988) *Community Care; Agenda for Action*, HMSO, London.

3. Ovenstone MK & Bean PT (1981) *A medical social assessment of admission to old people's home in Nottingham*, British Journal of Psychiatry, 139, 226–229.

4. Brocklehurst JC, Carty MH, Leeming JT & Robinson JM (1978) *Medical screening of old people accepted for residential care*, The Lancet, 15 July, 141–2.

5. Plant D (1977) *Caring for the Elderly*, GLC London.

6. DHSS (1981) *Care in the Community: a consultative document on moving resources for care in England*, DHSS p2, London.

7. Royal College of Nursing (1989) *Response to the Griffths Report of Community Care*, RCN London.

Further Reading

1. Bookbinder D (1991) *Housing Options for Older People*, Age Concern England, London.

2. *A Buyers Guide to Sheltered Housing*, Age Concern England and the National Housing and Town Planning Council, London.

Chapter 7

Financial Benefits for the Elderly

Martin Rathfelder B.Ed. (Leeds), B.A. (open)
Welfare Rights Officer
Manchester Royal Infirmary
Manchester
M13 9WL

Biosketch:

Martin Rathfelder works as Welfare Rights Officer at Manchester Royal Infirmary where he provides advice and representation to patients and staff. He is the author of How to Claim State Benefits and joint editor of Issues in Social Security, an electronic publication.

Introduction

Most developed countries have established systems for giving financial support to elderly and sick people.

The universality of the fear of poverty in old age has made financial provision electorally popular. The first British Pensions Act was passed in 1908 and as Beveridge noted *'The cost of pensions relative to the rest of Social Security will increase inevitably through increase in the proportion of people of pensionable age in the population*[1]*'.*

The nature of financial support available has important consequences for the ways in which it is possible for care to be provided. Because money has been easily available to pay for residential care but not to provide services in patients' own homes, enormous numbers of old people have been put into residential care, with little consideration of any alternative. It has been made difficult for hospitals to keep old people as in-patients on a long-term basis.

Within the space available it is only possible to sketch in the present financial support arrangements in the UK, and to indicate some of their consequences[2]. By the time this article is published some of the rules will have changed. Over the past twelve years there have been on average three or four substantial changes in the rules of the Social Security system each year, a rate of change which in itself gives rise to many difficulties both for claimants and for administrators.

Retirement Pensions

The system of compulsory National Insurance contributions for all, established in 1944, now provides a pension at a basic rate for almost everyone. The main exceptions are married women who, until 1977, were permitted to choose to pay only a token contribution, and people who have come from other countries and not worked for long enough in the UK. The pension scheme was based on the assumption that men would provide for their wives. That assumption is no longer universally shared, but a system of individual provisions has not yet been fully established.

The system of compulsory earnings-related pensions has now been in place since 1975 and that, together with the substantial increase in occupational pensions (protected to some extent against inflation), means that most people who have retired in recent years have more than just the basic pension to live on. The cost of earnings related pension has increased so the present government has reduced benefits for those relying on the state scheme who retire after 1999.

Their argument is that because present benefits are not paid for from accumulated capital, but by those who are presently working and contributing, by 1999 the numbers of those working in relation to those who have retired will be insufficient to maintain the present benefits[3].

Benefits for Disabled People

The priority is to support or replace the incomes of those of working age. Pensioners are expected to have made provisions for the infirmities of old age while they were working.

The central benefit for younger disabled people is the Disability Living Allowance. This replaced the former Mobility Allowance and Attendance Allowance in April 1992. It is in some respects more generous, but it is only available to those who become disabled and make a claim before their 66th birthday. There is a mobility component, which might be paid at either one of two rates, and a component for personal care needs which is paid at three different rates. Entitlement once established may continue for life. Older people must still apply for Attendance Allowance. This does not make any specific provision for mobility problems. It is not means-tested and it is not related to National Insurance contributions. There are three possible ways of qualifying:

1. Frequent attention throughout the day (or prolonged or repeated attention at night) in connection with bodily functions. A need for help with shopping or cleaning will not do because these are not bodily functions. Breathing, hearing, seeing, eating, drinking, walking, sitting, sleeping, getting in or out of bed, dressing, using the toilet are all bodily functions.

    A person with impaired senses or mental functioning might require help with such tasks as taking medicine, dealing with correspondence, reading or shopping, and such tasks would qualify if the patient was being helped to do such things rather than having them done for them. The patient must show that they need help throughout the day, not just when getting up and going to bed. At night, a need for attention more than once a night or for at least 20 minutes most nights would generally qualify.

2. Continual supervision throughout the day in order to avoid substantial danger to the patient or some other person, or a need for someone to be awake for prolonged periods or repeated intervals at night to avoid substantial danger. It is necessary to establish a risk of real harm such that supervision is required continually. It is largely those with impaired mental functioning who qualify by this route. A person who is fully aware of the risks of their condition and able to summon help if necessary would not normally qualify by this means.

3. Terminal illness. The patient must establish, by a doctors report, that they suffer from a progressive illness and that death from that illness within six months would not be unexpected. It is not necessary to predict the date of death and the patient need not be aware of the prognosis. Indeed the claim can be made without any involvement of the patient.

The highest rate, which is the same as the highest DLA care component is £46.70 for the day and night care. This is not sufficient to pay for very many hours of care commercially.

Benefits for Carers

Financial provision for those who care for sick and disabled people can be critical to the success of any care in the community policy. Most carers are women and are only able to devote care to their relatives because their husbands support them financially. Invalid Care Allowance (ICA) is paid at a rate of £35.25 a week[4] which is lower than unemployment benefit. Furthermore if the carer is getting any other benefit they will not get ICA as well. Since October 1990 anyone who was potentially entitled to ICA and claimed it became entitled to an increase of £12.60 in their Income Support. This too does not apply to carers over 65.

Means Tested Benefits

The other strand of the British benefit system is that which descends from the Poor Law and the workhouse. Parish relief eventually became National Assistance. In 1966 this became Supplementary Benefit and in 1988 the same system was re-christened Income Support. Income Support is largely computerised and requires little personal information to calculate. Unlike its predecessors it makes no attempt to match payments to the detailed circumstances of the claimant.

The basic subsistence levels of the scheme are based on those used by Seebohm Rowntree in his studies of poverty in York in 1899 and in 1937[5]. Rowntree was not attempting to establish a national minimum standard of living, but to show that some people were so poor as to be unable to maintain a decent standard of living no matter how efficient at budgeting they were. "*A definition of subsistence in the most stringent terms, adopted in the first place as a limiting case for the sake of an argument, subsequently became the administrative basis around which the post-war social security system was constructed[6]*".

No government since has been prepared to say what the basic rate of benefit was supposed to pay for. They have merely increased Rowntree's figures to allow for inflation. Rowntree assumed that the family would bake their own bread and live largely on vegetables. The only electrical device envisaged was a wireless. Beveridge did in fact make some small allowance for the fact that "*people in receipt of the minimum income required for subsistence will in fact spend some of it on things not absolutely necessary[1]*". It was assumed that old people needed less food but that it would be more expensive "*because of their failing mastication and digestion*". Furthermore, because there are so many old people "*It is dangerous to be in any way lavish to old age, until adequate provision has been assured for all other vital needs*". Even so, in the end it was decided "*for old persons it is reasonable to add a margin above the subsistence minimum*".

There are three means tested benefits available to pensioners: Income Support (which includes help with mortgage interest), Housing Benefit for rent and Council Tax Benefit. Although the last two are administered by local authorities the way the entitlement is calculated is very similar for all three benefits. A single person who is over 80 or qualifies as disabled, gets maximum help if their income is less than £64.20, a couple under 74 if their income is less than £101.05. Existing retirement pensions are made up to this level, or rent commitments are met to ensure that disposable income does not fall below it.

In the new streamlined means test established by the 1986 Social Security Act, *"There will be a general premium for all pensioners in recognition of the permanent loss of earnings[2]"*. This was accompanied by an extra premium for those over 80 or who were disabled before reaching pensionable age. In 1989 the Chancellor of the Exchequer introduced an intermediate premium for those aged 75–79. There is, however, no way for most pensioners who become ill or disabled after pensionable age to get the highest premium, until they reach the age of 80. The rationale is that the highest premium is compensation for premature reduction in earning power, but in practice injustice results.

Apart from the carer premium mentioned above there is one other premium which old people may get. When Income Support was introduced there was much complaint regarding a few very disabled people who got a lot of money out of the Supplementary Benefit system because of their multiple handicaps. In order to counter these arguments an additional premium was introduced by the House of Lords at a very late stage called the Severe Disability Premium.

The official publicity said that it was reserved for people who got Attendance Allowance and lived on their own, but this was not exactly what the law stated. It has proved very difficult to distinguish between groups of disabled people living together in what are sometimes termed minimum support homes (who were intended to have the extra premium) and disabled people living with their relations (who were not intended to have it). Patients cannot have this premium if someone claims Invalid Care Allowance for looking after them, nor if they share their home with other people who are not joint tenants or joint owners with them. The complexities of these rules mean that a careful plan needs to be constructed before the discharge of a newly disabled patient if the benefit income is to be maximised.

Health Benefits

Men over 65 and women over 60 are exempt from prescription charges but have to pay for eye tests and glasses, dentures and dental treatment unless they are poor enough to get help under the NHS low income scheme. Anyone who gets Income Support automatically qualifies for free optical and dental treatment. Anyone else may apply using the common means-test Form AG1. The assessment is very similar to the Income Support calculation. Applicants are given a certificate of poverty which is valid for 6 months and must be produced to qualify for help. The same certificate is also valid for claiming help with the cost of travelling to hospital for treatment and for visiting prisoners in prison.

Social Fund

In 1988 a fund was set up to take the place of the previous system of regulated grants. Claimants are entitled to help with the cost of a funeral if they get a means tested benefit and the deceased did not leave enough to cover the cost of a simple funeral. If the temperature at their local weather station does not rise above freezing point for seven consecutive days, pensioners will be awarded an extra £6 for each week of cold weather.

Other discretionary payments entitled Community Care Grants can be available from the local Social Security office budget. The needs of elderly disabled people generally have a high priority but at the expense of less deserving groups who are generally given loans rather than grants.

Independent Living Fund

This is a Government funded charity which will help pay for the cost of domestic help or personal care, up to £400 a week, if the patient is entitled to higher rate Attendance Allowance and gets Income Support, or if the cost of necessary care would reduce their income to below the Income Support rate. It can be a crucial element in a care package, but its resources are limited.

Financial Benefits for the Elderly

Practical Points

1. Over the last 15 years 3 or 4 changes in the rules of the Social Security system each year, have led to difficulties for staff and claimants.

2. Almost everyone qualifies for a basic pension. The main exceptions are married women who until 1977 were allowed to pay only a token contribution and immigrants with a short contributory record. Compulsory earnings related pensions were introduced in 1975 and the general increase in occupational pensions means that most people have more than a basic pension to live on.

3. Disability Living Allowance Mobility Component continues for life but only those who claim before the age of 66 can qualify.

4. Attendance Allowance or Disability Living Allowance Care Component is not means tested. There are three possible ways of qualifying. These include the need for frequent attention during the day or night in connection with body functions, continual supervision throughout the day and terminal illness.

5. Invalid Care Allowance is a benefit for carers.

6. There are three means tested benefits available to pensioners. These are Income Support, Housing Benefit and Council Tax Benefit.

7. Men over 65 and women over 60 are exempt from prescription charges but have to pay for eye tests and glasses, dentures and dental treatment, and fares to hospital, unless they are poor enough to get help under the NHS low income scheme. Anyone on Income Support automatically qualifies for free optical and dental treatment.

References

1. Beveridge W (1942) *Social Insurance and Allied Services Cmd 6404*, HMSO.

2. Those who are interested in a European perspective on the problems of financing an increasing elderly population are referred to: Johnson P (1989) *The costs and benefits of population ageing*, a paper presented to the International Colloquium on Opportunities and Challenges in an Ageing Society, Amsterdam.

3. *Reform of Social Security Cmnd 9518*, (1985) HMSO.

4. Secretary of State for Social Security. See Footnote below.

5. Rowntree S (1937) *The human needs of labour*, Longmans, London.

6. Kincaid JC (1973) *Poverty and equality in Britain*, Penguin.

Footnote: All benefit rates are weekly and are those from April 1995 to April 1996 (Personal Communication by the contributor of this article).

Chapter 8

Legal Problems and the Elderly

Dr John J Whitaker MB, CHB, MCRP
Consultant Physician
Department of Medicine for the Elderly
Harrogate District Hospital
Lancaster Park Road
Harrogate
HG2 7SX

Biosketch:

Dr Whitaker qualified from Edinburgh University in 1979. He trained in Medicine and Geriatrics in Edinburgh and Manchester prior to taking up Consultant Post in 1990.

Introduction

This chapter will cover those areas of the law in which the doctor working with the elderly may become involved. It concentrates on the law as it applies in England and Wales. The principles are similar in Scotland and Northern Ireland but details differ. Compulsory admission to hospital and guardianship are included, in addition to the supervision of the elderly person's financial affairs and the law as it applies to elderly drivers.

Compulsory Admission to Hospital

Reluctance to accept admission to hospital is often encountered with the elderly. A number of factors may underlie such reluctance. There may be associated depression or dementia (with lack of insight into the illness or the difficulties of staying at home). Fear of hospitals (especially so when the geriatric department is housed in the old workhouse or TB hospital) or fear of not being allowed to return home may be important. There may also be a wish to die at home. Most elderly people are amenable to pressure from doctors and relatives to accept admission to hospital, but if such persuasion does not work and it is believed that the elderly person could be helped by treatment in hospital which could not be delivered at home, there are two routes of compulsory admission to hospital:
1. Section 47 of the National Assistance Act (1948) as amended (1951).

2. Sections 2 to 5 of the Mental Health Act (1983) in England and Wales.

1 National Assistance Act (1948)

If a patient is mentally sound, the only means of compulsory admission is Section 47 of the National Assistance Act (1948) as amended (1951). It is used infrequently (about 200 times a year[1] in England and Wales).

This section covers *"removal to suitable premises of persons in need of care and attention"*. It applies to persons who:
(a) *"are suffering from grave chronic disease or, being aged, infirm or physically incapacitated, are living in insanitary conditions, and*
(b) *are unable to devote to themselves and are not receiving from other persons, proper care and attention."*

The 'medical officer of health' (now Consultant in Public Health) has to certify to the Local Authority that it is in the interests of any such person, or in the interests of preventing injury to the health of other persons or preventing serious nuisance to other persons that he/she be removed from his/her place of residence.

The original 1948 act required that 7 days notice be given before an application was made to a magistrates' court and the subsequent order lasted for 3 months. The 1951 amendment avoids the need for 7 days notice if it is felt that the situation is urgent. The Consultant in Public Health may apply to a magistrates' court or a single magistrate directly. The application has be be supported by a second registered medical practitioner. An order under the amended act lasts for 3 weeks only. This is the course which is usually followed.

Section 47 therefore allows a person without mental disorder to be removed from their home against their will. There is a great deal of controversy surrounding its use and, as mentioned previously, it is used rarely (about once per health district per year). Arguments revolve around personal liberty and the difficulty in defining 'insanitary conditions'. The lack of a right of appeal gives rise to concern. There is anxiety that Section 47 could be used to force admission to hospital when the basic problem is that the resources for community care are insufficient.

In the vast majority of cases in which Section 47 is used the person is over 65 years of age[2, 3, 4]. Most are taken from their home to hospital but some are admitted to Local Authority residential care directly. It has been estimated that in 50% of the cases in which it is used, the person is suffering from some form of mental disorder.

2 Mental Health Act (1983)

This act specifies the means by which mentally ill patients can be admitted to hospital, detained and treated without consent. The relevant sections are:

Section 2 – an application for admission for assessment.
This requires the written recommendations of two registered medical practitioners, one of whom is approved by the Secretary of State as having special experience in the diagnosis and

treatment of mental disorder. A patient admitted in this way may be detained for up to 28 days.

Section 3 – an application for admission for treatment.
This again requires the written recommendations of two registered medical practitioners, one of whom is approved as having special experience in the diagnosis and treatment of mental disorder. A patient admitted in this way may be detained for 6 months.

Section 4 – an emergency application.
This allows a patient to be admitted on the recommendation of only one doctor but it ceases to have effect after 72 hours unless a second medical recommendation is received within that time.

Section 5 – application in respect of a patient already in hospital.
The registered medical practitioner in charge of treatment (or another nominated medical practitioner) furnishes a report to the hospital managers to enable the patient to be detained for a period of 72 hours.

The Mental Health Act is rarely used in dealing with the elderly outside of psychiatric departments, although in certain circumstances it may be argued that admission under Section 4 may be more appropriate and less time consuming than invoking Section 47[5].

Guardianship

Sections 7 to 10 of the Mental Health Act (1983) cover guardianship, allowing compulsory care of mentally ill and mentally handicapped people in the community. A guardianship application may be made if a patient is suffering from mental disorder and *"it is necessary in the interests of the welfare of the patient or for the protection of other persons. . ."* that the patient should be received into guardianship.

Under the 1983 Act, the guardian has:
(a) *"the power to require the patient to reside at a place specifed. . ."*
(b) *"the power to require the patient to attend at places and times so specified for the purpose of medical treatment, occupation, education or training;"*
(c) *"the power to require access to be given . . . to any registered medical practitioner, approved social worker or other person so specified."*

The application is made by an approved social worker and must be supported by two doctors, one of whom is approved as having special experience in the diagnosis and treatment of mental disorder. The guardian is usually the local Social Services authority, or alternatively a named person approved by the local Social Services authority. The guardianship application lasts for 6 months initially, it may then be renewed for a further 6 months and subsequently it may be renewed annually.

Therefore, guardianship orders ensure that an old person with mental disorder receives care and protection rather than treatment. Although a guardian can require a patient to attend a place for medical treatment, the guardian cannot compel them to undergo treatment or give consent on the patient's behalf.

With the modifications to the guardianship orders in the 1983 Mental Health Act, there has been an increase in their use for those suffering from mental illness as opposed to mental handicap[9]. The number of orders remains small and there is local variation in their use. In its use in mental illness, most cases are elderly and the majority are suffering from dementias. It is a useful, although infrequently used means of providing care for people in the community where such care cannot be provided without compulsion.

Supervision of Financial Affairs

There are a number of ways in which the responsibility for managing the financial affairs of the elderly may be taken on by others. Power of Attorney, Enduring Power of Attorney and the Court of Protection will be discussed as these are the main areas where a doctor may become involved, particularly with regard to assessing the patient's mental capacity. Agency (by which an elderly person can nominate someone to act on their behalf for pension purposes) or Appointees (who can act on an elderly person's behalf with respect to Social Security claims) will not be covered. The Age Concern book *"The Law and Vulnerable Elderly People"*[6] summarises the means of representation and protection of the affairs of the frail elderly.

Power of Attorney

A Power of Attorney is a legal arrangement whereby one person (the 'donor') appoints another or others (the 'donee/s' or 'attorney/s') to act on his behalf while he is physically incapable of managing his own affairs. It cannot be created by someone suffering from mental incapacity and it loses its validity when the person creating it loses the mental capacity to manage their own affairs.

Enduring Power of Attorney

The Enduring Power of Attorney Act (1985) which came into force in 1986 in England and Wales allows the creation of an Enduring Power of Attorney which continues even after the donor has become mentally incapable of handling his or her affairs. It must be created while the donor is capable of understanding the nature and effect of creating an enduring power. If subsequently the Attorney believes that the donor is becoming mentally incapable, the Enduring Power of Attorney must then be registered with the Court of Protection. The role of the Court of Protection is to register the Enduring Power of Attorney and to consider complaints about its administration but it does not monitor the Enduring Power of Attorney as such. No medical report is needed for the creation of an Enduring Power of Attorney or its registration but medical assessment may be important if the Enduring Power of Attorney, or the need to register it, is challenged by relatives.

Court of Protection

If an Enduring Power of Attorney has not been created, the only way of managing the financial affairs of a person who is unable to do so for himself because of mental disorder is to apply to the Court of Protection. The Court of Protection is an office of the Supreme Court, the function of which is to manage and administer the property and affairs of people who, through mental disorder are incapable of managing their own financial affairs. The Court draws its powers from the Mental Health Act (1983) and the Court of Protection Rules (1984).

The person making the application to the Court of Protection is usually the nearest relative but if the nearest relative is unwilling or unable to do so, another involved person may apply. The patient's doctor will be asked to complete a medical certificate giving a diagnosis of the patient's condition and an explanation of why they cannot manage their own affairs.

The court can act by:

(a) Appointing a Receiver who takes control of the patient's financial affairs and property and acts on the patient's behalf in accordance with the Court's instructions.

(b) By a Short Procedure Order. If the patient's estate is straightforward or is less than £5000, the Court may, rather than to appoint a receiver, issue an order, usually to the person making the application, authorising the use of the patient's assets in a certain way for the patient's benefit.

In Scotland, the normal method of dealing with the affairs of an incompetent person is to petition the Court of Session for the appointment of a curator bonis, who carries out the same duties as a receiver in England and Wales.

In Northern Ireland, the equivalent of the Court of Protection is the Office of Care and Protection.

This account is no more than a brief outline. More detailed texts are included in the list of references[7, 8]. Legal advice should be taken before embarking on the above courses.

Fitness to Drive

In the UK, 35% of men and 5% of women over the age of 80 years currently hold driving licences. Over the next 15 years, these figures are forecast to rise to 63% and 14% respectively. Taken with the increasing numbers of the elderly over this period, there will be a dramatic rise in the number of elderly drivers. Older people drive less miles and consequently have fewer accidents in total, but the accident rate increases with increasing age and the older driver is more likely to be responsible for the accident.

In the UK, with regard to an ordinary driving licence, applicants have to declare that they are not suffering from:
(a) epilepsy,
(b) severe abnormality,
(c) liability to sudden attacks of disabling giddiness or fainting,
(d) inability to meet the prescribed eyesight requirements
or any other disability likely to cause the driving of a vehicle to be a source of danger to the public ('relevant disabilities'). The law also talks about 'prospective disabilities' which include any condition which, by virtue of its intermittent or progressive nature, may in time become a 'relevant disability'.

The UK driving licence states *"you are required to tell the Drivers' Medical Branch, DVLA . . . at once if you have any disability (includes physical or mental condition) which affects (or may in future affect) your fitness as a driver if you expect it to last more than 3 months"*. The onus is therefore on the licence holder to report to the Driver and Vehicle Licensing Agency any relevant disability or prospective disability previously notified which has become worse. Only temporary disabilities (eg fractured bones) not expected to last for more than 3 months are excluded from this obligation.

It is inappropriate to list here all the medical conditions which may affect driving and the recommendations associated with them. Doctors should refer to the 'red book'[10].

The licence is normally granted to run to the holder's 70th birthday. Subsequently it will be renewed every 3 years, based on a declaration of health from the licence holder. As stated previously, the onus is on the licence holder to inform DVLA of any change in their medical condition which will affect their fitness to drive. However, the patient's doctor needs to warn the patient that he/she is suffering from a disability which requires notification. The driver's duty to inform DVLA can only apply if he/she is aware of the condition. If the patient fails to notify DVLA and continues driving, the issue of confidentiality can arise. It is accepted that a doctor can inform DVLA directly, but only after having failed to persuade the patient to do so and having been unable to enlist the help of relatives. This can be a particular problem with patients who are dementing.

The advice with regard to specific medical problems and car driving is reasonably clear[10]. Various ageing changes (as opposed to specific diseases) also put the elderly at a greater risk of having an accident (deterioration in vision, reduction in muscle power, increased reaction time, difficulties with divided attention tasks etc). In the absence of any specific medical contra-indication it is not always clear as to when to advise the elderly driver to stop. There may be a conflict of loyalties. We want the elderly to remain active and independent and for many old people car driving is very important in maintaining their lifestyle and independence. On the other hand, we need to consider the interests and safety of the general public. If there are anxieties about an elderly person continuing to drive, they should

perhaps initially be advised to restrict themselves to driving in daylight, in good weather conditions, at off-peak times and uncongested roads. A second opinion from a colleague may be useful when it is felt that the time has come for the elderly person to stop driving. Perhaps the driver's insurance company will also exert some influence. In the case of disagreement about fitness to drive, there may be a place for a practical driving assessment.

There now follows two case histories – one regarding 'Guardianship' and the other with respect to 'Compulsory admission to hospital' – to illustrate the relevant points in these two situations:

Case History 1

Mrs T, aged 82, lived on a very remote farm, without mains water or electricity, in the Yorkshire Dales. Mr R, aged 81, had lived with her for over 40 years as her lodger. Mrs T was diabetic and had been dementing for a number of years. All offers of help from Social Services had been refused in the past, and they survived with the limited help which could be provided by a distant neighbour.

Mrs T did not comply well with the diet or drug therapy for her diabetes because of dementia. She was admitted to hospital early one winter with an acute worsening of her confusional state associated with hyperglycaemia. During the acute confusional episode she had attacked Mr R with a knife. A few days later, Mr R was admitted to hospital with severe heart failure. He was mentally clear but admitted that during the bad weather he did not take his diuretic therapy, to cut down visits to the outside toilet. This was the main reason for the deterioration in his heart failure.

Both patients' medical conditions were readily stabilised in hospital but it was obvious that their existence at home was becoming increasingly precarious, especially during the winter. Mrs T would not consider any option other than discharge home. Mr R admitted that he would rather move to Residential Care as he enjoyed company and felt that life on the farm had become too much of a struggle. However, as Mrs T insisted on returning to the farm, he felt obliged to accompany her.

After lengthy discussions with relatives, neighbours, general practitioner, district nurses, Social Services and Mr R, it was decided that the Local

Authority Social Services department would apply for a guardianship order so that Mrs T could be moved to a Local Authority residential home. It was felt that not only would she be risking her life by returning to the farm, without any insight into the risk due to her dementia, but that she would also be putting Mr R at an unacceptable risk in forcing him to return to the farm with her. The guardianship order was obtained and they both moved to residential care.

Case History 2

Mrs M is an 83 year old lady, without any significant medical history, who lived alone in a 2nd floor flat. She had always refused offers of help from Social Services in the past and coped with some support from her son who visited twice a week.

She developed congestive cardiac failure and uncontrolled atrial fibrillation and was started on digoxin and diuretic. Over the following 3 weeks she ate and drank very little. Her family had been buying food which was rotting in the fridge. She became incontinent of urine and faeces. She had told her family that she wanted to die and there was the suspicion that she was trying to starve herself to death.

When seen at home by a Consultant Geriatrician she had not eaten or drunk for 48 hours. She was painfully thin and dehydrated with peripheral circulatory shutdown, but there were no other significant findings on physical examination.

Mrs M refused admission to hospital. As she was physically incapacitated, living in insanitary conditions, unable to devote to herself proper care and attention and not receiving proper care and attention from others, it was felt that admission to hospital under Section 47 was justified.

In hospital her dehydration was corrected and she was found to have a urinary tract infection which was treated. As her physical condition improved it became obvious that she was depressed. This responded well to treatment. She was eventually discharged back to her own home.

References

1. Muir Gray JA (1981) *Section 47*, Journal of Medical Ethics, 7, 146–9.

2. Forster DP & Tiplady P (1980) *Doctors and compulsory procedures: Section 47 of the National Assistance Act 1948*, British Medical Journal, 280, 739–40.

3. Green M (1980) *Compulsory removal – a difficult decision to take*, Geriatric Medicine, January, 10, 41–5.

4. Fera JD, Hatton P & Renvoize EB (1989) *Is removal under Section 47 the way to deliver care?* Geriatric Medicine, May, 19, 69–72.

5. Murphy E (1984) *What to do with a sick elderly woman who refuses to go to hospital*, British Medical Journal, 289, 1435–6.

6. Greengross S (1986) *The Law and vulnerable elderly people*, Age Concern England.

7. Cretney S (1989) *Enduring Powers of Attorney. 2nd Edition.* Family Law, London.

8. Whitehorn NA (1985) *Court of Protection Practice. 11th Edition.* Longman, London.

9. Hughes G (1991) *Trends in guardianship usage following the Mental Health Act 1983*, Health Trends, 22(4), 145–147

10. Raffle A (1985) *Medical aspects of fitness to drive.* HMSO, London.

Chapter 9

The Role of General Practitioner in the Care of the Elderly

Dr D Brooks MD, FRCGP, DRCOG
General Practitioner
Peterloo Medical Centre
133 Manchester Old Rd
Middleton
Manchester
M24 4DZ

Biosketch:

Dr David Brooks is a General Practitioner in Middleton and an Associate Adviser in General Practice in the Department of Post-Graduate Medicine and Dentistry at Manchester University. His interests include vocational training for General Practice and continuing medical education. He has published widely.

Introduction

The role of the general practitioner in the care of the elderly is comprehensive and changing rapidly. It embraces disease prevention, health promotion and the clinical care of patients with acute and chronic illness. Moreover this must be considered in the light of the psychological and social circumstances which also affect health and well being. All of this must be delivered to a registered practice population for which the practitioner is responsible. A 'job definition' for a general practitioner is presented in appendix 1 and the reader might care to derive a list of tasks from this which could be said to be the responsibility of the general practitioner. It will inevitably be a lengthy list. Fortunately the practitioner does not work alone but in a team and the need for teamwork has been emphasised by two important pieces of legislation in recent years, the new 1990 contract for general practitioners and the National Health and Community Care Act of 1990[1,2]. These have had a pivotal effect on the practitioners' responsibilities. In many ways the general practitioner is the 'conductor' of a service 'orchestra' who will need to 'bring in' the services of a whole range of people with different skills in order to meet the health care needs of his patients at different times. This chapter will expand these themes and will provide a guide to the work of the general practitioner with older people.

Disease Prevention and Health Education

The 1990 contract for general practitioners required that all patients over 75 years be offered, either at home or at the surgery, an annual health check. The offer may be made orally or in writing but must be confirmed in writing and the response must be entered in the patients notes. All of this presupposes that something useful can be done by routine assessments on people who have not sought medical advice; it assumes that impairments that are currently producing or could conceivably produce handicaps or disabilities can be eased by timely intervention. Various types of interventions are listed in appendix 2.

We know that during any single year 90% of the over 75's are seen by the practice either at home or in the surgery. For this reason, case finding in this way is popular in general practice and is often seen as a cost effective method of tertiary prevention.

It is often assumed that because health care is a good thing more of it will be even better. However, particularly in the elderly much illness is iatrogenic and the concept of 'social iatrogenesis' introduced by Illich is not well understood by many medical workers. By our well intentioned actions we often take away from people the ability to look after themselves by medicalising their lives, often with little or no mandate.

The Concept of Unmet Need

It is well established that old people have many medical problems existing at the same time and that they tend to underreport them to medical advisers. This is complicated by the fact that doctors often miss them. Many if not most of these problems are not life threatening but tend to stop people doing things. There is some interference with the daily living activities of old people. The World Health Organisation has produced the following model.

impairment	...	disability	...	handicap
[the disease]		[functional loss]		[effect on daily living]

There are many studies which have looked at unmet need and attempted to support the need for screening. They have been reviewed and well summarised by Williams[3]. He concluded:

- that the evidence of unreported need is strong;
- that the evidence of benefit in terms of prevention or cure of illness is poor;
- that there is evidence that intervention leads to a better quality of life;
- that studies to demonstrate that handicap is reduced or prevented have yet to take place.

Organising a Screening Programme

There are three important questions:
1. What should be assessed?
2. How can it best be organised?
3. Who should do it?

Content

Under their terms of service general practitioners are required to provide each year the following services for patients aged 75 and over. The services may be provided by the general practitioner personally or by a practice team member.

There are seven major areas of assessment that are required. They are briefly summarised below.

Social and Home Assessment

The major question here is what social support is necessary and what is available? What need is there for support from relatives or carers and is there a need for home helps or meals on wheels etc. The home conditions should be reviewed. Is heating adequate and is a telephone needed?

Mobility Assessment

The major question here is how stable is the patient. Do falls occur and are they frequent? Can the patient get around in the house and outdoors? Previous strokes and arthritis would be relevant here of course. The need for special adaptations or walking aids should be considered.

Mental Assessment

Depression is common in the elderly as is confusion. Standard questions about name, age, address and date of birth or the name of the prime minister may well be appropriate in some patients but sensitivity is required as very many patients who are far from confused will find the questions insulting and it is all too easy to appear patronising.

Assessment of the Senses

Simple hearing and vision tests are often productive. Hearing impairment in particular is common and early referral is needed. When referral is late it is not surprising that so many patients put their hearing aids in a drawer. People get used to hearing loss and the new sensations produced by an aid may be unacceptable. Referral to ENT, audiology or ophthalmology departments may be needed. Cataract surgery is especially effective and a priority in the over 75's.
(Please see chapters on Deafness & Blindness).

Assessment of Continence

Urinary incontinence (which is more common) can often present as a smell of stale urine on entering a patient's home. If it is not a consequence of confusion or poor mobility the following principles should be borne in mind.
- Severe constipation with faecal incontinence.
- Urinary incontinence may be a product of glycosuria or prostatic hypertrophy.
- As with many symptoms in the elderly the medication should be reviewed, especially diuretics.
- Faecal soiling is often a consequence of severe constipation with impaction and overflow.

General Functional Assessment

This is an ambiguous term but it certainly includes current medical problems and their effect on activities of daily living. It also includes an assessment of how the patient functions as a member of a family or as a member of the community as a consequence of any medical problems. A major question is whether the patient is coping and what changes are taking place.

Review of Medication

(Please see chapter 38 on Prescribing).
Prescribing for the elderly needs special care but there are some relevant principles.
- Keep medication under regular review.
- Ensure that drug therapy is essential.
- Look out for adverse reactions.
- Use the minimum number of drugs in the correct dosage.
- Check on compliance.

How Can It Best Be Organised and Who Should Do It?

The general practitioner cares for a registered practice population. A list of patients over 75 can be provided by the Family Health Services (FHSA) but an age sex register either in manual form or on computer should be available in all practices to identify a target population. Much of this work can be done opportunistically during routine consultations. On average a general practitioner has 5 consultations a year with patients 65–74 and 6 with those over the age of 75. Required data can be entered in the records according to a suitable template based on a suitable history and appropriate examination. It is possible then to identify those who do not attend so that home assessment can be offered. This can be undertaken by a team member who could be a health visitor, district nurse or directly employed practice nurse. Appropriate training must be organised by the practice.

For an average list of 2,000 patients there should be around 130 patients 75 years and over who need to be seen annually. If they are to be seen at home this means three visits each week. However much of this can be done opportunistically using a geriatric screening card (appendix 3). Patients who are not seen can be reviewed by a nurse and patients with problems can receive a more detailed assessment.

Putting things Right

As a result of programmes of screening and case finding, examples of unmet need will be displayed which require attention. This may involve referral within the team (for example deafness due to earwax which can be dealt with by the practice nurse). Referrals outside the practice team to the chiropody services, the social services or to the hospital geriatric team may all be necessary in individual cases.

The National Health Service and Community Care Act 1990

During the last 20 years there has been a major but unplanned shift to community care. Long stay beds have decreased dramatically with little shift in resources. When associated with demographic changes and earlier discharge and increased demand from users and carers new thinking was indicated. The stated objectives are as follows:

- To promote the development of domiciliary, day and respite facilities to enable people to live in their own homes wherever feasible and sensible.

- To ensure that service providers make practical support for carers a high priority.

- To make proper assessment of need and good care management the cornerstone of high quality care.

- To promote the development of a flourishing independent sector alongside good quality public services (ie promote a mixed economy of care).

- To clarify the responsibilities of agencies and so make it easier to hold them to account for their performance.

- To secure better value for taxpayers money by introducing a new funding structure for social care.

The intention was that care managers should assess needs with users and carers on a multi-disciplinary basis and write and coordinate a care plan. Services should be bought from providers using a devolved budget. Unmet need was to be reported back in order to identify gaps.

The primary health care team were seen as ideally placed to act as care managers as well as providers. In practice, community multidisciplinary schemes have tended to act as referral agencies taking over the responsibility of assessment and management.

Clinical Problem Solving in the Elderly

Caring for patients with acute and chronic illness is a major responsibility of the general practitioner.

Consultation Tasks

Stott and Davis have identified four important consultation tasks.
1. Identification and management of the presenting problems.
2. Management of continuing problems.
3. Opportunistic anticipatory care.
4. Modification of help seeking behaviour.

Tasks 3 and 4 have been discussed but 1 and 2 are critical.

Appendix 4 identifies the elements of making a diagnosis and of management which need to be considered. The effect of age on the way the general practitioner approaches these tasks is worth attention.

Problem Identification

The process of making a diagnosis requires the generation of a list of hypotheses when faced with a patient's presentation. This is based on probability in a general practice context and results in a 'most likely, less likely, rare but important' list of categories. However, two major general practice specific factors influence this process – what we know about the patient already (from memory or the patient records) and the relationship we have with the patient. A series of discriminating questions follows which allow us to differentiate between the hypotheses and a focused examination and selective investigations complete the process. The history is the most important part of this.

However it is often the case that we cannot make a diagnosis in traditional medical terms. Psychological and social factors influence presentation and we may only be able to make judgements like 'urgent not urgent', 'serious not serious' and 'physical or psychological'. Follow up may be important in reaching a diagnosis. Old age may influence this process considerably.

It is likely that the general practitioner has a good deal of information available in memory or in the records of elderly patients. This may catalyse the above process and make problem identification easier or it may result in a biased judgement. Previous hospital records, previous general practitioner notes, information about the likes and dislikes, prejudices and personality of the patient and the family are all part of the decision making process particularly in relation to health beliefs, concerns and expectations. Indeed what we know already is often the best predictor of what will develop in the future and the list of current morbidity, a list of problems owned by the patient in physical, psychological and social terms should be easily available in general practice record systems.

Taking a history may be more difficult in the elderly, but helpful relatives and friends are usually available. Memory failure, deafness, poor concentration and a tendency to wander may all interfere with good communication. Physical examination is often difficult and frustrating, even when it is actually productive, and investigation is even more difficult in the presence of mobility problems. Fortunately the history is a very good guide to the need for examination and investigation and the availability of practice nurses to take blood specimens at home and pathology delivery services has greatly eased the work of the general practitioner. Remember also that good observation is a very productive source of examination information.

Problem Management

Reassurance, Explanation, Advice, Prescription, Referral, Investigation, Observation and Prevention are all management strategies that may be adopted in general practice. The first two are probably the most important and may need to be focused on the carer rather than the patient. Failure to achieve this may well result in an unnecessary referral to another agency. One certainly needs to bear in mind the limitations of old age but we should all remember that the right to take risks in pursuit of legitimate interests is a fundamental right and counselling might often be more appropriate than advice.

Prescribing is so important in the elderly that it deserves special consideration, as does communication with specialist colleagues.

Prescribing

Any list of patients with chronic major disease who are receiving long term medication will inevitably contain large numbers of old people. The monitoring of these patients and their repeat prescriptions is a major responsibility and should involve the primary health care team.

Computerised scripts can be delivered by team members and practice protocols can simplify the monitoring of the disease. A major protocol question should be, can any of the treatment be stopped? (Please see Chapter 38 on Prescribing).

Referral: there are many opportunities for communication between specialist geriatricians and general practitioners. These are listed in appendix 5.

The Training Needs of the General Practitioner in Geriatrics

In 1978 the Royal College of Practitioners and the British Geriatric Society published the report of a joint working party in the form of a statement on the training of general practitioners in geriatric medicine. They have since been updated and are presented in appendix 6. These training aims may be met during the 12 month attachment in general practice, during sessions on a release course and through experience as a SHO in a hospital geriatric post. About 40% of doctors who apply to the Joint Committee on Postgraduate Training for General Practice offer 6 months experience in hospital geriatric medicine. The College and the British Geriatric Society strongly endorse the need for protected teaching time, the identification of a named mentor to supervise training and regular and continuous assessment of learning need with feedback on performance.

Conclusion

This chapter can only present an outline of the work of the general practitioner with old people. It is hoped that there is sufficient information to enable the reader to gain some insight into the learning that is needed and that should be obtained in the hospital SHO posts in geriatric medicine and during the practice year.

References

1. Department of Health (1989) *General Practice in the NHS*. 1990 contract. DOH, London.

2. Department of Health (1990) *The National Health Service and Community Care Act 1990*, DOH, London.

3. Williams EI (1992) *Over 75: care, assessment and health promotion*. Radcliffe Medical Press Ltd, Oxford.

4. Fraser R (1987) *Clinical Method, a general practice approach*, Butterworths.

Appendix 1

A Job Definition for a General Practitioner

The General Practitioner is a licensed medical graduate who gives personal, primary and continuing care to individuals, families and a practice population irrespective of age, sex and illness. It is the synthesis of these functions which is unique. He will attend his patients in the consulting room and in their homes and sometimes in the hospital. His aim is to make early diagnoses. He will include and integrate physical, psychological and social factors in his considerations about health and illness. This will be expressed in the care of his patients. He will make an initial decision about every problem which is presented to him as a doctor. He will undertake the continuing management of his patients with chronic, recurrent or terminal illnesses. Prolonged contact means that he can use repeated opportunities to gather information at a pace appropriate to each patient and build up a relationship of trust which he can use professionally. He will practice in cooperation with other colleagues, medical and non medical. He will know how and when to intervene through treatment prevention and education to promote the health of his patients and their families. He will recognise that he also has a professional responsibility to the community.

Appendix 2

Some Definitions: Types of Intervention

Primary prevention	Stopping disease before it occurs, eg immunisation
Secondary prevention	Identifying problems (physical psychological or social) at a very early or presymptomatic stage when they are asymptomatic and by implication curable, eg cervical cancer.
Tertiary prevention	Early recognition of established problems so that their impact can be reduced or minimised.
Anticipatory care	This is a programme of care which combines all types of prevention as appropriate with health education in relation to life style and hazard avoidance. It is especially suited to the work of the general practitioner as much of it can be opportunistic. 'As we are together can we talk about . . .?'

Appendix 3

A Geriatric Screening Card

NAME

_____

ADDRESS

_____

NAME AND ADDRESS OF NEAREST RELATIVE

_____

CURRENT MEDICAL PROBLEMS

_____

MEDICATION

_____

Interview	Assessment
Smoking, alcohol, home conditions, help received, help required, continence	Appearance, mental state, bp, pulse, urine, vision, hearing, mobility

PLAN

_____

Appendix 4

Clinical Problem Solving (Fraser 1987[5])

Hypothetico Deductive Model of Clinical Problem Solving

presenting information   information already known

Pre diagnostic Interpretation

eg urgent/non urgent physical/psychological

↓   **HYPOTHESES**   ↓

Test each hypothesis by discriminating history

Revise, Rerank List Hypotheses

seek confirmatory evidence through appropriate (focussed) physical examination, investigations, ↓   use of time etc.   ↓

Diagnosis Confirmed or Not

Management Decisions

Reassurance

Advice

Prescription

Referral

Investigation

Observation

Prevention

Appendix 5

The Training Needs of the General Practitioner

Consultants–GP interface in the Management and Care of Patients

1. Lectures by Consultants/Specialists in Post-graduate Centres *or* in the community
2. Telephone advice; letters and investigation results, faxed *or* by ordinary post
3. Out-patients and specialist clinics (eg, osteoporosis, hypertension, Parkinson's disease clinics, etc)
4. Shared-care, eg, managing Diabetic patients
5. Protocol and Guidelines on common chronic medical problems (peptic ulcer, angina, etc)
6. Consultants working in the Community (Domiciliary Visits, visiting Nursing Home, working in GP Surgeries and doing out-patients in Community-Centres)
7. Open-access investigation of patients, eg, gastroscopy, Echo-cardiograms
8. Ultimately, admitting patients for further medical, rehabilitative or surgical management

Appendix 6

Objectives for the Training of General Practitioners in Geriatric Medicine

Amended from the report of the British Geriatrics Society and The Royal College of General Practitioners (Training General Practitioners in Geriatric Medicine (1)).

The care of the elderly has been re-ordered under the five areas identified in the *Future General Practitioner – Learning and Teaching* (9)):
1. Human development.
2. Human behaviour.
3. Medicine and society.
4. Health and diseases.
5. The practice.

At the conclusion of his/her vocational training the doctor should be able to:

Human Development

a. Describe, discuss, and compare the theories of ageing.
b. Describe and relate the physical, psychological, and social changes which may occur in old age.
c. Relate these changes to the physical, psychological, and social adaptations which the old person makes, and to the breakdown of these adaptations.

Human Behaviour

a. Describe the ways in which physical psychological, and social changes in the environment of the old person manifest themselves early as changes in behaviour.
b. Describe the tendency to disengage in old age, and the interplay between the previous personality and experience of the patient and the present tendency to disengagement.
c. Describe in terms of the patient's behaviour the consequences of an awareness of deterioration in sociability, motivation, mood, or sexual function.
d. Describe the effects of these behavioural changes in old age on family relationships.
e. Describe those changes in behaviour which may be the first manifestation of disease processes likely to occur in old age.

f. Exhibit appropriate attitudes to the care of old people, and manifest these attitudes in the doctor-patient relationship.
g. Demonstrate an awareness of recent progress in gerontology.

Medicine and Society

a. Describe the influence of culture and social class on the status of old people in the family and in society at large.
b. Describe how current medical education determines the personal care of the elderly by the profession.
c. Describe and illustrate the relationship between the attitudes of society towards old people, and the allocation of medical and social resources.
d. Describe the development of social and medical care for the elderly in our society.
e. Describe the major medical and social agencies, statutory and voluntary, and specify their particular activities and areas of concern in the care of the elderly.
f. Demonstrate the uses of epidemiology in the care of the elderly.
g. Describe the effects of government policy and the contractual obligations of general practitioners in the National Health Service for the care of the elderly.
h. Construct appropriate programmes of preparation for retirement.
i. Demonstrate an understanding of the needs of the informal carers of older people and how these can be met if the continuing well being of older people is to be maintained.
j. Describe the ethical aspects of care of older people and how they are taken into account in providing care through general practice.

Health and Diseases

a. Describe the physical factors, particularly diet, exercise, temperature, and sleep, which affect the health of the old person.

b.   Describe the social factors, including previous occupation, financial status, housing, social involvement, and marital status, which influence life in old age, and the interrelation between health status and social status.

c.   Describe the threats to the integrity of the old person, such as retirement, bereavement, isolation, institutionalisation, and impending death.

d.   Appreciate the importance of health education and health promotion in maintaining the health of older people and the practical implications for general practice.

e.   Describe the features, peculiar to the elderly, which modify the presentation of diseases, their course and management.

f.   Describe the management of the conditions and problems commonly associated with old age such as stroke, falls, Parkinson's disease, confusion etc.

g.   Illustrate the way in which a number of different disease processes commonly occur in the same old person.

h.   List the peculiar difficulties of taking a clinical history from an old person, with due regard to its slower tempo and possible unreliability, and the evidence of third parties, and demonstrate the appropriate skills required.

i.   Outline the special features of the clinical examination of elderly men and women.

j.   Demonstrate understanding of the changes in the normal range of laboratory values that are found in older people.

k.   Describe the special features of prognosis of diseases in old age and relate these to an appropriate plan for further investigation and management.

l.   Describe the way in which the management of disease processes in old age is influenced by the psychological state and the social situation of the old person.

m.   List the special factors associated with the absorption, metabolism, and excretion of drugs given to the elderly.

n.   Describe the hazards of drug treatment in old age, including the problems posed by multiplicity of drugs, non-compliance, and iatrogenic disease.

o.   Demonstrate an appreciation of the uses and the limitations of surgery and rehabilitation in the treatment of diseases of old age.

p.   Describe the special features of psychiatric diseases in old age, including the features of brain failure, and the effects of disorders of physical function on the mental state.

q.   Demonstrate the skills necessary to take a psychiatric history from an old person, including assessment of intellectual function (eg using short mental status questionnaires) and mood, and evaluation of the testimony of third parties.

r.   Demonstrate the skills required in the management of old people with a psychiatric disorder such as:
   (i)   deciding on the appropriate milieu of treatment;
   (ii)   listing the indications for specialist psychiatric or geriatric care;
   (iii)   describing the indications and procedures for compulsory admission;
   (iv)   assessing the quality and motivation of those persons available to care for the patient;
   (v)   advising on testamentary capacity, and advising on the management of affairs, eg by the Court of Protection.

The Practice

a.   Organise his/her practice for the benefit of his/her elderly patients so as to ensure ease of contact, appropriate timing of appointments, and satisfactory cover for emergencies, as well as provide information about these services and opportunities for older people and their carers to comment on these.

b.   Develop policies for the primary care team, so as to ensure control of repeat prescriptions, the appropriate use of screening or case-finding programmes, and the care of old people in all forms of residential accommodation.

c.   Develop systems and policies for the care of older people in all forms of residential accommodation.

d.   Advise individual patients about the available types of appropriate residential accommodation.

e.   Effectively use the various statutory and voluntary services for support of the elderly in the community.

f. Effect liaison and co-operate with the many different disciplines and persons involved in the care of the elderly.

g. Demonstrate an effective use of local hospital resources, including general hospital and general practitioner beds.

h. Demonstrate an understanding of the management of the transfer from one system of care to another, the complications that can arise and how they can be prevented and managed.

i. Ensure that the provision of care promotes the patient's sense of identity and personal dignity.

j. Demonstrate understanding of the obligations of the general practitioner under the 1990 contract to older people on the practice list, and the practicalities of how these can be fulfilled.

Chapter 10

Health Care of the Elderly in Developing Countries

G V Sridharan, MB, BS, MD, MRCP
Consultant Physician
Royal Oldham Hospital
Oldham, OL1 2JH

A Merriman MB, FRCP, FMCP(Nig)
Faculty of Community Medicine
University of Singapore
Singapore

V Dubey MB, BS
General Practitioner
Daltonganj
Bihar
India

Biosketch

Dr Venkat Sridharan graduated from Madras, India, and after dually accredited training in the UK has been working as a Physician in the Department of Adult Medicine, Royal Oldham NHS Trust, since 1992. His special interests include diabetes and endrocrinology but he has conducted extensive research on diseases of the liver and nervous system and has studied, by extensive travel, the various practices involved in Medicine for the Elderly in the developing and developed worlds.

Dr Anne Merriman joined the Universiti Sains Malaysia as an Associate Professor in 1983 and has pursued clinical research into diabetes in Malaysia after working as a Consultant Geriatrician in Liverpool. She has worked as a Senior Teaching Fellow in the Department of Community Medicine at the National University of Singapore and has extensive background training in Missionary Hospitals in Nigeria and Ethiopia. She received a Masters Degree from the School of Tropical Medicine, Liverpool regarding the needs of the elderly in India and has a special interest in Hospice care.

Dr Vishnu Dubey is a Senior General Practitioner in Bihar, India, and has wide experience in various needs of the elderly at a rural and urban level.

Introduction

The contents of this short chapter are arranged under several headings.

We begin by giving a brief comparative account of population increase in elderly people in developing countries compared to the United Kingdom, during the period 1985 to 2025.

We next discuss the *Changing Tradition and Culture* in developing countries.

The bulk of this chapter is formed by the discussion on *Existing Medical Care* which is described under:
a. rural;
b. urban; and
c. private health care.

Next, under *Existing Activity in the Care of the Elderly* we highlight the current and future trends in services and training of doctors and other professionals for the care of the elderly.

The chapter concludes by discussing the problems with, progress in, and advice for the development of services for the elderly in developing countries.

Background

The average survival time of human life over the last 100,000 years was generally believed to be about 20 to 30 years. Environmental hazards and infectious diseases were the main reasons for death in earlier times. The living environment and adaptive mechanisms have rapidly been changing, resulting in a mean life expectancy at birth of 74 years for the developed and 61 years for the developing nations of the world (Population Reference Bureau) in 1990. By the turn of the century China will have 86 million, and India 76 million people over the age of 60 years, not to mention other developing countries like Brazil, Nigeria, Indonesia, Kenya, Egypt, Pakistan etc, (Figure 1)[7] making the ageing population a critical issue in the developing countries in the near future.

Changing Tradition and Culture

In this chapter, the problems facing the elderly in eleven developing countries have been chosen as typical examples confronting the developing world and, have been compared with the United Kingdom, which has pioneered the care of the elderly for the industrialised world.

Figure 1

Percentage increase in the Elderly population 1985 to 2025

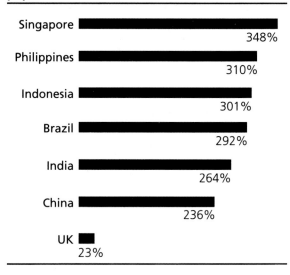

One major problem facing the developing world is its massive population. This is partly explained by illiteracy, lack of a social security system, high infant mortality and the use of child labour as an important source of income in some areas. The unequal distribution of wealth is likely to perpetuate itself despite the marked increase in gross national produce, because a larger proportion of any increase will be siphoned off by persons who are already wealthy. Traditionally, age had a value in itself and was synonymous with wisdom and made the society unique, priding itself on its veneration of the old. In India for example, caring for the old is considered by the Hindus, 'Punya', one path to salvation. In turn the elderly at home felt like institutions, fulfilling an important role as a bridge between their children and grand children; like conduits for building a 'sense of values in life' through explaining tradition and culture and took on themselves continuous child minding.

Like shifting sands, change has been altering the social landscape of the developing countries during the last twenty-five years. Urbanisation, the crunch on space, migration of youngsters in search of work to cities, visible assertion of individualism, inflation and the onset of a youth-worshipping culture have been responsible for the 'contraction' of the age-old joint family. This has meant displacement and marginalisation of the vulnerable elderly. The trend is likely to continue in the developing world, as the World Bank estimates a drop in number of poor (annual income less than $370) by the year AD 2000[6].

Existing Medical Care

Public health in most developing countries is primarily a State responsibility, but the central government sponsors and supports major national schemes for the prevention and control of diseases, and is committed towards schemes relating to sanitation, water supply and nutrition. Average Public health expenditure per head in the developing world is approximately $18.80 (ranging from $0.50 by Nigeria to $99.6 by Singapore), and is about 3.5% of total government expenditure (0.8 by Nigeria to 9.5% by Brazil). This would be an average of $4.5 billion per annum – corresponding figures for Britain are $614 per head, with 13.6% of total public expenditure, about $35 billion per annum, allocated to the National Health Service. (Table 1)[1,2]

Much of the medical care in the developing world is provided by practitioners of indigenous systems of medicine, for example, three fifths of

the total three quarters of a million registered medical practitioners in India are not trained in the western system of medicine but of Ayurvedic medicine. Most readers would be familiar with the Chinese indigenous system of medicine, and the systems in Africa, although exact numbers of such practitioners is not known. Besides these there are many other 'healers', who may or may not choose to call themselves doctors, many practising skills that have been handed down from one generation to another. Some governments have expressed a desire to foster indigenous forms of medicine, and research into traditional remedies is being encouraged[5].

The allopathic doctor–patient ratio is about 1:2998 (ranging from 1 per 616 in Egypt, to 1 per 7902 in Indonesia) – the comparable figure in the UK is 1:611. Many are private practitioners who live in urban areas and sometimes are working in one of several general hospitals (many of these hospitals are privately owned). For each hospital bed in the developing world there is an average population of 817 (ranging from 285 in Brazil to 1783 in Pakistan) compared with one bed for a population of 138 in the UK (Table 2,[1,2]). The inappropriate urban orientation of medical care identified by several countries is being rectified by a network of comprehensive primary health care services.

Table 1

Demography of some Developing Countries cf, UK (1991 Figures)

Country	Population in 2000 AD in millions			Male %	Female %	Urban %	Rural %	Life expectancy at birth		Average House-hold size	GNP billions $	Per Capita income $	Per Capita public health expenditure	
	Total	>60	<75					Male	Female				% GNP	actual $
UK	59.0	11.91	3.42	48.76	51.24	91.5	8.5	71.9	77.6	2.5	834	14,570	13.6	614.0
Brazil	187.5	11.06	2.06	49.87	50.13	75	25	62.3	67.6	4.3	375	2,550	9.5	49.5
China	1,283.0	86.00	16.67	51.60	48.40	52	48	68.1	71.0	4.2	393	360	NA	4.2
Egypt	64.4	4.6	0.64	51.09	48.91	44	56	59.0	62.1	4.9	32	630	2.5	13.0
India	1,042.5	67.76	13.54	51.68	48.32	28	72	58.1	59.1	5.6	287	350	1.8	1.1
Indonesia	214.4	9.4	2.14	49.77	50.23	26	74	54.9	57.7	4.9	87	490	1.8	1.7
Kenya	30.4	1.3	0.20	49.9	50.10	20	80	56.5	60.5	6.2	8	380	6.1	6.1
Malaysia	21.5	1.54	0.23	50.39	49.61	38	62	68.9	72.7	5.2	87	2,130	4.6	26.3
Nigeria	150.0	6.4	1.50	49.46	50.54	31	69	48.8	52.2	5.0	28	250	0.8	0.5
Pakistan	162.4	8.6	2.59	51.37	48.63	32	68	59.3	60.7	6.5	40	370	0.9	0.6
Philippines	77.0	4.6	0.77	50.23	49.77	43	57	62.8	66.4	5.5	37	630	4.1	4.2
Singapore	2.9	0.20	0.03	50.88	49.12	100	0	70.3	75.8	3.9	24	9,100	3.6	99.6

Table 2

Education and Health of some Developing Countries cf, UK (1991 Figures)

Country	Literacy %	Physicians 1 per population	Hospital Beds 1 per population	Per Capita calories per day	Causes of Death							
					Infection	Cancer	Endocrine system	Nervous system	CVS	Resp. system	GIS	Accidents
					Rate per 100,000 Population							
UK	100.0	611	138	3,218	4.9	281.4	18.9	21.5	536.6	122.4	35.5	38.1 .....
Brazil	79.3	685	285	2,280	37.2	52.4	13.0	6.7	156.2	48.3	22.0	69.2 .....
China	72.6	724	430	2,637	24.7	109.0	6.7	3.9	200.0	108.0	28.7	54.1 .....
Egypt	44.9	616	505	3,196	168.9	21.8	7.3	1.7	186.3	106.3	8.8	39.7 .....
India	43.5	2471	1130	2104	21.0	3.1	...	3.9	9.6	15.8	...	6.6 rural
Indonesia	74.1	7902	1512	2645	...	...	...	...	...	...	...	....
Kenya	59.2	7174	703	2016	...	...	...	...	...	...	...	....
Malaysia	72.6	2853	442	2665	55.0	53.3	9.0	5.6	122.8	38.9	12.8	70.8 .....
Nigeria	42.4	6573	1160	2083	...	...	...	...	...	...	...	....
Pakistan	25.6	2081	1783	2167	...	...	...	...	...	9.2	9.8	....
Philippines	88.7	1062	683	2238	179.8	30.2	13.4	...	100.6	...	...	16.8 .....
Singapore	87.6	837	360	2882	16.5	119.8	19.8	3.9	178.9	74.3	12.6	35.6 .....

(......... official figures N/A)

Rural Health Care

The developing world typically consists of nucleated villages scattered over several states, for example, 64,000 villages in the state of Tamil Nadu, in India. The infrastructure in the rural areas consist of primary health centres and subcentres, and a vast army of paramedics including multipurpose workers, village health guides and traditional birth attendants. Each health centre is staffed by two or three doctors and several auxiliary workers. Most have a few beds and the centre is orientated towards prevention rather than cure. These services have had less than optimal impact on the health status of the people and the reason for this includes poor leadership by doctors, poor supervision of para-medical workers, little accountability, inadequate and intermittent supply of medicines and vaccines.

There is also an element of consumer resistance due to a mixture of inaccessibility, cost (although the service is ostensibly free), and lack of trust. The hearts and minds of the medical profession have not been won over to the idea that community and preventive medicine should take priority.

Most are uninterested and hold little respect for their colleagues in community medicine. Reorientation of medical education was set up in some countries to shift the emphasis of medical training away from Western orientated medicine towards community health and preventive services. This was to be achieved by changing the undergraduate curriculum, by arranging weekly visits, and by senior medical staff and students conducting outpatients in an outlying rural health centre and thus fostering 'awareness' and promoting communication on both sides. It had been a dismal failure, at least in India, because established medical staff and the students have been against changing the curriculum and making the required visits, and the primary health centre staff have not been enthusiastic either. The Medical Council has been unable to persuade recalcitrant medical colleges to toe the line. Medical colleges are not an integrated part of the health care services in their area and come under the director of medical education, who may have little if any communication with the director of health services.

The location of the primary health centres and subcentres are not convenient for many people, who may have to take a day or several days off work, to get there. The loss of income coupled with the cost of travel may make them very reluctant to make the journey, especially if it is only, for example, for a routine check up. If there is need for long term treatment or supervision, repeat visits are so prohibitive that most 'fail to comply'. Compounding this issue, the consumer also has a locally based, cheaper choice of medical practitioner of indigenous medicine. There is

A GUIDE TO THE CARE OF THE ELDERLY

little concern to provide 24 hour service, and most centres are manned only intermittently. Mistrust of the services on offer is widespread, not least because family planning takes priority (it is encouraged by paid incentives and failure of health workers to carry it out is penalised). Many women are fearful of the whole concept of family planning, and those who have all too often seen young children and babies die do not share the enthusiasm for limiting their families. Any approach by such a worker, who has limited education and slavish outlook to his job, may be regarded with suspicion.

These centres are run 'from above' and hence the loyalties of the health staff concerned are with the higher authorities and not the villagers, with whom their relationship may be poor. The social divides between doctor, nurse, health worker, and the illiterate villagers all too often result in a failure to communicate effectively. By and large, villagers seek help only when really ill and the concept of preventive medicine is alien. They do not question the services on offer at the health centres, for they have little idea of what should be provided and no means of knowing (the services are not particularly user friendly) if the centre is meeting its objectives[3].

Only a small proportion of the hospital beds are in the rural sector, although this is where three quarters of the population live. Beds in the rural sector are largely in the equivalent of small cottage hospitals, and larger 250–500 bedded district hospitals, where facilities are basic, good nursing and auxiliary back up may be scarce, and specialist care is by necessity limited.

Urban Health Care

Millions of the developing world's 'exciting' middle class people live in urban areas, and are popularly known as the 'consumer boomers'. Patients have ready access to medical treatment in a variety of settings depending on what they can afford. Those who can afford little or nothing go to municipal dispensaries or state government hospitals. These hospitals are spartan, with massive bed capacity, and densely overcrowded, (a 40-bedded ward may have to house up to 80 patients). Para-medical staff may be in short supply and appropriate treatment, drugs, supplies of blood, x-ray and laboratory facilities are limited. Privacy and highly personalised care are impossible and the environment can be grim.

Employees of certain state or centrally run organisations and industries have their own hospitals and dispensaries, where medical care is provided free of charge. A good example is the Indian railway hospitals, which look after the 1.8 million railway employees and their dependants. One would be impressed by its cleanliness and orderliness and the attempt to soften the environment with a few pictures[3]. Other hospitals run on a charitable or voluntary basis, provide a combination of free and pay beds, and the administration is in the hands of some dedicated members, for example, monks.

Private Health Care

Although precise figures are hard to come by in the developing world, about two thirds of the expenditure on health is in the private sector, and about two thirds of doctors work as private practitioners. Some rent or buy a room in the high street and put up a board outside, others join together to run a small polyclinic. Private practice may be combined with work in the public sector and indeed it is advantageous to have a foot in both camps because the doctor can get his private patients investigated and treated free of charge in a state run hospital. This militates against the poor because the private patient invariably 'jumps the queue' over hundreds of his poor fellow countrymen and women waiting in the hospital queue.

Private establishments offer a wide choice of pay beds and provide privacy and personalised care, including full time nurses and private caterers. Such 'special beds' are also available in state hospitals, although in small numbers. The private hospitals run efficiently and profitably and the facilities are good and equipment up to date. Private hospitals are seen as good investments and are mushrooming in the big cities.

Existing Activity in the Care of the Elderly

Hospital based services for the elderly have been developed since 1965 in Alexandria University in Egypt and since 1978 in University of Madras, India. The units consist of a multidisciplinary team in the traditional sense, including social workers, and provides in-patient and out-patient service. They maintain reasonable public awareness via the media and are involved in productive research[4]. The first National Scientific Conference on Medicine for the Elderly was held in November 1990 and was organised by the Geriatrics Society of India.

Future Objectives

These departments have set themselves the objectives of achieving maximum public and political awareness of the need to care for the elderly population. They propose to organise regular community-based research (table 2 lists the varied prevalence of diseases causing death) to identify the needs of the elderly, to expand the undergraduate and post-graduate curriculum of medical graduate training in Geriatric Medicine in the University, and to conduct post-graduate examinations in Geriatric Medicine. Training nurses and other multidisciplinary members of the service, and motivating the existing staff to achieve maximum efficiency, to provide high quality care for the elderly are continued commitments of these departments. Establishing a 'Grey Brigade', (similar to – 'Grey Panthers' – the group of elderly Americans who fought for their rights) to organise a lobby to identify the needs of the elderly is being encouraged. Their demands include: 50% concession for public transport; establishment of health care services in the hospitals; a network of 'pay and stay' hostels for the elderly; and creation of a 'Grey skills Bank' where the aged can be converted from liabilities to assests by profiting from their vast experience.

Conclusions

The problems of the elderly in the developing world have several features in common. Climatic and geographical contrasts along with astonishing cultural, social and economic contrasts mingled with ignorance and illiteracy are, undeniably, important problems. Undoubtedly, improving the overall standard of education and literacy would do much to improve people's awareness of hygiene and health resources. While improving the economy, investing specifically on raising the levels of skills, creation of more jobs on sectors which make intensive use of labour, such as agriculture, and by applying technologies to make use of the country's natural resources, the political leadership should constantly reiterate

the implementation of population control. A much better deal for labourers and the awareness of the power of organisation of work force will lead to curative and preventive service.

Some of the general recommendations made by various representatives of the developing countries at the World Assembly on Aging during the summer, 1982 meeting, at Vienna[6] were as follows: *age prejudice* and discrimination needs to be combated by various means, including school level education and orientating the government and the private sector to regard all efforts to improve later life as medium-term investments in human capital; provision of health insurance for the needy; promotion of preventive geriatrics and an interdisciplinary approach to services; establishment of leisure and residential facilities for the elderly; preparation of the middle-aged for old age and education of the family members, and careers regarding normal ageing and common diseases in the elderly; promotion of positive attitudes toward themselves, their usefulness, and the role of work in their lives; establishment of a supreme council for the elderly; policies and coordinate programmes of care should be made, research on geriatrics should be increased, and medical curriculum should be revised to incorporate gerontology and geriatrics at under-graduate and post graduate level education; occupational therapy, vocational training, and part-time jobs should be made available for the elderly and the working population should be provided with training and encouragement in recreational activities; refresher courses for the family practitioners; and development of health workers who are motivated and committed to working with the elderly, and who live and work in the rural areas.

Some of the developing countries where bullock carts outnumber automobiles by a dozen to one, it is a notable achievement that they have been able to build jet engines, construct plutonium plants, design computers, develop rocket fuel, and manufacture transformers, steel machinery, oil rigs, electronic equipment, and television receivers. The effectiveness of a system is best achieved by its efficiency and unity of purpose and the developing world should change its orientation; a workable model in its own environment rather than copy a model from the developed world. However, the mistakes that have been learnt by the west could be applied most usefully in preventing loss of precious resources and time towards implementing many aspects of care of the elderly in the developing world.

Health Care of the Elderly in Developing Countries

Practical Points

1. The ageing population will be a critical issue in the developing countries in the near future.

2. The unequal distribution of wealth is likely to perpetuate itself despite the marked increase in gross national produce.

3. Average public health expenditure per head in the developing world is approximately $18.80 cf Britain $614.0.

4. Much of the medical care in the developing world is provided by practitioners of indigenous systems of medicine.

5. The rural health care has had less than optimal impact on the health status of people due to poor leadership by doctors, poor supervision of para-medical workers, little accountability and inadequate and intermittent supply of resources. The public do not question the services on offer as it is not user friendly. By and large villagers seek help only when really ill and the concept of preventive medicine is alien.

6. About two thirds of the expenditure on health is in the private sector (mainly in the urban areas) and about two thirds of doctors work as private practitioners. The private hospitals run efficiently and profitably and the facilities are good and equipment up to date.

7. The effectiveness of a system is best achieved by its efficiency and unity of purpose and the developing world should change its orientation to a workable model in its own environment rather than copy a model from the developed world.

References

1. Encyclopaedia Britannica (1991) *World data*.

2. Manorama (1991) *Volume XXVI: year book*, Kottayam, Kochi, Kerala–686 001, India. Reg. No. 40731/82. ISSN 0542–5778.

3. Richards T (1985) *Impressions of medicine in India*, Br Med J, 290, 1047, 1132, 1196, 1276 & 1329.

4. Natarajan VS (Personal communications), Dept. Geriatric Medicine, Madras Medical College, Madras, India–600 003, 1990–92.

5. Aluoch JA (1992) *Health care in Kenya: traditional medicine and modern medicine*, Proc Royal Coll Phy (Edn) 22, 120–122.

6. Selby P & Schechter M (1982) *Aging 2000: a challenge for society*, Sandoz Institute for Health and Socio-Economic Studies, Geneva, Switzerland.

7. Merriman A (1989) *Handbook of international geriatric medicine*, (**PG Economy Edition**), PG Publishing, Singapore.

Section B

Common Medical Problems in the Elderly

Chapter 11

Multidisciplinary Management of Falls in the Elderly

Dr D G MacMahon MBBS, FRCP
Consultant Physician
Barncoose Hospital
Redruth
Cornwall
TR15 3ER

Biosketch:

Dr Douglas MacMahon is a Consultant Physician with special responsibility for the elderly in Cornwall where he has provided specialist geriatric medical services since 1980. He qualified from King's College Hospital, London and moved to other training posts in Portsmouth, Aylesbury, and Oxford. He has developed a model of care for Parkinson's disease, and has pioneered the specialist nurse concept. Additionally, since 1990, he has undertaken additional managerial responsibilities, initially as Unit General Manager/Medical Director, for elderly services and subsequently, Medical Director for the Cornwall Healthcare NHS Trust. He is a keen advocate for the further development of Eldercare services, a term which he has adopted in preference to other adjectives. He has served on the British Geriatrics Society Council and Executive, and is now a member of the Policy Committee. He has been a member of the Royal College of Physicians Geriatrics committee, Parkinson's Disease Society Council, and now chairs its Nurse Steering Group. As Deputy Editor of *Care of the Elderly*, he has organised and chaired many National Conferences. His research interests are currently Parkinson's disease, Heart Failure, and Community Assessment and Rehabilitation. He has published widely in both professional and lay press, presented at meetings in GB, Europe, North America, China and Japan, and participated in Videos, Cassettes, and Teleconferences. He has been actively involved in policy issues eg with the Health Advisory Service and with the King's Fund.

Introduction

"Regia, crede mihi, yes est, Succerrere lapsis"
(It is a kindly act, believe me, to succour the fallen)

OVID, 43BC–17A

Attitudes have changed considerably since the introduction of Sheldon's[1] classic paper: *"The liability of old people to tumble and often to injure themselves is such a commonplace of experience that it has been tacitly accepted as an inevitable consequence of ageing, and thereby deprived of the exercise of curiosity"*. As a result of the attention that this subject has received, a fall is no longer accepted as a diagnosis in its own right, merely a symptom. We now recognise that in addition to pathophysiological changes related to the ageing process, almost every disease may present non-specifically to cause a fall, especially in the presence of environmental hazards.

Not only do falls present some of the commonest clinical problems to primary care teams but also one of the most frequent causes of admission to a geriatric unit. Their management embraces many of the fundamental principles underlying the multidisciplinary practice of geriatric medicine.

The prospect of falling still terrifies many old people as does the cascade of events that may follow: loss of liberty; admission to hospital, residential or nursing care; disability; or death. Families and friends worry about their elderly relatives falling, yet a balance between independence and security needs to be struck to avoid overprotective attitudes that deny the elderly their right to take risks.

How Common are Falls?

Statistics tend to hide the heterogeneity of the elderly, and must be interpreted cautiously. Several studies have shown falls occurring in between 25% and 35% of the elderly population each year with twice as many elderly women falling as men[2, 3, 4]. Even higher rates have been observed among residents of care homes[5]. A clear relationship exists between advancing age and increasing frequency of fall, the rate doubling in the two decades after the age of 65 years. After the first fall, the risk of a further one is increased.

Where do Falls Occur?

The distinction needs to be drawn between accidents and falls occurring in the domestic environment, and those that happen elsewhere. In contrast to younger people, most falls in the elderly occur in their home, and may go unreported.

The domestic fall is more likely to occur in the physically and mentally frailer, and although cushioned by floor coverings, may cause disproportionately severe injuries. Clark found that about 70% of the patients presenting with fractures of the femoral neck had fallen indoors, most commonly in the living room or bedroom[6].

Falls in the street, or shopping precincts are more likely to occur in physically and mentally fit subjects, and are therefore similar to those occurring in younger people, both in terms of aetiology, and subsequent morbidity and mortality[7].

In institutional settings, bedroom and bathroom are the most hazardous areas; transfers between bed, chair, toilet, and bath are the activities most associated with falls, although some even occur whilst resting[8].

Why Does the Fall Occur?

Falls commonly occur in childhood, with trivial injury sustained at worst. Once maturity is achieved, spontaneous falls occur less frequently. As age advances, the homeostatic mechanisms become blunted and postural instability becomes apparent. The functional result of ageing is a gait that is characterised by more sway, a shorter pace, and the tendency to fall. Neurological signs may be found: an abnormally flexed posture, loss of ankle jerks, reduced vibration sense, an action termor, benign memory loss, and a deficiency of upward gaze[9]. In addition to these changes, many diseases present in a non specific manner in the elderly. A fall may, therefore, represent a serious unexpected disease process or a minor precipitating problem on a background of a precarious domestic environment. Patients themselves are often uncertain of cause (table 1).

Intrinsic Risk Factor

There are a number of intrinsic factors pertinent to the elderly (table 2). Of the common specific conditions, the loss of balance is so characteristic of advanced Parkinson's disease that it is used as a guide to severity. Since it occurs in up to 2% of the elderly population it is a common cause of falls.

The characteristic 'drop attack' due to vertebro-basilar ischaemia, is thought to be a

Table 1

Self-Reported Causes of Falls
(after Prudham & Grimley Evans, 1981)[3]

Unknown

Dizziness

Loss of consciousness

Tripping

Legs giving way

Multiple (different causes)

Other definable

Table 2

Common *Intrinsic* Causes of Falls

Neurological

Cerebrovascular disease, (carotid and vertebrobasilar); Stroke; Transient Cerebral Ischaemia (TIA, Reversible Ischaemic Neurological deficit, cerebellar ataxia.

Autonomic failure, postural hypotension, carotid sinus hypersensitivity, normal pressure hyrocephalus.

Higher cortical function: dementia, toxic confusional states.

Epilepsy.

Peripheral nerves: peripheral neuropathy (eg diabetes, ethanol).

Extrapyramidal: Parkinson's disease, drug induced parkinsonism. Steele-Richarson-Olzewski (progressive supranuclear palsy).

Cardiac

Arrhythmias, silent Myocardial Infarcts, aortic outflow obstruction (stenosis, hypertrophic cadiomyopathy), emboli.

General

eg Metabolic – hypokalaemia, hyponatraemia, hypocalcaemia, hypoglycaemia), Haematological (eg Anaemia, acute or chronic).

Drugs

Sedatives, hypnotics, diuretics, antihypertensive and hypotensive agents.

Locomotor

Arthritis, shortening (old fractures, OA hip), muscle disorders, osteomalacia, onychogriphosis, gait abnormalities.

Visual problems

Cataracts, macular degeneration, diabetes.

common cause of falling. Cerebral blood flow may be compromised from hypotension or from more localised lesions such as aortic stensosi, or atheromatous carotid arteries from which emboli may also arise. These may cause a disproportionate problem in elderly people and provide the rationale for investigating falls for arrhythmias or other causes of transient loss, or reduction in cerebral perfusion.

Of the various risk factors, impaired mobility and the use of mobility aids are the paramount problems. Other contributory factors include foot abnormalities, arthritis, and muscular weakness causing failure to lock the extended knee joint. Declining vision, functional or mental impairment, a previous history of heart disease or stroke, all increase risk. Drugs contribute to risk, particularly tranquillisers and diuretics. Blind prescribing of vestibular sedatives cannot be condoned under any circumstance since they may exacerbate the problems by causing postural hypotension, drowsiness, or iatrogenic parkinsonism.

Extrinsic Risk Factors

Almost any hazard can contribute to an elderly person falling (table 3). They assume an extra importance in the more *vigorous* elderly for whom improved design and education could help, especially to reduce the incidence of falls resulting from common household hazards[12]. All members of the health-care team must be alert to these hazards when visiting the elderly in their own homes, or proffering advice.

Clinical Assessment

A good history (preferably confirmed by an accurate witness) is of great value and should reflect any previous history of 'funny turns', drug ingestion, disease processes (figure 1) which must be excluded before ascribing a fall to a simple slip or trip. Consideration must be given to the possibility of the fall being non-accidental, from criminal intent or abuse. This needs sensitive handling, with recourse to the appropriate caring and legislative authorities.

Examination

In addition to examining for external signs of fractures bruising and abrasions, attention should

Table 3

Common *Extrinsic* Causes Of Falls

Trips

Environmental: uneven flooring, stairs and steps, ramps, irregular footpaths, pavements, etc.

mobility aids (eg frames and sticks)

poor illumination

loose rugs or mats

trailing electrical (and telephone) wiring

pets

furniture, chairs

ill-fitting footwear

Slips

water

ice

foodstuffs (fats & oils)

Non-Accidental

Elderly abuse

criminal injury

Figure 1

Classification of Falls

after Lach et al[11]

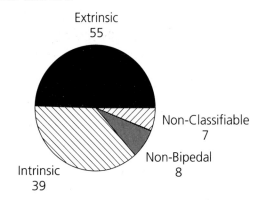

Extrinsic
55

Non-Classifiable
7

Non-Bipedal
8

Intrinsic
39

Non-Bipedal Fall = from bed or chair

be paid during the clinical examination for evidence of less obvious abnormalities, such as cardiac failure, arhythmias, tumours, cerebrovascular disease, extrapyramidal or other neurological signs. Dominant handgrip strength correlates well with fall risk, and should be assessed.

When the patient is able to stand, blood pressure should be recorded in both lying and standing positions, and examination is incomplete without a check on balance and gait. The 'Get-up and Go' test correlates well with formal tests of gait and balance and is useful once the patient has reached the point where they can comply with it[13].

Investigations

Investigations are directed at assessing causes and diagnosing complications. They should be requested only if their results will affect the management of the individual. If basic examination reveals an obvious abnormality, then appropriately selected X-rays will be required. A common catch is undisplaced fracture of pubic ramus or subcapital femur that is missed on the initial radiograph: any patient in whom the index of suspicion is high who is still unable to weight bear after 48–72 hours, should have a repeat X-ray.

A 12 lead ECG, and a check on Plasma Urea, Electrolytes, Sugar and Full Blood Count will usually be required, but can often be deferred until the routine laboratory run. Rarely will they affect management in the middle of the night. Liver function tests, bone profile and cardiac enzymes may also be of use, and reveal unsuspected pathology. Thyroid functions tests (deferred until convalescence to avoid factitious results) may also be revealing. An EEG, may be required to exclude epilepsy, particularly if a grand mal fit is witnessed, or if there is circumstantial evidence of epilepsy, such as a bitten tongue, urinary incontinence, or previous history of 'fits'.

Cardiac arrhythmias should be considered in patients with otherwise unexplained falls. The high background prevalence of arrhythmias implies that 24 hour cardiac tape (Holter) should be reserved for those patients with suggestive symptoms rather than a part of the routine investigation[14]. Stokes Adams attacks due to heart block are eminently treatable by pacemaker implantation.

A GUIDE TO THE CARE OF THE ELDERLY

CT or (NMR) scan may be required to confirm or refute a diagnosis of a treatable cause such as subdural haematoma, or normal pressure hyrocephalus, and may also be required in the investigation of other neurological causes.

Prognosis

A single fall does not necessarily indicate an imminent demise: whilst there is an increased mortality after a fall, many of the factors which lead to a fall are also markers of ill health. The excess mortality is around 10% in the subsequent three years[15].

Complications

Most falls occur without serious damage, even to the frailer elderly. When damage is sustained, a systematic review for complications is required.

Dehydration, chest and urinary infections are common coincidental finds, begging the question of whether they are the cause or the consequence of the fall. There is a real risk of hypothermia if the old person is unable to cover themselves (especially the scalp) in poorly heated or insulated housing.

Skin lacerations may be extensive with thin atrophic skin. The combined effects of age and solar exposure are exacerbated by corticosteroid treatment.

Soft tissue damage is common: muscle damage during a fall may be exquisitely painful, and may cause a fractitious rise in muscle enzymes, leading to difficulty in diagnosis of myocardial infarction. Rhabdomyolysis may be caused by the release of large quantities of myoglobin, causing transient, or more persistent renal failure. Judicious fluid replacement, with strict biochemical monitoring usually results in recovery.

Vascular damage sustained by inflexible vessels can cause profound blood loss or bruising. Fractures occur in approximately 10% of falls, particularly when risk is increased as a result of osteoporosis which increases bone fragility. Common sites include the distal forearm, the pelvis, and the neck of femur. After successful fixation most patients need at least some rehabilitation.

Head injuries are commonly sustained. A high index of suspicion of subdural haematoma should be raised by suggestive signs such as variable drowsiness and signs of raised intracranial pressure or hemiparesis. Management is greatly assisted with access to CT scanning.

Psychological

The psychological effect of a fall in which an elderly person has remained on the floor for a protracted period can be enormous. Anxiety, and transient cognitive impairment are common. Dementia may have been quietly progressing for a considerable period before the fall, but the sequelae of the fall often dictates a change of managements, and may lead to entry to residential or nursing care.

Multidisciplinary Management

A single fall in an otherwise fit old person if reported at all, may need only simple first aid measures. A follow-up visit by a member of the team is desirable. The failure to resume full activities should prompt a review, and perhaps referral to a day hospital or out patient clinic to ensure that remediable pathology has not been overlooked. If seriously injured, and unable to self-care, in-patient treatment will be required.

Medical assessment should be directed at background medical problems (active or non-active), and assessment of damage sustained at the time of the fall. If the pain from bruising or fracture is distressing, then analgesia is clearly essential.

Nursing needs change as the patient progresses and should therefore be regularly reviewed, incorporating views of relevant therapists. Initially, the priorities are pressure area care and the prevention of unnecessary loss of life skills, such as eating and drinking independently. As independence is regained, nurses must allow the patient to mobilise, taking limited risks in a controlled environment to prepare for their homegoing.

Cot sides should be reserved for exceptional circumstances since paradoxically they may increase the risk of damage. Similarly, the use of chair restraints is usually inappropriate, although adapted chairs may be of use for selected individuals.

Nurses may fear legal problems when elderly patients fall in hospital but completion of an accident form should not be taken as a criticism of care. Rehabilitation entails an acceptance of risk that competes with the need for safety. The individual risk/benefit should be a team decision well annotated on the care plans.

Physiotherapy is mainly addressed at the restoration of mobility and function. After a full assessment, therapy may entail graduated exercise, with the use of aids or appliances as appropriate. Passive exercise will be followed by increasingly active exertion, mobilising with a walking frame; progressing to walking sticks. The choice of appliance is best assessed by an experienced therapist working within the team.

Attention to **re-education** and exercises that will help the person to get up from a fall are also of great importance. To practice getting up from the floor under supervision in a safe environment may allow the patient to start thinking more positively about returning home. Discharge planning may be prolonged, and should usually entail a home visit. For those returning to live alone, the installation of an alarm system or a cordless telephone may give added reassurance both to the patient and their family.

Occupational Therapists have two main roles in this context. First, they aid functional recovery, assessing the need for specialised equipment, staff, or training carers. Next is their assessment of the home environment, making them key members of the home visit team. They will not only be checking for access, for ability to cope with the 'activities of daily life' – washing, dressing, eating, food preparation, transfers to bed or chair – but will also be looking to remove hazards, and check or adjust the heights of bed and/or chairs.

Social Workers help to identify and overcome social, financial or emotional problems. They help to assess whether a home discharge is a viable proposition, and ensure that domiciliary care is available. Alternative placement arrangements may need to be considered in respect not only to the needs of the patient, but also of the carers.

It is clearly essential that co-operation between the relevant authorities occurs to ensure that all necessary aids and appliances are provided at the time of discharge. Many Health Districts utilise Liaison nurses to facilitate nursing care after discharge.

The Dietitian, Chiropodist, Orthotist, and Specialist Nurses may each be involved in individual cases. Following in-patient mobilisation, some follow-up may be beneficial. The Day Hospital is often invaluable, although if transport is a problem, a domiciliary visit by the nurse or therapist may be more cost effective and acceptable to the patient.

Conclusion: Prevention is Better than Cure!

It is recognised that compared to those who do not fall, fallers are more likely to have had contact with their GP within the preceding month. This suggests that there are possibilities for avoidance if the appropriate risk factors are sought.

Preventative measures should include rationalisation of medication and attention to risk factors during routine screening visits. The reported benefit of a moderate exercise regime in the improvement of muscular strength may suggest other ways of prevention. Indeed, the simple act of attendance at a day centre or day hospital may have a similar, albeit modest, effect.

All healthcare workers involved in the care of elderly people have a responsibility to promote the reduction of falls. If attention is paid to identifying and minimising the risk factors commonly encountered by this client group, the occurrence of falls with all their attendant problems may be reduced.

Multidisciplinary Management of Falls in the Elderly

Practical Points

1. One third of the elderly population fall each year, yet most require minimal medical attention.

2. Although many falls are due to a combination of factors, there are two basic causes – intrinsic (ie, physical causes) and extrinsic (environmental and side-effects of medications).

3. A thorough assessment of the patient (ie, history, physical examination, appropriate investigations and any complications due to a fall) should precede the management.

4. Management should involve the whole multidisciplinary team working together to assess, treat, rehabilitate and re-educate the patient.

5. Prevention of falls includes encouraging exercise, keeping drug therapy to a minimum and positively looking for and addressing the various risk factors.

References

1. Sheldon JH (1960) *On the natural history of falls in old age*, Br Med J, 1685–90.

2. Prudham D & Grimley Evans J (1981) *Factors associated with falls in the elderly: a community study*, Age & Ageing, 10, 141–146.

3. Campbell AJ, Reinken J, Allan BC & Martinez GS (1981) *Falls in old age: a study of frequency and related clinical factors*, Age & Ageing, 10, 264–70.

4. Blake AJ, Morgan H, Bendall MJ, et al. (1988) *Falls by elderly people at home: prevalence and associated factors*, Age & Ageing, 17, 365–372.

5. Gryfe CI, Amies A & Ashley MJ (1977) *A longitudinal study of falls in an elderly population. I Incidence and morbidity*, Age & Ageing, 6, 201–10.

6. Clark ANG (1968) *Factors in fracture of the female femur*, Gerontologia Clinica, 10, 257.

7. Grimley Evans J (1988) *Falls and Fractures*, Age & Ageing, 17, 361–4.

8. Ashley MJ, Gryfe CI & Amies A (1977) *A longitudinal study of falls in an elderly population. II Some circumstances of falling*, Age & Ageing, 6, 211–20.

9. Broe GA & Creasey H (1989) *The Neuroepidemiology of Old Age*, in: The Clinical Neurology of Old Age, R Tallis (ed), John Wiley & Son, 51–65.

10. Nevitt MC, Cummings SR, Kidd S & Blac D (1989) *Risk factors for recurrent nonsyncopal falls. A prospective study*, JAMA, 261, 2663–8.

11. Lach HW, Reed AT, Arfken CL, Miller P, Paige G, Birge SJ & Peck WA (1991) *Falls in the elderly: reliability of a classification system*, J Am Ger Soc, 39, 197–202.

12. Speechley M & Tinettie M (1991) *Falls and injuries in frail and vigorous community elderly persons*, J Am Ger Soc, 39, 46–52.

13. Mathias S, Nayak USL & Isaacs B (1986) *Balance in elderly patients: the "Get-up and go" test*, Arch Phys Med Rehab, 67, 387–389.

14. Rosado JA, Rubinstein LZ, Robbins AS, Heng MK, Schulman BL & Josephson KR (1989) *The value of Holter monitoring in evaluating the elderly patient who falls*, J Am Ger Soc, 37, 430–4

15. Campbell AJ, Diep C, Reinken J & McCosh L (1985) *Factors predicting mortality in a total population study of the elderly*, J Epidemiol Community Health, 39, 337–42.

16. Aniansson A, Ljundberg P, Rundgren A & Wetterqvist H (1984) *Effect of a training programme for pensioners on condition of muscular strength*, Arch Gerontolog Geriatr, 3, 229–41.

Further Reading

1. Tallis, R (ed) (1989) *The clinical neurology of Old Age*, John Wiley & Son.

2. Tideisksaar R (1989) *Falling in Old Age: its prevention and treatment*, Springer, New York.

3. Andrews K (1987) *Rehabilitation of the older adult*, Edward Arnold.

Chapter 12

Dyspnoea

Martin J Connolly, MD MRCP
Senior Lecturer Honorary Consultant Physician in Medicine and Geriatrics
University of Manchester
Barnes Hospital
Cheadle
Cheshire
SK8 2NY

Biosketch:

Martin J Connolly MBBS(Hons), MD, MRCP is a Senior Lecturer in Medicine (Geriatrics), University of Manchester and Honorary Consultant Physician, Manchester Royal Infirmary and Barnes Hospital, Cheadle, Cheshire. His clinical and research interests include asthma and obstructive airways disease in old age, stroke disease and physical signs in geriatric medicine.

Introduction

"Old persons are also at certain times readily seized; and being seized . . . it requires but a slight inclination of the scale to lay them on the bed of death".

> Aretaeus, the Cappadocian on 'Pneumodes . . . a species of asthma'[1]

Dyspnoea is the unpleasant awareness of breathing. It is a symptom and *not* a physical sign, and it must be distinguished from tachypnoea (rapid breathing). An individual may *appear* dyspnoeic and not complain of being breathless. A classical example of this is the tachypnoea associated with metabolic acidosis. Conversely, patients with an apparently normal breathing pattern may complain of dyspnoea. Not all dyspnoea is due to cardio-respiratory pathology (table 1).

The mechanisms of dyspnoea remain to be fully elucidated. It is likely that a combination of factors are involved, and/or that different mechanisms pertain to different clinical situations. Sensory input from the lungs is transmitted by three different types of receptor: the J receptor, the irritant receptor and the stretch receptor. Stretch receptors are certainly involved in the appreciation of dyspnoea produced by breathing air enriched with carbon dioxide and J receptors may be associated with dyspnoea caused by pulmonary oedema. Irritant receptors are involved in the production of unpleasant respiratory sensations.

The perception of elastic and resistive loads to the thorax, and of tactile sensation and joint movement, is probably important in the perception of dyspnoea. Also relevant is the perception (by chemoreceptors) of hypoxia[2]. However, central processing aggregates and controls all these respiratory inputs and has a major effect on the sensation of breathing. This may be modified by psychological and other cortical influences.

Elderly persons have impaired perception of dyspnoea, at least in some circumstances. Subjective awareness of acute bronchoconstriction produced by methacholine challenge is impaired in elderly asthmatics and normals[3], and the elderly may also appreciate chronic bronchoconstriction less well[4]. The mechanism(s) of any impaired awareness of respiratory difficulties in old age is unclear. It may relate to age-related reduction in activity of stretch receptors, or chemoreceptors[2], impaired perception of elastic and resistive respiratory loads, impaired perception of joint movement and tactile sensation or

Table 1

Differential Diagnosis of Acute Dyspnoea in Old Age

Exacerbation of ROAD* (or of other chronic lung disorder)	
Acute Pulmonary Oedema	
Pulmonary Embolism	
Pneumonia	
Pneumothorax	
Aspirated Foreign Body (or fluids)	
Laryngeal or Tracheal Tumour	Stridor
Angioneurotic Oedema (drugs, insect bites)	
Metabolic Acidosis (eg Diabetic ketoacidosis)	
Panic Attack or other psychological disorder[6]	
Acute Neurological Event (eg cervical fracture, Guillain-Barre syndrome)	
Shock Syndrome	

* ROAD—Reversible Obstructive Airways Disease

abnormalities in central processing. In addition to these physiological changes elderly people may have a reduced expectation of exercise tolerance, and/or a diminished exercise capacity as a result of unrelated conditions (eg musculoskeletal or neurological) which may further contribute to underreporting of dyspnoea by the elderly.

The Scale of the Problem in Old Age

Despite the likely reduced awareness of the symptom (or of the perception of its importance), dyspnoea is one of the most common clinical complaints of elderly patients. For every 1,000 people over the age of 65 in England and Wales, there are over 700 GP consultations per year for respiratory complaints[7]. Over 30% of all acute medical admissions in this age group are for respiratory disease. Respiratory conditions are responsible for 23% of all male deaths and 14% of all female deaths in the over-65's[7]. Of all housebound elderly living in the community and considering themselves disabled, respiratory and cardiac conditions were cited as the cause of disability in over 30% (versus stroke in just over 15%)[8].

Acute Dyspnoea

Acute dyspnoea in old age is thus a common clinical problem, both in general practice and acute hospital-based medicine and geriatrics. The following section discusses presentation, investigation and management of the commonest causes of acute breathlessness in elderly people. Chronic dyspnoea is not within the remit of this chapter.

Acute Exacerbation of Chronic Airways Limitation (including asthma)

The concept of "episodic variable wheezing" as a working definition of asthma is less useful in elderly patients than in the young. Asthma in old age may be associated with only limited lability and reversibility, and often produces chronic persistent airflow obstruction[9]. Asthma may begin at any age, and late-onset asthma in the old is usually non-atopic, under-diagnosed and poorly treated. Differentiation from smoking-related chronic airways obstruction and asthma in middle or late life is clinically difficult and often unhelpful. On the other hand, the degree of reversibility, whatever the underlying pathophysiology, is of prognostic import[10]. It is thus useful to consider the concept of reversible obstructive airways disease (ROAD). ROAD includes obstruction showing ≥15% spontaneous variability or improvement following treatment. The prevalence of ROAD in the elderly may be as high as 41%[11], and acute exacerbations of ROAD are responsible for over a quarter of all elderly acute medical admissions.

The clinical presentation of acute exacerbations of ROAD in old people is atypical. Impaired awareness of acute bronchoconstriction in the elderly[3] contributes to poor control of the chronic condition, and to late presentation during exacerbations[5]. Furthermore, physical signs on examination are often unreliable. This may be partially the result of physician bias, leading to an over-classification of elderly obstructive patients as emphysematous (and by implication, less reversible[12]). Moreover, elderly ROAD patients during acute exacerbations have less tachycardia and pulsus paradoxus than younger patients with similar degrees of hypoxia and airways obstruction[5]. The combination of impaired awareness of bronchoconstriction by the patient and lack of reliability of physical signs in assessing severity may result in an underappreciation of

the seriousness of an exacerbation by both patient and physician, and contribute to the much higher mortality of acute exacerbations of ROAD in old age[13]. The poor reliability of other physical signs, such as lung crepitations[14] in acutely ill elderly patients makes assessment even more difficult.

Assessment must therefore depend chiefly on objective testing and not reliance on misleadingly reassuring symptoms and signs. Most elderly patients with ROAD will first come to medical attention (especially hospital attention) during an acute exacerbation. In light of the impaired appreciation of acute bronchoconstriction in the elderly, old persons who *are* acutely breathless at rest or with little exertion should be referred urgently for hospital assessment. *Objective* measurement is essential. This chiefly depends on measurement of arterial blood gases and regular peak expiratory flow (PEF) estimations. A low-reading peak-flow meter may be particularly helpful in old age. The belief that elderly persons cannot produce reliable peak-flow readings is widespread but erroneous, though they often need more tuition. The only significant limitation to the production of reliable peak-flow measures by elderly people is acute or chronic confusion.

Admission chest radiograph may or may not be helpful in the assessment of *younger* asthmatic patients. However, in elderly patients admitted with acute exacerbations of ROAD, we have found that there is a high prevalence of clinically unsuspected though significant pathology (eg coincident cardiac failure, TB, lung abscess) on admission chest X-ray in these circumstances (unpublished data). Most severe exacerbations of ROAD in this age group *are* infective. Moreover, the chest X-ray may not only differentiate other causes of wheeze (eg pulmonary oedema, bronchogenic carcinoma, inhaled foreign body), but may also reveal other precipitating factors such as pneumothorax.

Urgent blood tests should include urea and electrolytes. Breathless patients are often dehydrated, due to excessive respiratory and sweating losses, and reduced intake associated with dyspnoea. Dehydration is difficult to assess clinically in the elderly, although the presence or absence of axillary sweating may aid in this[15].

Revised national guidelines for acute asthma assessment and treatment have recently been published[16]. These are almost directly applicable to elderly patients with acute exacerbations of

ROAD. As discussed above, it is stressed in the new guidelines that patient distress or features of severe asthma (table 2) may not always be present. In the elderly, in particular, tachycardia is less marked for any given degree of hypoxia or airway obstruction[5], and predicted 'normals' for peak flow are less reliable, generally being derived from extrapolations from younger patients, although recent directly derived data is likely to be more representative and valuable[17]. Conversely, confusion is commoner in elderly patients with less severe degrees of airway obstruction, and by no means specific to life threatening disease.

Whilst eucapnia or hypercapnia is a worrying feature in young asthmatics and suggests the need for artificial ventilation, its prognostic import in *smoking-related* ROAD is less dire. However, the significance of a normal or high pCO_2 in elderly obstructed patients with a minimal smoking history is the same as in young asthmatics.

The treatment of acute exacerbations of ROAD should also essentially follow the published national guidelines for acute asthma[16].

Acute treatment aims to reverse underlying causes of deterioration (eg pneumothorax or infection) with supportive treatment to alleviate bronchoconstriction, oedema, airway plugging, and to reverse hypoxia and hypercapnia, together with the prevention or treatment of complications. The national guidelines suggest flow charts for asthma management. In terms of elderly

patients, these are the *minimum* that should be followed. It is likely that the presence of multiple pathologies or poor social factors may necessitate hospital admission in an elderly person that would be unnecessary with the same clinical features in a young adult.

Nebulised beta$_2$-agonists (terbutaline 10mg, or salbutamol 5mg) should be given 4 hourly (including overnight). Corticosteroids should be administered immediately (hydrocortisone 200 mg (intravenously) ±30–60 mg oral prednisolone), unless there is severe infection and objective evidence of only minor airways obstruction. Oxygen should be given according to blood gas results. Eucapnic or hypercapnic patients, without other life-threatening features will need 24–28% oxygen initially, with repeat assessments of blood gases, preferably within an hour. However, the smoking-history should be clearly established to ensure that eucapnic or hypercapnic 'pure' asthmatics are not overlooked at this stage. Those without a smoking-history and with low initial pCO_2, should be given 40–60% oxygen. Infection, when present or suspected, should be treated with appropriate antibiotics, which will usually include a broad spectrum beta-lactam, and for hospital-acquired infections should also 'cover' gram-negative enterobacteria (see section on Pneumonia). This review, however, does not attempt to produce detailed guidelines on antibiotic use in these circumstances and the reader is directed to a comprehensive review on this topic[18].

Nebulised ipratropium bromide (Atrovent) may produce additional bronchodilatation when given with a nebulised beta$_2$-agonist. The ideal dose for the elderly is not established, although 500 micrograms 4–6 hourly is the optimum for younger patients. Both the response to beta-agonist and to ipratropium decline with age. However, there is some evidence that the decline in ipratropium response is less rapid than that of beta-agonist response, such that beyond the age of 60 years ipratropium produces greater bronchodilatation than beta-agonists[19].

The use of intravenous aminophylline remains controversial. It should be used with extreme caution in the elderly and never in those currently taking oral theophyllines without a previous estimation of theophylline levels. The recently published national guidelines[16] suggest the use of intravenous aminophylline infusion

Table 2

Features of Severe Asthma[16]

Features of Severe Asthma

Too wheezy or breathless to complete sentences in one breath

Respiratory rate ≥25 breaths/minute

Heart rate ≥110 beats/minute

Peak flow ≤50% of predicted normal or best

Life Threatening Features

Peak flow <33% of predicted normal or best

Silent chest, cyanosis or feeble respiratory effort

Bradycardia or hypotension

Exhaustion, confusion or coma

A GUIDE TO THE CARE OF THE ELDERLY

(750–1500 mg over 24 hours) for patients who are desperately ill on first assessment, or who have failed to improve rapidly with standard treatment. Most of the studies on methylxanthines have not included elderly patients. However, some studies in older people with chronic airways limitation have shown improvements in respiratory function and dyspnoea, which may be related to improved respiratory muscle performance and reduced breathing workload. There is renewed interest in methylxanthines following a report showing that the use of intravenous aminophylline in acutely ill ROAD Sufferers, who were also receiving corticosteroids and beta-agonist, markedly reduced hospital admissions[20]. An alternative may be intravenous beta$_2$-agonist infusion, on the assumption that nebulised doses are failing to reach the intrapulmonary receptors of severely obstructed patients.

During the course of treatment, continued objective observation is mandatory. Peak flow charts, whilst often not showing marked diurnal variation, will be helpful in assessing overall response. It should be recognised, however, that lung function is not of itself a major independent predictor of activity level, and that improvements in activities of daily living and walking distance (measures familiar to geriatricians) are equally, if not more, important in the later stages of recovery.

Pulmonary Embolism

Pulmonary embolism is a disease of old age. In the Prospective Investigation of Pulmonary Embolism Diagnosis Project (PIOPED), over half the subjects with proven pulmonary emboli were over the age of 65[21]. Deep venous thrombosis (DVT) develops in 70% of patients with lower limb paralysis due to acute stroke. In the absence of prophylaxis, approximately half of patients undergoing elective hip surgery developed deep vein thrombosis[21].

Although lower limb DVT is usually the source of pulmonary embolism, the signs of DVT may be minimal or lacking. Despite the fact that symptoms of pulmonary embolism are not significantly different in elderly as compared to younger subjects, the diagnosis of pulmonary embolism is often difficult, especially in the presence of pre-existing cardio-respiratory disease.

The classical pattern of pulmonary embolic symptoms (dyspnoea, chest pain, circulatory collapse) is seen with similar frequencies in elderly and younger subjects, and accounted for over 80% of cases in the PIOPED study[21]. The other 20% were usually diagnosed on the basis of radiographic findings, such as basal atelectasis, pleural opacities or pleural effusion.

A normal ventilation/perfusion scan suggests that pulmonary embolism is very unlikely. Conversely, a high probability ventilation perfusion scan (eg normal ventilation with multiple segmental perfusion deficits) is probably adequate for diagnosis. However, many or most studies in elderly patients with previous cardio-respiratory pathology produced intermediate or indeterminate results. In the presence of DVT, it is arguable that anticoagulation is necessary in any case, and that an absolutely proven diagnosis of pulmonary embolism is unnecessary. Non-invasive methods of imaging leg veins are preferable in elderly patients. Impedance plethysmography, with or without B-mode ultra sonography, is of comparable sensitivity and specificity to contrast venography[22]. Recent audit experience on our own integrated medical-geriatrics unit has indicted that establishing or refuting a suspected diagnosis of lower limb DVT by non-invasive means is associated with a reduced length of stay.

Where accurate diagnosis of pulmonary embolus *is* necessary, it is noteworthy that up to one third of patients with low or intermediate probability scans *do* have pulmonary embolism[35]. Pulmonary angiography is the definitive test, but may be difficult in the confused or critically ill, and dangerous in the presence of impaired renal function or raised pulmonary artery pressure. The overall complication rate, however, does not appear to be greatly elevated in old age[22].

Simple investigations in pulmonary embolus are usually of limited help in diagnosis. Standard 12 electrocardiogram shows right heart strain in only 6% of cases[23]. The standard blood gas abnormalities of hypoxia, coupled with a low pCO$_2$, are helpful if seen, but in elderly patients other cardio-respiratory problems may complicate the picture.

Anticoagulation is the treatment of choice in old age. This should initially be with intravenous or high-dose subcutaneous heparin for 5–7 days, aiming to increase the activated partial thromboplastin time (APTT) to 1.5 to 2 times the control. Maintenance therapy is with oral anticoagulation (usually warfarin) aiming for a prolongation of the international normalised ratio (INR) to between 2.0 and 3.0[24]. Recent evidence suggests that duration of anticoagulation need not be as prologued as previously thought. For a DVT following surgery, anticoagulation for four weeks is currently recommended[24]. In the absence of a *persisting* precipitating factor, anticoagulation for DVT and/or pulmonary embolism is recommended for three months[24].

For massive or multiple pulmonary emboli with haemodynamic imbalance, there is a high acute mortality. When 25–50% of the pulmonary arterial tree is obstructed, the six-hour mortality approaches 85%[25]. Anticoagulation is of little benefit in these circumstances as it is the haemodynamic impairment which is life-threatening. Thrombolytic therapy and/or aggressive surgery may be indicated in *some* elderly patients. The mortality of percutaneous or open embolectomy is high – 25–80%[25]. Such procedures should be reserved for those elderly patients without other significant cardio-respiratory impairments or other disease processes (ie those well enough prior to the embolic event to survive what is major surgery).

Acute Pulmonary Oedema

The commonest causes of acute pulmonary oedema in elderly people are listed in table 3. Ischaemic heart disease (with or without myocardial infarction) is the commonest cause of cardiac pathology and of pulmonary oedema in the elderly in Britain and other western countries. Indeed approximately one in five men and one in ten women over the age of 65 suffer from ischaemic heart disease and are thus at risk of developing pulmonary oedema given suitable precipitating or decompensating factors (table 3).

Prior to acute presentation, many patients will have chronic, less severe, symptoms. The most common, though least specific, of these is general tiredness and lethargy, though other classical symptoms of cardiac failure may be present (breathlessness on exertion, orthopnoea, paroxysmal nocturnal dyspnoea, and ankle oedema). However, impaired perception of breathlessness in the elderly[3], together with decreased activity levels consequent upon other pathologies in old age, may reduce the sensitivity of these early symptoms.

Table 3

Commoner Causes of Acute Pulmonary Oedema in Old Age

Acute myocardial infarction

Non-infarctive ischaemia

Arrhythmia (ag acute atrial fibrillation)

Mitral valve disease (± arrhythmia) (± infective endocarditis)

Intravenous fluid overload

Poor compliance with anti-failure therapy

Drug related (eg non steroidal anti-inflammatory agents, beta-blockers, calcium antagonists)

Decompensation during other acute illness (eg respiratory infection)

High output failure (eg anaemia, thyrotoxicosis, Paget's disease)

When compensatory mechanisms fail, the acute presentation is most typically that seen in younger patients with extreme breathlessness, worsened by lying flat, cough, wheeze, anxiety and distress, sweating and (very commonly) acute confusion. Physical signs have been grouped into 'major criteria' and 'minor criteria', for the diagnosis of congestive cardiac failure[26]. The major criteria in terms of physical signs are neck vein distension, clinical (or radiological) evidence of cardiomegaly, gallop rhythm, hydrothorax, and crepitations (rales). Minor physical sign criteria comprise pedal oedema, hepatomegally, pleural effusion and tachycardia greater than 120 beats per minute. These physical signs are generally applicable in the elderly; however, bilateral basal crepitations are of limited specificity and sensitivity in this age group[14], and tachycardia is often less marked in response to hypoxia[2].

Investigations

In view of the lack of specificity and sensitivity of crepitations, an acute admission chest X-ray is mandatory in the assessment of suspected pulmonary oedema in old people. The ECG is not helpful in confirming the diagnosis of cardiac failure, but will often give valuable clues as to the aetiology. Cardiac enzyme series over three days is essential for retrospective assessment of aetiology. Emergency estimation of plasma urea and electrolytes (including potassium) is essential and assessment of blood gases is also recommended. Full blood count is useful to exclude mild to moderate anaemia, and a very high peripheral white blood cell count may indicate co-existent infection, as the combination of respiratory infection and cardiac failure is not unusual. However, a slightly raised white count is not uncommon following acute myocardial infarction.

Efforts should be made to obtain a postero-anterior (PA) chest radiograph, to enable accurate assessment of cardiac size. However, many patients are too ill to stand for a PA X-ray. The next best compromise is an erect antero-posterior (AP) sitting film. This is almost always of inferior radiographic quality, but an erect film (patients should be erect in any case) enables reasonable assessment of upper lobe veins, although it does produce apparent cardiomegaly, because of the change in the patient position relative to the film, and a reduced focus distance, both of which result in magnification of the cardiac outline.

A typical bat's wing appearance is well known, but more subtle changes, most particularly Kerley B lines (fluid in the interlobular septa) should be noted.

Despite changes in the microscopic structure of the myocardium and reduction in cardiac function with age, there have been no consistent age-related changes in the cardiac contour described on plain chest radiography. However, reduction in size of the thorax (chiefly due to a more vertical position of the ribs), ossification of the costal cartilages, and cardiac and aortic calcification may complicate radiological assessment.

Treatment of acute pulmonary oedema in old age is little different from that in younger patients. If not already upright, the patient should be sat up immediately. High-dose oxygen (40–60%) should be administered via a mask or nasal canulae. The latter are often preferable in very anxious patients. A venous canula should be inserted and the patient given intravenous diamorphine (2.5–10 mg), and an anti-emetic. A loop diuretic should be administered, remembering that elderly patients not chronically treated with diuretics can be extremely sensitive to their effects. Initially 40 mg of Frusemide should be tried in these patients. Only after these initial measures should further investigations be pursued. A 12-lead ECG plus rhythm strip is essential at this stage. This will not only allow assessment of treatable arrhythmia but is also necessary in the assessment of possible acute myocardial infarction. Elderly patients with acute myocardial infarct benefit from thrombolytic therapy with low-dose aspirin and streptokinase according to the normal assessment criteria adopted for younger patients. The elderly should not be denied thrombolytic therapy[27,28]. In practice this will mean that most elderly patients with acute MI should be admitted to a coronary care unit for 12–24 hours. Such admission in itself is known to reduce mortality from myocardial infarction in elderly patients. Oxygen flow rates should be adjusted according to blood gas results, particular care being given to those with coincidental smoking-related chronic obstructive airways disease. Patients should be catheterised to enable accurate assessment of urine output, and should be attached to a cardiac monitor.

In the context of acute myocardial infarction, atrial fibrillation as a complication is extremely common and very often resolves with treatment of acute pulmonary oedema within a few minutes to hours. However, when atrial fibrillation is the primary precipitant of pulmonary oedema, it should be treated acutely. Before administration of digoxin, hypokalaemia should be excluded or (if possible) corrected. Oral digitalisation takes many hours to be effective, and even intravenous digoxin will not produce improvement for at least six hours following infusion. Intravenous digoxin, where administered, should be given by slow intravenous infusion (250–500 micrograms over two hours). Intravenous amiodarone is an alternative.

Following improvement in the patient's acute state, continued regular monitoring is necessary, together with further investigations to establish the aetiology. Repeat cardiac enzymes daily over the next 72 hours are required. Where the cause of the event is not immediately obvious, continued cardiac monitoring, followed by a 24-hour taped ambulatory ECG recording may be indicated to look for arrhythmia events. Many, but not all, patients will need continued anti-failure therapy.

The elderly in particular should be mobilised as early as possible and the physiotherapist should be notified within 24 hours of admission. Excessive sodium in the diet should be avoided. Those unable to mobilise early should receive prophylactic sub-cutaneous heparin (calcium heparin 5,000 units bd) to reduce the risk of DVT, whilst any drugs that may lead to cardiac decompensation (table 3) should be discontinued if possible.

Pneumonia

Pneumonia is commoner, and has a higher mortality among the elderly, even excluding terminal pneumonia, "the old man's friend". Pneumonococcal pneumonia, for example, has a case fatality of over 35% (versus less than 10% in young adults), and has four times the incidence in the over 65's. The prognosis of bacteraemic pneumonia has improved little in the last generation[29]. The risk factors, bacterial pathogenesis and management of community acquired and nosocomial (hospital acquired) pneumonias have distinct differences, and thus community acquired and nosocomial pneumonias will be discussed separately. There is little UK-research on the pattern of nursing-home-acquired pneumonia, although in the USA the pattern in nursing homes resembles more that of hospital-acquired disease than community-acquired disease.

Community Acquired Pneumonia

Haemophilus influenzae and *Streptococcus pneumoniae* are the commonest causes of community acquired pneumonia in the elderly in Britain[29,30]. Atypical infections, although not uncommon in the United States, are rarer in the elderly in Britain, although *Staphylococcus aureus* may be a problem after influenza epidemics, and Mycoplasma may be commoner in adults in general during epidemics (approximately every four years). In addition, influenza pneumonia itself is not uncommon in the elderly[29].

Dyspnoea as a presenting feature occurs in at least 60% of patients[29]. Tachypnoea in particular is an early and sensitive physical sign[32]. Other respiratory symptoms, particularly pleuritic chest pain, are less common in the elderly than in the young[31]. Conversely, non-specific symptoms and signs are much commoner in old people, particularly the previously cognitively impaired[29,30].

In the light of the non-specific presentation, and the lack of specificity of crepitations as a physical sign[14], chest X-ray is mandatory and is indeed the single most useful investigation in the acutely confused elderly patient without physical signs, suggesting a diagnosis in nearly a quarter of cases[33].

Antibiotic treatment should be instituted early[29,30] and should be chosen to cover *Streptococcus pneumoniae* and Haemophilus influenzae. During influenza epidemics and Mycoplasma epidemics suitable extra cover should be included. Ciprofloxacin should never be employed as a blind single agent for pneumonia, as it does not reliably kill *Pneumococcus*. Treatment should *not* be delayed by awaiting the collection of sputum for culture, as in early pneumonia sputum is difficult to obtain. Blood cultures should be performed and may diagnose pneumococcal infection in up to 30% of patients[29,30]. Counter-current immune electrophoresis of sputum or urine may also help diagnose pneumococcal infection retrospectively[29,30]. The reader is directed to a more detailed review of antibiotic treatment of this area[18].

Other treatment comprises oxygen, as indicated by blood gas measurements and careful intravenous rehydration which as well as giving general support may also assist mucus clearance.

Resolution of radiological abnormalities following pneumonia in the elderly may be slow – nearly a third of chest X-rays remaining abnormal over three months after admission[30]. Thus, unless there is failure of *clinical* resolution, over-zealous further investigation should not be prompted by slowly-resolving chest X-ray. Failure to improve clinically may be due to unusual or 'atypical' infection (including TB), aspiration, bronchial obstruction by foreign body or carcinoma, pulmonary embolic disease, immunological disorder (eg Wegener's granulomatosis, bronchiolitis obliterans), malignancy (lymphoma, broncho-alveolar carcinoma) or drugs (eg amiodarone).

Nosocomial Pneumonia

Nosocomial pneumonia is second only to urinary tract infection in terms of its frequency as a hospital-acquired infection. It has an incidence of 1.5 to 8% in the acute sector and about 8% in long-term care[14].

Symptoms and signs are not significantly different from those in community acquired infection, although they may be more frequently complicated by underlying respiratory or other conditions.

Gram-negative infection is a particular problem in hospital-acquired disease, and indeed are the most frequently identified pathogens accounting for more than half of all cases[18]. Clearly therefore, antibiotics should be chosen to cover gram-negatives and intravenous second- or third-generation cephalosporins are an appropriate first choice[18]. In the neurologically impaired

A GUIDE TO THE CARE OF THE ELDERLY

(especially acute stroke) or obtunded, aspiration is extremely common (eg 40%–60% of acute stroke subjects and 50%–70% in motor neurone disease[34]). Detailed advice on prevention is beyond the scope of this chapter and the reader is referred to a recent review[34]. However, the presence or absence of the gag reflex is not a reliable predictor of aspiration risk. Patients in at-risk groups should be placed 'nil-by-mouth', hydrated intravenously and speech therapy advice sought urgently (the same day). In the presence of established pneumonia in these circumstances, intravenous metronidazole should be added to an intravenous broad-spectrum antibiotic (eg a beta-lactam) in order to reliably cover aspirated mouth anaerobes.

Summary

Despite the fact that dyspnoea is less well perceived in older persons, it remains one of the commonest acute presenting complaints of elderly patients, reflecting the high prevalence of cardiorespiratory pathology in this age group. Tachypnoea (>24 breaths/minute) is an extremely sensitive though non-specific physical sign. In light of atypical clinical presentation and, in many cases, the unreliability of clinical signs, assessment and monitoring of the acutely breathless elderly patient must include objective investigation at an early stage.

Dyspnoea

Practical Points

1. Dyspnoea is a symptom, not a physical sign.

2. Elderly people may be less subjectively aware of acute dyspnoea.

3. Reversible obstructive airways disease may have a prevalence of up to 40% in old age.

4. Elderly patients present late with acute bronchoconstriction, and accurate assessment depends on objective measurement (PEF and blood gases).

5. Deep venous thrombosis occurs in up to 70% of patients with leg paralysis due to stroke.

6. The duration of anti-coagulation on the embolism or deep venous thrombosis need not be as long as previously thought[24].

7. Bilateral basal crepitations have low sensitivity and specificity in ill elderly patients, and thus urgent chest X-ray is mandatory in assessment.

8. Dyspnoea occurs in over 60% of cases of pneumonia in the elderly, but other 'localising' features are less common.

9. Aspiration pneumonia is not uncommon – risk factors include neurological disease and/or impaired consciousness.

References

1. Brewis RAL (ed) (1990) *Classic Papers in Asthma. Volume One. The Evolution of Understanding.* Science Press Ltd, London, 1–3.

2. Kronenberg RS, Drage CW. (1973) *Attenuation of the ventilatory and heart rate responses to hypoxia and hypercapnia with aging in normal man.* J Clin Invest Pathol Res Pract, 52, 1812–9.

3. Connolly MJ, Crowley JJ, Charan NB, Nielson CP, Vestal RE (1992) *Reduced subjective awareness of bronchoconstriction provoked by methacholine in elderly, asthmatic and normal subjects as measured on a simple awareness scale,* Thorax, 47, 410–3.

4. Renwick DS, Connolly MJ (1994) *Lung function and quality of life in old age – an epidemiological survey,* Age & Ageing, 23(Suppl 1), 8–9.

5. Petheram IS, Jones DA, Collins JV (1982) *Assessment and management of acute asthma in the elderly: a comparison with younger asthmatics,* Postgrad Med J, 58, 149–51.

6. Landahl S, Steen B, Svanborg A (1980) *Dyspnoea in 70-year old people,* Acta Med Scand, 207, 225–30.

7. Clinical Epidemiology, National Heart and Lung Institute (1988) *Respiratory disease in England and Wales,* Thorax, 949–54.

8. Hunt A. (1976) *The elderly at home. A study of people aged sixty-five and over living in the community in England in 1976,* Office of Population Censuses and Surveys.

9. Braman SS, Kaemmerlen JT, Davis SM (1991) *Asthma in the elderly. A comparison between patients with recently acquired and long-standing disease.* Am Rev Respir Dis, 143, 336–40.

10. Kawakami Y, Kishi F, Dohsaka K, Nishiura Y, Suzuki A (1988) *Reversibility of airways obstruction in relation to prognosis in chronic obstructive pulmonary disease,* Chest, 49–53.

11. Banerjee AK, Lee GS, Malik SK, Daly S (1987) *Underdiagnosis of asthma in the elderly.* Brit J Dis Chest, 81, 23–9.

12. Dodge R, Cline MG, Burrows B (1986) *Comparisons of asthma, emphysema and chronic bronchitis diagnoses in a general population sample,* Am Rev Respir Dis, 133, 981–6.

13. Committee on Safety of Medicines (1992) Report of the beta-agonist working party. Medicines Control Agency, London.

14. Connolly MJ, Crowley JJ, Vestal RE (1992) *Clinical significance of crepitations in elderly patients following acute hospital admission: a prospective study,* Age & Ageing, 21, 43–8.

15. Eaton D, Bannister P, Mulley GP, Connolly MJ (1994) *Axillary sweating in clinical assessment of dehydration in ill elderly patients,* Br Med J, 308, 1271.

16. British Thoracic Society, British Paediatric Association, Research Unit of the Royal College of Physicians of London, King's Fund Centre, National Asthma Campaign, Royal College of General Practitioners, General Practitioners in Asthma Group, British Association of Accident & Emergency Medicine, British Paediatric Respiratory Group (1993) *Guidelines on the Management of Asthma,* Thorax, 48 (Suppl) 1–24.

17. Enright PL, Kronmal RA, Higgins M, Schenker M, Haponik EF (1993) *Spirometry reference values for women and men 65 to 85 years of age. Cardiovascular Health Study,* Am Rev Respir Dis, 147, 125–33.

18. Woodhead M (1995) *Respiratory infections in the elderly,* in: Respiratory Disease and the Elderly Patient, Connolly MJ (ed), Chapman and Hall, London (in press).

19. van Schayck CP, Folgering H, Harber H, Maas KL, van Weel C (1991) *Effects of allergy and age on responses to salbutamol and ipratropium in moderate asthma and chronic bronchitis,* Thorax, 46, 355–9.

20. Wrenn K, Slovia CM, Murphy F, Greenberg RS (1989) *Aminophylline therapy for acute bronchospastic disease in the emergency room.* Ann Intern Med, 115, 241–7.

21. PIOPED investigators (1990) *Value of the ventilation/profusion scan in acute pulmonary embolism. Results of the prospective investigation of pulmonary embolism diagnosis (PIOPED),* JAMA, 263, 2753–9.

22. Stein PD, Facc AG, Saltzman HA, Terrin ML (1991) *Diagnosis of acute pulmonary embolism in the elderly,* J Am Cardiol Clin, 18, 1452–7.

23. Dalen JE (1991) *Clinical diagnosis of acute pulmonary embolism. When should a V/Q scan be ordered?* Editorial, Chest, 100, 1185–6.

24. Research Committee of the British Thoracic Society (1992) *Optimum duration of anti-coagulation for deep vein thrombosis and pulmonary embolism*, Lancet, 340, 873–6.

25. Mitchell JP, Trulock EP (1991) *Tissue plasminogen activator for pulmonary embolism resulting in shock; two case reports and a review of the literature*, Am J Med, 90, 255–60.

26. McKee PA, Castelli WP, McNamara PM, Kannel WB (1971) *The natural history of congestive cardiac failure: the Framingham Study*, N Engl J Med, 285, 1441–6.

27. ISIS-2 (Second International Study of Infarct Survival) Collaborative Group (1988) *Randomised trial of intravenous streptokinase, oral aspirin, both, or neither among 17,187 cases of suspected myocardial infarction*, Lancet, ii:349–60.

28. Anglo-Scandinavian Study of Early Thrombolysis (ASSET) (1988) *Trial of tissue plasminigen activator for mortality reduction in acute myocardial infarction*, Lancet, ii:524–30.

29. Venkatesan P, Gladman J, MacFarlane JT, et al (1990) *A hospital study of community acquired pneumonia in the elderly*, Thorax, 45, 254–8.

30. The British Thoracic Society and The Public Health Laboratory Service, (1987) *Community-acquired pneumonia in adults in British hospitals in 1982–1983: a survey of aetiology, mortality, prognostic factors and outcome*, Q J Med, 239, 195–20.

31. McFadden JP, Price RC, Eastwood HG, Briggs RS (1982) *Raised respiratory rate in elderly patients: a valuable physical sign*, Br Med J, 284, 626–7.

32. LaCroix AZ, Lipson S, Miles TP, White L (1989) *Prospective study of pneumonia hospitalizations and mortality of US older people: the role of chronic conditions, health behaviors and nutritional status*, Public Health Rep, 104, 350–60.

33. Puxty JAH, Andrews K (1986) *The role of chest radiography in the evaluation of "geriatric giants"*, Age & Ageing, 15, 174–6.

34. Park C, O'Neill PA (1994) *Management of neurological dysphagia*, Clin Rehabil, 8, 166–74.

35. Pioped Investigators (1990) *Value of the ventilation/perfusion scan in acute pulmonary embolism. Results of the prospective investigation of pulmonary embolism (PIOPED)*, JAMA, 263, 2753–9.

Chapter 13

Psychology of Ageing

Dr Elspeth A Stirling MA, MSc, PhD
Consultant Psychologist (older people)
Tayside Clinical Psychology Department
Royal Dundee Liff Hospital
Dundee
DD2 5NF
Scotland

Biosketch:

Elspeth Stirling has worked as a Clinical Psychologist in services for older people for fifteen years, much of it at Brighton Clinic, Newcastle Upon Tyne. She has contributed to clinical care, training and service initiatives to enhance the opportunities for older people to continue to develop irrespective of even a serious illness or disability.

Introduction

Human beings proceed through adult life on a developmental trajectory, and late life is a particularly challenging period psychologically. There are new tasks to be taken on in late life. There are also multiple changes in health, wealth, status and independence. The psychological tasks arise from:

1. Multiple losses of relationships through death and separation.
2. Loss of home or the threat of.
3. Facing the end of life and having life experiences and core beliefs acknowledged.
4. Conflicts about families.
5. Disappointments with occupation.
6. Surviving in age-incompetent surroundings, in a world which is not age-friendly.
7. A greater need to rely on others for important aspects of one's life, commonly caused by ill health or disability.

Clinical psychologists who specialise in the care of the elderly should be available in each Health District, though this is not always achieved. The work of the clinical psychologist includes day-to-day clinical casework, training, consultancy and projects in research and service development. The specialist psychologist will bring to bear a range of clinical and scientific methods for the objective measurement and treatment of problems in a developmental framework.

Cognitive and behavioural assessment is carried out. Treatments, training and advice are provided on problem behaviours, skills retraining, withdrawal, confusion, depression, bereavement, anxiety, stress and other problems of the individual or carers. An increasingly effective and practical use of the psychologist is in planning and development in elderly people's services.

Primarily Developmental Needs and Problems

Until recently, survival into one's 70's and 80's was an unusual phenomenon. In contrast, today's survivors are the first generation to experience survival as 'normal'. Consequently, psychology is now able to recognise the particular problems of the very mature psyche. These include:

Choice and Control

Multiple losses in later life can cause feelings of loss of control, leading to depression and anxiety.

Cognitive therapy and behavioural psychotherapy can be particularly relevant; these focus on the present and aim to restore a sense of effectiveness and control. In residential and hospital settings the psychological techniques of **goal-planning** offer a particularly practical method of help. Here an individual plan is devised which focuses on step-wise achievements; this can be successful in treating generalised apathy and depression.

Legacies of the Past

Some lifestyles that were sustainable whilst health was good become lethal when health deteriorates permanently. Old habits can become a threat to survival. For example in a relationship where one partner had been dominant, the changed health of one may destroy that previous balance causing stressful role reversal or role loss. The partners struggle to restore the old system but repeatedly fail. Psychological intervention would usually focus on finding a new system instead and may include family therapy.

Some individuals find that disability itself undermines the core beliefs of a lifetime. Other causes might be the prejudiced attitudes which they internalise from others. **Reminiscence** may be used as a therapy by psychologists with the aim of strengthening these beliefs.

Special Needs

There is considerable variation in the range of responses of older people to the effects of illness. The objective of psychological intervention is to enhance the capacity of the elder and of their environment to adapt positively.

Dementia-Related Needs

Both elder and family are helped by specific and clear information. The significance of psychometric assessment is that it provides information which has practical value. It makes it possible to distinguish patterns of residual abilities and therefore give guidance on continuing activities. The person living with dementia is a constant challenge to our capacities to provide high quality support and care. **Reality Orientation** can be effectively taught to staff as a means of minimising the damage that dementia does to the personal awareness and dignity of the person. For staff who are giving care to the most seriously impaired **Validation Therapy** can be introduced. Psychological advice on **environmental modifications** can limit stress and disproportionate underfunctioning.

Stroke-Related Needs

Residual 'invisible' impairments in cognitive or perceptuo-motor functions are often mistakenly attributed to poor motivation. Except in motor and language functions other damage may be 'invisible' until investigated. For example, distortion of depth and distance perception may be the cause of refusal to walk. Or the purposeful execution of an action, such as dressing, is impossible because the meta-skill of sequencing is lost (despite the component skills being intact). These need to be identified specifically, so that practical advice can be given on ways round the problem.

Extreme psychological reactions in the aftermath of stroke, whether denial or depression may require a psychological form of help. For example depression has been reported as more common following right-brain stroke damage.

Primarily Physical Health Problems

Anxiety can aggravate the symptoms caused by a physical illness including pain. Or symptoms may come under the control of other stimuli, causing them to be disproportionately troublesome. In either way they exacerbate the disabling effect of the illness. Psychologists can specially adapt the usual methods of anxiety management to the particular situation caused by the physical illness.

Where there are respiratory or circulatory system disorders, for example, the commoner breathing control and muscle control methods may need to be replaced by alternative relaxant techniques. Or if there is circulatory insufficiency there may be limited concentration and memory span, requiring specially tailored methods.

Bowel and mobility conditions similarly give rise to secondary psychological anxiety, and may be alleviated by appropriate psychological treatment of the anxiety component.

Primarily Psychological Problems

Of the many stressors of later life **bereavement** is the one most likely to be suspected as causing psychological problems. However only where grief has become complicated is it usually appropriate for intervention to be considered.

Since there is no blueprint for the process of grieving, the signals of complicated grieving may lie in the objective circumstances of the loss. The complexity (or conflict) in the relationship, or avoidance/separation around the time of the loss may be relevant signals.

Long-ago losses can look temptingly like 'unresolved losses'. However, the chances are that the grief is as powerfully rooted in feelings about the future or re-evaluating the present, as it is in past life experiences. The psychologist's assessment can identify the 'real' problem and lead to more effective treatment.

The psychologist will often be involved in assessing and helping with grief reactions in an advisory capacity. They will be able to offer guidelines on what is expectable or complicated, and on the implications for intervention. In this way, direct referral and the implication that grief is 'unnatural' is avoided. In some cases, suicidal behaviour or distorted cognitions over a long time period suggest a different approach involving the psychologist directly.

Carers

Psychologists have carried out significant research into the processes by which carers for elderly people either tolerate strain or break down. The **carers's subjective view** of the situation emerges as being critical. Their perceived control over the situation and their perception of how supportive people are (as contrasted with the numbers of people), are key factors.

This knowledge is applied in practice to enhance the capacity of carers to cope. For example through carers' groups or individually, cognitive strategies and problem-solving strategies can be taught and shared. These influence stress and restore the care giver's ability to find meaning in the care giving situation.

Some elderly people will have only formal (paid) care givers. Here also there is a need to address strain and subjective job satisfaction. When involved in either teaching or clinical consultation the psychologist will usually function as visibly as possible. The aim, as with informal care givers, is to reinforce that meaningful care can be given even where the most profound impairments exist.

Organisational and Service Development Roles

Clinical psychologists working with services for elders are still relatively scarce. The most practical way to ensure maximum benefit is to involve them in key areas across teaching and planning activities, **as well as** in key clinical areas. It is possible only to touch on the wider role here.

Planning

The psychologist can be a full or co-opted member of joint planning or development teams. This enables the research and knowledge base of psychology to be applied to elderly people's services. An analogy might be made with Services for People with Learning Difficulties which drew on psychological models in the development of new community care. The successful implementation of appropriate community care for older people will depend on a similar paradigm shift in services, towards an integrated approach to health, psychological and social needs.

Evaluation of Services

PASS (Programme Analysis of Service Systems) is an example of a system which can be used together with the service providers to look at the service's response to its users' needs. Psychologists are trained in other systems appropriate to service evaluation and quality of life evaluation.

Training and Teaching

"Clinical psychologists do not always work directly with patients and clients, even though what is done is for their benefit. A psychologist may put a proposed solution into practice in person, face to face with the patient, or through supporting the activities of other people such as the patient's family or the other professionals involved in the problems" (MPAG, 1990). As part of this broader role a significant part of the clinical psychologist's work with elderly people is training and teaching other professional groups and care givers. Both by demonstration 'on-the-job' and by more organised arrangements, psychologists will enable others to take more effective account of psychological issues and help

them to provide an improved standard of psychological care. Carers and professionals are increasingly demanding a more positive approach to the challenges posed by illness and disability in later life. Positive psychological approaches are increasingly being taught with the aim of providing health and social care gains through high quality and cost effective services.

Glossary of Terms

Cognitive therapy: a relatively new psychological therapy which is based on the principle that moods are created by 'cognitions' or *thoughts*. The aim is to teach new ways of thinking and to eliminate the negative distorted thinking which causes the depression or anxiety.

Behaviour therapy: actually a *range* of psychological techniques which are based on the principle that the majority of behaviours are alterable through adjusting the environment. The emphasis is on explicitly building up new patterns to replace ineffective patterns of behaviour, systematically tailored to the individual situation.

Goal planning: an approach involving a number of techniques for *assessing* the exact and individual *needs and strengths* of a person, *designing a programme* to meet those needs coherently and evaluating the effectiveness of the programme. Used in relation to 'problem behaviours' or generally where there is a reduced level of ability.

Reality orientation: a psychological approach which aims at reducing confusion, memory loss and disorientation by providing information (such as signs, memory aides) and by carers giving verbal and non-verbal stimulation to assist a person in regaining an awareness of their own identity and surroundings.

Validation therapy: an approach for communicating with severely disorientated and confused elderly people which focuses on validating their underlying feelings rather than on the factual reality.

Psychology of Ageing

Practical Points

1. The work of the Clinical Psychologist includes clinical casework, training, consultancy, research and evaluation and service development.

2. The psychological problems of older patients may be intricately bound up with the organic and or social factors.

3. Although doctors may feel overwhelmed by the psychological problems of patients, time spent in dealing with them is effective – removing obstacles to recovery, relieving unnecessary distress and in the long-run by reducing the doctor's work-load.

4. Common situations where psychological interventions alleviate problems include depression and anxiety, the dementias, stroke, carer and family stress, bereavement, trauma and prevention of further disability after physical illness.

5. Apart from Clinical Psychologists, other professionals who deal with psychological problems include Psychiatrists and Physicians for the elderly, General Practitioners, Social Workers, Nurses and a whole range of formal and informal carers. Psychologists work with all of these to enhance health gains and offer positive gains in quality of psychological care.

6. Needs of carers must not be overlooked – a psychological approach offers practical benefits, preventing breakdown of the care situation and enhancing carers' coping skills.

7. Priorities of older people are more likely to include the importance of home, relationships being lost, core beliefs and adjusting to reliance on others.

References

1. Manpower Planning Advisory Group (1990) *Report on Clinical Psychology*, Department of Health.

Bibliography

1. Garland J (1987) *Working with Elderly* in J S Marzillier & J Hall (eds), What Is Clinical Psychology?, Oxford University Press.

2. Wolfensberger W & Thomas S (1978) *PASS: A method for the quantitative evaluation of human services*, National Institute of Mental Retardation, Canada

3. Woods R & Britton P (1985) *Clinical Psychology with the Elderly*, Croom Helm.

4. Marcus AC, Murray Parkes C, Tomson P & Johnston M (1989) *Psychological Problems in General Practice*, Oxford University Press.

5. Miller E & Morris R (eds) (1993) *The Psychology of Dementia*, John Wiley & Sons, New York.

6. British Psychological Society (1994) *Purchasing Clinical Psychology Services*, Briefing paper No 5: Services for older people, their families and carers.

Chapter 14

Sexuality in the Elderly

Dr Ivor L Felstein MB ChB
Senior Hospital Medical Officer
Department of Medicine for the Elderly
Bolton General Hospital
Minerva Road
Farnworth
Bolton
BL4 0JR

Biosketch:

Doctor Felstein, a former consulting editor of the British Journal of Sexual Medicine, is the author of four books on human sexuality. His pioneering 'Sex in Later Life' was translated into five languages and he has contributed chapters on sex and ageing to major volumes on both sides of the Atlantic. A member of the Institute of Psychosexual Medicine of London, he nevertheless takes an eclectic view of sex therapy for psychological and physical sex dysfunctions seen in his private practice. He lists his current hobbies in 'Who's Who in Europe' as movies, book collecting and grandfathering.

Introduction

Medico-social understanding of sexuality in older men and women has long been thwarted by at least eight elemental myths or misunderstandings (table 1).

The strength of these received notions alongside the absence of accurate and reliable assessments of sexual activity, needs and expressions, delayed fuller appreciation of elderly sexuality until a mere thirty years ago.

Neither the pioneer questionnaire studies of Kinsey and co-workers in the USA in the late 1940s nor the pioneer photographic and physiological measurement studies of Masters and Johnson in the USA in the 1960s provided satisfactory statistics or scientific yardsticks on interest, capacity, frequency, expression and dysfunction of sexuality after sixty[1,2]. Certainly, in the early 1960s, North Carolina physicians in general practice, Newman and Nichols, persuaded the Journal of the American Medical Association to publish their remarkable assessment of sexual activity in elderly patients on their medical list.

The definitive medical stimulus to take such information seriously came from professor Eric Pfeiffer in the Duke University study of ageing in North Carolina.

Human sexuality impinges on many medico-social specialities. These include: gynaecology, pharmacology, psychiatry, clinical psychology and genito-urinary medicine, as well as sociology itself.

Medicine for the elderly – the 'traditional' speciality called geriatric medicine – tended to adopt the negative asexual attitudes mentioned at the beginning of this chapter. Not until the 1980s did serious reference and textbooks give a clear mention of sex in later life, having finally grasped the significance of a nationally retired population of 12 to 14 per cent whose 'members' were still mentally and physically active in all directions. Clear signals were offered in the United Kingdom from several sources in different geographical areas. My own study, Sex in Later Life, appeared in 1971 from Manchester. Dr Ann Gilmore reported her studies from north Glasgow in 1976, while Maddison reported his work at Teddington, Middlesex in 1973[3,4]. The national organisation, SPOD (sexual problems of the disabled and elderly) promoted research and counselling on sexual dysfunction among older men and women in Great Britain. The British Journal of Sexual Medicine, originally pioneered by Dr Eric Trimmer in London in the early 1970s included a steady stream of important papers on ageing and sexology, physiological and dysfunctional, diagnostic and therapeutic.

Most importantly, the foregoing studies, reports and papers showed how many of the received views on sex and ageing really were myths and misunderstandings. No longer can GPs and hospital doctors dismiss complaints of sexual dysfunction in old people by the denigrating comment 'What do you expect at your age?' Older men and women can expect to have their sexual needs and dysfunctions considered alongside their general health needs and dysfunctions.

Possible Age-Related Changes in Sex Organs in Men

Quantitive and qualitative changes have been recorded in both sexes but the speed of change and degree of change remains, as with other body systems, very individual. The standard phases of human coitus established by Masters and Johnson are arousal, plateau, orgasm/ejaculation and rest or refractory phases. There is functional change in the sex organs with age (table 2).

Table 1

Common Myths about Sexuality in the Elderly

1. A belief in a fixed endpoint beyond which sex is neither desired nor possible.

2. An insistence that decline in physical fitness and health is likely to preclude overt sexual expression.

3. A view that the imbalance of gender – many more women than men reaching old age – foils sexual partnerships and contacts.

4. A youth-provoked notion that the changed physical external appearance in ageing negates any likely sexual attraction between sexes.

5. An inaccurate assessment that the menopause causes not just ovarian shutdown but libido shut-off.

6. A superstitious belief that ejaculation in later years discourages longevity and encourages physical weakening.

7. A view that long married partners lose all mutual sexual interest, preferring food and external leisure interests.

8. A medical/nursing attitude that the need to use drugs and medication for various illnesses of later years invites iatrogenic ablation of sexual capacity almost invariably.

Despite these acknowledged changes, a qualitative sense of sexual enjoyment can be well-maintained into very senior years. This may reflect reduced expectations of older men or it may point to a more relaxed and non-competitive view of sexuality for men in later life. In sex therapy and sex counselling practices among older individuals, it is nevertheless more likely to be the man in a heterosexual partnership who seeks help when difficulties of dysfunction arise. No matter what changes in his external physical state – wrinkles, greying, scalp loss – most men link their power of erection with their sense of maleness/virility. Older female partners do encourage their men to seek help more often now than in past decades, both to continue their mutual sexual pleasure and because they are aware of the virility element.

Possible Age-Related Changes in Women

In women, effects of ageing on the coital phase necessarily reflect the oestrogen depletion at and after the menopause (which itself is variable to the individual woman) in addition to age physiological changes. These are listed in table 3.

Factors Influencing Sexual Expression

Medical and sociological studies have confirmed that the presence of an able and willing partner (marital partner or not, as the case may be) encourages continuation of sexual expression and sexual outlet into very senior years. Oppositely, the absence of an able and willing partner is linked with far reduced partner sexual contact as well as regular sexual outlet. It need not preclude absence of sexual interest or the practice of masturbation, for example; older men and women, partnered or not, may opt out of sexual activity or sexual expression for the reasons listed in table 4.

Sexual Problems in Later Years

The main difficulties and dysfunctions of sex in older men and women can be listed under the same general heading as those of earlier years (table 5).

Table 2

Possible Age-Related Changes in Sex Organs

1. Reduced speed of arousal. This may be influenced by altered capacity in vision, hearing and smell function, and by reduced vibration sense in the elderly penis.

2. Reduced penile length and turgidity as well as in plethoric state and angle of erection. This may be influenced by arteriosclerosis, reduced muscle power and tone and lowered arousal itself. Elevation of the testicles in coitus is less marked too.

3. Pulse, blood pressure and respirations still increase during the three initial phases. Reduced fitness levels may augment these responses and reduce 'staying time' for the individual older man.

4. Two stage ejaculation – into the rear of the urethra then out of the urethra – persists but need not take place with a full erection, and the total ejaculation may diminish by as much as 50 per cent.

5. The rest or refractory phase – during which further male arousal and ejaculation cannot proceed – becomes longer with each decade.

6. Serum testosterone – produced by the testicles and the adrenal glands – usually increases during coital activity, acting both as an arousal and a maintenance hormonal mechanism. The androgen levels decline slowly but surely with the years, though absolute levels vary. Atheroma, drug medications, and various illnesses may adversely influence the testosterone levels. Yet testosterone is the key to emotional and physical sex drive, capacity and interest. This is true for both genders.

Table 3

Possible Age-Related Changes in Women

1. Reduced speed and intensity of sexual arousal (paralleling the effects in men). The traditional view has it that women take longer to arousal than men at any age and the differential continued into senior years, but any evidence remains anecdotal.

2. Oestrogen depletion reduces vulva-vaginal lubricity in both the non-stimulated and stimulated states. Atrophic lining changes alter local sensitivity and may contribute to lower/slower response or alternatively to 'turn-off' sex drive for women.

3. Clitoral engorgement, nipple erection and breast swelling may all be reduced. The vaginal 'ballooning and tenting' in the plateau phase, described by Masters and Johnson, are less apparent. In both genders, the sex flush and sexual sweating may be much reduced or lost as a regular response.

4. The physiological markers – pulse, blood pressure and respiration parallel those noted for older men. Power of orgasm and multiple orgasms become less evident. The rest phase increases as well.

Important Organic Sources of Dysfunction

In older men and women, the source of sexual difficulties increasingly shifts from the psyche to organic; a likely psychological overlay is frequently present in any organic dysfunction as well. Certain disorders are of adverse influence and are listed in table 6.

Psychological/Psychiatric Sources of Dysfunction

There are important psychological and psychiatric sources of dysfunction which are listed in table 7.

An Approach to Management

One or more of any of the organic and psychological causes can be combined for either or both partners. Age in any case increases the risk of multiple illness and need for multiple medication. Sex therapy requires therefore a careful general medical history, a careful sexual history, a clear account of drugs taken, and other 'help' already tried. Various techniques and therapies are listed in table 8.

Table 4

Factors Influencing Sexual Expression

1. Onset and persistence of physical and emotional illness.
2. Fear of accelerating the ageing process.
3. Depressed or absent libido.
4. Lack of pleasure and enjoyment in sexual acts.
5. Partner 'turn-off' due to external or ablative changes in the man or woman.
6. Medication-induced sexual dysfunction or suppression of libido.
7. Absence of privacy due to environmental change.
8. Self-view of age as a time of disengagement socially and sexually.
9. Societal and peer disapproval.
10. True sexual aversion (phobic anti-sexual state).
11. A religious view that sex is only for procreation.

Table 5

Sexual Problems in Later Years

1. Short-term or prolonged decline or loss of sex drive.
2. Faulty control of presentation of erection, ejaculation or both in men.
3. Faulty orgasm in the female subject.
4. Altered quality of sexual experience: painful sex, unexpected sexual demands, repetitive patterns, for example.
5. Sexual deviation: homosexual 'coming out', early dementia, fetishism, for example.

Help for any of the foregoing may be sought from the family practitioner known to the patient or from a 'stranger' GP, for example, to avoid embarrassment. The GP trained in sex counselling and sex therapy may undertake his/her own psycho-sexual and organic sexual assessment. Alternatively, referral may be made to a professional sex therapist, clinical psychologist, psychiatrist, genito-urinary specialist or gynaecologist as considered appropriate. Both the presenting patient/client and his/her partner require interviewing and counselling if possible.

Table 6

Important Organic Sources of Dysfunction

1. Diabetes mellitus, whether insulin dependent or not. Its effects include the results of diabetic autonomic neuropathy, diabetic athero-sclerosis, and diabetic-derived local balanitis and vulvitis.
2. Hormone deficiency. This includes hypothyroidism, hypopituitarism, declining testosterone production for example.
3. Neurological disorders may variably affect libido, catecholamine function and spinal reflex/autonomic nerve function. These include stroke, parkinsonism, dementia, degenerative cord disease, spinal artery disease, head injury and cord trauma.
4. Hypertension alone or with the additive effect of hypotensive medication.
5. Alcoholism.
6. 'Mechanical' interference, for example, hip and spinal osteoarthritis, chronic bronchitis, angina.
7. Drug side-effects. These may be 'expected', for example: the use of anti-androgens like cyproterone or oestrogen in prostatic cancer. The side-effects may initially be unexpected, for example: the effects of thiazide diuretics, H2 antagonists, and anti-depressants.

Table 7

Psychological/Psychiatric Sources of Dysfunction

1. Anxiety neurosis/anxiety state.
2. Fear of failure (even after one episode of failed erection).
3. Depressive illness.
4. Sexual aversion (Partner phobia).
5. Other phobic state, eg venerophobia.
6. Fear of pain during coitus.
7. Partner cosmetic change or disability 'Turn-off'.
8. Fear of provoking illness relapse eg post-coronary.

Table 8

Techniques and Therapies

The approaches include:

1. Talking out/brief psychotherapy.
2. Behavioural therapy.
3. Psychoanalysis.
4. Sensate focus therapy.
5. Institute of Psychosexual Medicine interview therapy.
6. Instructional aids: pamphlets, books, videos.
7. Appropriate short-term use of oral medication eg anti-depressants, tranquillisers. Hormone replacement therapy/local oestrogen therapy, intracavernous injection medication: papaverine, phentolamine, prostaglandin El.
8. Vascular flow assessment/possible operative correction.
9. Vacuum aid/Penile implants.
10. Medication control of 'mechanical' problems like osteoarthritis, angina, chronic bronchitis.
11. Pre-operative counselling and post-operative counselling in pelvic/perineal/genital operations where sexual dysfunction may be wrongly or occasionally anticipated.
12. Post-illness counselling.
13. Pre-retirement sex counselling should be part of contemporary 'health in retirement' programmes.

References

1. Kinsey AC et al. (1948) *Sexual Behaviour In The Human Male*, Philadelphia, Saunders.
2. Masters WH & Johnson VE (1966) *Human Sexual Response*, Little Brown, Boston.
3. Gilmore A (1976) *Age & Sexuality*, Modern Geriatrics, 6, 35–38.
4. Maddison J (1973) *Hormone Therapy & Age*, Brit J. Sex Med, 1, 44–47.

Further Reading

1. Cole M & Dryden W (1988) *Sex Therapy in Britain*, Open University Press, Milton Keynes.
2. Coope J (1984) *The Menopause*, Dunitz, London.
3. Felstein J (1980) *Sex in Later Life*, Granada Pub, London.
4. Felstein I (1986) *Dysfunctions: Origins & Therapeutic Approach in Sexuality in Later Years*, Academic Press, New York, 223–247.
5. Felstein I (1986) *Understanding Sexual Medicine*. MTP/Kluwer Pub, Lancaster.
6. Greengross W & Greengross S (1989) *Living, Loving & Ageing*. London Age Concern.
7. Kahn HG & Holt JH (1990) *A–Z of Women's Sexuality*, Facts on File, New York.

Chapter 15

Nutrition in the Elderly

Dr Arup K Banerjee FRCP (Lond). FRCP (Edin). FRCP (Glasg).
Honorary Lecturer in Geriatric Medicine
University of Manchester
Consultant Physician
Bolton General Hospital
Minerva Road
Farnworth
BOLTON, BL4 0JR
U.K.

Biosketch:

A medical graduate from the University of Calcutta, India, Dr Banerjee obtained virtually all his post graduate clinical training and experience in the United Kingdom. He had also spent a few years as a lecturer in Medicine in the University of Malaya, Kuala Lumpur. His main research interests and publications have been in the fields of Blood Disorders, Nutrition, Upper GI Tract and Service/Care delivery for the Elderly, and he has contributed chapters to a number of text books in Geriatric Medicine and in Blood Disorders. He is President, British Geriatric Society.

Introduction

A balanced nourishing diet is essential for people of all age groups. An adequate nutritional intake is especially important for the ill, as this is an essential prerequisite for the success of any therapeutic intervention[1]. This is all the more relevant in the elderly because as a client group they tend to harbour and suffer multiple and major illnesses. In this context, it must be appreciated that most of the fit and active elderly living in the community in this country do not have any major nutritional deficiencies; specific problems, however, do occur in certain vulnerable groups. For the maintenance of good quality health in the elderly, proper dietary advice needs to be given and a discussion on nutrition, therefore, is very necessary.

Dietary Requirements

A large number of studies and surveys have been carried out over the years to determine the levels of various nutrient intakes among the elderly. The 'ideal' requirements can be difficult to define. Perhaps these should be the minimum levels of nutrients necessary to prevent any overt clinical malnourishment. The British Department of Health, following several surveys[2] have pronounced on daily food energy and nutrient intake levels for the elderly (table 1). These widely accepted recommendations probably strike a balance between the 'usual' intakes and the 'minimum' requirements.

The Recommended Daily Allowance (RDA), published by the National Research Council of the United States, if applied to the elderly population is likely to identify subnormal intake of total energy and almost all nutrients, although the energy proportions of protein, fat and carbohydrates remain closer to the RDA[3]

One or two specific areas deserve special mention:

Protein:

Despite the steady diminuation in the fat-free lean body cell mass in old age, various other biological, environmental and social factors still warrant a need for adequate protein intake. It has been suggested[4] that the appropriate protein allowance should provide 12–14% of the total daily energy intake. This amount would retain and maintain a positive nitrogen balance. Eleven percent of the total protein requirement should ideally be provided by essential aminoacids. Accordingly, the global protein intake in the elderly is not too different from that in the younger adult.

Vitamin D, Calcium and Other Minerals:

Most dietary surveys reveal a sub-optimal intake of Vitamin D. As sunlight is the main source of this vitamin, the housebound and the institutionalised subjects happen to be the most vulnerable.

Table 1

British Department of Health Recommended Daily Intake

	Males		Females	
	55–74	75+	55–74	75+
Energy (MJ)	10	9	8	7
Protein (G)	60	54	47	42
Thiamine (mg)	1.0	0.9	0.8	0.7
Riboflavine (mg)	1.6	1.6	1.3	1.3
Nicotinic Acid (mg)	18	18	15	15
Ascorbic Acid (mg)	30	30	30	30
Vitamin D (mcg)	10	10	10	10
Calcium (mg)	500	500	500	500
Iron (mg)	10	10	10	10
Vitamin A (mcg)	750	750	750	750

A GUIDE TO THE CARE OF THE ELDERLY

Subsequently, the calcium balance and homeostasis is also affected. Absorption of calcium from dietary source may diminish with age[5].

No definite recommendation is available for Potassium; an adequate balanced diet containing fresh fruit is usually enough to compensate the normal daily losses. The importance of the trace elements Copper, Zinc, Magnesium, Iodine etc should not be forgotten as these elements are valuable ingredients of several enzymes and hormones and influence the body's immune status.

Water:

Although not a provider of energy, adequate fluid and water intake is essential. The sensation of thirst may diminish with age and accordingly the severely infirm may not drink enough for their daily needs. This situation may get worse with pathological fluid loss, eg vomiting and diarrhoea, or subsequent to febrile illnesses and diuretic drug therapy.

Fibre:

These are indigestible carbohydrate or carbohydrate-like substances, recognised to be an essential dietary requirement. Although fibres can adversely affect the absorption of calcium its overal benefits on bowel action, prevention of colonic cancer and in the glucose metabolism far outweigh its marginal drawbacks. Unfortunately, even in 1985, the Department of Health did not make any official pronouncement on their recommended intake.

Malnutrition: Incidence, Causes and Evaluation

As mentioned before, malnourishment is difficult to define. If one accepts the Department of Health recommended dietary intake levels and looks at the situation globally for all elderly people in this country, relatively few will be found to be 'subnourished'. Specific nutrients may cause some concern. For example, the intake of Vitamins C and D will probably be found to be inadequate in many. The average elderly person, free from any chronic physical and mental disability and living in the community in the United Kingdom is adequately nourished. Furthermore, even when selective nutrient dietary deficiencies are identified, frank clinical manifestations of malnourishment are extremely rare[6].

The situation is, however, different among certain vulnerable groups. Any 'case-finding' for malnutrition should, therefore, be targeted to these cohorts. The main factors which may have either a direct or an indirect causal role are shown in table 2.

Malnutrition is a consequence of *Diseases and Poor Diet*.

Old people with physical and/or mental impairments and disabilities, housebound, socially isolated and financially deprived should ideally be visited by statutory service staff under the aegis of either their General Practitioner or the Social Services Department. A 'check list' (table 3) is available[8].

The new General Practitioner contract on elderly home surveillance and over-75 screening could be a vehicle for this kind of programme.

Table 2

Factors Influencing the Nutritional Status in the Elderly[6, 7]

1.	Physical disorders; immobility
2.	Mental disorders; dementia
4.	Social Inadequacies: isolation, marital status, financial constraints, erroneous dietary beliefs, poor housing with inadequate kitchen and storage facilities. Poverty
5.	Alcohol abuse
6.	Alone on Supplementary Benefit

Table 3

Check List for Nourishment 'At-Risk'

1.	Sudden unexplained change in weight
2.	Reduction in the number of main meals in the week.
3.	Lack of fruit/vegetables/juices
4.	Wastage of food
5.	Lengths of period between meals
6.	Difficulties in shopping and storage

Maintenance of positive health is one of the priorities of 'Health of the Nation' campaign by the Government of the United Kingdom and a properly structured nutritional monitoring should be a part of it. Perhaps the practice nurses, health visitors or care managers should be more vigilant and check their clients' food stocks and shopping baskets from time to time!

Possible components of a nutritional monitoring programme are as follows.

Dietary intake surveys and measurements:

Comparison of the 'recommended' intake with the 'actual' intake can be achieved with questionnaires which could be filled either by the elderly client, if able, or even by the carers or by a professional, eg Health Visitor, Practice Nurse or a community based Dietitian. The actual nutrient intakes can then be calculated, validated and analysed.

Clinical evaluation:

Evaluation can be carried out at home, at GP surgery or at community based health clinics. In addition to identifying overt signs of malnutrition certain simple measurements can be useful, eg body weight and height to determine Quatelet index (Weight (kg) ÷ Height (m)^2) the normal range of which is 20–25; the tricepts skinfold thickness; and upper arm circumference. Grip strength can be indicative of body strength and potassium status although there may be considerable individual variations. These anthropometric measurements, eg mid-arm circumference, arm-muscle circumference, corrected arm-muscle area and other indices are often used by both clinicians and researchers to assess nutritional status.

Laboratory tests:

Various haematological and biochemical data have been correlated with nutritional status but these 'expensive' investigations have all in all not been found to be of any great value; other variables, eg concurrent illnesses, medication etc influence these results.

Measurements of Vitamins:

Measurements of Vitamin C, Folate, B$_{12}$, Vitamin D etc do not necessarily reflect the true body status. These measurements may be helpful as research tools only in strictly scientifically controlled situations.

Nutrition and Dementia

With up to 10% of the total elderly population suffering from some form of organic brain failure this is an important area of concern. Some[9] suggest that in approximately a quarter of cases this dementing process may be at least partially reversible with measures including dietary manipulation. Energy and/or protein malnutrition is overt in nearly half of cases[10] with consequent severe weight loss. Dietary intake is lower than in non-demented controls. Although this nutritional inadequacy among the dements is multifunctional, recent research suggests that certain biochemical and metabolic derangements in their neuro-transmitter system may have an influencing role. Specific deficiencies of certain vitamins eg Folate have also been noted.

The Institutionalised Elderly

With the recent huge increase in the number of residential and nursing home beds in the United Kingdom, the situation is changing fast. Most of the dietary surveys have so far been carried out on the residents of either long stay wards or Social Services homes and have identified a dietary intake of reduced quantities[11] without any significant protein-energy malnutrition[12]. The privately registered 'homes' claim to provide a more homely environment with personal service and better choice. Whether residents of these private homes are stimulated and encouraged to eat a proper diet and whether their individual difficulties are carefully assessed, ought to be monitored and audited.

Management and Food Supplementation: In Institutions and Hospitals

All elderly patients should have a full dietary review. This should be an integral part of medical examinations and the complete assessment process. Any physical and/or mental handicap which may have an effect on feeding and on the preparation of meals (if applicable) should be thoroughly assessed. This could be carried out by a multidisciplinary team including Dietitian and Occupational Therapist. The edentulous elderly may have a special problem. Their specific needs should be properly met and in many instances the intervention of the Orthodontist to ensure provision of properly fitting dentures is invaluable. As well as looking at the process of cooking and feeding etc, appropriate health education advice on the importance of an affordable well balanced diet should be given. The psychology of eating can be very important. The food may be adequate and well balanced but the actual preparation and presentation may leave a lot to be desired. Timing of meals, the quantity served, perhaps too heavy a breakfast, a relatively short gap between mid-day meal and afternoon tea and then a long overnight gap are a few institutional routines which may require some modification to meet individual taste and living style.

Dietary advice is routinely rendered only in specific situations eg diabetes, kidney disorders etc. Like drug counselling, perhaps, diet counselling should be a routine exercise. As mentioned earlier, overt malnutrition is not an issue amongst our general institutionalised population. Some deficiencies in specific vitamins eg Vitamin C, D and Nicotinic Acid, however, have been identified[13]. Supplementation with whole food (eg Complan) increases intake of protein, vitamins and minerals, but does not fully correct these specific deficiences. This suggests that whole food supplements, although helpful to a certain degree, may not necessarily fulfil the total dietary need; specific vitamin supplements may still be required.

In the Community

The vulnerable section needs to be targetted and adequately assessed. Any health visiting/case finding programme should include dietary enquiries and a visit to the kitchen and inspection of the larder. The principles, as outlined in relation to hospitalised patients, should apply and any problems should be remedied. The meals-on-wheels service can be a life-line for many disabled elderly and their contents and presentation should be carefully monitored. Patients attending Day Centres and Day Hospitals can be given dietary advice. Many such centres run WRVS shops supplying basic food stuff. For the more ambulant, luncheon clubs provide both social and dietary relief!

Certain Specific Issues

Ascorbic Acid (Vitamin C):

Even the 'normal' elderly are significantly deficient in their Ascorbic Acid status compared to that in the young[14]. This is more overt among those who live alone, and are physically and mentally infirm. The deficiency is more pronounced during winter months due to inadequate access to fresh fruit and vegetables. Despite this biochemical Ascorbic Acid deficiency, fortunately very few actually develop symptoms of frank scurvy. Deficiency of Ascorbic Acid does, however, have an adverse effect on wound healing, certain immune activities and on platelet functions[14]. An adequate dietary intake of Ascorbic Acid is, therefore, important and in certain at-risk groups supplementation may be essential.

Vitamin D:

Deficiency of Vitamin D is common in the elderly and is more prevalent among certain groups especially those living in institutions or living alone with severe infirmity and chronic disabilities. Defective bone mineralization from Vitamin D deficiency gives rise to osteomalacia and may make some[15] more prone to fractures. Apart from bone changes, Vitamin D deficiency can cause muscle weakness and immobility. Even in sunnier climates, biochemical deficiency of Vitamin D is common among the elderly; therefore, importance of dietary intake must not be forgotten. Where supplementation is required, oral intake along with environmental sun lamp therapy should be considered.

Calcium and Vitamin D supplementation (see minerals) is becoming increasingly important for osteoporosis-prevention programmes.

Vitamin B Group:

Thiamine deficiency can give rise to mental confusion. Careful enquiry should be made into the patient's alcohol-intake habits. Various nutritional disorders are associated with and can be compounded by chronic alcohol abuse which should be handled appropriately. Deficiencies in Nicotinic Acid[13], Folate and other members of the Vitamin B Group have been observed; some such deficiencies are not always due to dietary inadequacies – coincidental drugs and antibiotics intake may be responsible from time to time.

Minerals:

Minerals, eg Calcium and Iron are well studied. As the deficiency signs are well known and easily recognised, supplementation and other treatment measures are usually taken without delay. Long-term Calcium supplementation to prevent post-menopausal bone loss has been a subject of wide discussions and deliberations. A recent study of long term milk consumption found that frequent milk consumption (as a proxy for adequate calcium intake) before the age of 25 increases hip bone mineral density in middle age and older women[16]. The importance of other trace elements has been emphasised earlier.

Obesity:

In any discussion on nutrition, problems and prevalence of obesity should not be forgotten. This is a fairly common problem in the elderly[2] and may be metabolically linked with the causation of disorder, eg diabetes and hypertension. Apart from the basic inconvenience of excessive weight such as those affecting mobility and activities of daily living, obesity can influence the natural history of osteoarthrosis, cardiopulmonary disorders and upper GI conditions, eg hiatus hernia. At the same time, an overweight individual with excessive fat in the body may remain deficient in important nutrients, minerals and vitamins. Reduction of weight can be difficult and may warrant a multidisciplinary approach. Specific supplementation may be indicated to overcome deficiencies.

Antioxidant Vitamins:

Although not a specifically nutritional issue, over the past decade, there has been a great deal of speculation on the cancer and cardiovascular disease preventing effects of antioxidant vitamins, eg beta carotene (ProVitamin A) and Vitamin E. It has been hypothesised that the scavenging of free radicals in excited oxygen molecules might prevent cancer causing damage to DNA, and that antioxidants can prevent atherogenesis. Unfortunately, more detailed and larger studies are needed before such benefits can be proved[17].

Nutrition Support to Patients with Dysphagia

Artificial hydration and nutritional support are fairly common practice for very frail elderly with neurological dysphagia. Naso-gastric tube and IV or SC infusion are widely used. For carefully selected patients, precutaneous endoscopic gastrostomy is a procedure which is usually tolerated well and can be used as a nutritional adjunct.

Conclusion

Malnutrition is not widely prevalent among the elderly living in this country. Certain vulnerable groups may have particular problems with specific nutrients which may require vigilance, education and in some instances intervention. Nutritional monitoring ought to be an integral part of regular community health checks and home visits. Adequate dietary advice and counselling should also be an essential part of total in-patient care.

There still remains many unanswered questions and more research is required in this field.

Nutrition in the Elderly

Practical Points

1. The average elderly person living in the UK and free from chronic mental and physical disability is adequately nourished. Frank clinical manifestations are rare.

2. Most dietary surveys reveal a sub-optimal intake of vitamin D. As sunlight is the main source of this vitamin, the housebound and the institutionalised are most at risk of calcium imbalance and homeostatis.

3. Apart from physical and mental illnesses (dementia and depression, for example), the other factors leading to nutritional deficiency include disability, poverty, social isolation, bereavement and faulty diet.

4. Case finding for malnutrition should be restricted to vulnerable groups which include those with mental and physical disabilities, those who are socially isolated and housebound and the financially deprived.

5. Clinical assessment includes overt signs of malnutrition, the Quatelet index, triceps skinfold thickness, upper arm circumference and grip strength.

6. Thin and frail people do badly in the face of illness. So, frail elderly living alone and especially on supplementary benefit are especially at risk and need extra nutritional support.

7. Poor dentition and oral hygiene are part and parcel of the overall nutritional assessment in a patient.

8. Health Professionals including Doctors do not seem to be fully aware of nutritional deficiency in their patients. Besides, complexity of nutritional problems in patients needs to be fully realised.

References

1. Isaksson B (1975) *Future Trends in Clinical Nutrition*, Bibl. Nutr. Dieta, 21, 163–177.

2. DHSS (1985) *Recommended Daily Amounts of Food Energy and Nutrients for Groups of People in the UK*, Report on Health & Social Subjects, 15, HMSO, London.

3. Sjogren A, Osterberg T & Steen B (1994) *Intake of energy, nutrients and food items in a ten year cohort comparison and on a six year longitudinal perspective: a population study of 70 and 76 year old Swedish people*, Age & Ageing, 23, 108–112.

4. Young V (1990) *Amino Acids and Proteins in Relation to Nutrition of Elderly People*, Age & Ageing, 19 (Suppl), 10–24.

5. Heaney RP, Gallagher JC, Johnston CC, Neer R, Parfitt AM & Wheldon GD (1982) *Calcium Nutrition and Bone Health in the Elderly*, Amer. J. Clin. Nutr, 36, 986–1013

6. Steen B & MacLennan WJ (1991) *Nutrition in Principles and Practice of Geratric Medicine. 2nd Ed*, Pathy MSJ (ed), 319–340, Wiley, Chichester.

7. Davies L (1990) *Socioeconomic, Psychological and Educational Aspects of Nutrition in Old Age*, Age & Ageing, 19 (Suppl), 37–42.

8. *Assessment Kit for Meals-on-Wheels and Alternative Services*, Gerontology Nutrition Unit, Royal Free Hospital, School of Medicine, London

9. Hedner K, Gustafson L, Steen G & Steen B (1987) *Screening of Patients admitted to a Geriatric Hospital with Supposed Organic Dementia*, Compr. Gerontology, 1, 55–60.

10. Sandman PO, Adolfsson R, Nygren C, Hallmans G & Wilenblad B (1987) *Nutritional Status and Dietary Intake in Institutionalised Patients with Alzheimer's Disease and Multiinfarct Dementia*, J. Amer Geront Soc, 35, 31

11. Vir SG & Love AHG (1979) *Nutritional Status of Institutionalised and Non-Institutionalised Aged in Belfast*, Amer J. Clini. Nutrit, 32, 1934–1937

12. Banerjee AK, Brocklehurst JC & Swindell R (1981) *Protein Status in Long-stay Geriatric In-Patients*, Gerontology, 27, 161–166

13. Banerjee AK, Brocklehurst JC, Wainwright H & Swindell R (1978) *Nutritional Status of Long-stay Geriatric In-patients Effects of a*

Food Supplement, Age & Ageing, 7,
237–243

14. Banerjee AK & Etherington M (1974) *Plate-let Function in Elderly Scorbutics*, Age & Ageing, 3, 97–105

15. Compston JE, Vedi S & Croucher PI (1991) *Low Prevalence of Osteomalacia in Elderly Patients with Hip Fractures*, Age & Ageing, 20, 132–134

16. Murphy S, Khaw KT, May H & Compston JE (1994) *Milk Consumption and Bone Mineral Density in Middle Aged and Elderly Women*, Brit Med J, 308, 939–941

17. The Alpha Tocopherol, Beta-Carotene Cancer Prevention Study Group (1994) *The Effect of Vitamin E and Beta-carotene on the Incidence of Lung Cancer and Other Cancers in Male Smokers*, New Eng J Med, 330, 1029–1035

Chapter 16

Dental Care of the Elderly

Dr J R Drummond, BDS, BMSc, PhD
Clinical Lecturer

Dr J P Newton, BSc, BDS, PhD
Clinical Senior Lecturer

Professor R Yemm, BDS, BSc, PhD
Clinical Professor and Honorary Consultant

Department of Dental Prosthetics and Gerontology
Dental School
University of Dundee
Dundee
DD1 4HN

Biosketch:

John R Drummond, James P Newton and Robert Yemm all work within the Department of Dental Prosthetics and Gerontology, Dundee Dental School, University of Dundee. As well as being practising clinicians they all have a basic science qualification that has led to an interest in the science of geriatric dentistry. They have published widely in a range of scientific and dental research journals on applied neurophysiology, structural changes in the oral tissues with age and in clinical technique development. Recently they edited a 'Color Atlas and Textbook of Dental Care of the Elderly' which was published by Mosby-Wolfe.

Dental State of The Elderly

Although more elderly people are retaining their natural teeth, the major dental problem of the elderly in the United Kingdom is edentulousness. The latest adult dental health survey shows that although edentulous levels are falling, they are still very high[1]. Around 65% of those over the age of 65 remain edentulous although this varies from only 57% in the south of England to 80% in the north of England. For those over the age of 75 nearly 80% are edentulous, again showing a variation between the south of England (73%) and the north of England (90%). The numbers of elderly retaining some natural teeth have increased considerably over the last few decades although many of these teeth are poorly supported by the periodontal structure, have extensive dental restorations or dental decay. It is also clear that social class, income levels and education are important influences on the condition of any remaining teeth. The condition of dentures in many elderly patients is very poor and up to one third may be wearing dentures that were constructed over 20 years ago. Associated with denture problems in the elderly is a high incidence of candida infection of the palatal mucosa, fibrous hyperplasia and traumatic ulceration. Oral carcinoma, although only 2–3% of all malignancies (in the UK), is most commonly found in the elderly and unfortunately the prognosis remains relatively poor.

Age Changes in the Mouth

A number of age related changes in the mouth and surrounding structures are relevant to treatment considerations.

The enamel, dentine and pulp of the tooth all undergo changes with age although most of these changes are related to the incremental effects of wear, habit and disease. In elderly persons' there is an increased concentration of fluoride in the surface enamel which increases resistance to caries. With age there is also a reduction in the size of the tooth's pulp chamber and in extreme cases there may be complete calcification of the root canals. These changes therefore make root canal therapy more difficult to complete to a satisfactory level.

The oral mucosa shows a number of changes with age that are clinically relevant. It has been shown, for example, that lingual mucosa undergoes a 30% reduction in mean thickness from youth to old age[2]. Many elderly people have prominent sublingual varicosities and sub-epithelial sebaceous glands. It is important that these structures are recognised as being a normal finding and not related to disease.

Changes in the mandibular and maxillary alveolar bone are also important as continuing resorption leads to an increasing inability of some patients to cope with dentures. Loss of alveolar bone is normal following the loss of natural teeth but proceeds at an unpredictable rate and can vary considerably between individuals. Basal jaw bone is also lost in a process identical to osteoporosis and there is generally a good correlation between jaw osteoporosis and that found in the long bones.

Although it is often stated that salivary flow decreases with age there is little evidence for this in the major salivary glands. Histologically there is a well documented loss of acinar elements in the salivary glands although this does not seem to effect function[3]. Although there is doubt whether ageing affects salivary glands *per se*, many elderly people suffer from xerostomia. Most cases of xerostomia in the elderly are related to drug intake and there are over 600 prescribable drugs that reduce salivary secretion. Less common causes of xerostomia in the elderly include Sjogren's syndrome and the effects of head and neck radiation therapy. Xerostomia is a distressing condition for the patient which may lead to extensive rapidly developing caries as well as denture looseness and discomfort.

There is evidence that jaw muscles are affected by the ageing process. There is a reduction in masticatory muscle bulk with age[4], as well as an increase in muscle contraction time. When the natural dentition is lost and patients become edentulous there is a further reduction in jaw muscle size suggesting a decrease in the masticatory force which can be, or is being, utilized[5]. Other studies suggest that the elderly use their jaw muscles with less precision and this probably contributes to a number of chewing problems particularly amongst denture wearers[6].

There is some evidence to suggest that dental state will modify food intake although a good dentition is not an absolute necessity for good nutrition. Many elderly denture wearers do however select (or are given) a soft diet and enjoyment of certain foods is often greatly impaired.

Approaches to Treatment

Although some groups within the population need less restorative care, most elderly will need more. Many of these will have already suffered from extensive dental disease and their future restorative requirements will continue to be very large even in terms of the maintenance of present restorations. With the provision of partial dentures and complete dentures at a much greater age, treatment needs to be effective and to allow for the fact that patients may be relatively intolerant of change and less able to learn new skills.

For these reasons, various duplication and replication techniques for the provision of replacement complete dentures have been developed which enable the dentist to provide the necessary prescription for the new appliances while incorporating desirable features of the old[7,8]. In this way, edentulous patients are able to tolerate gradual rather than sudden changes in denture shape and form, thus maintaining optimum oral function for mastication and speech.

Similar principles should be applied to the provision of partial dentures with careful assessment of how long the remaining natural dentition is likely to last and consideration should be given to partial denture design which is realistic for that patient. The denture copying philosophy can be extended to partial dentures and is usefully applied when extraction of natural teeth becomes necessary with either the use of immediate denture extraction procedures or pre-extraction records[9,10,11]. Where transition to complete denture wearing is inevitable, overdenture techniques provide at least a temporary and sometimes a long term advantage. This involves removal of the pulp tissue from the chosen teeth, filling the root canal with an inert material, decoronating the tooth and covering the root face with a suitable filling material. The retention of roots on which appliances are supported (and sometimes retained) gives confidence to the patient and retains alveolar bone. In some carefully chosen cases, the use of osseointegrated implants may be considered in a similar role.

Where teeth are retained it seems likely that the principal argument will be for relatively simple forms of treatment. The provision of extensive crown and bridge restorations, if not carefully constructed, may render teeth more susceptible to a deterioration in oral hygiene and the patient more liable to sudden breakdown in oral function in the event of subsequent failure.

Management of new caries seems likely to become a significant need with root surfaces exposed by periodontal disease being particularly susceptible[12].

Use of modern adhesive restorative materials with simple and minimal cavity preparation has revolutionised the treatment and maintenance of the elderly dentition[13]. Some materials, such as glass ionomer cements have the additional advantage of releasing fluoride, which may help prevent new carious lesions. A further problem with the retained elderly dentition is that of tooth wear or loss of tooth substance which manifests itself in a small percentage as gross attrition; this is often associated with the loss of posterior teeth such that function is restricted to a small occluding surface area. Extensive application of complex restorative treatment involving crowns and bridges is contra-indicated in many elderly patients and maintenance of posterior occlusal support and oral function by other means such as the provision of a partial denture may be more appropriate[14].

Some elderly patients with natural teeth may be susceptible to gingival disease as a consequence of diminishing oral hygiene[15]. The need for self care is obvious but so too is the requirement for assistance to be given when limitations in mobility or manual dexterity restrict the patient's own capabilities. This can be given in the form of modified oral aids or direct involvement of caring staff.

It is also essential that elderly patients are encouraged to attend on a regular basis, as surveys have shown that only a small minority attend the dentist regularly even when some natural teeth remain[1]. This is particularly disappointing as the profession has been advocating that regular attendance provides the ability to prevent some problems developing. This is applicable not only to the dentate, but also to edentulous patients, where not only the state of the appliances but the general health of the mouth can be reviewed.

Although most old people live as independent healthy individuals within the community a minority is institutionalised or house bound as a result of debilitating physical, medical or psychiatric problems. Recent studies have shown that the oral health of these groups is particularly poor[16]. However, portable equipment is now available (though expensive) so that more aspects of dental treatment can be carried out in the home. Many dental surgeons are already prepared to undertake home visits and others should be encouraged with, if necessary, the sharing or renting of equipment to provide a regular, satisfactory and cost-effective care to this group of the elderly.

Prospects for Dental Care of the Elderly

Over the next few decades there will continue to be a large increase in demand for dental treatment from elderly people. There is little doubt that the new generations of elderly will have a much greater dental health awareness and be much more sophisticated in their treatment demands. Fewer elderly people will consider the loss of natural teeth and the provision of dentures as reasonable. Whilst the retention of the natural dentition in the elderly is usually preferred, the consequences of failure and breakdown of the dentition may be serious. Rapidly developing caries and peridontal disease may often follow a serious medical crisis when there has been a breakdown of dental self care. Patients who have to be rendered edentulous late in life almost invariably find dentures difficult to adapt to and are thus very difficult to treat. Another problem that the dental services will have to face is the increasing numbers of patients who are house bound or institutionalised. Most of these patients at present are edentulous and the treatment relatively straightforward in terms of the portable equipment required. As increasing numbers of elderly patients keep some natural teeth, the range of treatment required will be much wider and less easy to provide away from a dental surgery. The increased work involved in maintaining dental health and oral function of the elderly is certain to be significantly greater than the reduction of treatment needs in some child patients. Given this and the increasing dental awareness of the whole population, it is questionable whether sufficient numbers of dentists are currently being trained in the United Kingdom.

The majority of dental services for elderly people are provided by General Dental Practitioners under the National Health Service Regulations. A substantial percentage of the cost of treatment has to be paid by the patient unless they are exempted on grounds of low income.

Increasingly GDPs are withdrawing from the NHS and in some parts of the UK it is difficult to receive dental care other than on a private basis. This change will reduce the availability of dental care to the elderly as they are, on the whole, less able to pay for private or insurance based care. Domiciliary care can be provided by GDPs although complex restorative care cannot easily be carried out in a setting other than a dental surgery. Community dental officers are now increasingly concerning themselves with treating elderly people although the numbers of community dentists are relatively low. Referral of elderly people to hospital based specialists is possible in areas of the country where these facilities exist. Services tend to only be available in the larger cities and at the moment there are no specifically trained consultants in geriatric dentistry.

Dental Care of the Elderly

Practical Points

1. About 65% of the over 65's remain edentulous. This figure rises to 80% in those currently over the age of 75.

2. Elderly people should be encouraged to attend for dental care on a regular basis. Apart from cost, many of them fail to seek advice for a combination of reasons, such as ignorance, anxiety, confusion and poor mobility.

3. Supervision of oral conditions, seen in different types of systemic diseases and also some local conditions, should be regarded as complimentary to overall dental care. Care must be taken with prescribable drugs which could reduce salivary secretion.

4. The institutionalised and house-bound have a poor dental attendance record – many aspects of dental health treatment can be carried out in the home.

5. The role of the Dental Hygienist in dental care of the elderly is much the same as the role of the Diabetic Nurse in the case of diabetics.

6. More training to medical and dental undergraduates about dental care of the elderly is needed.

References

1. Todd JE & Lader D (1991) 1988 *Adult Dental Health*, OPCS, HMSO, London.

2. Scott J, Valentine JA, Hill A, Balasooriya BAW et al. (1983) *A quantitative histological analysis of the effects of age and sex on human lingual epithelium*, J Biol Buccale, 11, 303

3. Drummond JR (1987) in: *The Ageing Mouth. Morphological changes in human salivary glands*, Ferguson DB (ed), Karger, Basel, 31

4. Newton JP, Abel RW, Robertson EM & Yemm R. (1987) *Changes in human masseter and medial pterygoid muscles with age: a study by computed tomography*, Gerodontics, 3, 151

5. Newton JP, Yemm R & Abel RW (1993) *Changes in human jaw muscles with age and dental state*, Gerodontology, 10, 16

6. Yemm R, Newton JP & Lewis GR (1985) *Age changes in human muscle performance* in: Current Topics in Oral Biology, Lisney, SJW and Matthews, B (eds), Bristol University Press, 17

7. Davenport JC & Heath JR (1983) *A copy denture technique*, Br Dent J, 155, 162

8. Duthie N & Yemm RJ (1985) *An alternative method of recording the occlusion of the edentulous patient during construction of replacement dentures*, Oral Rehab, 12, 161

9. Drummond JR, Duthie N & Yemm R (1983) *An immediate denture technique for replacing the last natural teeth*, Br Dent J, 155, 297

10. Newton JP, Quinn, DM & Sturrock, KC (1986) *An approach to complete immediate dentures*, Dental Practice, 24, 1

11. Quinn DM, Yemm R, Ianetta RV, Lyon FF & McTear J (1986) *A practical form of pre-extraction records for construction of complete dentures*, Br Dent J, 160, 166

12. Wallace MC, Retief DH & Bradley EL (1988) *Prevalence of root caries in a population of older patients*, Gerodontics, 4, 84

13. Wilson AD & MacLean JW (1988) *Class V and class III restorations*. in: Glass Ionomer Cement, Quintessence Publishing Co Inc, Chicago, pp 143–157.

14. Kidd EAM & Smith GBN (1990) *Why restore teeth?* in: Pickard's Manual of Operative Dentistry, Oxford Medical Publications, 17

15. Abdellatif HM & Bunt BA (1987) *An epidemiological investigation into the relative importance of age and hygiene status as determinants of periodontitis*, J Dent Res., 66, 13

16. Hoad-Reddick G, Grant AA & Griffiths CS (1987) *Knowledge of dental services provided: investigation in an elderly population*, Comm Dent Oral Epidemiol, 15, 137

Further Reading

Drummond JR, Newton JP & Yemm R (1995) *Color Atlas and Text of Dental Care of the Elderly*, Mosby-Wolfe, Times Mirror International Publishing.

Chapter 17

Blindness

Dr Jeffrey Kwartz DO, FRCS, FRCOphth
Senior Regristrar
Manchester Royal Eye Hospital
Oxford Road
Manchester
M13 9WL

Biosketch:

Dr Jeffrey Kwartz is a Senior Registrar at Manchester Royal Eye Hospital, Manchester and has been a Fellow in Corneal and External Eye Disease at University of Toronto, Canada, 1994. Research interests: Anterior Segment Disorders; Contact Lens related problems; Anterior Segment ultrasound. Publications: Corneal crystallisation; Diplopia following head injury; Corneal ulceration in relation to disposeable contact lenses; Corneal transplantation for pseudophakic corneal oedema.

Introduction

Visual impairment is a disability which falls on a relatively high proportion of the elderly population. Analysis of recent blind and partial sight registration statistics in England and Wales shows that over 84% were over the age of 65[1].

In Great Britain blindness has the statutory definition "*so blind as to be unable to perform any work for which eyesight is essential*". This is taken as not having visual acuity more than 3/60 in the better eye or a greatly reduced visual field. Ocular disease appears to rise exponentially with age as does the risk of a combination of more than one ocular disease. Systemic diseases present frequently in old age and it is often said that every systemic condition has an ocular manifestation.

Here the common age-related ocular conditions are considered:

Age Related Macular Degeneration

Age related macular changes represent the commonest causes of visual impairment in the elderly. The macula (posterior pole) is an active metabolic area responsible for central vision. It shows several ageing changes, the most important being drusen. The pale white spots are deposits of sub-retinal hyaline material. They are usually quite benign but may predispose to the development of subretinal neovascularisation.

Blurred central vision with fine vision and reading difficulty may progress to a central scotoma. The patient often notices distortion in image shape (metamorphopsia) and size which is usually minified (micropsia).

There are two main types of macular degeneration:
1. Dry, involutional, atrophic type.
2. Wet, exudative, disciform type.
Both types are confined to the posterior pole. Reassurance that total blindness will not ensue should be given. Low visual aids may offer some help.

In the dry atrophic form there is degeneration of the retinal pigment and underlying capillary network with overlying retinal photoreceptor dysfunction. Ophthalmoscopy reveals pigmentary disturbance and atrophic patches.

Disciform macular degeneration is often more severe. It is characterised by the presence of a sub-retinal neovascular complex which can grow into and through the retina. New vessels frequently leak serous fluid (oedema) along with lipid precipitation (exudates). The fragile complexes may break and bleed under or through the retina. The end stage of the disease often leaves a white atrophic macular scar (disciform). Diagnosis and treatment is assisted by intravenous fluorescien angiography. Neovascular membranes eccentric to the fovea are treated by destruction with laser photocoagulation before foveal involvement[2]. Unfortunately, the elderly present with advanced disease which is often untreatable. There is a risk of the second eye becoming involved which has been calculated at 10–12% per year[3]. There is a similar risk of further subretinal neovascularisation in treated eyes. Patients are instructed to monitor their central vision and told to report urgently if they have new visual symptoms either in their treated eye or the other eye.

Glaucoma

Glaucoma is a group of conditions characterised by raised intraocular pressure, cupping (excavation) of the optic nerve head and visual field loss. Exceptions include 'ocular hypertension' where high pressure exists without the other changes, and 'low tension glaucoma' where normal pressure is associated with cupping and glaucomatous visual field defects.

Glaucoma is classified according to its aetiology: primary glaucoma is subdivided into open (chronic simple) and closed angle. Around one third of glaucoma is closed angle. The secondary glaucomas are a small but significant group with raised intraocular pressure secondary to ocular disease or therapy, eg. cortiscosteroids. Glaucoma is found in about 1% of Europeans above 40 years of age and rises to 7–10% at 70 years[4]. Glaucoma-risk increases in first degree relatives.

The drainage angle between cornea and iris root is inspected with a special contact lens, a gonioscope. Intraocular pressure is measured with the Goldmann contact tonometer as the standard. Less accurate non-contact tonometers (air-puff) are available.

Intraocular pressure shows diurnal fluctuation. There is no definite safe pressure and individuals vary as to what their optic nerves will tolerate before damage ensues. Nerve head inspection and visual field assessment is required for diagnosis and monitoring therapy. Characteristic changes in optic nerve head relate to its size, colour, shape, symmetry and the optic cup to disc ratio (usually recorded as a decimal fraction). Accurate visual field assessment utilizes computerised perimeters. Patient attention and cooperation is needed for several minutes and may not be obtainable in frail or uncooperative patients[5]. Monitoring then emphasises the other clinical indicators of glaucoma.

Closed angle glaucoma is caused by anatomical predisposition to aqueous humour outflow obstruction. Predisposing factors include a very short eye (hypermetropia = long-sightedness) and enlargement of the lens with age or cataract. Aqueous outflow is often obstructed when the pupil is mid-dilated and an acute attack frequently presents with severe pain, nausea, vomiting, red eye and a fixed, nonractive, mid-dilated pupil. Corneal oedema produces visual loss and early or chronic subacute attacks may produce coloured haloes around lights. Emergency ophthalmic intervention aims to lower pressure, overcome pupillary obstruction to aqueous outflow with an iridotomy and protect the contralateral eye.

Open angle (chronic simple) glaucoma is a painless disease with progressive cupping of the optic disc and associated permanent visual field loss. Central vision is disturbed late in the disease. The objective of management is to halt this progression.

Medical treatment aims at reducing aqueous production with topical beta blockers or increasing outflow with miotics (eg pilocarpine) or sympathomimetics (eg adrenaline). Oral acetazolamide reduces aqueous production but has side effects which patients often find troublesome. Filtration surgery (trabeculectomy) is used when medical control fails or as a primary form of treatment. Disease progression is related to treatment failure or poor compliance, a common problem in the glaucomatous population.

Cataract

Cataract is defined as an opacity in the ocular lens. It may not necessarily produce visual symptoms. The lens (greek = phakos) grows throughout life and becomes more rigid with a reduction in the ablity to focus for near. This age related accomodation loss (presbyopia) is managed with optical correction.

The lens responds to metabolic and physical insults by a loss of optical clarity. 'Senile cataract' becomes almost universal in people in their 90's[6]. There are several patterns of lens opacities which have different effects on vision. Central browning of the lens due to lens protein oxidation is known as nuclear sclerosis. An alteration in refractive index can cause a shift in refraction which may allow reading without glasses, the 'second sight of old age'. This visual improvement is frequently short lived and heralds lens changes that reduce visual acuity. Sectorial alterations in lens proteins produce cortical spoke opacities. Acuity is often preserved until the visual axis is interrupted. Proliferation of lens fibres on the posterior capsule produces posterior subcapsular opacities. This is also seen with prolonged use of topical or systemic corticosteroids. Opacities at the back of the lens produce severe visual disturbance. Sometimes the elderly present late with a total white, opaque 'mature' cataract.

Diagnosis should be made after pupil dilation by checking for an obstruction in the red reflex. Closer inspection reveals the type of cataract.

Microsurgical techniques of cataract extraction with intraocular lens implantation produces gratifying results with prompt visual rehabilitation. Timing of surgery is determined by visual requirements and not by any need for the cataract to 'mature'. Excessive glare, contrast reduction or monocular diplopia may warrant surgical intervention before a significant reduction in visual acuity. Rendering the eye 'pseudophakic' with a plastic intraocular lens has resolved the optical problems of aphakia (no lens). Aphakic correction necessitates thick 'cataract glasses' or contact lenses. Pseudophakia and low surgical risks in the elderly has reduced the threshold at which both the surgeon and patient are willing to undertake surgery[7]. Although visual impairment from cataract is treatable it remains a major cause of blindness worldwide.

It would be appropriate, at this stage, to discuss the post-operative care and surgical complications of cataract surgery in some detail. This is because it is such a common procedure now that General Practitioners will be looking for guidance, as they are responsible for care of these patients after their discharge from hospital.

Surgical Complications of Cataract Surgery/Post-Operative Care

Cataract surgery is a common procedure which in the vast majority of patients goes well with no significant complications. Informed consent should include an explanation of the devastating but rare causes of permanent visual loss which includes expulsive haemorrhage and intraocular infection. Intraoperative complications should be recognised and managed appropriately by the ophthalmic surgeon. There is a move towards shorter hospitalization and day case surgery. Post operative complications (table 1) need prompt identification and referral for ophthalmic assessment.

Post-operative complications are now briefly discussed:

1. Bacterial Endophthalmitis

This serious complication can present early in the post-operative period and needs urgent treatment. The patient presents with visual loss, photophobia and ocular pain. The eye and even surrounding tissues are swollen and inflamed and there is a loss of the red reflex due to media opacification. A hypopyon, white cells forming a level of pus in the anterior chamber, is often visible. Vitreous aspiration with urgent microbiological investigation and antimicrobial therapy is needed. Organisms such as *Propionbacter acnes* or *Staphylococcus epidermidis* may produce a late chronic endophthalmitis.

Table 1

Post-Operative Complications

1.	Bacterial Endophthalmitis
2.	Intraocular Haemorrhage
3.	Wound Related Problems:– Inflammation Dehiscence: leak or iris prolapse Astigmatism
4.	Corneal Oedema
5.	Cystoid Macular Oedema
6.	Lens Related Problems
7.	Glaucoma
8.	Retinal Detachment
9.	Posterior capsule opacification

2. Haemorrhage

Haemorrhage into the anterior chamber may produce a fluid level of blood, hypaemia. This is caused by bleeding from the iris or cataract wound. Haemorrhage into the vitreous cavity necessitates retinal examination to eliminate retinal detachment.

3. Wound Problems

Significant leak of aqueous through a corneal wound may produce excessive tearing, a shallow anterior chamber and is a pathway for intraocular infection. If the leak is beneath the conjunctiva a filtering bleb is formed. The resultant hypotony or shallowing of the anterior chamber warrants wound resuturing.

Wound dehiscence results in prolapse of iris, and occasionally, other ocular contents. A peaked pupil along with tissue prolapsing through the wound is evident and urgent surgical repair is required.

4. Corneal Oedema

A single layer of endothelial cells on the back surface of the cornea pumps out fluid and helps maintain corneal clarity. These endothelial cells do not divide and if lost by surgical trauma there is a limit after which surviving cells cannot compensate for those lost. Superior corneal oedema (striate keratopathy) is usually temporary. In the presence of pre-existing endothelial pathology or continued trauma from an old style of intraocular lens the corneal oedema may be permanent (bullous keratopathy) and a corneal transplantation becomes necessary. There is natural loss of endothelial cells and corneal oedema may not appear until years after intraocular surgery.

5. Cystoid Macular Oedema

This is caused by several factors including inflammation, vascular incompetence and vitreous traction. Macular oedema with visual blurring is usually transient and subclinical but some patients develop significant visual impairment 1–4 months following surgery. Treatment can involve surgery with release of vitreous traction if present after vitreous loss at initial surgery. Medical management involves reducing inflammation with periocular steroids and non-steroidal anti-inflammatories and attempting to dry up the macula with oral acetazolamide. Treatment is not always successful and visual reduction may be permanent.

6. Lens Related Problems

Retained crystalline lens material induces inflammation and is seen as fluffy white material in the pupil or anterior chamber. Treatment consists of topical steroids and occasionally surgical removal.

The artificial intraocular lens replacement may not be perfectly centred in the capsular bag of the crystaline lens and the bag itself may be unstable. Resulting visual disturbance may be due to lens decentation or displacement back into the vitreous cavity. This often warrants surgical reintervention.

7. Glaucoma

Transient raised intraocular pressure is not unusual in the early post operative period and is usually asymptomatic. A sustained pressure rise may be related to anterior chamber abnormalities, pupil block, ingrowth of conjunctival epithelium through the wound or as a response to topical steroids.

8. Retinal Detachment

Although a rare complication, urgent surgical intervention is necessary to avoid permanent visual loss. Patients present with visual loss, flashing lights (photopsia) and visual floaters. This can occur from soon after surgery to many years later. Predisposing factors include high myopia, preexisting retinal problems and vitreous loss at time of surgery.

9. Posterior Capsule Opacification

This common occurrence reduces vision with the formation of an 'after cataract' secondary to fibrosis of the capsule along with epithelial cell proliferation. It is more common in children and can occur in up to 50% of adults up to several years following surgery. When vision is reduced significantly an opening is made in the posterior capsule with the Neodymium YAG laser. This out-patient procedure carries a low risk of cystoid macular oedema and retinal detachment.

Postoperative care of the patient varies between ophthalmic units and usually involves topical steriod and antibiotics for several seeks. The patient often wears a protective ocular shield at night. The patient is given instructions to report back to the ophthalmic department if they experience significant pain or visual loss. Best visual acuity may not be attained until spectacles are prescribed which is frequently at around 2 months following surgery. Tight sutures are often removed at this point to reduce astigmatism and a later repeat refraction is then necessary. Most activities not involving heavy straining or a high risk of ocular trauma can be performed. The move towards phakoemulsification with a smaller incision hastens visual rehabilitation while producing less astigmatism with a stable, strong and safer wound.

Diabetes (see chapter 26 on Diabetes)

Diabetic eye disease is more common after the presence of the disease for greater than 10 years. Elderly, non insulin dependent diabetics may present with ocular signs at diagnosis. Early detection and appropriate intervention aims to prevent a potentially blinding process[8]. Diabetes appears to attack the retinal capillary microcirculation. Microaneurysms (dots) may leak fluid causing macular oedema. The risks of visual loss may be reduced if prompt laser treatment is initiated to seal the leaking microaneurysms or 'dry up' the oedema near the fovea. Proliferative retinopathy is a manifestation of significant retinal ischaemia. Ischaemic retina is recognised by the presence of cotton wool spots and irregular, tortuous dilated retinal veins. The neovascular proliferation results in optic disc and peripheral retinal venous fibrovascular outgrowths. These complexes may bleed causing haemorrhage and contraction produces tractional retinal detachment. Fibrovascular growth on the iris surface (rubeosis iridis) and into the drainage angle causes intractable glaucoma. Reduction of the neovascular response by laser ablation of the ischaemic peripheral retina may cause regression of the fibrovascular complexes. Laser photocoagulation aims to avoid the devastating consequences of neovascularisation and reduce the need for complex intraocular microsurgery[9].

Myopia

Visual loss in high myopia may be secondary to myopic chorioretinal degeneration. Myopic disciform macular degeneration and associated haemorrhage (Foster-Fuch's spot) is often less severe than routine disciform degeneration[10].

Other Eye Conditions

Vascular Diseases

Retinovascular occlusive events occur with increasing frequency in the elderly[11]. Patients usually present with sudden blurring of vision.

Arterial Occlusions are either embolic or arteritic in nature. Almost one half of patients have carotid artery disease. Other associations include atherosclerosis, hypertension, diabetes and valvular heart disease. Early on the retina appears pale and swollen and the offending embolus may be visible. Urgent manoeuvres to encourage migration of the embolus include ocular massage, intraocular pressure reduction and arterial dilation by rebreathing carbon dioxide. These manoeuvres, however, are rarely successful[12]. Transient visual obscuration (amaurosis fugax) are taken seriously as they represent small emboli that spontaneously dislodge and indicate an increased risk of stroke.

Vascular occlusion of the optic nerve head in anterior ischaemic optic neuropathy (AION) may be arteritic or non-arteritic. In arteritic AION clinical indicators of temporal arteritis are usually present along with, but not invariably, a raised erythrocyte sedimentation rate. Urgent medical therapy with systemic steroids in high doses (starting dose 80mg daily) is initiated to reduce visual loss and protect the contralateral eye. Diagnosis should ideally be confirmed with temporal artery biopsy. Non arteritic AION, on the other hand, does not respond to steroids. Besides, there is an increased risk of the second eye becoming involved.

Retinal vein occlusions involve the central retinal vein or produce specific patterns distal to a branch vein occlusion. Visual disturbance is associated with retinal vascular tortuosity and intraretinal haemorrhage. Most venous occlusions are related to compression by the adjacent artery. This is worsened by hypertension, arteriosclerosis and glaucoma. Evidence of systemic disease causing a thrombotic tendency should be sought. Laser retinal ablation aims to reduce the risks of retinal ischaemia. Peripheral retinal neovascularisation is associated with branch retinal vein occlusion and rubeotic glaucoma with central retinal vein occlusion.

Neurophthalmology

Visual disturbance may be secondary to pathological insults to the visual pathways or oculomotor nerves. The common causes are either ischaemia or intracranial space occupying lesions.

Orbit

Tumours of the orbit present with displacement of the globe. Common tumours include lymphoma, pseudotumour, lacrimal gland tumours and secondary metastatic deposits. Computerised tomography along with histopathological diagnosis is mandatory for effective management. Dysthyroid ophthalmopathy is the commonest cause of presentation with unilateral or bilateral exophthalmos (proptosis).

Lids

Basal and squamous cell carcinomas are common on the eyelids[13]. Oculopolastic surgery involves a curative excision with eyelid reconstruction. Surgery aims to prevent corneal damage secondary to exposure in non recovering facial palsies and eyelid eversion (ectropion) or recurrent mechanical trauma from eyelid inversion (entropion).

Helping the Visually Handicapped

Blind or partially sighted registration alerts the Social Services department in the patient's home area. Although this may ease access to appropriate aid it is not dependant on registration[14]. Additional benefits include transport concessions, income tax relief and increased supplementary benefit. Visual loss, especially in the elderly, is often a frightening experience producing a sense of isolation and helplessness. Local support groups and voluntary organisations such as the Royal National Institution for the Blind provide invaluable aids, advice and support. Homes for blind people are also available.

Blindness

Practical Points

1. The ophthalmologist's definition of blindness does not coincide with the patients feared perception of blindness as complete blackness with no useful vision. The patient can often be reassured that complete blindness is rare.

2. The main causes of blindness in the elderly are glaucoma, cataract, diabetes and myopia.

3. Pupil dilation is necessary for proper examination of eyes. It is safe in all patients except extreme long-sightedness (thick magnifying glasses) and previous cataract surgery with pupillary supported lenses.

4. Elderly patients may not complain of ocular pain when expected such as in acute angle closure glaucoma or corneal ulceration.

5. A red eye should be stained with fluorescein dye to look for the dendritic staining of Herpes Simplex.

6. Glaucoma is often a silent and insidious blinding condition and should be screened for, especially if there is a family history of the disease.

7. Early laser photocoagulation offers therapy in some forms of macular degeneration. Patients with macular disease should be instructed to monitor their central vision.

8. Cataract removal should depend on a patient's visual requirements rather than any specific reduction in visual acuity. Also modern ophthalmic techniques and anaesthesia allow successful surgery in virtually all elderly patients.

9. Topical steroids cause cataracts, glaucoma and may worsen Herpes Simplex keratitis. They should only be prescribed in conjunction with an ophthalmologist.

References

1. Evans JR & Wormald RP (1993) *Epidemiological Function of BD8 Certification*, Eye, 7, 172–9

2. The Moorfields Macular Study Group (1982) *Treatment of Senile Disciform Macular Degeneration: a single-blind randomised trial by argon laser photocoagulation*, Br J Ophthalmol, 66, 745–53.

3. Teeters VW & Bird AC (1973) *The Development of Neovascularization of Senile Disciform Macular Degeneration*, AM J Ophthalmol, 76, 1–18.

4. Popovic V (1982) *The Glaucoma Population in Gothenberg*, Acta Ophthalmol, 60, 745–58.

5. Michaels DD (1992) *Ocular Disease in the Elderly*, in: Vision and Aging. 2nd ed. Rosenbloom AA Jr, Morgan MW, (eds) Butterworth-Heinemann, Boston 111–59.

6. Falcoln M (1992) *Eye Problems in the Elderly*, Practitioner, 236, 178–83.

7. Adler AG & Kountz DS (1990) *Eye Surgery in the Elderly*, Clin Geriatr Med, 6, 659–67.

8. Packard RBS & Kinnear F (1991) *Post operative Complications*, in: Manual of Cataract and intraocular lens surgery. 1st ed. Churchill Livingstone, Edinburgh, 107–122.

9. Friedman SM & Rubin ML (1992) *Diabetic Retinopathy: New Therapies to Prevent Blindness*, Geriatrics, 47, 71–81.

10. Shilling JS (1986) *Macular Degeneration*. in: The Eye and its Disorders in the Elderly, Caird FI, Williamson J (eds), Wright, Bristol, 95–100.

11. Delaney WV Jr. (1993) *Ocular Vascular Disease: In-officer Primary Care Diagnosis*, Geriatrics, 48, 60–9.

12. Augsburger JJ & Magargal LE (1980) *Visual Prognosis following Treatment of Acute Central Retinal Artery Obstruction*, Br J Ophthalmol, 64, 913–7.

13. Sternberg I & Levine MR (1985) *Cysts, Tumours and Abnormal Postitions of the Eyelids in the Elderly*, in: Geriatric Ophthalmology, Kwitko ML, Weinstock FR (eds), Grune & Stratton, Orlando, 139–70.

14. Croft C (1992) *Helping Visually Handicapped People*, Practitioner, 236, 192–4.

Chapter 18

Hearing Loss in the Elderly (Deafness)

Dr S D G Stephens M Phil, FRCP
Welsh Hearing Institute
University Hospital of Wales
Cardiff
CF4 4XW
Wales

Biosketch:

Dr Dafydd Stephens is Consultant in Audiological Medicine and Director of the Welsh Hearing Institute at University Hospital of Wales. He has been Consultant in Audiological Medicine since 1976 when he was appointed to the Royal National Nose, Throat and Ear Hospital and then moved to Cardiff in 1986. His particular interests are in audiological rehabilitation, tinnitus and genetic deafness. Over the years much of his work has been concerned with hearing problems in the elderly and has also been concerned with the development of pre-retirement screening programmes and direct referral programes in this field. He is Chairman of the British Association of Audiological Physicians and Vice-President of the International Association of Physicians in Audiology.

Introduction

Hearing loss in the elderly is extremely common, affecting the majority of elderly people and increasing exponentially with age. Most elderly people are reluctant to seek help for this and both they and their families suffer considerably as a result. It is important for professionals to detect any hearing disability as early as possible and encourage appropriate referral for rehabilitative help. Such an approach based on preretirement screening for hearing disability is both acceptable and effective.

Prevalence

Within this chapter I shall follow the WHO[1] definitions of hearing disablements as discussed by Stephens and Hétu[2]. Within this context *Impairment* may be defined as an audiometric deficit measurable in a clinic or laboratory using psychophysical or physiological techniques. Most commonly it is considered in terms of an elevation of the hearing threshold but it may be reflected as impaired speech discrimination or frequency resolution.

Auditory Disability refers to the hearing problems experienced by the individual. These most commonly reported[3] are those of hearing conversation, hearing the television, doorbells, telephone bells, etc. Usually the first indication of disability noted and reported by the individual is difficulty hearing speech in noisy places.

Finally *Handicap* is the effect of the hearing loss on the individual's life. This may be a social withdrawal, effects on the marital relationship, depression or anxiety. Handicap is very much dependent on the socio-cultural environment of the individual and also on the reaction of the spouse, family member, carer or other Significant Others (SOs).

While the OPCS Survey[4] has identified that hearing disability is the second most common disability after musculoskeletal problems, the MRC National Study of Hearing[5] has indicated an even greater prevalence when considering the response to identical questions.

Prevalence of Hearing Impairment

The most extensive study of hearing impairment is the MRC National Study of Hearing[5]. That study highlighted a prevalence of hearing impairment higher than previous reports. It indicated that the prevalence of a mild or worse hearing loss (>25 dB) in the better hearing ear increased from 19% in the 51–60 age group to over 60% in the 71–80 age group. The equivalent figures for the worse ear were 34% in the 51–60 age group rising to 72% in the 71–80 group.

For a moderate-severe hearing loss (>65 dB) the comparable figures were 1% rising to 4% in the better ear, but 4% rising to 12.5% in the worse ear. Furthermore, in his extensive analyses of the determinants of hearing level, Davis[5] found that age was far and away the biggest factor, followed by social class, high levels of occupational noise exposure and gender. Thus an individual from a working class background is twice as likely as one from a white collar background to have a hearing loss even when noise and other factors are controlled for. Males are more likely than females to have a mild hearing loss but equally likely to have a moderate to severe loss.

Prevalence of Hearing Disability

Various studies[6,7] have indicated that, for a given level of hearing impairment, elderly individuals are less likely to complain of hearing difficulties than younger people. Thus the prevalence of hearing disability does not rise as dramatically with age as does hearing impairment. Hence in the Cardiff Health Survey[8], in response to the question 'Do you have any difficulty with your hearing' 22% of people in the 51–65 age group answered 'yes' with 31% of those aged over 65. However, in the 80+ age group the prevalence does rise to 50%. The main other determinant of this prevalence, was again social class.

Within this population, the commonest problem listed as the 'Most troublesome problem' was difficulties with the television and radio (22%) followed by general conversation, listed by 20%.

The Prevalence of Tinnitus

Tinnitus may be defined as a sound or sounds originating in the head and perceived by the patient in the ear, ears or head. Most commonly it arises from a disorder of the inner ear and the hearing level at high frequencies has been shown to be the best predictor of occurrence[9].

The experience of tinnitus is very common, occurring in some ⅓ to ½ of adults, but significant persistent tinnitus is found in some 10–14% of adults[9,10]. Its prevalence is more than twice as great in those individuals aged over 60 than in younger people. It is present always or often in 21% of people in the 60–79 age group[10].

When we question patients complaining primarily of tinnitus as to the effects of tinnitus on them, 59% complain of effects on their hearing, 46% on their sleep and 44% on their mental state and 25% on their concentration[11]. This therefore plays an important role in the disabling and handicapping effects of hearing loss.

Causes of Hearing loss

Many studies have been performed on causes of hearing loss in the elderly. It is all too easy to attribute the hearing loss to 'Presbyacusis' which is largely a dustbin for unexplained and inadequately investigated hearing loss. While undoubtedly there is an increased prevalence of unexplained hearing loss with increasing age, the majority of elderly patients presenting to their GPs and audiology clinics have additional causes for their hearing loss on top of any purely age effects.

Most age-related hearing loss stems from inner ear problems with a smaller proportion resulting from changes in the middle ear, cochlear nerve, and central auditory pathways. In many elderly patients there is more than one identifiable cause, such as noise exposure and ototoxicity, or underlying genetic factors. Table 1 shows the results of

aetiological determination in two elderly populations examined by the author[12]. It may be seen from this that in ¼ to ⅓, the underlying cause stems from a middle ear disorder; although in elderly individuals these may be manifest primarily by cochlear hearing losses secondary to the underlying pathology.

The inner ear problems stem frequently from trauma, mainly noise exposure, acoustic trauma (primarily gunfire) and head injury, together with vascular problems, genetic and metabolic disorders. It is often difficult to tease out the different components when an individual's ears may have been exposed to a range of different insults. Furthermore, many metabolic and other effects are mediated by interference with the blood supply to the cochlear end-arteries. In this context the one systemic factor to consistently surface in epidemiological studies of hearing loss in the population has been blood viscosity[13].

While many genetic hearing disorders such as otosclerosis are well understood, with an increasingly ageing population the occurrence of late onset dominant hearing loss is becoming more apparent[14]. These may be identified by taking a careful family history as members of the same family may show the same pattern of hearing loss. An example of such a family tree is shown in figure 1.

Neoplastic disorders causing hearing loss are rare. Unilateral hearing loss may be caused by a vestibular schwannoma (acoustic neuroma) but the incidence of these is about 1:100,000 population per year. In other patients hearing loss may stem from metastases of lung, breast and stomach neoplasms and may also occur in chronic leukaemia.

Table 1

% of Hearing Loss by Aetiology

| | Conductive Hearing Loss | | | Sensorineural Hearing Loss | |
	London	Cardiff		London	Caridff
Otitis Media	33	21	Vascular	19	27
Otosclerosis	5	4	Noise/trauma	12	15
			Genetic	9	8
			Metabolic	3	7
			Ototoxic	1	3

Figure 1

Family tree of genetic late onset hearing loss

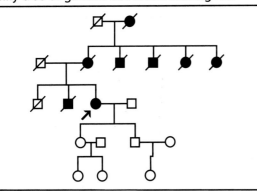

Medical and Surgical Treatment of Hearing Loss

With the aetiologies outlined above it is apparent that there is little scope for the surgical management of hearing loss in the elderly. Even in the disorders such as otitis media and otosclerosis, most of the hearing loss is cochlear and hence not amenable to surgery. The two exceptions to this may be in the case of clean dry perforations in which fitting a hearing aid with earmould may result in a recurrence of infection causing greater problems. This may be avoided by a judicious myringoplasty. In healthy individuals with a major hearing loss caused by otosclerosis and with a significant middle ear component, a sta-pedectomy may be justified to facilitate an effective hearing aid fitting.

Medical treatment likewise has a limited role in the management of hearing problems in the elderly. In general, management of an underlying metabolic disorder such as myxoedema, hyper-lipidaemia, or Paget's disorder may slow down the progress of the hearing loss but is most unlikely to result in any significant improvement to the hearing.

Audiological Rehabilitation

Entry into the rehabilitative process

From the above, it may be appreciated that the main line of approach to the management of hearing loss in the elderly is one of rehabilitation. One of the main problems is that most elderly patients do not present for rehabilitation in an audiology clinic until they have had a hearing disability for some 10–15 years. By this time they are generally in their early 70s, have quite a significant hearing loss and have been causing considerable problems for their family and friends. Even within health care systems such as the UK where hearing aids are available free of charge, only about a fifth of patients who could benefit from them actually possess them.

Gilhome-Herbst, in two studies,[15,16] has found that amongst patients aged 70 and over with at least 35 dB hearing loss in two separate populations in London and Wales, cared for by excellent GPs, only 23% had hearing aids. 25% of the remainder denied any disability, 22% admitted a disability but had done nothing about it, and 29% had consulted their GP but not been referred on for rehabilitative help. Subsequent interviewing of the group not referred on indicated that, in the majority of these, their motivation was very low and the GP had judged that they were unlikely to accept any rehabilitative intervention.

Various approaches have been suggested for encouraging people to use hearing aids or seek other rehabilitative help earlier, mainly aimed at endeavouring to reduce the stigma associated with hearing impairment and hearing aids. However, even in countries with enlightened social attitudes such as the Scandinavian countries, hearing aid use is little greater than in the UK.

A different approach, which has been used, is to screen for hearing disability in the pre-retirement age group (aged 50–65). The rationale behind targetting this group has been discussed by Davis[17], who initiated the first intervention in Cardiff. The result of that and subsequent studies have been discussed by Stephens and Meredith[18] who found that it was possible to screen individuals for hearing disability from the GP age/sex register using a simple two question approach enquiring about hearing disability and tinnitus. This postal approach had good sensitivity for detecting those prepared to use hearing aids. A simple forced whisper voice test of the hearing of those admitting disability had good specificity in deciding the acceptors, although a retrospective analysis indicated that handicap levels was the best predictor of ultimate hearing aid use. This approach was cost-effective and trebled the level of hearing aid use in the three socially different populations.

It is arguable that a screening procedure, aimed at a rehabilitative intervention of this nature needs to be targeted towards disability and handicap rather than towards impairment both on ethical and on pragmatic grounds.

The Process of Audiological Rehabilitation

Audiological rehabilitation, to be effective, must be considered as an entirety rather than in terms of individual components such as hearing aids or cochlear implants. Such instruments have a unique role within the rehabilitative process, but are of little value applied in isolation.

Audiological rehabilitation may be defined as a *problem solving process* aimed at *reducing disability* and *minimizing handicap*. As such it has a variety of components which should be applied in an integrated manner. Goldstein and Stephens[19] developed a management model of this process, which has been updated in figure 2.

In this figure, it may be seen that the process comprises three major components of evaluation, integration and decision making and remediation: defining the problem; making relevant decisions; and implementing the solution. Evaluation and remediation may further be divided into important subcomponents which address different elements of the evaluation and remedial sections.

Evaluation

This is the process of obtaining all the relevant information about the individual which will be necessary for optimal rehabilitation. This information may be obtained in different ways, by observation, by questioning, and by testing. Different approaches may be relevant for different parts of the evaluation process.

Evaluation can be split into the four components:
a) disability and handicap assessment;
b) communication status;
c) associated variables; and
d) related conditions.

Essentially the first of these is concerned with defining the problems experienced by the patient. The second defines the raw material with which the Therapist has to work. The third is concerned with the psychosocial aspects of the patient which will define the overall approach necessary. Finally, related conditions is the identification of

Figure 2

Management Model of Audiological Rehabilitation Process

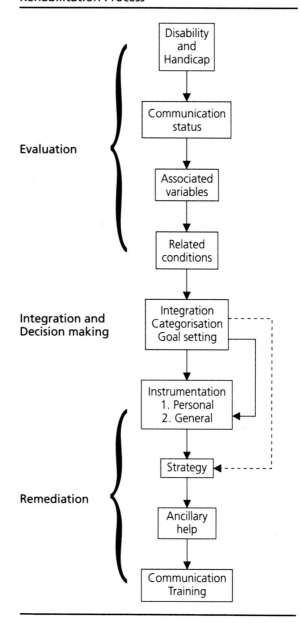

the manipulative and aural conditions which will influence the details of the rehabilitative process.

Disability and handicap are usually assessed by direct questioning or by using the open-ended problem questionnaire approach.

Table 2

Communications Status
Auditory – comprises various relevant measures of auditory impairment.
Visual – visual acuity, use of spectacles, speech-reading (Lipreading) abilities.
Speech Production – different aspects of this eg phonology, semantics, pragmatics, syntax.
Manual – includes different types of gesture and sign language.
Non-verbal communication
Previous Rehabilitation – what has been done before in an attempt to help the patient.
Overall – an integration of the individual components in the optimal communication mode.

Communication status assesses the various aspects of communication skills and communication potentials of the patient. Its different components are shown in table 2.

Associated variables are the elements of the patient's attitudes and lifestyle which influence the overall approach to rehabilitation which it may be necessary to take in the particular case. The most important components are 1) psychological and 2) sociological.

Psychological components are mainly related to the personality and specific attitudes of the individual.

Sociological factors are determined by Significant Others and their attitudes, together with the influences of the social class and the society in which the individual lives.

Related conditions comprises three components: 1) mobility; 2) upper limb function and 3) related aural pathology. These will have an influence on the detailed aspects of the rehabilitative approach to be adopted, particularly the choice of instrumentation.

Integration and Decision Making

In this stage, the information acquired in evaluation must be pulled together to provide the basis for decisions about the management of the patient. This section comprises the three elements of: 1) integration; 2) categorisation and 3) goal setting.

Categorisation of the patient entails the therapist making a decision which will have important ramifications for the direction of the remedial process. Broadly, we can divide the patients into four categories:

Category 1 – These individuals are positively motivated towards the rehabilitative process with no apparent complicating factors either expressed by the patient or anticipated by the therapist.

Category 2 – These individuals are also positively motivated, but there are complicating factors which are likely to lead to a more prolonged rehabilitation.

Category 3 – This group wants help, but may be resistant to one or more relevant parts of the rehabilitative process, eg hearing aids.

Category 4 – These patients come to the clinic as a result of pressure from long-suffering Significant Others [SOs]. They deny disability and will not be prepared to accept intervention.

Following this, the next activity is for the therapist and patient, often together with a SO, to define *goals* which are important for the patient and potentially achievable, and to consider how these goals may be best accomplished.

Remediation

This component comprises the four components: 1) instrumentation; 2) strategy; 3) ancillary help and 4) communication training. As shown in figure 1, some aspects of this may be bypassed in Category 3 and a few Category 2 patients.

Instrumentation comprises a consideration of and selection and fitting of personal instruments and of general instruments (environmental aids/assistive listening devices). The *personal instruments* will usually be hearing aids, but may also include vibrotactile aids and cochlear implants in profoundly and totally deafened patients. A characteristic of all these instruments is that they are specifically selected for and fitted to the individual concerned and used in a variety of different circumstances.

A GUIDE TO THE CARE OF THE ELDERLY

Environmental aids or assistive listening devices may be used to supplement personal instruments or, under certain circumstances, to replace them. These are summarised in table 3.

Strategy consists of elaborating with the patient, and appropriate SOs, how the goals defined earlier can best be achieved, given the personality of the patient and those around them. In particular, it is concerned with defining appropriate *hearing tactics* – ie discussing how the patient can manipulate his/her environment in order to hear better.

Ancillary help is concerned with involving other professionals in giving additional support to the patient which is beyond the skills of the rehabilitative team. This may entail the *medical* treatment of other illnesses, *psychological* help, and *social work* support, which, under the terms of the Chronically Sick and Disabled Persons Act (1980), can provide appropriate environmental aids.

Communication training may be of short duration, particularly for Category 1 patients, but in other patients it may continue for days, weeks, months or even years until the patient and therapist are happy that they are managing as well as possible. In all cases, however, it is important to consider four components: 1) information provision; 2) skillbuilding; 3) instrumental modification and 4) counselling.

Information provision is necessary to help the patient accept and adjust to their hearing loss.

Skillbuilding is classically thought of in terms of speechreading and auditory training. For many elderly people, patient training in the fitting and use of their hearing aids may be critical. Whatever the skill, the training should be maintained until the individual is performing optimally, given his/her degree of impairment.

Instrumental modification entails reviewing and modifying the instrumentation provided for the patient in the light of their experience with it.

Counselling involving both the patient and Significant Others, is an important ongoing part of the rehabilitative process. Different problems are discussed as they arise.

Finally, it is essential to consider appropriate **outcome measures** to assess the effectiveness of what has been done. This can be approached in terms of: 1) patient satisfaction; 2) reduction in disability and handicap; 3) improved performance in specific skills; and 4) improved quality of life.

Table 3

Types of Environmental Aids

Electronic Speech	Alerting/Warning Systems
Telephone amplifiers	Telephone bells
Television aids	Doorbell systems
Public address systems	Baby alarms
Loop systems	Smoke alarms
	Alarm clocks

Hearing Loss in the Elderly (Deafness)

Practical Points

1. Hearing disability in the elderly is very common and increases with increasing age.

2. The disability and handicap may be increased by the presence of tinnitus.

3. Many causes of hearing loss in the elderly are easy to identify by simple history taking and clinical examination and this helps the patients to accept their disability.

4. There are rarely effective surgical and medical interventions.

5. Seek to detect hearing disability early and encourage the patients to accept intervention by an effective audiological clinic.

6. Endeavour to ensure that the audiological clinic has a comprehensive approach to rehabilitation and is not merely a hearing aid fitting centre.

References

1. World Health Organization (1980) *International Classification of impairments disabilities and handicaps*, World Health Organization, Geneva.

2. Stephens D & Hétu R (1991) *Impairment, disability and handicap in Audiology: towards a consensus*, Audiology, 30, 185–200.

3. Barcham LJ & Stephens SDG (1980) *The use of an open-ended problems questionnaire in auditory rehabilitation*, Br J Audiol, 14, 49–54.

4. Martin J, Meltzer H & Elliott D (1988) *OPCS Surveys of disability in Great Britain, Report 1, the prevalence of disability among adults*, HMSO, London.

5. Davis AC (1989) *The prevalence of hearing impairment and reported hearing disability among adults in Great Britain*, Int J Epidemiol, 18, 911–917.

6. Merluzzi F & Hinchcliffe R (1973) *Threshold of subjective auditory handicap.* Audiology, 12, 65–69.

7. Gatehouse S (1991) *The role of non-auditory factors in measured and self-reported disability*, Acta Otolaryngol Suppl, 476, 249–256.

8. Stephens SDG, Lewis PA & Charny M (1991) *Assessing hearing problems within a community survey*, Br J Audiol, 25, 337–343.

9. Coles R, Davis A & Smith P (1991) *Tinnitus: its epidemiology and management*, in: Presbyacusis, Hartvig-Hensen J (ed). Danavox, Copenhagen, 377–402.

10. Axelsson A & Ringdahl A (1989) *Tinnitus – a study of its prevalence and characteristics*, Br J Audiol, 23, 53–62.

11. Stephens SDG, Lewis PA & Sanchez L *Tinnitus complaint behaviour and its measurement*, in: 'Proceedings of the 2nd International Meeting in Audiology for the Mediterranean Countries', Thessaloniki, 853–861.

12. Comlay C & Stephens SDG (1989) *Hearing problems*, in: Geriatric Medicine: problems and practice, Pathy MSJ & Finnucane P (eds). Springer-Verlag, London, 177–188.

13. Gatehouse S & Loew GDO (1991) *Whole blood viscosity and red cell filterability as factors in sensorineural hearing impairment in the elderly*, Acta Otolaryngol Suppl, 473, 37–43.

14. Stephens SDG (1982) *What is acquired hearing loss in the elderly*, in: Acquired hearing loss and elderly people, Glendenning F (ed). Beth Johnson Foundation, Keele, 9–26.

15. Humphrey C, Gilhome Herbst K & Faruq S (1981) *Some characteristics of the hearing impaired elderly who do not present themselves for rehabilitation*, Brit J Audiol, 15, 23–30.

16. Gilhome Herbst KR, Meredith R & Stephens SDG (1991) *Implications of hearing impairment for elderly people in London and Wales*. Acta Otolaryngol, Suppl 476, 209–214.

17. Davis AC (1987) *Epidemiology of hearing disorders*, in: Scott Brown's Otolaryngology 5th Ed. Vol 2, Stephens D (ed). Butterworths, London, 90–126.

18. Stephens D & Meredith R (1991) *The Afan Valley Audiological Rehabilitation Studies*, in: Presbyacusis and other age related aspects, Jensen JH (ed). Danavox, Copenhagen, 323–335.

19. Goldstein DP & Stephens SDG (1981) *Audiological rehabilitation: management model I*, Audiology, 20, 432–452.

Chapter 19

Osteoporosis and Fractures

Dr Anthony D Woolf BSc, FRCP
Consultant Rheumatologist
Royal Cornwall Hospital
Infirmary Hill
Truro
Cornwall
TR1 2HZ

Mr J P Hodgkinson
Consultant Orthopaedic Surgeon
North Manchester Healthcare NHS Trust
Central Drive
Crumpsall
Manchester
M8 6RL

Biosketch:

Dr Anthony D Woolf has been Consultant Rheumatologist at the Royal Cornwall Hospital, Truro since 1987. He graduated from the London Hospital Medical College and trained in rheumatology at the Hammersmith Hospital, Guy's Hospital, Royal National Hospital for Rheumatic Diseases, Bath and Bristol Royal Infirmary. His research interests are osteoporosis and early arthritis and publications include 3 books on osteoporosis and original and educational papers on a spectrum of rheumatic diseases.

Mr J P Hodgkinson graduated from Victoria University, Manchester in 1977 and obtained FRCS England in 1982. He has been Senior Registrar in Orthopaedic Surgery in North Western Regional Health Authority. He subsequently obtained Fellowship in revision hip surgery at the Hip Centre, Wrightington Hospital in 1987. He was appointed Consultant Orthopaedic Surgeon at North Manchester General Hospital in 1988. His special interests are lower limb arthroplasty and revision hip surgery and his research and publications include trauma, joint arthroplasty and medico-legal aspects of soft tissue injuries.

Introduction

Osteoporosis is not a new nor recently recognised bone disorder. Osteoporotic vertebrae have been found in neolithic burial mounds. Woolf & Dixon (1990) found examples as early as the sixth century AD when Paulas Aeginata described a condition of the bone which was typical of osteoporosis[1]. In 1824 Astley Cooper stated that in old age, bones 'become thin in their shells and spongy in their texture[2]'. In addition he noted that fractures of the neck of the femur often occurred after only minor trauma. It was not however until 1940 that osteoporosis was linked with the post-menopausal state[3]. The scale of the problem related to osteoporosis has, however, become recognised only in recent years.

Definition and Presentation

Osteoporosis is defined as a decreased amount of bone but it is usually not recognised until it presents itself clinically as a fracture in the elderly with subsequent pain, disability and increased mortality. These fractures are not only a consequence of the fragility of bone but also of trauma, usually a fall, and both these increase with age. The most common presentations of osteoporosis are fractures of the vertebrae, hip or wrist with resultant pain, disability and risk of further fracture. There are in the order of 130,000 vertebral fractures, 40,000 distal forearm fractures and 50,000 proximal femur fractures a year in Great Britain, most of which are in the elderly and in part due to osteoporosis. There is also an age related increase in fractures of the proximal humerus, lateral tibial plateau and pubic rami.

Women more often sustain osteoporotic fractures not only because of the link between bone loss and the menopause but also because of their greater life expectancy. It is projected that by the year 2031 the number of elderly people (over 65 years) in the United Kingdom will increase to 13.6 million which represents 22% of the total population, with a greater increase in the very elderly. The risk of fracture rises twenty fold from 65 to 85 years[4]. As a consequence, it is estimated that proximal femoral fractures will increase by 15% in a decade, but there is also an unexplained trend which, if maintained, means there could be a 50% increase of these fractures

in a decade. Without effective preventative and therapeutic intervention the socio-economic costs of osteoporosis will increase considerably. This involves many specialities including family practice, endocrinology and gynaecology at its earlier stages; and orthopaedics, rheumatology and geriatrics once fracture has occurred.

Osteoporosis and Fractures

Fracture is a consequence of both osteoporosis, that is loss of bone mass with micro architectural deterioration, and of falling with loss of protective responses. In the elderly, falling determines who does or does not fracture as the majority have an osteoporotic skeleton. Prevention of fracture therefore involves both maintaining bone mass and preventing falls. The lower the bone mass, the higher is the risk of fracture[5].

Bone Mass

The quality of the skeleton is influenced at all stages of life. Dent described osteoporosis as a disorder of ageing with its origin in paediatrics[6]. Bone mass increases with growth and development until 25–30 years and begins to decline from 40–45 years with a period of rapid loss in women during the perimenopausal years. The bone mass in the elderly is the most important determinant of whether a fall results in fracture. This in turn is determined by the peak bone mass at mid-life, age at onset of loss and rate of that loss. The peak bone mass is a result of genetic potential, the attainment of which depends on adequate oestrogen exposure, diet and skeletal loading. Lifetime exposure of oestrogen is important for the developing skeleton as late menarche, early menopause or any prolonged period of secondary ammenorrhoea will result in a reduced bone mass. A lack of dietary calcium or of exercise are also associated with a reduced bone mass. The onset of loss is largely determined by the menopause and hormone replacement therapy will maintain bone mass and, if taken long-term, reduces risk of future fracture[7]. The rate of loss is affected by other specific factors such as excess corticosteroids, immobility and excess thyroxine.

With bone loss there is thinning of cortical bone and of the trabeculae of cancellous bone resulting in them losing their connectedness and strength. This microarchitectural deterioration results in increased fragility. This loss of bone is a consequence of an imbalance between osteoblastic resorption and osteoblastic formation, processes that continue throughout life. With ageing there is a gradual decline in formation, and there is a period of rapid resorption during the perimenopausal years. Resorption is also increased by cortiscosteroids and immobility.

Falls

Falls are common in the elderly; 1 in 4 over 65 years will fall in the subsequent year and 5% will result in a fracture. Half occur in the home and they are usually from a standing height. There are some preventable causes such as sedatives or arrhythmia's but more commonly there is a generalised neuromuscular deterioration. The circumstances of any fracture must be carefully considered so that any cause of falling can be treated.

In conclusion, the bone mineral content determines who is at risk of fracture, but its actual occurrence is usually a consequence of trauma.

Types of Fracture and their Treatments

Fracture of the Wrist

These fractures are the commonest between 50 and 70 years. A Caucasian woman has a lifetime risk of sustaining this fracture. They are usually caused by a fall on an outstretched hand and present with pain, swelling, deformity and loss of function of the affected hand. The classic fracture is the Colles fracture, which causes a dinner fork deformity of the distal radius. However, other fractures of the distal radius may occur and if the fracture line enters the wrist joint the patient is likely to be left with permanent restriction of movement of the joint. Wrist fractures are usually treated by immobilisation in a short arm plaster cast for a period of about six weeks. If the fracture is severely displaced or angulated then manipulation under anaesthetic is required before application of the plaster cast. Manipulation is ideally carried out under general anaesthetic, although local anaesthetic techniques are sometimes more appropriate. The open reduction and internal fixation of a wrist fracture is rarely indicated.

Patients occasionally require physiotherapy to improve function and it is quite common for them to continue to experience some discomfort and slight swelling for up to one year.

More prolonged symptoms can occur if an algodystrophy (Sudek's atrophy) develops.

However, these fractures usually heal satisfactorily with patients regaining good function of their hand in the majority.

Fracture of the Hip

Fractures of the neck of the femur are very common in elderly patients with a lifetime risk of 15% of Caucasian women. These fractures usually occur after minor trauma although some are stress fractures occurring spontaneously which, in turn, causes the patient to fall to the floor. Twenty five to 30 per cent of these elderly patients with fractures of the hip will die within 6 months, 50% will suffer increased disability and 20% will lose independence.

Fractures of the neck of the femur can be classified into intra-capsular (subcapital) and extra-capsular. There are two main types of intra-capsular fracture: displaced and undisplaced. Undisplaced sub capital fractures are usually treated by internal fixation of the fracture using metal screws. Displaced sub capital fractures can be treated by manipulation and internal fixation but there is a signficant risk that the patient may develop avascular necrosis of the femoral head. Therefore, in patients over the age of seventy years the primary treatment of choice is hemi-arthroplasty. In patients under the age of sixty years most surgeons would attempt manipulation and internal fixation, accepting the risk of developing avascular necrosis. If at some later date this does develop, then a total hip replacement will become necessary. In patients between the ages of sixty and seventy years, a total hip replacement is often the primary treatment of choice for a displaced subcapital fracture. Extra-capsular fractures include trans-cervical, basal and intertrochanteric. These are best treated by open reduction and internal fixation using a dynamic hip screw and plate.

The advantages of surgical treatment for hip fractures is that the patient is usually able to mobilise within twenty-four to forty-eight hours of their surgery. This reduces the significant complications which occur when an elderly patient is confined to bed. Early surgery with prompt attention to medical problems is important. However, complications including pressure sores, chest infections, deep venous thrombosis and deep infections still occur. Early postoperative geriatically orientated rehabilitation is effective at achieving functional independence[8].

Fractures of the Shoulder

Fractures of the neck of the humerus usually occur after a fall on an outstretched arm. These fractures are often very comminuted involving both the greater and lesser tuberosities. Occasionally such fractures are associated with a dislocation of the shoulder joint. The fractures cause significant pain and bruising which often extends down to the elbow. There is often a considerable swelling of the arm and movements of the shoulder is reduced.

These fractures are usually treated conservatively in a broad arm sling for approximately three weeks. As the acute pain resolves, the patient is encouraged to mobilise the shoulder as much as possible. Patients are often left with signficant stiffness of the shoulder although this causes only minimal functional disability. Severely comminuted fractures of the neck of the humerus and fracture dislocations occasionally require surgical treatment and it is sometimes necessary to perform a hemiarthroplasty. In these cases intensive physiotherapy is required and their function may continue to improve for up to two years after surgery.

Fractures of the Knee

Fractures of the lateral tibial plateau in elderly patients with osteoporosis occur most commonly after a minor valgus strain of the knee. These fractures cause pain, swelling and deformity of the knee joint and are diagnosed by radiograph.

If the amount of depression of the lateral tibial plateau is minimal, then the patient can be nursed in a plaster cylinder or femoral cast brace. The advantage of a brace is that it allows flexion at the knee which also maintains mobility.

If the depression of the tibial plateau is greater than 1 cm then open reduction, internal fixation and bone grafting is probably indicated. The aims of this type of surgery are to reduce the risk of osteoarthritis developing in the knee joint and also to restore normal anatomy. If the patient does develop significant osteoarthritis of the knee

joint, then the total knee replacement which may become necessary has a higher chance of success if there is not significant loss of bone stock.

Fracture of the Pelvis

Fractures of the superior and inferior pubic rami do occur in elderly patients with osteoporosis after only minor trauma. These fractures require no specific treatment and rarely cause discomfort for more than a few weeks.

Fractures of the Spine

Osteoporotic wedge fractures are fairly common and usually cause acute pain and stiffness of the back. There may be radicular distribution of pain. These fractures are almost always treated conservatively with bedrest and analgesics. Opiates may be required, and calcitonin 100 units daily for 3 weeks may reduce the acute pain. The severe pain settles spontaneously in most within a few weeks and the patient should be encouraged to mobilise as soon as possible. These fractures do not usually cause any neurological deficit. There may be chronic pain relating to the mechanical changes consequent to the fracture. Vertebral fractures are also frequently asymptomatic and are identified either incidentally on an X-ray or due to the consequent loss of height and stoop. This chronic vertebral osteoporosis can result in chronic back pain, neck pain, reflux oesophagitis, stress incontinence, intertrigo within the redundant skin-folds and a feeling of fullness when eating. There may be pain resulting from the lower ribs impinging within the pelvis. The splinting of the rib cage may also result in breathlessness.

Management of Osteoporosis

The management of osteoporosis does not only involve the treatment of fractures. These heal normally. They may however result in chronic pain and disability which must be recognised and treated. The risk of further fracture must also be reduced. One of the highest risk factors for future fracture is having already sustained an osteoporotic fracture.

The cause of the fall must be identified and corrected if possible, although they usually result from a generalised neuromuscular deterioration. Generalised exercise programmes may reduce the risk of falling. Skeletal strength must also be increased or at least further deterioration prevented.

Any treatment that reduces bone loss or even causes an increase in bone mass must also be shown to influence risk of future fracture before it can be considered effective in the management of this condition. It is possible to increase bone mass without any change in strength if structurally irrelevant trabeculae are thickened.

Hormone replacement therapy prevents bone loss at this later stage of life but there is no data as to whether further fractures will be prevented[9]. The difficulty is that women over 60 years of age seldom find the return of menstruation acceptable and there is a higher risk of breast tenderness with the initiation of oestrogen therapy at this age. However, once established HRT is well tolerated and it should be strongly recommended to those who have had a hysterectomy. Low levels of habitual physical activity are associated with risk of hip fracture, whilst exercise will increase bone mass in the elderly and may reduce risk of falling and of fracture of the hip[10]. Moderate or vigorous exercise is necessary to increase bone mass which raises the question of compliance in the elderly. The role of calcium is contentius but studies do show that it has most benefit in established osteoporosis, in particular if the person has been on a low calcium diet and supplements of 1 gm daily are recommended. Recent studies have shown that sodium fluoride does not significantly reduce vertebral fractures, despite an increase in vertebral bone mass, and it may increase the risk of non-vertebral fracture[11]. Calcitonin will increase bone mass and intranasal formulations are being developed, but fracture prevention remains to be proven. Bisphosphonates are a group of drugs that inhibit the activity of osteoclasts. They are absorbed on to the mineralised surface of bone and block its absorption. Etidronate disodium given as a cyclical regime for 2 weeks every 3 months increases bone mass and appears to reduce risk of further vertebral fractures[12, 13]. Vitamin D supplements, but not in pharmacological doses, have also been shown recently to reduce future fractures risk although earlier studies have had varied results[14].

There are now treatments that reduce bone loss and reduce risk of further fracture but the relative merits of them are not yet established.

The main factor limiting the use of all of these treatments however, is a failure to recognise patients suffering from osteroporosis. Although trauma plays a major role in many of these fractures, it is the underlying osteoporosis that allows the fracture to occur. Further fractures will result in increased disability and mortality and attempts must be made to prevent these. Any postmenopausal fracture should be considered osteoporotic once other causes are eliminated and treated appropriately.

Osteoporosis and Fractures

Practical Points

1. Any post-menopausal fracture should be considered osteoporotic once other causes are eliminated and treated appropriately.

2. In keeping with the general health of the person, increased physical activity should be advised at all ages.

3. The pain due to vertebral fractures settles spontaneously between 4 to 6 weeks. This does not preclude the use of Calcitonin, analgesics and initial bed rest.

4. The cause of falls – physical, medications or environmental, either singly or in combination – should be identified and corrected, where possible.

5. Although the role of calcium is contentious, its use nevertheless is indicated in those with established osteoporosis, particularly if the person has been on a low calcium diet.

References

1. Woolf AD & Dixon A St J (1990) *Osteoporosis: A Clinical Guide*, Martin Dunitz, London.

2. Morgan DB (1983) *The epidemiology of osteoporosis* in: Osteoporosis: a multidisciplinary problem, Dixon A St J et al (eds) Academic Press, London, 127–32.

3. Albright F, Smith PM & Richards AM (1941) *Postmenopausal Osteoporosis – its clinical features*, JAMA, 116, 2456–74

4. Grimley Evans J, Prudham D & Wandless I (1979) *A Prospective study of fractured proximal femur: incidence and outcome*, Public Health, 93, 235–241.

5. Johnstone CC, Slemede CW & Melton LJ (1991) *Clinical use of bone densitometry*. N Eng J Med, 324, 1105–1109.

6. Dent CE (1976) *The management of the Menopause and Post-menopausal Years*, in: Campbells (ed) MTP Press, Lancaster, 221.

7. Fogelman I (1991) *Oestrogen; the prevention of bone loss and osteoporosis*. Br J Rheumatol, 30, 276–281.

8. Kennie DR, Reid J, Richardson IR, et al. (1988) *Effectiveness of geriatric rehabilitative care after fractures of the proximal femur in elderly women: a randomised clinical trial*, Br Med J, 297, 1083–86.

9. Christiansen C & Lindsay R (1990) *Estrogens, Bone Loss and Prevention*, Osteoporosis Int, 1, 7–13.

10. Gerber NJ & Rey B (1991) *Can exercise prevent osteoporosis?*, Br J Rheumatol, 30, 2–4.

11. Riggs BL, Hodgson SF, O'Fallon WM, et al. (1990) *The effect of fluoride treatment on vertebral fracture rate in osteoporotic women*, N Engl J Med, 322, 802–809.

12. Storm T, Thamsborg GM, Steiniche T, et al. (1990) *Effect of intermittent cyclical etidronate therapy on bone mass and fracture rate in women with postmenopausal osteoporosis*. N Engl J Med, 322, 1265–1271.

13. Watts NB, Harris ST, Genat HK, et al. (1990) *Intermittent cyclical etidronate treatment of postmenopausal osteoporosis*. N Engl J Med, 323, 73–79.

14. Tilyard MW, Spears GFS, Thompson J & Dorey S (1992) *Treatment of Postmenopausal osteoporosis with calcitriol or calcium*, N Engl J Med, 326, 357–62.

Chapter 20

Arthritis and Musculo-Skeletal Disorders

Dr A Bhalla BSc, MD, FRCP
Consultant Rheumatologist
The Royal National Hospital for Rheumatic Diseases
Upper Borough Walls
Bath
BA1 1RL

Dr B Shenstone MBBS, FRACP
Consultant Rheumatologist
Concord Hospital
Concord NSW
Australia 2139

Biosketch:

Dr Ashok K Bhalla has been a Consultant Rheumatologist at the RNHRD since 1989. He graduated from the University of Manchester and did further training at the Middlesex Hospital and from 1981 to 1984 was a Clinical and Research Fellow at Massachusetts General Hospital and Harvard Medical School. Apart from general rheumatology, his interests include osteoporosis and he heads the Metabolic Bone Unit. His research interests include the effects of early joint inflammation on bone turn over, the differentiation of bone cells, the interactions of Vitamin D with the immune system and management of chronic pain.

Dr Shenstone is currently Consultant Rheumatologist at Concord Hospital in Australia. Between 1990 and 1992 he was a Sir Jules Thorn Fellow at the Royal National Hospital for Rheumatic Diseases. During this time he undertook research work on the effects of rheumatoid arthritis and early joint inflammation on generalised osteoporosis. He also investigated the effects of joint inflammation and inflammatory mediators on bone turnover. On his return to Australia Dr Shenstone has continued work on similar lines and has set up the assays for bone turn over in his laboratory.

Introduction

Musculoskeletal disorders are common causes of disability in the elderly in whom management poses several problems including distinguishing changes of normal ageing from pathology altered expression of familiar rheumatic diseases, coexistence of other chronic illnesses, increased iatrogenic potential of drugs and the psychosocial implication of chronic disease. The frequency of nonfatal chronic rheumatic diseases, often with onset in earlier years, results in increased prevalence in the elderly. Additionally, several rheumatic diseases are more frequent (osteoarthritis, polymyalgia rheumatica, giant cell arteritis and chondrocalcinosis); others are less frequent including seronegative spondylarthropathy and connective tissue diseases (CTD).

This chapter outlines the principles of management and then provides an overview of common and important rheumatic diseases and their manifestations in the elderly.

Principles of Management

The aim is to control disease, maximise function and provide relief of symptoms. This involves making a correct diagnosis and assessment of disease activity and functional impairment.

Diagnosis

Initial assessment determines whether symptoms arise from muscles, joints or periarticular structures. Diseases are distinguished by pattern of onset and chronological progress of symptoms, pattern of joint involvement (table 1), pain characteristics and associated constitutional and extraarticular symptoms.

Musculoskeletal pain may be inflammatory, mechanical, malignant or 'psychogenic' in nature. Inflammatory pain is present at rest, worsens with activity and, when severe, disturbs sleep. It fluctuates with disease severity and is associated with joint stiffness, most marked in the morning and improved by exercise. Constitutional features of malaise, weight loss, fever and sweats may accompany it. Causes include infection, rheumatoid arthritis (RA), crystal arthropathies and CTD. Mechanical pain is related to joint use, worse towards the evening, relieved by rest and not associated with prolonged stiffness or constitutional symptoms. The commonest cause is osteoarthritis (OA). Malignant pain is constant, progressively more severe, present at rest and may disturb sleep. 'Psychogenic' pain tends to be constant with variable idiosyncratic exacerbating and relieving factors associated with depression, general fatigue and sleep disturbance. Constitutional and extra articular symptoms define a systemic rather than a localised problem and may provide diagnostic clues (table 2).

Table 1

Patterns of Joint Involvement of Arthritis in the Elderly		
	Acute	Chronic
Monoarticular	Infection Crystal Associated Disease Trauma Onset of Polyarticular Disease Avascular Necrosis Seronegative Spondyloarthropathy	Osteoarthritis Chronic Infection Soft tissue – tears – degeneration Sarcoid Pigmented Villonodular Synovitis
Assymetrical Oligoarticular	Tophaceous Gout Infection Onset of Polyarticular Disease Seronegative Spondyloarthropathy	Osteoarthritis
Polyarticular	Onset Chronic polyarthritis Polymyalgia Rheumatica	Rheumatoid Arthritis Primary Generalised Osteoarthritis Polymyalgia Rheumatica

A GUIDE TO THE CARE OF THE ELDERLY

Radiological examination of the joint may be normal in the early stages but later may help differentiate erosive from degenerative disease and changes do not necessarily correlate with symptoms. Laboratory investigations may indicate an inflammatory process (ie elevated ESR, plasma viscosity, C-reactive protein, thrombocytosis and normochronic normocytic anaemia) and allow disease activity to be assessed. Appropriate laboratory tests will be needed to help monitor for complications of drug therapy. Some tests need to be interpreted with caution: rheumatoid factor is present in 18% of the elderly without disease, and asymptomatic *ANA* positivity and hyperuricaemia are common.

Examination of synovial fluid may be diagnostic in septic and crystal arthritis and also help categorise the joint involvement as inflammatory or non inflammatory. Inflammatory effusions appear cloudy or turbid, with low viscosity and a high white cell count (WCC) (3,000–75,000/ml) with greater than 50% polymorphonuclear leukocytes while non-inflammatory effusions are clear with a high viscosity and a low WCC

(200–2,000/ml). Blood stained effusions may result from trauma, bleeding disorders, pyrophosphate arthropathy, severe destructive arthropathy of any cause and pigmented villonodular synovitis.

Synovial biopsy is not usually helpful except to exclude chronic infection (eg tuberculosis) or tumours. Biopsy of appropriate tissues is important in the diagnosis of polymyositis, amyyloidosis, vasculitis and sometimes in giant cell arteritis.

Assessment of Disease Activity

After making the correct diagnosis, the activity of the disease is assessed to determine indications for treatment, and follow response. In inflammatory conditions, useful features include duration of early morning stiffness, progression of joint involvement, constitutional symptoms, extra articular symptoms, degree of synovitis, laboratory indices of inflammation and radiological changes. Functional impairment can be assessed by joint examination, simple task performance,

Table 2

Extra Articular Manifestations of Arthritis and Associated Conditions

Constitutional	Fever, Sweats, Weight Loss	Infection, RA, Malignancy, CTD*, Vasculitis
Skin	Erythema nodosum	Infectous, Sarcoidosis, Inflammatory Bowel Disease
	Nodules	RA
	Tophi	Tophaceous Gout
	Facial Rash	Dermatomyositis, SLE
	Psoriasis	Psoriatic Arthritis
	Livedo reticularis	Polyartenti Nodosa, Vasculitis secondary to RA, SLE, Sclerodema
	Purpura	
Ocular	Keratoconjunctivitis sicca	RA, CTD
	Iritis	Seronegative Spondyloarthopathy, Sarcoid
		Giant Cell Arteritis
Digital	Raynaud's Phenomenon	Scleroderma, SLE, MCTD
	Clubbing	Hypertrophic Osteoarthropathy Bacterial Endocarditis
	Gangrene	Vasculitis
Muscular	Proximal Muscle Weakness	Polymyositis/Dermatomyositis
Cranial	Headaches, scalp pain & tenderness	Giant Cell Arteritis
Renal	Hematuria, proteinuria	CTD, Endocarditis
Cardio-Respiratory	Haemoptysis	Wegener's Granulomatosis, Pericorditis (SLE, RA). Fibrasing Alvoclitis
	Oypnoca	

*CTD = corrective tissue disorders (eg SLE, Scleroderma, Sjogren's Syndrome)

(eg hand grip strength, walking time) and ability to perform activities of daily living, assessed by questionnaire such as the Health Assessment Questionnaire (HAQ) or by detailed evaluation by an occupational therapist.

Management Strategies

Symptom relief and maximising function may involve a range of modalities including physical methods, drug therapy and surgery. The approach used depends upon patient expectation and motivation, the disease process, severity of symptoms, coexistent diseases and the availability of therapeutic modalities.

Physical Methods

Physical methods include rest, physiotherapy, lifestyle modification and biomechanical devices. Rest may range from using a walking stick in OA of knee to complete bed rest and joint splinting in inflammatory arthritis. Bed rest or joint splinting is followed by a passive and later active exercise programme to avoid complication of stiffness and loss of joint movement which itself will interfere with rehabilitation. Physiotherapy is used to reduce pain and restore function by exercise programmes, manual methods and electromechanical techniques. An important goal is the restoration and maintenance of muscle strength with subsequent joint support. Hydrotherapy allows exercises to be carried out in a supported environment combined with heat therapy. Lifestyle modification may involve dietary education, such as reduction of weight or reduction of alcohol intake. Occupational therapists assess an individual's functional capacity, suggest methods and provide aids to make task performance easier, or advise about environmental adaptation to maximise a patient's independence. Biomechanical devices include splints, orthotic devices and braces which provide functional improvement and pain relief by correcting deformity or instability and providing extra support around a joint or region.

Drug Therapy

Drugs used for arthritis can be considered in four groups – analgesics, nonsteroidal anti inflammatory drugs (NSAIDs), corticosteroids and disease-modifying agents.

Analgesics have no anti-inflammatory or disease modifying properties and are used for pain relief. Non narcotic analgesics have relatively few side effects and are most useful in the relief of mechanical pain (ie OA) or as an adjunct to NSAIDs.

NSAIDs have analgesic and anti-inflammatory but no disease-modifying properties. They have a wide range of adverse side effects and the benefits expected must be weighed against potential side effects. The acute adverse effects of NSAIDs on renal function and gastrointestinal tract are more likely to occur in the elderly. Acute renal failure is more likely to occur in an elderly patient with pre-existing cardiac or renal disease or who is on diuretics. Gastrointestinal ulceration and bleeding is more common in patients over 60 years, in females and in those with previous history of peptic ulcers. In such circumstances, benefits and toxicity should be assessed carefully and prophylaxii with an H_2 receptor antagonist or misoprostol considered.

Corticosteroids have potent anti-inflammatory effects but also significant short and long-term side effects. They can be administered intravenously, orally or intra articularly. Intra articular injections are best used when synovitis is restricted to one or only a few joints and may obviate the need for NSAIDs. They provide rapid relief of symptoms which may last many months. They should be avoided if joint infection is suspected. There is no consensus about the frequency of intra-articular steroids but a balanced approach is necessary and regular evaluation of clinical responses is required and too regular usage avoided. Oral corticosteroids may be needed to treat PMR, polymyositis and SLE. The lowest dose necessary to control disease activity should be used, but if this is not possible a steroid sparing agent (eg azathioprine, methotrexate) should be considered. Steroids should be withdrawn gradually over a period of weeks to months with careful monitoring of disease activity. It is a common mistake to withdraw steroids too rapidly in patients with PMR as recurrence of symptoms soon occurs. Intravenous steroids pulse are usually used for acute complications of disease where irreversible organ damage may occur or for acute polyarticular flare-up of RA.

Disease modifying drugs alter the course of the rheumatic diseases; the term is applied to agents used in the treatment of RA and include gold,

D-penicillamine and immunosuppressive drugs (eg azathioprine, methotrexate, cyclophosphamide). The indications for use are in general no different for the elderly compared to younger patients. Their onset of action is slow, taking up to 10 to 20 weeks for maximal effect. These agents are significantly more toxic than NSAIDs and require regular monitoring.

Surgery

Septic arthritis requiring urgent joint drainage and cervical spinal cord compression in RA is an indication for acute surgical intervention. In most other situations pain relief and improvement of function, particularly the maintenance of independence, are the main indications for surgery.

Common and Important Rheumatic Conditions in the Elderly

Osteoarthritis

OA can be classified as primary with no known cause or secondary to other predisposing factors. It is characterised by localised loss of cartilage associated with subchondral bone changes of sclerosis, pseudocyst and osteophyte formation. It is the commonest form of arthritis, slightly more common in women than men, with an increasing prevalence with age. Most individuals over the age of 75 have radiological changes of OA. Pain, swelling, instability and loss of function are the main symptoms. The pain has mechanical features, although rest and nocturnal pain occur in advanced cases. Signs include muscle wasting, joint swelling, deformity, crepitus and decreased movement and instability. Laboratory investigations are normal. Synovial fluid is non inflammatory. Joints most commonly affected include cervical and lumbar spine, distal and proximal interphalangeal joints (DIP, PIP), carpometacarpal joints (CMC), hips, knees and feet, particularly the first metatarsophalangeal joints (MTP). The most common pattern in elderly women is a polyarticular involvement of the DIP, PIP, CMCs, knees and spine. Hip and knee disease with or without spinal involvement is common in men.

The diagnosis of OA in peripheral joints is usually straightforward although a common mistake is to accept radiological features of OA as the cause of a patient's symptoms despite an inconsistent history or physical examination. Atypical

distribution of joint involvement such as the elbow or shoulder suggests secondary OA. Treatment is symptomatic and includes patient education, weight reduction, physiotherapy, occupational therapy and drug therapy including simple analgesics, low dose NSAIDs and/or intra articular steroids. Surgery is considered for severe pain inadequately relieved by conservative therapy or functional disability threatening independence.

Osteoarthritis in the spine causes cervical and lumbar spondylosis. Most individuals over the age of 65 have radiological changes of spondylosis with osteophyte formation and disc space narrowing and the majority are asymptomatic. Symptoms are often of chronic recurrent diffuse mechanical pain, sometimes with nerve root entrapment. Physical signs include limitation of movement, reproduction of pain with spinal movement and occasionally signs of nerve root entrapment.

Lumbar disc protrusion, osteophyte formation around facet joints and hypertrophy of the ligamentum flavum lead to narrowing of the spinal canal, most commonly in the lumbar region, causing the syndrome of spinal canal stenosis characterised by symptoms suggestive of intermittent claudication. The diagnosis can be confirmed by CT scan or by magnetic resonance imaging.

Treatment for back pain includes rest for short time only followed by physiotherapy including hydrotherapy and postural exercises, simple analgesics or low dose NSAIDs. Surgery is reserved for few individuals with progressive neurological deficit.

Rheumatoid Arthritis (RA)

A chronic inflammatory joint disease, sometimes with extra articular features, characterised by chronic inflammatory hypertrophy of synovial tissue potentially affecting all joints, tendons and bursae with a synovial lining.

The peak age of onset is between 35 and 50; however 10% of cases start after the age of 60. Consequently, in the elderly the disease spectrum ranges from active recent onset disease to longstanding chronic disease with multiple joint deformities and systemic complications.

Joint involvement is characteristically symmetrical and polyarticular with hands, wrists, feet, knees and hips being the most commonly involved joints. Initially there may be pain without joint swelling which usually develops within a few months. Tenosynovitis may be prominent, particularly involving the flexor and extensor tendon sheaths of the wrists and fingers. Onset in the elderly may be insidious, with a slow progressive symmetrical onset or acute and polyarticular with constitutional symptoms; or constitutional onset when extra articular features dominate; or the polymyalgic onset indistinguishable from polymyalgia rheumatica in the initial stages.

With persistent synovitis joint destruction, instability and deformity ensues and pain takes on mechanical features. Local complications include popliteal cyst formation in the knee which may rupture and resemble a deep venous thrombosis, atlantoaxial subluxation or subluxation of the lower cervical spine causing cervical cord compression and rupture of the extensor tendons of the hand.

Extra-articular features of RA include constitutional symptoms, rheumatoid nodules, leg ulcers, nail fold infarcts, anaemia, splenomegaly, keratoconjunctivitis sicca, pleurisy, pericarditis and vasculitis. They are more common in seropositive patients with severe articular disease.

X-rays of the hands and feet are helpful in following the progress of the disease. In early disease there is soft tissue swelling, juxta articular osteoporosis, joint space narrowing and marginal erosions and later this leads to loss of joint space, subchondral bone cysts and bone collapse and joint subluxation. New bone formation is not a feature.

Laboratory tests reveal an anaemia of chronic disease, reactive thrombocytosis, elevated ESR and acute phase reactants. A low white cell count and platelet count may be associated with Felty's syndrome or marrow suppression due to drugs. Rheumatoid factor is present in 60–80% of patients and may indicate extra articular complication as does a positive antinuclear antibody.

The course of RA is variable and unpredictable. In general, an onset with an acute or polymyalgic presentation tend to have a good prognosis while high titre rheumatoid factor, early erosion, rheumatoid nodules and extra articular involvement indicate a poorer outcome.

Management includes patient education, rest of inflamed joints followed by physiotherapy, NSAIDs, local steroid injections of joints and tendon sheaths, and disease suppressing agents.

Crystal Deposition Diseases

Arthropathies due to the presence of intra-articular crystals are of three main types: gout, calcium pyrophosphate deposition disease and hydroxyapatite deposition disease. They may be asymptomatic, cause an acute inflammatory synovitis or chronic destructive disease.

Gout

Gout, characterised by the presence of mono-sodium urate crystals in articular tissue, increases in incidence with increasing levels of hyperuricaemia and principally occurs in middle age. In the elderly, a common cause of hyperuricaemia and gout is the use of diuretics.

The classical features in middle age are a period of asymptomatic hyperuricaemia followed by an acute inflammatory arthritis, usually monoarticular and affecting the big toe, followed by the uncommon development of tophi. In the elderly, acute attacks are uncommon and, if present, occur in hands, feet and knees and tophi are more common, usually seen over the interphalangeal joints of the hand, in association with Heberden's and Bouchard's nodes.

Diagnosis is clinical and confirmed by demonstrating urate crystals in synovial fluid and tophi. X-ray findings in acute gout are non specific with soft tissue swelling and juxta articular osteoporosis but tophaceous gout may lead to joint space narrowing, sclerosis, and cyst formation.

Treatment of the acute attack involves the cautious use of NSAIDs or sometimes colchicine. Urate lowering drug should only be used for persistent recurrent attacks of gouty arthritis. NSAIDs and allopurinol are potentially toxic drugs in the elderly, especially in those with compromised renal function. If gout is secondary to diuretics, their need should be evaluated carefully and these drugs can often be discontinued.

Calcium Pyrophosphate Deposition Disease (CPPD)

The deposition of CPPD crystals in articular cartilage increases with age and radiologically appears as chondrocalcinosis. Clinically presentation may be acute or chronic. The typical presentation is acute synovitis identical to gout (pseudogout), a common case of acute monoarthritis in the elderly. The commonest site is the knee followed by wrist, shoulders and ankles. There may be pyrexia, leucocytosis and the joint is warm and red suggesting septic arthritis which must be excluded by culture of synovial fluid. Attacks may follow intercurrent illness or surgery. In 10% of cases, more than one joint may be involved and transient less severe attacks are common. Occasionally severe destructive disease occurs, particularly in the hip, shoulder or knee.

Diagnosis is suggested by X-ray changes of chondrocalcinosis and confirmed by finding CPPD crystals in the synovial fluid.

There is no specific treatment with acute attacks being treated with NSAIDs or intra-articular steroids once sepsis has been excluded. General management is the same as for osteoarthritis.

Hydroxyapatite (also basic calcium phosphate) Associated Arthritis

Hydroxyapatite (HA), the main mineral constituent of bone and teeth, may be deposited in areas of tissue damage and is commonly seen in the region of the supraspinatus tendon and rotator cuff of the shoulder with a radiological frequency of 7% in the elderly. Occasionally it causes severe acute inflammation of the subacromial bursa, periarticular tissue or joint itself.

HA crystal identification is difficult requiring specialised techniques such as X-ray diffraction or electron microscopy. Crystals have been found in association with osteoarthritis although their significance remains unclear. An unusual form of a rapidly destructive large joint arthritis in the elderly has been described ("Milwaukee shoulder" or "apatite associated destructive arthritis"). The shoulders, knees and hips are most commonly affected with remarkably few associated symptoms. Joints may be large, cool, often with bloodstained joint effusions and X-ray shows marked destructive changes with little sclerosis or osteophyte formation. Laboratory investigations are unhelpful and treatment is symptomatic.

Polymyalgia Rheumatica (PMR) and Giant Cell Arteritis (GCA)

PMR is a clinical syndrome characterised by pain and stiffness of the hip and shoulder girdles, associated with constitutional symptoms and lacking evidence for a primary muscle disorder. GCA is a granulomatous vasculitis of medium sized arteries, with numerous clinical features including those of PMR. The disorders may overlap; features of GCA are seen in 10–15% of temporal artery biopsies from individuals with PMR but without clinical features of GCA. Both conditions occur after the age of 50 and females are twice as frequently affected as males.

Onset of PMR may be insidious or abrupt with pain and stiffness affecting muscles around the neck and shoulders, upper arms, buttocks and thighs. Morning stiffness is common. Constitutional symptoms include low grade fever, night sweats, anorexia, malaise and weight loss. Muscle weakness is not a feature though this may be difficult to ascertain due to pain and stiffness. Mild large joint synovitis may occur and whether small joint synovitis is associated with PMR or related to a polymyalgic onset of RA is controversial.

GCA is manifest by headache, scalp tenderness, visual disturbance, constitutional symptoms and in up to 50% of cases, symptoms of PMR. Sudden blindness occurs in 5% of patients. Less common manifestations include claudication of jaw or limbs, aortic arch syndrome and vertigo, depending on the artery involved.

Laboratory investigations reveal an elevated ESR, plasma viscosity, CRP and other acute phase reactants with a normocytic anaemia, thrombocytosis and an elevated alkaline phosphatase. Rheumatoid factor, creatinine phosphokinase, EMG and muscle biopsies are normal. Temporal artery biopsy may confirm the diagnosis of GCA but lesions are patchy in distribution with segments of normal artery between involved areas.

Corticosteroids are the treatment of choice for both disorders. When GCA is suspected, doses of 40–60 mg of prednisolone daily should initially be used due to the risk of sudden blindness. Patients with PMR start on lower doses 10–15 mg prednisolone daily and have dramatic relief of symptoms. After 2–4 weeks, the dose is slowly reduced depending on symptoms and ESR. PMR is said to be self limiting diseases lasting 12–24 months.

Septic Arthritis

Septic arthritis is not uncommon in the elderly, particularly those who are debilitated, or who have pre-existing joint disease. Staphylococci followed by gram negative bacilli are the commonest causative organisms. Diagnosis is not difficult if the patient is acutely unwell with a red hot swollen and painful joint. However, in debilitated patients the presentation may be atypical with mild constitutional symptoms, multiple joint involvement and with joint symptoms being relatively unimpressive. Diagnosis is made by joint aspiration and gram staining of fluid followed by culture, and should be done whenever septic arthritis is suspected. Blood and urine should also be cultured. Laboratory investigations reveal a neutrophil leucocytosis in 50–70% of patients and an elevated ESR. Initial X-rays are often normal but are a useful baseline for comparing further changes including joint space narrowing, subchondral bone destruction and periostitis. The differential diagnosis of acute monarthritis includes infection, crystal synovitis, acute haemorrhages and acute reactive arthritis.

Most cases arise from haematogenous spread and a diligent search should be made for the portal of entry to aid antibiotic choice. Immediate administration of appropriate antibiotics in adequate doses, after cultures have been taken, is essential followed by and splinting to immobilise the joint in a functional position. Joint drainage by needle aspiration is done daily if fluid remains purulent. For inaccessible joints, lack of response to antibiotics and thick pus, open or arthroscopic drainage should be considered. In general parenteral antibiotics are given for 2 to 4 weeks followed by oral antibiotics for 4–6 weeks. As symptoms improve, physiotherapy is introduced to maintain a normal range of movement and prevent contractures. Functional outcome is largely dependent upon the speed and appropriateness of therapy.

Musculoskeletal Manifestations of Malignancy

Joint symptoms during malignancy may arise from direct involvement of bone or joint or be part of the non metastatic manifestation of malignancy.

Bone pain from metastatic infiltration is characteristically persistent, becoming progressively more pain, and disturbs sleep. There may be constitutional symptoms and symptoms related to other organ involvement. Primary tumours of bones or articular structures are extremely uncommon. Malignant infiltration of articular structures is also rare but may occur with myeloproliferate and lymphoproliferative disorders.

Non metastatic manifestations of malignancy may be myopathic or arthropathic in nature. Myopathic syndromes include polymyositis, dermatomyositis, myasthenia gravis, Eaton-Lambert syndrome and asthenia related to type II fibre

atrophy. Polymyositis is manifest by progressive symmetrical muscle weakness usually most pronounced in the neck and girdle muscles. Dermatomyositis has muscle involvement as for polymyositis with additional cutaneous features of a dusky red rash overlying the elbows and dorsum of the IP and MCP joints (Gottron's papules), or a heliotrope rash of the eyelids. Laboratory features include elevated muscle enzymes (CPK and aldolase) and characteristic EMG and muscle biopsy changes. An association between polymyositis and malignancy has been disputed but patients with dermatomyositis have a definite increase in the risk of cancer.

Articular symptoms of malignancy include hypertrophic osteoarthropathy, secondary gout and a polyarthritis resembling RA. Hypertrophic osteoarthropathy is a syndrome with periostitis of the long bones, clubbing of fingers and/or toes and occasionally an oligo or polyarticular synovitis, which may precede symptoms related to malignancy. Periostitis causes deep-seated burning pain, worse with dependency of the limb and improves with elevation. X-rays may confirm the diagnosis of periostitis affecting the shaft of the long bones particularly the wrist, ankles and knees. Treatment of the malignancy results in marked improvement. NSAIDs or steroids may be helpful for symptomatic relief.

Secondary gout due to hyperuricaemia from high cell turnover is not uncommon in the myeloproliferative disorders. Its clinical features have been covered earlier.

A polyarthritis generally resembling RA may precede presentation of malignancy. Onset may be explosive and joint involvement may be RA-like, asymmetrical or monoarticular. Rheumatoid factor is negative although positive ANA may be found. Treatment of the underlying malignancy may result in resolution of the symptoms.

Arthritis

Practical Points

1. Rheumatic disorders are very common – up to 40% of elderly people may have this disorder.

2. Osteoarthritis and Rheumatoid Arthritis are two giants among arthritic disorders.

3. A careful history and relevant clinical examination is very important in making a diagnosis of several of these disorders.

4. The management of osteoarthritis and Rheumatoid Arthritis is multidisciplinary.

5. NSAIDs (Non-steroidal anti-inflammatory drugs) have potentially serious side-effects. Greatest caution is necessary in prescribing them.

6. In view of dramatic response of Prednisolone in both polymyalgia rheumatics and cranial arteritis, its use is indicated not only therapeutically but also diagnostically in these conditions.

7. Elderly patients with severe arthritis should not be denied benefits of surgery, say, osteotomy or arthroplasty, if other measures fail.

Further Reading

1. Dieppe PA, Doherty M, McFarlane DG & Maddison PJ (1985) *Rheumatological Medicine*, Churchill Livingstone, London.

2. Doherty M & Dieppe P (1986) *Crystal deposition disease in the elderly*, in: Clinics in Rheumatic Diseases, Kean WF (ed) WB Saunders, London, 12, 1, 97–116.

3. Caldwell DS (1989) *Musculoskeletal syndromes associated with malignancy*, in: Textbook of Rheumatology, Kelly WN, Hams ED, Ruddy S, Sledge CB (eds) WB Saunders, Philadelphia.

4. Fries JF (1989) *Assessment of the patient with rheumatic disease*, in: Textbooks of Rheumatology, Kelley WN, Harris ED, Ruddy S, Sledge CB (eds), WB Saunders, Philadelphia.

5. Harris ED (1989) *The clinical features of rheumatoid arthritis*, in: Textbook of Rheumatology, Kelley WN, Harris ED, Ruddy S, Sledge CB (eds). WB Saunders, Philadelphia.

6. Hollingworth P (1988) *Rheumatology*, Heinemann Medical Books. London.

7. Hopperfield S (1976) *Physical examination of the spine and extremities*, Applenton-Century-Crofts, New York.

8. Kean WF, (1986) *Arthritis in the Elderly*, in: Clinics in Rheumatic Deseases, Kean WF (ed), WB Saunders, London.

9. Maddison PJ, Isenberg DA, Woo P & Glass DN, (eds) (1993) *Oxford Textbook of Rheumatology*, Oxford Medical Publication, Oxford.

10. Sanders PA & Grennan DM (1990) *Nonsteroidal anti-inflammatory drugs versus simple analgesics in the treatment of arthritis*, in: Bailliere's Clinical Rheumatology, Bellamy N (ed). Bailliere Tindall, London. 4, 371–386.

Chapter 21

Urinary Incontinence

Dr Jean Robinson MBChB, MD, FRCP
Consultant Physician in Geriatric Medicine
Withington Hospital
South Manchester University Hospitals NHS Trust
Nell Lane
Manchester
M20 2LR

Biosketch:

Dr Robinson was appointed Lecturer (Honorary Consultant) in Geriatric Medicine at Withington Hospital, Manchester in 1982 and subsequently Consultant Geriatrician in 1985. She has been responsible for running a specialist urinary incontinence clinic. A Fellow of the Royal College of Physicians (FRCP) of London in 1991, Dr Robinson has several publications to her credit, mainly on urinary incontinence and related topics. She has been teaching not only undergraduate and post-graduate doctors, but also health visitor students and rehabilitation therapists.

Introduction

Incontinence of urine is a symptom that leads to embarrassment, shame and social isolation.

Prevalence

In hospitals, incontinence occurring at least once each day can be expected in 25% of elderly patients on acute wards and in at least 40% of elderly patients in long-term care wards[1, 2]. Prevalence does not increase with advancing age for patients in hospital, but is rather more common in women than men.

In the community, leakage of urine occurring daily or more often is to be expected in about 5% of the elderly and is found more commonly in women than men. Prevalence does increase with increasing age for patients in the community: 1.7% for men aged 70–74 years and 6.2% for those aged 85 years and over 4% in women aged 70–74 years and rising to 13.8% in those aged 85 years and over[3].

Consultations should provide an opportunity for patients to tell us about this distressing symptom and we should then evaluate the problem appropriately.

Causes and their Treatments

Elderly patients may have several reasons for the development of incontinence. There are two major categories for causes of urinary incontinence in the elderly:

1. Pathologies affecting the bladder and urethra, and their neurological control.
2. Physical and mental disabilities preventing easy access to toilet facilities.

Causes and treatments aimed at regaining continence are indicated in table 1.

Assessment

History

Important points in the history include:

1. Recent onset of incontinence with increased frequency of micturition and discomfort on voiding which suggest acute urine infection.
2. Haematuria may occur with bladder calculus or tumour.
3. Continuous leakage of urine is likely in the presence of vesico-vaginal fistula.
4. If cough stress leakage is the only urinary symptom then urethral weakness is likely.
5. A complaint of constipation may indicate the presence of faecal impaction.
6. Known illness may be relevant: eg diabetes mellitus that may be associated with peripheral neuropathy and underactive detrusor function (or simply with polyuria); Parkinson's disease that may be causing impaired mobility and poor dexterity.
7. Medications may be contributing to the incontinence problem: eg night sedation which may prevent the patient from waking when his bladder is full; diuretic medication which may lead to marked urgency of micturition and consequent incontinence if there is any impairment of mobility.

Physical Examination

Important points in the examination include:

1. A palpable bladder indicates incomplete emptying, due either to outflow obstruction or underactive detrusor function.
2. Faecal masses or tumours may be palpable in the abdomen.
3. Rectal examination may reveal faecal impaction, prostatic enlargement or tumour.
4. Vaginal examination will identify prolapse (and so suggest urethral weakness as a cause of incontinence). The presence of pinpoint haemorrhages and eroded areas on the vaginal mucosa indicates oestrogen deficiency.
5. Neurological assessment will identify upper motor neuron lesion that may be accompanied by detrusor instability, peripheral neuropathy with which under-active detrusor function may be associated, or other more complex neurological problems.
6. Observation of mobility and dexterity may disclose that incontinence is inevitable if assistance with toileting is not available. The reasons for impaired mobility and/or dexterity must then be sought.

Mental State Assessment

1. Anxiety may be precipitated by a move to a new environment. The consequent uncertainty about location of the lavatory, and when visits will be permitted, may provoke incontinence.

Table 1

Causes of Urinary Incontinence and Their Treatment

Cause		Treatment
Bladder Disorder	acute urine infection	antibiotics
	atrophic trigonitis	oestrogen
	calculus	surgery
	tumour	surgery
	fistula (may be malignant)	surgery
Urethral Abnormality	weakness (in women)	pelvic floor exercises/surgery
	obstruction eg by prostatic enlargement	surgery
	eg by faecal impaction	enemas, diagnosis of cause
Neurological Deficit	idopathic detrusor instability, detrusor instability associated with demonstrable neurological disease	timed voiding
	underactive detrusor function	intermittent self-catheterisation/ indwelling urethral catheter
	other complex detrusor/urethral dysfunctions	depends on specialist urodynamic assessment
Physical Disability	impaired mobility/dexterity	improved mobility treat specific disease eg Parkinson's disease aids eg walking frame, commode easily removed clothing review medications eg diuretics, sedatives
Mental Disability	anxiety	reassurance
	acute confusional state	treatment of underlying disease
	depression	antidepressant therapy
	dementia	timed voiding

2. Depression can so retard the patient that he simply sits in the chair and wets himself.
3. Dementia may provoke incontinence, simply because a patient cannot remember where to find the lavatory. If he has severe dementia he may not be aware of the difference between his armchair and the lavatory seat.

Urinalysis

1. Glycosuria will warn that poorly controlled diabetes mellitus may be leading to polyuria and incontinence in those patients with some impairment of mobility.
2. Haematuria would suggest a tumour or calculus.

Urine Microscopy and Culture

1. Urine infection (more likely to be significant if leucocytes are present on microscopy) will be identified.
2. Red cells, particularly in the absence of infection, suggest bladder tumour or calculus.

Specialist Assessment

The most frequently performed specialist investigations are uroflowmetry (to identify patients with low urine flow rate which may be due to bladder outflow obstruction or underactive detrusor function), cystometrography (to evaluate detrusor muscle function) and cystoscopy (to identify intravesical pathology such as tumour or calculus). Particularly for patients where bladder outflow obstruction is suspected, it is necessary to assess renal function (by blood urea and creatinine estimations).

Specialist evaluation is likely to be necessary in the following circumstances:
1. Male patients after treatment/exclusion of urine infection, faecal impaction and/or mental disability preventing easy access to toilet facilities.
2. Female patients with predominantly stress incontinence.
3. All patients with continuous incontinence.
4. All patients with haematuria.
5. All patients with intractable incontinence that cannot be accounted for by an obvious irremediable condition, eg severe dementia.

Regaining of Continence

Specific treatments aimed at the regaining of continence are indicated in table 1. Oestrogen deficiency results in atrophic changes in the bladder trigone and urethral mucosa, as well as the vaginal mucosa. If pinpoint haemorrhages and eroded areas are identified on the vaginal mucosa then it is reasonable to treat with oestrogen. Oral ethinyloestradiol 5 micrograms daily for one month is sufficient to mature the epithelium of post-menopausal women[4]. Vaginal oestrogen preparations produce physiological blood levels of oestradiol and oestrone, and suppress the levels of luteinising hormone and follicle stimulating hormone[5]. Therefore, it would appear that intravaginal oestrogen creams exert their biological effect through delivery to the target cells by the circulation and, consequently, systemic side effects of oestrogens are not likely to be reduced by using vaginal preparations. Ethinyloestradiol is available in 10 microgram tablets. If ethinyloestradiol 10 micrograms daily for 3 weeks is insufficient to produce a vaginal mucosa of normal appearance then treatment should be changed to a combined oestrogen and progestogen preparation eg Prempak-CO.625, in order to minimise the risk of development of endometrial carcinoma. Oestrogen may be administered by a self-adhesive patch. Transdermal oestradiol 25 micrograms daily result in significant rise in serum oestradiol concentration; however, the beneficial effects of both transdermal and oral oestradiol on vaginal mucosa were

lost within four weeks of stopping treatment that had been given for a four week period[6]. Hence, it seems likely that longterm benefits would require longterm treatment. Therefore, oestrogen and progesterone would be needed. Specialist gynaecological advice should be considered where oestrogen treatment is contemplated.

Women with urethral weakness may benefit from pelvic floor exercises. However, the best response to this treatment is seen in young women with mild incontinence[7].

Detrusor instability is likely to be present in about 50% of elderly women with urinary incontinence[8]. Over the years, many drug treatments have been used in the expectation that they will suppress this instability. Any that have been carefully studied in an elderly population have been found no more effective than placebo in curing incontinence. Timed voiding is widely advocated as an appropriate management for incontinence associated with detrusor instability. For this regime to be effective, the patient must void before the bladder has filled to a volume when an uninhibited contraction would occur. A chart should be kept for a few days to determine the frequency of urinary incontinence. Then, the timed intervals between voiding must be shorter than the intervals between recorded episodes of incontinence. A study of 20 elderly men with detrusor instability showed that 85% were much improved with regard to urinary incontinence after a 2 hourly voiding regime was established[9].

Keeping Patients Comfortable

Appliances

Collecting Appliances
Urine collecting appliances are available only for men. The appliance must fit snugly around the penis without causing constriction and conduct the urine to a collecting bag. A pubic pressure urinal requires considerable manual dexterity in order for it to be fitted onto the body satisfactorily. The sheath (condom) urinal is fitted directly on to the penis; the sheath is either self-adhesive or attached with adhesive tape. An appliance is most likely to be of benefit to a patient who fully appreciates the need for the appliance and can fit it himself.

Pads and Pants

These can be used for both men and women. The aim is to keep the patient's skin dry and to avoid leakage of urine on to the clothes. Therefore, it is necessary to have a non-wettable surface next to the patient and a plastic layer outside the padding. The pads must be appropriate in size and absorbency for the patient's needs.

Catheters

A catheter may be used for intractable incontinence if appliances and pads and pants are unsatisfactory. The risks of acute and chronic pyelonephritis may be acceptable for an elderly, frail patient with an expected life span of only a few years. Catheters for long-term use should be inert and smooth; pure silicone or latex coated with silicone elastomer are satisfactory[10]. These catheters are suitable for use over periods of up to 12 weeks. A size 12Ch (Charriere) catheter provides optimal drainage and larger size catheters are likely to cause discomfort[11, 12]. Catheters with a balloon capacity of 5 ml should be used; larger sized ballons have been stated to cause bladder irritation and spasms with resultant leakage of urine past the catheter[13]. Bladder washout with a weak acid solution (eg Uro-Tainer Suby G) may be of benefit in reducing catheter encrustation. It has been found that long-term catheterised patients who suffered blocked catheters were more likely to have alkaline urine[14]. There is no clinical data available to dictate the frequency of bladder washouts for patients susceptible to catheter encrustation and blockage. Antiseptic washouts should not be routinely used for patients with long-term catheters; this practice may lead to selection of drug resistant organisms.

The urine drainage bag should not be visible; it may be attached to the leg or suspended from an apron attached to a waistband. The bag should be replaced with a new one if there is any leakage of urine from the bag or any smell of urine associated with it.

Odour Control

The distressing, offensive smell of stale urine can be almost totally avoided if the patient's skin is washed and dried before new pads are put on and wet pads, clothes and linen are promptly removed from the patient and placed either in cold water with added antiseptic solution or sealed in polythene bags. A high fluid intake should be encouraged as dilute urine has little odour, particularly if it is free from infection.

Appropriate evaluation of the sympton of urinary incontinence will clarify the underlying causes and indicate appropriate treatments that may cure the problem. If incontinence cannot be cured then it must be contained in such a way that the patient is comfortable and confident that no one around him can know of his problem.

Urinary Incontinence

Practical Points

1. Urinary incontinence is common in the elderly. Approximate assessment and management will ensure that continence is regained or, at least, a marked improvement in the symptom is achieved.

2. Like headache or chest pain, incontinence is a symptom that may result from a variety of medical, surgical and psychiatric conditions – that it is part of normal ageing is a myth.

3. Urodynamic studies are performed only in selected patients after a careful assessment of urinary incontinence.

4. Timed voiding can effect marked improvements in the majority of patients with detrusor instability.

5. Drugs, so far, have proved disappointing in the management of urinary incontinence.

6. Access to continence services should be open to all patients needing such help, irrespective of their place of abode – hospital, residential and nursing homes or their own homes.

References

1. Sullivan DH & Lindsay RW (1984) *Urinary incontinence in the geriatric population of an acute care hospital*, J Am Geriatr Soc, 32, 646–50.

2. Isaacs B & Walkey FA (1964) *A survey of incontinence in elderly hospital patients*, Gerontologia Clinica, 367–76.

3. Vetter NJ, Jones DA & Victor CR (1981) *Urinary incontinence in the elderly at home*, Lancet, 2, 1275–7.

4. Mandel FP, Geola FL, Lu JKH, et al. (1982) *Biologic effects of various doses of the ethinyloestradiol in post-menopausal women*, Obstet Gynecol, 59, 673–9.

5. Rigg LA, Hermann H & Yen SSC (1978) *Absorption of estrogens from vaginal creams*, N Engl J Med, 298, 195–7.

6. Billett J, Burton R, Miodrag A & Castleden CM (1991) *Oral or transdermal oestrogen for atrophic urovaginitis?* Age & Ageing, 20 (Suppl 1), 6

7. Wilson PD (1981) *The value of physiotherapy in the treatment of genuine stress incontinence*, in: Female genuine stress incontinence. An objective study of aspects of its aetiology, investigation and conservative treatment, (MD Thesis) University of Glasgow, 210–31.

8. Staskin D, Ouslander J, Zimmerrn P & Raz S (1985) *The clinical and urodynamic characteristics of an elderly female population*, J Urol, 133, 145A.

9. Sogbein SK & Awad SA (1982) *Behavioural treatment of urinary incontinence in geriatric patients*, Can Med Assoc J, 127, 863–4.

10. Blacklock NJ (1986) *Catheters and urethral strictures*, Br J Urol, 58, 475–8.

11. Ebner A, Madersbacher H, Schober F & Marbeger H (1985) *Hydrodynamic properties of Foley catheters and its clinical relevance*, in: Proceedings International Continence Society, 15th meeting. London, 217–8.

12. Roe BH (1986) *Patients' perceptions of their catheters and study of urine drainage systems*, (M Sc Thesis), University of Manchester.

13. Blannin JP & Hobden J (1980) *The catheter of choice*, Nursing Times, 76, 2092–3.

14. Kunin CM, Chin QF & Chambers S (1987) *Indwelling urinary catheters in the elderly*, Am J Med, 82, 405–11.

Chapter 22

Pressure Sores and Leg Ulcers

Dr E Freeman FRCP FRCP(E)
Consultant Geriatrician
University Hospital of South Manchester
Nell Lane
Didsbury
Manchester
M20 8LR

Biosketch:

Dr E Freeman is Consultant Geriatrician, University Hospital of South Manchester and Honorary Associate Lecturer, University of Manchester. The present chapter arises mainly from tutorials to medical students and the interesting feedback in their questions and comments. Other personal interests have included respiratory diseases in old age with several publications on that topic.

Pressure Sores

Aetiology

When compressional, shearing or frictional pressures occlude capillaries, the resulting ischaemia and infarction produces pressure sores. The mean intra-capillary pressure is 25–30 mmHg; the essence of pressure sore management is to prevent tissue pressures becoming high enough for long enough to cause infarction.

Compression is weight divided by surface area, so its effects are greatest over bony prominences. Increasing the weight bearing surface area is the rationale underlying the use of water beds and soft cushions.

Shearing stresses arise from the movement of parallel planes of the body relative to their parallel axes. For example, in a patient partly sitting up in bed, the skeleton and soft tissues tend to slide relative to the skin which is held in place by frictional contact. Shearing stresses thus set up may occlude capillaries crossing tissue planes.

Friction particularly affects the skin over the coccyx and the heels, eg by sliding down a chair.

Incidence and Prevalence

About 20% of geriatric admissions are at substantial risk of developing a pressure sore and over 70% of all sores occur in the aged population. They are mostly acquired in hospitals within two weeks of admission so this is an acute problem and not one especially of long-stay wards.

On geriatric wards, about 20% of acute patients and 10% of long-stay residents have a pressure sore at any one time. Sores in other departments are of lesser severity and frequency. About a quarter of hospital sores and half of community ulcers last for over six months.

There has been no national survey of the problem but prevalence is approximately 40–85 per 100,000 population.

Risk Factors

All geriatric admissions need assessing, specifically for vulnerability to pressure sores. Re-assessment is necessary whenever the medical condition worsens. Particular attention should be paid to any of the causes of impaired movements, sensory loss and poor arterial perfusion. (Table 1)

The risk of a sore developing depends upon both the time at risk and the pressure. Long periods on unyielding surfaces in operating theatres, casualty or X-ray departments and on transport trolleys is an often overlooked iatrogenic contribution. Many hospital mattresses are too firm. The geriatric principle of early mobilisation is sometimes over-enthusiastically applied: sick people are at higher risk of pressure sores while seated rather than lying.

Urinary incontinence is not of itself a risk factor but its underlying cause is likely to be so.

Clinical Pathology

The earliest warning of a deep sore may be no more than surface reddening, which, if it blanches on pressure, suggests reversibility; palpable induration suggests otherwise. Persisting pallor is of similar significance. Necrosis begins near bone, involves deep muscle and may extend to bone, joint cavities and subcutaneously. When the pressure is relieved, most sores heal spontaneously though slowly.

Normal Healing

In clean experimental wounds, elastic tissue contraction speedily reduces the cavity; an inflammatory exudate appears and becomes organised while granulation tissue forms and extends to cover the base of the wound. Epithelial cells migrate from its edge to cover the surface.

Table 1

Risk Factors for Pressure Sores	
Diminished Movements	Reduced level of consciousness Stroke/paralysis Pain, eg fracture Advanced dementia
Impaired Sensation	Stroke Sensory neuropathies Paraplegia
Poor Perfusion	Dehydration Hypotension Septicaemia Peripheral vascular disease

Effects of Ageing

In old age, the breaking strength of healed incisional wounds is lessened. Contraction, capillary regeneration and epithelialisation are slowed. Local oxygen utilisation is impaired.

Impaired Healing

The factors likely to inhibit wound healing are summarised in table 2.

Clinical

Most sores occur over bony prominences in the lower half of the body. The site says something about causation and hence, about management, eg ischeal tuberosities from sitting; greater trochanter from lying on the side etc.

Even large sores are usually painless, or painful only during the first few days. Lesions over a lateral malleolus may cause persisting pain, perhaps because of periosteal irritation. The site and severity of each sore should be recorded; perhaps using a simple grading system. (Table 3).

A photograph, tracing or measurements are useful for monitoring purposes.

Complications

The main complication is infection. A spreading cellulitis around the edge indicates a likely streptococcal cause. In deeper sores, anaerobic organisms are sometimes detected by the odour.

Table 2

Factors Likely to Inhibit Wound Healing

Reduced Arterial Pressure	
Reduced Oxygen Delivery	anaemia
	hypotension
	arteriosclerosis
Reduced Oxygen Utilisation	old age
Substrate Deficiency	vitamin C deficiency
	hypoalbuminaemia
Inappropriate Dressings	Eusol
Continuing pressure	tight packs

Table 3

A Grading System for Pressure Sores

Grade I	persisting erythema
Grade II	oedema, blistering and epidermal loss
Grade III	full skin thickness
Grade IV	subcutaneous involvement

Osteomyelitis and septicaemia are not rare. The yellow exudate on a wound surface is sometimes misdiagnosed as infective but when infection is present the usual local or systemic signs will be apparent. Septicaemia should be suspected if the patients general conditions worsens. Routine wound swabs for bacterial culture are unhelpful. They usually yield a mixed growth of contaminants.

Different Diagnosis

Even at the common sites of pressure sore occurrence there will be alternative diagnostic possibilities, these being mainly:
1. Neoplasms, especially basal and squamous cell carcinomata.
2. Discharging lesions, such as haematomata, bursitis, ischeo-rectal abscess and osteomyelitis
3. Vasculitis.

Management

Prevention has been mentioned in the section on 'risk factors'. A careful watch for persisting pallor or erythema in vulnerable areas is essential. The treatment of an established sore consists of relieving the pressure on it, getting it clean and keeping it so. Most sores will then heal themselves.

Dehydration should be countered vigorously and early intra-venous infusion may be needed. Anaemia, sub nutrition and causes of poor peripheral perfusion and oxygenation will need appropriate treatment.

Most local infections are controllable with broad spectrum penicillins. Local antibiotics should be avoided except in special circumstances, eg local Gentamycin application may be useful in pseudomonas infection, clinically obvious by the green colour. Even then, such infections usually clear without antibiotics when predisposing causes, such as maceration, resolve.

Sores of Grades I and II need little more than the relief of pressure and local protection.

For lesions on the trunk a pressure relieving mattress (see later) will be best. Padded ankle or elbow protectors are available. A wedge of foam (Lennard pad) under the calf will keep a vulnerable heel off the mattress: a bed cradle to take the weight of blankets off the feet will then be essential to prevent foot drop. If pressure can be satisfactorily relieved, there may not be a need for any dressing, except to protect from incontinence or to absorb oedematous transudate. Measures to reduce local oedema will be needed or continuing maceration will inhibit healing and predispose to infection.

Grade III and Grade IV sores require careful consideration of exudate/eschar removal, choice of local application and selection of pressure relieving device.

Excavating wounds should be palpated, using a sterile glove, to assess the amount of exudate and necrosis, the suitability for debridement, the quality of underlying tissue and the presence of deep extensions.

Wound Care

Some surface exudate is present as a part of normal healing and need not be deliberately removed unless it becomes organised into a hard eschar. Even then it will eventually separate spontaneously, if slowly. Healing time will be reduced by debridement of surface eschar and necrotic tissue, though this may need to be repeated. A variety of local applications are available for cleansing or antiseptic purposes. Clean wounds do not need them though, in practice, it is difficult to resist the temptation to put something on it. Superficial lesions can be protected with a semi-permeable film (Opsite, or similar). Sugar Paste (or honey) is a good general purpose application which encourages exudate separation by osmosis and has an antibacterial action by reducing local water vapour pressure.

In hospital practice, frequently changed saline soaks are best for surface cleansing but are uncomfortable and require much nursing time. Betadine powder or ointment has a useful iodine-releasing antiseptic quality. There are many others of similar efficacy. Absorbent microbeads (Debrisan or Iodosorb) are useful for cleaning very moist sores but are highly expensive. They are ineffective on congealed exudate or hard necrosis. A suitable plan for initiating treatment is outlined in table 4.

The use of proteolytic enzymes, hydrogen peroxide and local antibiotics/antiseptics is rarely necessary.

In slow to heal Grade III and IV ulcers, additional benefit may come from the physiotherapeutic use of ultra-violet A (sterilising, slough removal and improved healing), ultrasound (slough removal and improved healing) or ozone therapy (cleansing and pain relief).

Pressure Relief

'At-risk' patients can be managed with regular turning, a large cell ripple mattress or air bubble mattress. Such devices are useful only for prevention and not always very reliable; a heavy patient may bottom out on the underframe. Feeling between underframe and mattress will check for the latter. Patients with truncal ulcers are best managed with bed rest: the sitting position is much riskier and an inappropriate urge towards early mobilisation should be resisted. Treating established ulcers requires one of the more advanced (and expensive) support systems. Those with a double layer of large cells which are set in groups to allow controlled sequential inflation and deflation are effective (Pegasus Airwave: Huntleigh Medical). Also highly effective, but very heavy and difficult for routine nursing, are

Table 4

Pressure Grade and Treatment Plan	
Grade I	protect surface, if necessary, with Opsite or similar
Grade II	as above, or use semi-occlusive dressing, eg Granuflex. Kaltostat etc.
Grade III	clean the ulcer. Debride if needed. Use semi-occlusive dressing or thick Sugar Paste.
Grade IV	clean with saline soaks or thin Sugar Paste. Debride if needed. When clean, fill with thin Sugar Paste or *lightly* pack with absorbent dressings. Do *not* pack tightly.

water beds with thick water tables (Beaufort-Winchester). The Mediscus Low Air Loss bed uses a controlled rate of airflow through support cells to maintain a pre-set and adjustable pressure; cardiac patients can be nursed on it. The Clinitron Air Support System circulates warm air through a supportive container of microbeads. The skin of incontinent patients stays dry as urine drains through the beads.

When patients are sat out, some thought should be given to their positioning and the choice of suitable furniture. Sitting with the legs raised on a stool puts the saddle area and heels at risk and should be discouraged. Thick foam, gel cushions and alternating pressure cushions are available.

Venous Ulcers

The basic causes of venous ulcers are incompletely understood. The two main factors are chronic venous hypertension and incompetent perforating veins. Local tissue damage occurs when capillary hyperpermeability allows fibrinogen through the wall, leading to the deposition of a peri-capillary fibrin cuff. Additionally, entrapment of white cells in capillaries in regions of venous insufficiency promotes local damage, either by mechanical obstruction to blood flow or through the release of toxic white cell factors.

Leg Veins

The venous pressure in a resting leg is determined by hydrostatic factors. On standing, it slowly rises to equal that in the right atrium. In normal people the pressure falls rapidly with exercise; when there is venous insufficiency, the fall is slower and incomplete.

The main superficial veins draw blood from subcutaneous venous plexuses. A valve is situated where these plexuses drain into a main vein and if it becomes incompetent superficial varicosities result. Venous ulcers hardly ever occur when only the superficial veins are incompetent. Blood flows from the superficial veins into the deep veins through perforating veins, which contains valves to prevent reflux. When the perforating veins are functioning normally, ulcers are rare.

Proximal flow up the deep veins is promoted by a series of muscle pumps: throughout the leg the muscles are arranged in compartments for this purpose. In old age, leg ulcers are usually associated with incompetence of both deep veins and perforators. This incompetence usually happens after a deep vein thrombosis (DVT), but it may take five to fifteen years before the effects of the DVT show themselves in the post-phlebitic syndrome, which includes ulcers. During that time, organisation of a thrombus with either destruction of valves or incomplete recanalisation of the vein leads to functional incompetence or obstruction to flow or both. Venous hypertension with incompetent perforating veins allows reversal of normal blood flow and distends superficial veins. The number of open capillaries increases as a result and their walls exhibit increased permeability. Fibrinogen and other large molecules pass across the wall and that which cannot be cleared is laid down as a peri-capillary layer of fibrin. The slowed capillary circulation allows sludging of leukocytes and these release damaging proteolytic enzymes.

Incidence and Prevalence

About 1% of the adult population has had a venous ulcer at some time and about 1.5 per 1,000 population is under treatment for such at any one time. Onset is before age fifty in about 40% and in them the male:female ratio is 1. With advancing age, ulcers become much more common in women. About 1% of old women have an active leg ulcer. Despite treatment 20% will be uncured after two years and 8% or so after five years.

Clinical

Venous ulcers are shallow with an irregular contour and without a raised edge. The common site of occurrence is near the medial or lateral malleolus but sometimes elsewhere on the lower leg. A venous ulcer on the foot implies co-existing arterial insufficiency. The chief differential diagnosis is from arterial ulcers and the distinction is essential in a condition mainly treated by compressive dressings. The older the patient, the more likely are the two conditions to co-exist and an arterial contribution cannot always be excluded without measurement of arterial pressures at the ankle. (Table 5).

Table 5

Arterial and Venous Ulcers

Favours Venous	Favours Arterial
proximal to foot	usually on foot
	painful
eased by elevation	eased by dependency
other venous signs (eczema, liposclerosis)	other arterial signs (dystrophic skin, nails)
may be large	h/o coronary, stroke etc.
good arterial pulses	ankle/brachial pressure ratio <0.9

Symptoms and Signs

Ulcers become painful when inflamed and may be uncomfortable at other times; especially after prolonged standing. Pain in the leg while walking may be due to venous claudification or a sub-acute compartment syndrome. Hypertrophic osteoarthropathy occurs rarely. Skin changes are common, especially varicose eczema which includes scaling, erythema and dystrophic skin. A brownish pigmentation is due to the deposition of haemosiderin from erythrocyte leakage. In severe calf-pump failure, lipodermatosclerosis may develop and constrict the lower calf; it can be felt as a firm, sometimes woody, texture. Its onset is insidious but at an early stage there may be erythema which is often misdiagnosed as cellulitis.

Oedema is often bilateral and systematic causes need distinguishing. It inhibits ulcer healing.

Management

Compressive bandaging and supportive hosiery are the mainstays of treatment. After the ulcer has been cleaned, as discussed under 'pressure sores', graduated pressure bandaging is applied from the base of the toes to below the knee. Modern four-layer bandaging gives impressive results but not all district nurses have the time or skills. A lesser procedure can be tried in uncomplicated cases ie a non-adherent dressing then a crepe bandage then graduated compression elastic bandaging. To maintain the tension, redressing every 2–3 days in necessary.

For long-term prevention, the patient is measured for graduated pressure elastic stockings. A spare pair will be needed for washing.

The elastic compression reduces capillary permeability, improves venous return, enhances fibrinolysis and relieves discomfort. Below-knee length is sufficient. Various grades of compression are available but few old people will tolerate the higher degrees and many either will not wear such stockings or cannot get them on. Doubled-over tubigrip is a poor alternative. Elastic stockings should be worn throughout the day and preferably put on before rising from bed.

Other treatment

The androgen analogue Stanazolol enhances fibrinolysis and may improve lipodermatosclerosis but does not improve ulcer healing. Several months of treatment are needed but fortunately virilising effects are uncommon at the usual dose of 5 mgm bd. Oxpentifylline (Trental) 400 mgm tds influences fibrinolysis and white cell adhesiveness and probably ulcer healing rates.

Ultrasound and ozone have been mentioned in the section on pressure sores. For gravitational oedema, bed-end elevation by 9″ plus an hour daily lying with the legs elevated will help, if tolerated. A long acting diuretic can be tried. Mechanical compression, eg flowtron, gives short-term benefit. To get healing started in an oedematous leg there may be no alternative to a period of bed rest.

Varicose eczema may necessitate low strength corticosteroid application. It has to be remembered that such patients may have had years of treatment with local applications and they are very vulnerable to contact dermatitis. Even so, there is an occasional use for impregnated zinc bandages, especially in uncooperative patients and those who interfere with their dressings.

In old people, unexpected failure to heal should always prompt thoughts about compliance. Many welcome nurses visits or Day Hospital attendances as their only social contacts and are loathe to give up their ulcers.

Pressure Sores and Leg Ulcers

Practical Points

1. A carefull assessment of pressure sores/leg ulcers is essential before initiating treatment. This includes a knowedge of their duration, site, type (arterial or venous), condition (superficial or deep; clean or sloughy), presence or absence of infection and any associated medical condition.

2. Too much reliance should not be put on result of bacterial swabs to select an antibiotic. Local wound conditions such as cellulitis and/or lymphangitis are more useful pointers to the presence of infection.

3. Treatment of an established sore involves relieving the pressure, getting it clean and keeping it clean. Most ulcers then heal themselves.

4. It is the whole patient and not only the leg ulcer/pressure sore which needs treating. General measures include nutritional support (vitamins, high protein diet and blood transfusion, if necessary), treatment of associated medical conditions and patients' education.

5. As the 'best treatment' of pressure sores is their prevention, adequate trained staff and equipment (alternating pressure air mattresses, for example) to attend to at-risk group of patients should be ensured.

6. Compressive bandaging and supportive hosiery are the mainstays of treatment for venous ulcers.

Further Reading

1. Bader DL (ed) (1990) *Clinical practice and scientific approach*, Pressure Sores. Macmillan.

2. Eklof B, Gjores JE, Thulesius O & Bergvist D (1989) *Controversies in the management of venous disorders*, Butterworth.

3. Janssen H et (eds) (1991) *Wound healing*, Wrightson Biomedical.

4. Daniel RK, Priest DL & Wheatley DC (1981) *Etiologic factors in pressure sores: an experimental model*, Arch. Phys. Med. Rehab., 62, 492–498.

5. Burnand KG, Whimster I, Naidoo A & Browse NL (1985) *Pericapillary fibrin in the ulcer-bearing skin of the leg: the cause of lipodermatosclerosis and venous ulceration.* Brit. Med. J., 285, 1071–1072.

6. Thomas PRS, Nash GB & Dormandy JA (1989) *White cell accumulation in dependent legs of patients with venous hypertension: a possible mechanism for trophic changes in the skin*, Brit. Med. J., 296, 1693–1695.

Chapter 23

Dementia

Professor Brice Pitt MD, FRCPsych
Psychiatry of Old Age
St Mary's & The Royal Postgraduate Hospital Medical Schools
Academic Unit of Psychiatry
St Charles' Hospital
London
W10 6DZ

Biosketch:

Brice Pitt, MD BS (London), FRCPsych, DPM, is Professor of the Psychiatry of Old Age at St Mary's & the Royal Postgraduate Medical Schools, London. He was formerly Consultant Psychiatrist with a special interest in old age at the London Hospital, E1 and Senior Lecturer in the Psychiatry of Old Age at St Bartholomew's Hospital, EC1. He was chair of the Section of the Psychiatry of Old Age at the time the speciality was recognised by the Royal College of Psychiatrists & the Department of Health. Author of 'Psychogeriatrics' (1974 & 1982) and editor of 'Dementia in Old Age' (1987) (all published by Churchill Livingstone), his research interests are in the identification of depression in old age, liaison psychiatry and memory disorders.

Introduction: Prevalence

Dementia is the most dreaded and disabling affliction of later life. Extremely rare in those under 50, after that age it is ever more common: one in 20 of those over 65 and no less than a fifth of those in their 80s are affected[1]. As octogenarians are likely to increase by 40% in the next 10–20 years, and as there is no cure in sight for most dementias, the implications are ominous. The disorder is devastating, reducing the sufferer to ignominious helplessness and the family to frustration and dismay.

The prevalence in those admitted to general and geriatric wards and to residential and nursing homes is very much higher than in the community. 30% of those aged 65 or more on general hospital wards are demented, and up to 60% in geriatric wards and homes[2,3]. This is because demented people neglect themselves and are accident-prone. They get hypothermic, suffer burns, falls and fractures, take medication for other important disorders (heart failure, diabetes) irregularly and have a low threshold for delirium. Once in hospital they stay longer than other old people because of difficulties in making appropriate arrangements for their discharge; the momentum of community care is often lost very soon after the patient's admission[4]. While in hospital, problems which may arise from the demented patient's erratic behaviour, like wandering, interference, resistance to care and abuse, may be compounded by the negative attitudes of staff – resentment, irritation, fear, and rejection.

Clinical Features

The mental function especially affected in dementia is cognition, comprising memory, orientation, intellectual grasp, language and other skills; there is often a personality change too. Troublesome behaviour, such as incontinence, wandering and aggression, and psychiatric symptoms like depression, hallucinations and delusions, are usually thought to be secondary to the cognitive defects: for example, it is surely depressing to realise that one's mind is going, and it is easy to blame others for taking what one has lost or mislaid. (Figure 1).

Cognitive Changes in Dementia

Memory and Orientation

Memory loss is usually the first and most striking indication of dementia. Sometimes it develops

Figure 1

Aide Memoire for the Mental Functions Affected by Dementia

My Old Grandfather Converses Pretty Badly:

    M=emory

    O =rientation

    G =rasp

    C =onverses

    P =ersonality

    B =ehaviour

quite suddenly, for example after a stroke, but more often it is insidious, and more obvious at first to those who have not seen sufferers for a while than to those who live with them. Often a strange environment, for example a holiday location, makes painfully obvious defects which had been hardly noticed in the familiar setting of home.

Tradition has it (Ribot's Law) that the most recent memories are the first to go, and this is probably true. However, it is more difficult to check the accuracy of what is said to have happened many years ago than that which is said to have occurred yesterday. Episodic, or personal, and semantic, or general knowledge memory are both affected, so that the sufferer not only forgets the day and date, where he is and with whom (disorientation in time, space and person), his age and even his birthday but also who is the monarch and the years of the World Wars. As the dementia advances there is a tendency to live in the past. Octogenarians insist that their mothers are still alive, and angrily reject the spouse of some 50 years as an intruder.

Intellectual Grasp

Reason dwindles in dementia, so that the failing memory cannot be helped by logical deductions. 'Your mother's still alive? Well, how old is she?' *"Eighty."* 'And how old are you?' *"Eighty."* Tests like defining 'bridge' and 'opinion', or explaining how a table and a chair, or a plant and an animal are alike, or calculating change help to bring out deficiencies in intellectual grasp, as does the Clock Test: all these are found in CAMCOG, a comprehensive mental test which is part of the CAMDEX examination[5].

Communication

Serious name-finding difficulties, not only for people but for objects and concepts, are a feature of dementia and can cause great difficulties in communication. The understanding of words may also be impaired, so that the sufferer becomes ever more foreign to his own language. Reading and writing may be affected as much as speech. Usually, obvious language difficulty is apparent only late in the disorder, when it progresses to uncomprehending incoherence. However, it is likely that more subtle problems are present from an early stage[6].

Personality Change

It is not clear how often the personality changes in dementia, or even whether the change is necessarily for the worse; the latter is more likely to be brought to professional attention, so may seem more common than it really is. It is normal and appropriate to react to a failing memory by becoming rather more reclusive, avoiding unnecessary and possibly challenging social encounters, and more dependent and readier to let others take decisions. However, tactlessness, aggression and, occassionally, sexual disinhibition can cause great embarrassment and distress. *"She won't wash, and she used to be scrupulously clean."* *"She uses words I never knew she knew"*. As the dementia progresses, Shakespeare's 'second childishness' becomes painfully apparent, and the previous personality is submerged in emotional vacuity and inarticulate inertia. However, some sufferers preserve their social facade and small talk to a remarkable degree at first, and brief encounters may quite fail to detect the emptiness and disarray behind a gracious or jocular exterior.

Behavioural and Psychiatric Disorder

Wandering, incontinence, angry outbursts, stubborn denial that there is a problem and sleep reversal, being drowsy by day and restless at night, are among the most troublesome forms of disturbed behaviour. There is rarely a single explanation for any of these. Incontinence, for example, may be due to not having had the foresight to evacuate before a long journey, severe constipation with overflow, a bladder infection, diabetes, diuretic drugs, loss of cortical control,

not caring any more, not knowing where to go or how to find the lavatory or how to use it.

Psychiatric disorder was prominent in the patient examined in 1901 by Alois Alzheimer[6], whose description of the associated microscopic changes in the brain was eventually recognised in the concept 'Alzheimer's Disease'. She presented with paranoid ideas and auditory hallucinations, as well as the more traditional features of dementia. Visual hallucinations are not uncommon in dementia, especially at nightfall. Television may act as a hallucinogen – the little people on the screen seem real and can move off the screen and into the house, where they may be rather cherished, or feared and resented as intruders!

Stresses on Carers

A good half of those who suffer dementia are sustained by informal carers, usually family (most commonly the spouse or a daughter), less often friends or neighbours. The help given by these carers makes the difference between survival in the community or the necessity for institutional care (or, of course, death from neglect, which is not unknown). Carers, motivated by bonds of affection and duty, cope at considerable emotional cost: most suffer anxiety and depression to the same degree as that shown by psychiatric out-patients[7].

Categories of Dementia

The division of dementias into senile and presenile forms, according to whether they arise after or before the age of 65, is obviously arbitrary. Presenile dementias are, on the whole, more diverse, more rapidly disabling and more likely to be familial, but there are none which do not occur in later life too.

Alzheimer's Disease

Once confined to one of the commonest presenile dementias, the term has now been extended to most senile dementias because the abundance of amyloid plaques and neurofibrillary tangles in the brain described by Alzheimer characterise both. As it is hardly ethical to biopsy the brain, the diagnosis can only be confirmed post-mortem, and is made clinically by a history and mental state typical of dementia and the exclusion of other disorders. The course is inexorable, but the length varies from a year or two to more than 10. Life is shortened much more when the onset is early.

The brain is shrunken in Alzheimer's as in all dementias. At the biochemical level, nearly all the neurotransmitters are reduced, especially acetyl choline: cholinergic treatments (see below) seek to redress this.

The distinction between mild, early Alzheimer's and normal forgetfulness in old age is not always easy. One difference is that in normal forgetfulness one can be reminded of what one has forgotten, whereas in Alzheimer's it is as if it had never happened[8].

Despite a huge current research programme, the list of known risk factors for Alzheimer's, apart from age, is disappointingly meagre. Sometimes it is familial, especially the presenile form. However if an identical twin gets the disease, his genetically identical twin will not necessarily do so, so the gene cannot be wholly responsible. Recently, the locus of the gene for a rare familial variety has been identified by researchers at St Mary's Hospital, London, on chromosome 21[9]. This is interesting because people who have an extra chromosome 21, ie sufferers from Down's Syndrome, all develop the characteristic brain changes of Alzheimer's Disease if they survive into their fifth decade[10]. Other families with early onset Alzheimer's Disease have been linked to a locus on chromosome 14[11]. Serious head injury seems to increase the risk of dementia in later life[12] and is rapidly followed by plaque formation. Women seem slightly more susceptible, not only because they outlive men by five years. People of low intelligence and limited education perform poorly the kind of screening tests used to detect possible dementia (eg the Mental Test Score[13]) but this is not the same as being more at risk of Alzheimer's, which is no respecter of persons. Among environmental causes aluminium, which is at the heart of the amyloid plaque, is still under suspicion, especially as there is a weakly positive association between the prevalence of Alzheimer's and the amount of aluminium in the drinking water[14], but overall the evidence is not very persuasive. It may be true that smokers are somewhat protected from the disease, or from its diagnosis: they could well be more likely to be labelled as having Vascular Dementia simply because they smoke; or, of course, smokers may not, as a rule, live long enough to become demented!

It is now apparent that Apolipoprotein E4, the gene for which is on chromosome 19, is a risk factor for late-onset Alzheimer's Disease[15].

Vascular (Multi-Infarct) Dementia

This is the commonest presenile, and the second most common senile dementia. It proceeds by fits and starts, as small blood vessels in the brain are blocked by thromboses or emboli. Risk factors are much better established than for Alzheimer's: being male, a smoker, overweight, having high blood pressure, diabetes, blood vessel disease elsewhere (eg in the heart and feet) and having any kind of stroke[16].

Lewy Body, Parkinson's, Creutzfeld-Jakob's, Gerstmann Straussler's, Huntington's, Niemann-Pick's and AIDS

It now appears that some patients previously diagnosed as Alzheimer's disease, but with a relatively rapid, quasi-delirious course, some clouding of consciousness and excessive sensitivity to neuroleptics are suffering from Lewy body disease[17]. It has, indeed, been suggested that this is the second most common dementia in late life. In this disease the Lewy bodies in the neurones of the basal nuclei precede the onset of Parkinson's disease. Also, despite Parkinson's original description of the 'shaking palsy', which left cognition intact, dementia is a common complication of the disease which bears his name[18].

The rare, debilitating Creuzfeld-Jakob disease occurs in familial, acquired and sporadic forms. An agent – the prion – has been shown to transmit the disease experimentally to Rhesus monkeys and from one human to another by meningeal grafts, corneal transplants and growth hormone[19]. This is a spongy encephalopathy, like BSE (bovine spongy encephalopathy) of which, however, there is as yet no human case on record. Gerstmann-Straussler disease is analogous, but still rarer, almost always hereditary, associated with cerebellar ataxia, runs a much slower course and instead of a spongy encephalopathy there are prion protein amyloid plaques in the brain.

Huntington's Chorea is a hereditary, autosomal dominant disorder in which a moderate dementia and involuntary twitching develop usually in middle or later life; depression, suicide and personality disorder are common in younger members of Huntington's families. In Niemann-Pick's Disease personality change – becoming selfish, callous, thoughtless and disinhibited – because of disease of the frontal lobes precedes the other features of dementia. Dementia is often a feature of AIDS[20].

Reversible Dementias

All the above are degenerative dementias which are bound to get worse over time. There are, however, a few dementias in which deterioration can be arrested or even reversed. They include neurosyphilis; communicating hydrocephalus (often following a previous brain injury, haemorrhage or infection, which affects the drainage of cerebrospinal fluid into the venous system) in which the blockage can be by-passed by a shunt into a vein or the abodominal cavity; benign space-occupying lesions like sub-dural haematoma and meningioma; hypothyroidism; and early alcoholic dementia, which may be mitigated by vitamins B and abstinence. The commonest reversible dementia, however, is the 'pseudodementia' of severe depression, where major cognitive difficulties can respond dramatically to antidepressant drugs or even ECT (see below).

Diagnosis and Differential Diagnosis

The history and the mental state are of most importance in the diagnosis of dementia. A history, from a reliable, knowledgeable informant, of cognitive deterioration over a period of months or years, with forgetfulness, loss of former skills, word-finding difficulties and vagaries of behaviour to the fore, is typical. Questions about how the patient manages through the day, and from day to day, with what assistance and from where are highly relevant.

The use of a test in assessing the mental state is highly desirable: it gives a measure of cognition and a baseline. The best of the short tests is the Mini Mental State Exam [21]; it is reasonably comprehensive, well validated and internationally known. Scores below 24/30 suggest significant cognitive impairment, but are influenced by education, literacy and intelligence. The mental state also includes the patient's manner and appearance, mood , any delusions or hallucinations, the likely intelligence and insight.

Physical examination, the haematological and biochemical profiles, ECG and sometimes chest X-ray, CT brain scan, EEG and neuropsychological testing are also part of the dementia screen. If the patient is seen at home then its state and the living circumstances can be very revealing.

The main disorders from which dementia should be distinguished are delirium and depression.

Delirium has a short course (days or a week or two) and is often associated with a severe physical illness. Consciousness and cognition fluctuate, visual hallucinations may be prominent, and the delirium ends fairly soon in death or full mental recovery. Demented people, however, are at risk of delirium if they get physically ill[22].

Depression has a shortish course (weeks or months) and there may well be a previous history and a precipitating stress like bereavement or physical illness (eg stroke). The patient is unhappy, uneasy, off-hand, self-disparaging and has little desire to live; anorexia, weight loss, feeling worse in the morning and insomnia with early waking are typical. Agitation, retardation, severe guilt and suicidal impulses, hearing hostile voices and delusions ('I'm the worst person in the world' 'I'm ruined' 'I ought to be shot' 'They're going to get me' 'I've no insides') are less common. Cognitive impairment is rarely more than moderate, and 'don't know' answers are characteristic, while confabulation and dysphasia are not.

Many demented people, however, are also depressed, but are not able to explain how they feel. The Depressive Signs Scale[23] is designed to record behaviour which may indicate depression.

Prognosis

The earlier in life the dementia, the worse its effects on life expectancy. The dementias of old age incur more mortality from neglect than from the primary process. Thus, demented old people who are all alone will die sooner than those well cared for in the bosom of their family.

However, the progress of demetia is inexorable, though the pace varies between disorders and different people with the same disorder. The end-point is an almost total loss of memory, speech and comprehension, with extreme dyspraxia and immobility, requiring total care. However, most patients die of something else before reaching this pitiful last stage.

New Treatments

At present, prospects look brightest for vascular dementia. Smoking, obesity, hypertension and diabetes can all be brought under control, and regular low dose aspirin can safely reduce the tendency of the blood to form clots[24,25].

Despite huge research endeavour by the drug companies, no very useful drug for the memory problems at the core of Alzheimer's Disease has yet been found. Enthusiasm for tacrine, which increases acetyl choline available to nerve receptors by negating the enzyme which destroys it, has waxed and waned. It helps the failing memory of sufferers from Alzheimer's more than placebo, but there is little overall improvement in the activities of daily living, and some risk of liver damage. Benzodiazepines cause amnesia, and drugs which have an opposite effect at the benzodiazepine receptors in the brain show promise. Antioxidants to combat superoxide radicals, destructive to brain cells; an 'ACE inhibiting' drug, the effects of which on the kidney suggest that it might have a comparable biochemical action in the brain; a ganglioside (GM-1) which can reduce the degeneration of the nerve cells which use acetyl choline; and an antibiotic which may promote the activity of a centre concerned with cortico-cortical pathways are all under consideration[26]. The present position, though, is that the promise shown by these drugs in animal experiments is very feebly reflected in people with dementia.

Managing Dementia

The primary health, social, specialist, voluntary and private services have, potentially, much to offer. The GP screens his patients over 75 for dementia, and can arrange further assessment and planned support in association with Social Services and the local old age psychiatric team (or geriatric if the patient has significant physical illness or disability). Memory clinics specialise in the early identification of dementia and trials of new drugs. Meanwhile old drugs – tranquillisers, sleeping tablets, antidepressants – can be helpful if used judiciously. Thioridazine, 10–100 mg up to t.i.d. is the most widely favoured tranquilliser; temazepam 10–20 mg nocte the most often used hypnotic; and lofepramine 70–140 m daily is a useful, well tolerated antidepressant. Day care

and respite admissions can considerably ease the burden and stress on carers. Home helps, meals on wheels, community nursing, alarm systems and sheltered housing all help to keep the demented person safely at home, where most will fare best. In the UK, an attendance allowance is a gesture towards payment to informal carers, though increasingly patients are required to pay the costs of their own care, be it in an institution or at home, while they have the means.

While demented people generally do best in their own homes, some are too disabled and demanding and their carers (if any) are too stressed for them to stay there. Continuing care should be speedily provided when needed – in a psychogeriatric or geriatric ward, a residential or a nursing home according to need, means and availability. However, in many countries with large populations of the elderly (including the UK) an equitable means of providing enough of such care has yet to be found.

Acknowledgement

This chapter is partly based on an article written by the author for the Observer magazine, published on 2nd February 1992.

Dementia

Practical Points

1. Dementia is the most dreaded and disabling affliction of later life.

2. Memory loss is usually the first and most striking indication of dementia.

3. Diagnosis of Alzheimer's Disease is made clinically by a history and mental state typical of dementia and exclusion of other disorders. The diagnosis, however, can only be confirmed post-mortem.

4. Multi-infarct (vascular) Dementia is the second most common senile dementia. At present, prospects look brightest for vascular dementias.

5. Out of few reversible dementias (see text), the 'pseudo-dementia' of severe depression is the commonest.

6. The earlier in life the dementia, the worse its effects on life expectancy.

7. No very useful drug for the memory problem at the core of Alzheimer's dementia has yet been found.

8. The primary health, social, specialist, voluntary and private services have, potentially, much to offer in managing dementia.

References

1. Livingston G, Hawkins A, Graham N, Blizard B & Mann A (1990) *The Gospel Oak Study: prevalence rates of dementia, depression and activity limitation among elderly residents in Inner London*, Psychological Medicine, 20, 137–146.

2. Anderson DN & Philpott RM (1991) *The changing pattern of referrals for psychogeriatric consultations in the general hospital – an eight-year study*, International Journal of Geriatric Psychiatry, 6, 801–807.

3. Mann A, Graham N & Ashby D (1984) *Psychiatric illness in residential homes for the elderly: a survey in one London borough*, Age & Ageing, 13, 257–265.

4. Pitt B (1991) *The mentally disordered old person in the general hospital ward*, in: Handbook of Studies in General Hospital Psychiatry. Judd F, Burrows G & Lipsit D (eds) Elsevier Biochemical, Amsterdam.

5. Roth M, Huppert F, Tyms E & Mountjoy CQ (1988) *CAMDEX: The Cambridge Examination for Mental Disorders in the Elderly*, Cambridge University Press.

6. Alzheimer A (1907) *Uber eine eigenartige Erkrankung der Hirnride*, Allgemeine Zeitschrift fur Psychiatrie, 64, 146–148.

7. O'Connor DW, Pollitt PA, Roth M, Brook C & Reiss B (1990) *Problems reported by relatives in a community study of dementia*, British Journal of Psychiatry, 156, 835–841.

8. Kral VA (1978) *Benign senescent forgetfulness*, in: Alzheimer's Disease: Senile Dementia and Related Disorders. Katzman R, Terry RD, Bick KL (eds) Raven Press, NY.

9. Goate A, Charlier-Harlin MC, Mullan M et al. (1991) *A missense mutation in the amyloid precursor protein gene segregates with familial Alzheimer's disease*, Nature, 349, 704–706.

10. Ellis WG, McCulloch JR & Corley J (1974) *Presenile dementia in Down's syndrome: ultrastructural identity with Alzheimer's disease*, Neurology, 24, 101–106.

11. Schellenberg GD, Bird TD, Wijsman et al (1992) *Genetic linkage evidence for a Familial Alzheimer's disease locus on chromosome 14*, Science, 258, 668–671.

12. Heyman A, Wilkinson WE, Stratford JA et al. (1984) *Alzheimer's Disease: a study of epidemiological aspects*, Annals of Neurology, 15, 335–341.

13. Hodkinson M (1972) *Evaluation of a mental test score for assessment of mental impairment in the elderly*, Age & Ageing, 1, 233–238.

14. Martyn CN, Barker DJP, Osmond C et al. (1989) *Geographical relationship between Alzheimer's disease and aluminium in the drinking water*, Lancet, i, 59–62.

15. Poiriea J, Pavignon J, Bovthilwea D et al. (1993) *Apolipoprotein E and Alzheimer's Disease*, Lancet, 342, 697–699.

16. Hachinski VC, Iliff LD, Zilkha E et al. (1975) *Cerebral blood flow in dementia*, Archives of Neurology, 32, 632–637.

17. Forstl H & Levy R (1991) *FH Lewy on Lewy bodies, Parkinsonism and dementia*, International Journal of Geriatric Psychiatry, 6, 757–766.

18. Smith RJ & Mindham RHS (1987) *Dementia in disorders of movement*, in: Dementia in Old Age. Pitt B (ed) Churchill Livingstone, Edinburgh and NY.

19. Corsellis JAN (1979) *On the transmission of dementia: a personal view of the slow virus problem*, British Journal of Psychiatry, 134, 553–559.

20. Esiri MM & Kennedy PGE (1992) *Viral disease of the nervous system*, in: Greenfield's Neuropathology (5th edn.) Adams JH, Duchen LW (eds) Arnold, London 17.

21. Folstein MF, Folstein SE & McHugh PR (1975) *Mini-mental state: a practical method of grading the cognitive state of patients for the clinician*, Journal of Psychiatric Research, 12, 189–198.

22. Pitt B (1991) *Delirium*, Reviews in Clinical Geronotology, 1, 147–157.

23. Katona CLE & Aldridge CR (1985) *The DST and depressive signs in dementia*, Journal of Affective Disorders, 8, 83–89.

24. Katona CLE (1989) *Multi-infarct dementia*, in: Dementia disorders: advances and prospects. Katona C (ed) Chapman & Hall.

25. Meyer JS, Rogers RL, McClintic K et al (1989) *Randomized clinical trial of daily Aspirin therapy in multi-infarct Dementia. A Pilot Study*. Journal of American Geriatrics Society, 37, 549–555.

26. Bowden DM (1990) *Treatment of Alzheimer's disease. Molecular pathology versus neurotransmitter based therapy*, British Journal of Psychiatry, 157, 327–330.

Chapter 24

Care of the Terminally Ill (Palliative Care)

H. Anderson MBChB, MRCP, MD
Consultant in Medical Oncology and Palliative Care
CRC Department of Medical Oncology
Christie & Wythenshawe Hospitals
Wilmslow Rd
Withington
Manchester
M20 4BX

Biosketch:

Dr H Anderson qualified at Manchester University in 1976 and obtained the MRCP (UK) in 1980. She worked as a research registrar at the Christie Hospital and wrote her MD (1984) on 'Infection in the immunocompromised host'. She spent some time working in Sobel House in Oxford in 1990. Her current appointment is as a consultant in Medical Oncology and Palliative Care at Wythenshawe and Christie Hospitals in Manchester. Her main areas of work are lung and bowel cancer, palliative care and teaching.

Introduction

Terminal or palliative care is the active total care of patients whose disease is not responsive to curative treatment. Control of pain and other symptoms, psychological, social and spiritual problems is paramount. The goal is achievement of the best quality of life possible for patient and family. Although palliative care has been founded on the research and treatment of cancer patients, the same principles apply to all patients with a life-threatening illness. It is worth remembering in this context, however, that in the western world cancer is the second commonest cause of death, coronary artery disease being the first[1].

The uniqueness of an individual derives from a complex interaction between personality, religious beliefs, culture and previous experience. Different individuals with an apparently similar problem may have different experiences of pain or distress. Much of this is due to the uniqueness of the individual together with influence from the environment. Social isolation, emotional distress, anger and fear may all influence a patient's symptoms and the patient or carers' ability to cope.

Thus communication skills are very important in the management of palliative care. The doctor's role changes from cure to care. Care takes time, because you need to listen. It is important to remember the body language of listening so that the patient or carer will 'open up' and explain the real concerns that may be influencing symptoms and ability to cope hence the importance of having allocated enough time, sitting down, touch (eg shaking the hand) and eye contact. The doctor needs skills to interpret and explain the cause of symptoms, 'break bad news', facilitate hope (eg that a symptom can be improved), recognise and allay unfounded anxiety, appreciate the importance of sexuality and body image and identify stress in carers. Doctors have to recognise and appropriately handle normal responses to bad news and death including anger, guilt, denial and collusion. Family support is important, including preparation for death and help during bereavement.

Teamwork in palliative care is essential, and care is multi-disciplinary. The community team of GP and district nurse liaise with the hospital staff, Macmillan nurse, welfare rights officer, social worker, physiotherapist, occupational therapist, religious advisor, pharmacists, hospice staff and of course, the patient and family. In an effective team, communication between members is good[2]. A key worker system may be used. Each team member has expertise which is recognised and valued by other members of the team.

Although many patients express a wish to die at home, most will die in hospital or a hospice. Improvement in symptom control and more help in the home, eg trained volunteers and nurses (district nurses, Macmillan and Marie Curie nurses), in conjunction with hospice day care and respite care may help more patients to die comfortably at home.

This chapter deals with the more common symptom–control problems. It should be noted that apart from symptomatic medical therapy, other measures which alleviate various symptoms, *either* singly or in combination, include radiotherapy, chemotherapy, surgery, attendance at pain clinics and psychological interventions. Ethical issues are discussed in a separate chapter (Chapter 37: Law, Ethics and The Elderly).

Pain

This is an unpleasant sensory and emotional experience. Pain threshold may be raised by several factors eg sleep, rest, sympathy, understanding, companionship, diversional activities, reduction of anxiety, treatment of depression, hope, knowledge and explanation. Moderate or severe pain is experienced by one third of cancer patients on active treatment and 60–90% of patients with advance cancer[3]. Pain may be due to the cancer, the treatment (eg radiotherapy induced dysphagia or chemotherapy associated mucositis) or concomitant problems (eg arthritis, dyspepsia and angina). A thorough history, especially in relation to Provocative and Palliating factors, Quality of pain, Radiation, Severity and Temporal factors (PPQRST), in conjunction with a physical examination which looks at the sites of pain, local soft tissue or bone tenderness, limitation of joint movement, sensory changes, skin temperature, trigger points, tumour masses and abnormal neurological findings will help to determine the cause of pain. Pain charts may be used to record and reassess the sites and severity of pain.

It is very important to explain the cause of pain(s) to the patient, the proposed treatment and potential side effects. Some patients believe pain is inevitable with cancer, others may believe that the presence of pain prevents them from harming a diseased area. Others may believe that narcotics are harmful. The patient's understanding of pain and beliefs should be explored when explaining the cause of pain and proposed treatment.

Investigations may be necessary to determine the cause of pain and thus the most appropriate treatment. Pathological fractures of long bones are most quickly palliated by surgical intervention and radiotherapy is very useful for bone metastases and spinal cord compression. However, there is no reason to wait for the results of investigations before commencing analgesics. These should be prescribed according to the World Health Organisation's (WHO's) 'analgesic ladder'[4]. The first step includes non-narcotics and anti-inflammatory drugs (paracetamol or non-steroidal anti-inflammatory drugs). The second step is comprised of the weak opioids, eg co-proxamol and dihydrocodeine, and the third step of the strong narcotics, eg morphine and diamorphine. Medication is given orally unless the patient cannot swallow or is vomiting. If pain is not controlled at the maximum dose and schedule, switching to another analgesic on the same step in the analgesic ladder will be ineffective. Table 1 shows the oral morphine sulphate solution equivalent doses of several opioids. Pethidine and dextramoramide are unsuitable for long-term use because they have a short half life.

Once narcotics are prescribed, patients should routinely be given laxative because although opioid induced drowsiness or nausea are transient, constipation does not improve with time. Other side effects of narcotics include sweating, dry mouth, itching, dizziness, reduced cough reflex, mood changes and small pupils.

Starting Morphine Elixir or Sevredol

The recommended starting dose of oral morphine is 5–10 mg, 4–6 hrly. For patients failing on co-proxamal (two tablets are equivalent to 6 mg morphine) oral morphine 10 mg 4–6 hrly will be necessary. The dose may be doubled at bedtime to avoid the 2 am dose. If the first dose is ineffective, the dose may be increased by 50%.

Converting Morphine to MST

MST is a more convenient long acting morphine preparation that is prescribed every 12 hours. Once a patient's pain is controlled on oral morphine elixir, conversion to MST may be carried out: the total 24hr dose of oral morphine in mg is divided by two, eg oral morphine 10 mg every 4 hrs = 60 mg daily = 30 mg MST bd.

Parenteral Analgesics

Diamorphine is usually given subcutaneously and is preferred to morphine as it is more soluble and

Table 1

Oral Morphine Equivalent Doses

Oral agent and dose		Duration of actions (hrs)	Dose oral morphine
Buprenorphine	0.2 mg	8	10 mg
Coproxamol	two	4–6	6 mg
Codeine	120 mg	4–6	10 mg
Diamorphine	5 mg	4–5	7.5 mg
Dihyrocodeine	90 mg	3–4	10 mg
Dextromoramide	5 mg*	2–3	10 mg
Methadone	5 mg**	8–12	7.5 mg
Pethidine	80–100 mg*	2–3	10 mg
Phenazocine	5 mg	6–8	25 mg

*Short half life means poor analgesia long term
**5 mg single dose = 7.5 mg oral morphine, long half life – repeated dosing 5 mg = 15–20 mg oral morphine.

can be given in a small volume for injection. If given as a 24 hour subcutaneous infusion the total daily dose of diamorphine required is one third the total daily dose of oral morphine, eg MST 90 mg bd = 180 mg morphine daily – or 60 mg diamorphine over 24 hrs. The effect of a single bolus of diamorphine, parenterally, lasts 4 hrs. Thus a patient on MST 90 mg bd needs 60 mg diamorphine over 24 hrs or 10 mg every 4 hrs, for pain control.

Morphine Resistant Pain

It is recognised that certain types of pain do not respond fully to morphine, especially those caused by nerve damage eg post herpetic neuralgia, phantom limb pain and nerve-infiltration pain. In these patients co-analgesics are used, eg tricyclic antidepressants, corticosteroids and anti-epileptic drugs:
1. Tricyclic antidepressants eg amitriptyline 10–25 mg nocte increasing over 4–7 days to 50 mg, then weekly increases to a maximum of 75 mg or until toxicity is reached (drowsiness, dry mouth, problems with micturition or confusion). Dothiepin is less toxic and given at 50 mg increasing to a maximum of 150 mg at night.
2. Corticosteroids are of great help with nerve compression eg cord compression or pain from a pancoast tumour. Dexamethasone 8 mg–16 mg daily may convert opioid resistant pain to an opioid sensitive one.
3. Anticonvulsants eg sodium valproate 200 mg nocte building up every four days to 600 mg at night may also be helpful in neuropathic pain. Sodium valproate has a longer half life than carbamazepine and has a similar mode of action. Sodium valproate may be given as a once daily dose. If carbamazepine is prescribed in addition to a tricyclic antidepressant, accumulation of both drugs may occur.
4. Local anaesthetic agents eg flecainide or mexiletine may occasionally be used. These agents are contraindicted in the presence of congestive cardiac failure because of their negative inotropic effect. Side effects include confusion and myoclonus.

Sympathetic Mediated Pain

This type of pain is due to partial injury to the sympathetic afferents eg a Pancoast tumour. A burning or cold area is described and observed; and X-rays may show osteopenia. The superficial burning is felt in areas of arterial distribution and not nerve distribution. Sympathetic nerve blockade may help.

Bone Pain

Bone metastases may be opioid semi-responsive. NSAIDs and radiotherapy are helpful. If a patient has a pathological fracture of a long bone, consideration should be given to surgical fixation. An injection of steroids and local anaesthetic into the site of tenderness due to rib fractures may help reduce pain.

Subcapsular Haemorrhage into the Liver

This pain is acute and severe. It usually is associated with an area of local tenderness in the right hypochondrium. If the patient is already on narcotic analgesics, 2–3 times the usual dose may be needed for a few days and then gradually reduced to former levels. Corticosteriods are often helpful.

Muscle Spasm

Painful spasms may not resolve with analgesia alone. Muscle relaxants eg lioresal (baclofen) 5–10 mg tds, dantrolene 25 mg daily gradually increasing over 1–2 weeks to a maximum of 75 mg tds, or clonazepam 0.5 mg at night slowly increasing to 1–4 mg if confusion is not a problem, may be helpful.

Intractable Pain

Some patients may have pain which is difficult to manage and advice should be sought from the pain clinic or palliative care team.

Oral Problems

Patients with terminal illness often develop oral problems. Some of the causes of dry mouth are listed in table 2. The dryness may be relieved by mouthwashes, frequent sips of fluids, artificial saliva eg salivix, glandostane topical spray and sweets to stimulate salivation eg peardrops.

Table 2

Causes of Dry Mouth

Medication	tricyclic antidepressants
	phenothiazines
	anticholinergic agents
	anti-histamines
	opioids
	unhumidified oxygen
Metabolic problems	hyperglycaemia
	hypercalcaemia
Infection	candidiasis
	parotits
Radiotherapy	to the head and neck
Mouth breathing	dyspnoea,
	metabolic acidosis
Collagen diseases	

Mucositis may be caused by chemotherapeutic agents, radiotherapy, infection by candida or herpes simplex virus, or apthous ulceration.

Oral candida may occur in the elderly or in debilitated patients especially if they are taking oral antibiotics or steroids. Either classical white plaques or a generalised soreness and erythema associated with angular stomatitis may be seen. Topical therapy with nystatin or amphotericin lozenges is suitable for mild cases but systemic therapy for five days with fluconazole (50–100 mg) or ketoconazole (200–400 mg) is convenient and effective for moderate and severe infections.

Herpetic mouth infections are fairly common in debilitated patients on chemotherapy or high-dose steroids. The mouth lesions are well circumscribed, painful, non-erythematous ulcers with a white base, often seen on the lateral border of the tongue in addition to the mucous membranes. They respond well to acyclovir.

If patients have weight loss due to illness, the dentures may no longer fit and cause traumatic oral ulceration. A dental opinion should be sought in these circumstances. Patients complaining of a bad taste in their mouth may have a coated, furry tongue. This may be helped by chewing pineapple chunks (the proteolytic enzymes help remove the fur) brushing with a soft toothbrush dipped in a solution of bicarbonate of soda, or by using cider and soda water mouthwash. A disordered sense of taste is common and difficult to treat. Patients may complain that everything tastes metallic, bland, bitter, too sweet or too salty. Bitterness may be caused by foods rich in urea. This may be helped by marinating red meat before cooking. Altering the diet (eg more spicy food, Pickles, or fresh fruit) may help. Another approach is for the patient to suck sweets so that a more acceptable taste is left in the mouth.

Nausea and Vomiting

Nausea or vomiting are distressing symptoms that may lead to anorexia, weight loss and cachexia. Causes of nausea and vomiting are

Table 3

Causes of Nausea and Vomiting

1. Medication – anticancer chemotherapy, digoxin, opiates, steroids, NSAIDs, antibiotics (eg cotrimoxazole, metronidazole), oral iron, theophylline and carbamazepine
2. Radiotherapy.
3. Biochemical abnormalities – hypercalcaemia, hyperglycaemia, uraemia.
4. Infections – eg urinary tract infection
5. Gastric problems – eg hiatus hernia, peptic ulcer, gastritis, blood in the stomach, irritable bowel syndrome.
6. Raised intra-abdominal pressure – eg ascites, intra-abdominal tumour, hepatic enlargement (eg heptatic metastases).
7. Bowel obstruction – adhesions, malignancy, faecal impaction.
8. Raised intracranial pressure – cerebral haemorrhage or metastases.
9. Vestibular disorders – Meniere's disease, viral labarynthitis.
10. Coughing
11. Severe pain – eg myocodial infarction
12. Fear and anxiety

shown in table 3. The treatment of chemotherapy associated nausea and vomiting has been greatly improved by the 5HT3 anagonists and the recognition that dexamethasone is useful in reducing both acute and delayed emesis after chemotherapy. The treatment should be tailored to the cause if it can be identified. It may be necessary to use more than one class of antiemetic (table 4). Vomiting due to metabolic problems eg uraemia and hypercalcaemia may need high doses of haloperidol (2.5.–20 mg daily). Rectal prochloroperazine or domperidone, buccal prochloroperazine-buccastem 3 mg, and haloperidol drops for oral mucosal absorption (2 mg/ml and 10 mg/ml) are useful for patients unable to swallow. Transdermal hyoscine – Scopaderm TTS will slowly release 0.5 mg hyoscine into the systemic circulation over 72 hours. Several drugs, eg hysocine, cyclizine, midazolam, metoclopramide, and haloperidol may be given by subcutaneous injection or infusion.

Gastric Compression (Squashed Stomach Syndrome)

Dyspepsia with early satiation after eating, heartburn, nausea and vomiting (especially after meals), epigastric fullness and discomfort, flatulence, hiccup and anorexia may all be due to a small stomach (eg post gastrectomy, gastric cancer, linitis plastica), or by compression of the stomach by hepatomegaly, retroperitoneal tumour or enlarged retroperitoneal nodes. The

Table 4

Antiemetic Agents

Class	Use	Example
Antihistamines	brain metastases bowel obstruction motion sickness menieres disease	cyclizine 50 mg 8 hrly
Butyrophenones	uraemia hypercalcaemia chemotherapy radiotherapy opioid	haloperidol 0.5–3 mg daily 5–20 mg for uraemia
Phenothiazine	chemotherapy	prochloroperazine 5–10 mg 8 hrly
	radiotherapy	chlorpromazine 25–50 mg 8 hrly
Anticholinergics	brain metastases	hyoscine hydrobromide 0.3 mg or 0.4 mg s/c
	bowel obstruction	buscopan 10–20 mg 6–8 hrly
	motion sickness	scopaderm
Dopamine antagonist	chemotherapy	domperidone 10–20 mg 8 hrly
	opioids, oesophageal reflux	metoclopramide 10–20 mg 8 hrly
Benzodiazepines	anxiety anticipatory vomiting	diazepam 2–5 mg 8 hrly lorazepam 1–2 mg before chemotherapy
Steroids	brain metastases chemotherapy radiotherapy	dexamethasone 1–4 mg 6–8 hrly
5HT3/Serotonin antagonists	chemotherapy radiotherapy	ondansetron 8 mg 8–12 hrly (or granisetron 1 mg bd or tropisetron 5 mg daily)

A GUIDE TO THE CARE OF THE ELDERLY

patient needs a clear explanation of the mechanics of the problem, along with advice to take small frequent meals, sitting rather than reclining, in addition to an antiflatulent (eg asilone 10 mls after meals and at bedtime), metoclopramide 10 mg half an hour before meals to encourage gastric emptying, analgesia as necessary and antiemetics, eg cyclizine 50 mg eight hourly.

Weight Loss

Cachexia is seen in about a third of all cancer patients, but is more common in those with bronchial or gastric tumours. Weight loss may be a reflection of tumour burden or be a non-metastatic manifestation of malignancy. It is frequently associated with conditions leading to eating-difficulties – ill fitting dentures, oral candidiasis, anorexia, feeling easily full, nausea or vomiting. Treatment includes correction of any underlying cause and dietary advice. Meals should be small and frequent. Liquids should be as nutritious as possible. Patients with dysphagia may need liquidised meals. Oral steroids (prednisolone 10–30 mg daily or dexamethasone 2–4 mg daily) may improve the appetite. Recent studies with progestagens (medroxyprogesterone acetate and megestrol acetate) have shown that weight gain occurs in cachexic patients[5, 6].

Hiccups

Persistent hiccups are disabling, reducing appetite and causing insomnia. The causes of hiccup include gastric distention (by tumor or gas), diaphragmatic irritation, phrenic nerve irritation, cerebral tumours and uraemia. Pharyngeal irritation may abort the attack – this is achieved by sipping fluids slowly, drinking from the wrong side of a cup, placing a cold key down the back of the neck, (this hyperextends the neck and stimulates the pharynx), or by direct stimulation of the pharynx with a wooden spatula. If these measures fail, increasing the pCO2 may abort the attack (by eg rebreathing into a brown paper bag or by breath holding) Occasionally it may be necessary to prescribe oral lioresal 5–10 mg or chlorpromazine 25 mg.

Subsequent prevention of hiccups may include peppermint water to relax the lower oesophageal sphincter, an antiflatulent, metoclopramide as a gastric emptying agent, lioresal (baclofen) 5–10 mg bd or tds as a muscle relaxant, chlorpromazine 25 mg tds as a central nervous system depressant or steroids, if cerebral metastases are implicated as a cause.

Constipation

This is a common problem in the elderly and in terminal illness, being aggravated by poor diet, low fluid intake, immobility, and drugs. Impacted faeces can cause abdominal colic, distension, or even subacute bowel obstruction. Anorexia, lethargy and confusion may accompany constipation. Faeces proximal to the obstruction may liquify to seep around the impaction and cause overflow incontinence. The clinical assessment of constipation or diarrhoea includes examination of the abdomen and rectum. If faecal impaction is present, either suppositories (eg bisacodyl or glycerine) or enemas (eg phophate enema) will be necessary. Occasionally manual removal of faeces may be necessary under light sedation (ie midazolam or diazepam). Dietary advice should be given stressing the importance of a higher fluid intake, fruit juices and roughage (eg porridge). Table 5 shows the classes of drugs used to treat and prevent constipation.

Intestinal Obstruction

Patients with intra-abdominal malignancy may develop bowel obstruction. Therapy is aimed at reducing vomiting and relieving bowl spasm and pain. Surgery may be performed if obstruction is at one site only, or is due to adhesions, especially if the onset was acute and the patient was well beforehand. Bowel stimulants should be discontinued (eg metoclopramide, or senna). Emesis may be controlled by cyclizine given orally (50 mg 8–12 hrly) or subcutaneously (100–150 mg over hrs). If nausea persists haloperidol or chloromazine maybe helpful. An antispasmodic agent, eg hyoscine, may be given sublingually or subcutaneously. Analgesia should be maintained and stool softeners prescribed to prevent constipation.

(See Chapter 30 on Gastrointestinal Malignancy and Chapter 32 on Surgery in the Elderly).

Dyspnoea

Dyspnoea is a common problem in the management of a terminally ill patient. A medical history and clinical examination will help to determine the cause, along with chest radiographs, and blood tests, as clinically indicated. Causes of dyspnoea are shown in table 6. Treatment depends upon the underlying cause. Therapeutic drainage of pleural or pericardial effusions or ascites will result in rapid benefit. If re-accumulation of fluid within the pleural cavity occurs, pleurodesis should be considered. Steroids are useful in the therapy of lymphangitis carcinomatosa (prednisolone 50 mg daily or dexamethasone 8–16 mg daily, reducing generally to as low a maintenance dose as possible). Steroids are also helpful in addition to radiotherapy or chemotherapy for stridor or superior vena caval obstruction (eg dexamethasone 8–16 mg daily reducing to a lower maintenance dose). Oxygen should also be considered. The physiotherapist can teach the patient relaxation and 'breathing exercises'. A modification of lifestyle may be necessary (eg ironing while sitting down). Dyspnoea at rest is a most distressing symptom for the patient and their carers. This will often be associated with anxiety and will respond to diazepam 2–10 mg or midazolam subcutaneous infusion 10–30 mg over 24 hours. The central respiratory drive caused by anoxia will be reduced by oral morphine 5 mg, 4–6 hourly, or diamorphine 10 mg/24 hours by subcutaneous infusion. These measures often reduce patient's feelings of distress. Patients with dyspnoea often have a dry mouth, so attention should be given to oral hygiene and oxygen may need to be humidified. During the last few days of a patient's terminal illness, oral secretions may build up in the back of the mouth causing very noisy, moist sounding respiration. This may be treated with anticholinergic agents, eg hyoscine 0.4 mg given subcutaneously.

Cough

A cough is present in half of all patient dying from malignant diseases. It is a common symptom associated with chronic bronchitis, asthma, left ventricular failure, chest infection and post-nasal drip. From the history, a differential diagnosis should be sought and treatment given as appropriate. Dry cough associated with stridor due to bronchial carcinoma may be helped by intraluminal or external beam radiotherapy, or chemotherapy. In either case steroids (dexamethasone 8–16 mg daily) often also helps reduce cough and dyspnoea.

Antitussive agents may be required, eg simple linctus which may reduce pharyngeal irritation, and cough suppressents, eg pholcodeine or methadone which have a direct action on the central nervous system. Steam inhalations, alone or with benzoin tincture (Friar's balsam) or methanol and eucalyptus may help those with a cough productive of thick tenacious sputum. Chemical mucolytic agents, eg carbocisteine (mucodyne), have been tried. Nebulised saline may palliate a troublesome dry cough. If this fails, try nebulised bupivacaine (marcain) 0.25% ie 25 mg/10 mls–5 mls 4–8 hrly to block the cough receptors. It has an unpleasant taste, causes oral numbness and may make swallowing difficult for a time. Bupivacaine is given by a nebuliser or pulmasonic inhaler.

In addition to the above measures, patients with cough are usually more comfortable sitting propped up. The physiotherapist may be able to provide advice in the form of 'breathing exercises', relaxation, chest percussion and postural drainage.

Skin problems

Dying patients are often concerned about their appearance, not only about physical changes in body shape (eg visible masses, mastectomy, cachexia) but also about their complexion and skin colour. Terminally ill patients may be pale (due to anaemia, and lack of sunshine), cyanosed, jaundiced, or have a sallow complexion (secondary to uraemia, pernicious anaemia or myxoedema). Attention to make up for ladies and to the colour of clothes may be helpful in boosting morale.

Pruritus may be due to concurrent diseases (eg eczema, infection, uraemia, diabetes), drug allergy, obstructive jaundice, or the malignancy (eg Hodgkin's disease). Dry itchy skin is a common symptom. The itch may be reduced by applying emulsifying cream (eg Boots E45), reducing or cutting out the use of soap, avoiding prolonged hot baths, patting the skin dry rather than rubbing it and the avoidance of scratching. Crotaminton cream (eurax) has a mild antipuritic and anti-scabetic properties and may be helpful. Antihistamines at night may help if patients have insomnia due to itching. In patients with obstructive jaundice, stanozolol 5 mg daily may be tried.

Table 5

Oral Therapy for Constipation
1. Bowel stimulants eg senna, codanthrusate (normax).
2. Bulk forming laxatives eg methycellulose or ispaghula (fybogel or regulan).
3. Bowel lubricants eg liquid paraffin.
4. Faecal softeners eg docusate or codanthrusate.
5. Osmotic laxatives eg lactulose.
6. Salines eg magnesium salts (Epsom salts, milk of magnesia).

Patients with skin tumours may have superficial infection of the tumour mass which may bleed and discharge. Radiotherapy may be helpful in reducing the bleeding and tumour size. Oral metronidazole 200–400 mg tds reduces the odour associated with anaerobic infections. Bacterial swabs for culture and sensitivity will help to rationalise antibiotic therapy. In general, topical antibiotics are not used because they tend to cause skin sensitivity. Charcoal dressings applied over standard dressing will help to absorb the odour. Patients with troublesome breast cancer/chest wall tumours may respond to a change of hormone therapy or palliative chemotherapy. If bleeding is a problem (eg epistaxis, skin bruises) then the patient's platelet count and blood clotting tests may show deficiencies that may readily be reversed by a platelet transfusion or vitamin K. Patients on steroids easily develop skin bruising.

Oedema

Gravitational oedema is frequently seen in patients with reduced mobility eg following a stroke. Oedema may complicate cardiac failure, varicose veins and deep venous thrombosis. Other causes include hypoproteinaemia, superior and inferior vena caval obstruction, and pelvic masses. Lymphodema may occur after mastectomy, block dissection of the axilla or groin, after radiotherapy to the axilla or groin or may follow malignant obstruction of lymphatic vessels. Therapy is symptomatic, with treatment of the underlying cause. Patients with lymphoedema are prone to cellulitis and skin thickening. Early treatment of skin infection is necessary. Skin creams, eg E45, are used to keep the skin soft. Gentle massage will stimulate superficial lymphatic flow, gentle exercise will prevent stiffness while compression hose may reduce swelling[7]. Pneumatic compression therapy and compression bandaging are also helpful in some cases. Macmillan nurses and mastectomy councillors are often familiar with these techniques. Diuretics do not usually have a role in the management of lymphoedema unless lymphoedema is aggravated by the administration of steroids or NSAIDs (Non-steroidal anti-inflammatory drugs.)

Psychiatric Problems

Patients with advanced physical disease will gradually become less able to perform normal tasks. They may also have financial problems due to an inability to work and increased expenditure because of their illness. Furthermore, they may lose self esteem through loss of their role in the household or through a new and unpleasant body image that they strive to accept. Pain may be debilitating, and the family unit may be under considerable strain.

It is not surprising, therefore, that about 30% of cancer patients suffer from significant anxiety or depression at some time during their illness[8]. Older patients perceive these psychiatric problems as a failing and frequently will not report the problems to the doctor or nurse. Anxiety and depression can be managed conventionally. Midazolam, can be used as a subcutaneous infusion (20 mg–30 mg over 24 hrs) in terminally ill patients with agitation. Confusion, delerium and dementia are other distressing symptoms, more so for the carers. The causes of these should be sought and treated appropriately.

Raised Intracranial Pressure

The typical symptoms of raised intracranial pressure are early morning headaches with vomiting.

Table 6

Causes of Dyspnoea (See Chapter 12, on Dysponoea)

Acute
Pulmonary oedema
Infection
Trauma
Pneumothorax
Fractured rib(s)
Pleurisy
Asthma
Pulmonary emolism
Metabolic acidosis
Superior vena caval obstruction
Infiltration and occlusion of the main airways

Chronic
Obstructive airways disease
Emphysema
Asthma
Congestive cardiac failure
Pleural effusion
Ascites
Anaemia
Lung metastases
Lymphangitis carcinomatosa
Abdominal masses
Anxiety

Other neurological symptoms and signs may also be present, eg poor memory, motor weakness, change of personality, impaired intellect, incoordination weakness and falls. Dexamethasone 4 mg qds relieves symptoms by reducing cerebral oedema. If vomiting is a problem, the first dose should be given parenterally. If there is no benefit after 7–14 days the therapy should be discontinued. If there is benefit, the dose should be gradually reduced to a maintenance dose that will control symptoms. Patients should be warned about the side effects from steroids. Prophylactic H2 antagnosits may be necessary, especially in patients with previous dyspepsia.

Palliative cranial irradation may help to control the symptoms but will cause alopecia. Analgesics should be given for the pain, and also antiemetics and anticonvulsants as indicated. Patients should be instructed not to drive.

Spinal Cord Compression

If a patient develops back pain with leg weakness and problems with bowel or urinary problems the diagnosis of spinal cord compression should be considered. This is a medical emergency, and neurosurgeons will decompress the spinal cord if the lesion is at a single site and the patient had a reasonable quality of life beforehand. Surgical intervention may prevent a patient dying paraplegic. High dose steroids should be given at the time of diagnosis (dexamethasone 16 mg daily). Radiotherapy may be helpful alone or after neurosurgery, and chemotherapy is helpful in some malignancies (eg myeloma and lymphoma). Physiotherapy is necessary for rehabilitation in those who have received active therapy. In patients with irreversible cord compression physiotherapy may help prevent stiffness and bedsores. Aids are available and are described in a catalogue from the 'Disabled Living Foundation'.

Metabolic Problems

Hypercalcaemia will cause nausea, vomiting, polyuria, polydipsia, confusion and ultimately coma and death, if left untreated. Its treatment includes rehydration and bisphosphonate therapy with treatment of the underlying cause, if possible[9]. Hypercalcaemia may occur as a non-metastatic manifestation of malignancy, and when corrected the patient's quality of life will improve. Other metabolic problems include hyponatraemia causing weakness or confusion, and renal failure which may be associated with vomiting. These will need appropriate therapy.

Subcutaneous Infusion Therapy

Parental analgesia is often necessary for dying patients who cannot swallow or have troublesome vomiting. Intravenous therapy is not always convenient, and many drugs and indeed fluid may be given by subcutaneous infusion. Portable syringe drivers are available for hospital or home use (eg Graseby pump). Several drugs may be given subcutaneously eg metoclopramide (30–60 mg/day), haloperidol (5–20 mg/day), hyoscine (0.8–1.2 mg/day), and midazolam (20–30 mg/day). Other agents may be infused subcutaneously, eg cyclizine, and dexamethasone, but these may cause local skin irritation. Diamorphine is compatible with metoclopramide, haloperidol, hyoscine or cyclizine[10]. Sites suitable for subcutaneous infusion therapy are the upper chest, upper outer arm, abdomen and thighs. A daily change of infusion site may reduce the tendency to form sterile granulomas which, although red and unsightly, are not usually painful.

Conclusion

Control of symptoms enables a terminally ill patient to face death more comfortably. A good doctor-patient relationship and communication skills are essential. The aim is for the patient to be as active as possible and for as long as possible. Poor symptom control often means that relatives cannot cope looking after the patient at home and may have problems after bereavement.

References

1. Smyth JF (1991) *Oncology*, in: Davidson's Principle and Practice of Medicine, 16th Edition, Churchill Livingstone.

2. Robinson L & Stacy R (1994) *Palliative care in the elderly: setting practice guidelines for primary care teams*, BS Gen Practice, 44, 461–464.

3. Foley KM & Sundaresan N (1985) *Management of cancer pain*, in: Cancer principles and practice of oncology. Devita VT, Hellman S & Rosenberg SA (eds). 2nd Edition, 1940–1961.

4. WHO (1990) *Cancer pain relief and palliative care*. Report of a WHO expert committee. WHO Technical Report Series, 804, Geneva.

5. Talbot DC, Slevin ML, Joel SP, Stubbs L, Plant H, Allbright A, Lynch D & Hemmings B (1988) *A randomised, double blind, placebo controlled trial of medroxyprogestrone acetate (MPA) in cancer cachexia*, B J Cancer, 58, 267.

6. Tchekmedyian NS, Tait N, Moody M & Aisner J (1987) *High-dose megestrol acetate. A possible treatment for cachexia*, JAMA, 257(9), 1195–1198.

7. Badger C (1987) *Lymphoedema. Management of patients with advanced cancer*, The Prof Nurse, (Jan) 100–102.

8. Derogatis LR, Morrow GR, Fetting J, Penman D, Piasetsky S, Schmale AM, Henrichs M & Carnicke CM (1983) *The prevalence of psychiatric disorders among cancer patients*, JAMA, 249, 751–757.

9. Ralton SH, Gallacher SJ, Patel U, Dryburgh FJ, Fraser WW, Cowan RA & Boyle IT (1989) *Comparison of three intravenous bisphophonates in cancer-associated hypercalcaemia*, Lancet, ii, 1180–1183.

10. Allwood MC (1984) *Diamorphine mixed with antiemetic drugs in plastic syringes*, B J Pharm Practice (March), 88–90.

Further Reading

1. Tycross RG & Slack SA (1990) *Therapeutics in the terminally ill*. 2nd Editions, Churchill Livingstone.

2. Regnard CFB & Davies A (1986) *A guide to symptom relief in advanced cancer*, Haigh & Hochland Ltd Manchester.

3. Working Party on Clinical Guidelines in Palliative Care. *Guidelines for managing cancer pain in adults 1994*. The National Council for Hospice and Specialist Palliative Care Services.

Chapter 25

Elder Abuse and Neglect

Barbara E Cammer Paris, MD
Assistant Professor of Geriatrics and Medicine
Department of Geriatrics and Adult Development
Mount Sinai Medical Center
New York
New York 10029
USA

Biosketch:

Barbara Paris is Assistant Professor of Geriatrics and Medicine at the Mount Sinai School of Medicine in New York City, Medical Director, Coffey Geriatrics Associates and former medical consultant to the Mount Sinai Hospital Elder Abuse Team. Dr Paris has also published articles related to peripheral vascular disease, health promotion and disease prevention, and end of life decisions.

Introduction

Abuse of the elderly has been documented over many centuries throughout the world, however, mistreatment by family members has, in the most recent decade, received heightened attention from governmental agencies and health care providers[1, 2]. This has resulted in a greater awareness of abuse and neglect of the elderly, but there remains a very large number of undetected cases[3]. This chapter focuses on the role of professionals in detection, assessment and intervention in cases of abuse and neglect of the elderly residing in the community, where it is both most likely to go unnoticed, and to occur at the hand of a family member.

Definitions

Abuse can occur either as a continuum throughout life or its onset may occur in later life. Although there is no universal definition of the term 'elder abuse' in the literature both in terms of a specific age of onset and in terms of what constitutes abuse, it may be categorised as psychological, financial, physical, intentional and unintentional[2, 4, 5, 6]. Table 1[7] is an overview of various types of mistreatment. It should be noted from this table that neglect is also considered a type of mistreatment. While the signs and symptoms outlined on this table can be due to factors other than abuse or neglect, a clustering of several of these may be suggestive of mistreatment[8]. Often, several types of mistreatment occur simultaneously and, over time, are also likely to escalate both in frequency and severity.

Categorisation of the type of mistreatment is helpful in planning intervention. For example, an illiterate spouse caring for a frail, elderly, medically complex patient cannot read the label on the medication bottle and consequently dispenses the medication incorrectly, leading to an untoward side effect in the patient. This situation is characterised as unintentional neglect, as there is no intent to harm the patient. In this instance, the intervention might be education of the caregiver regarding proper dosage of the medication. In other situations, there is deliberate intent to harm, inflict physical pain, emotional suffering or take advantage of another person to fulfil one's own needs. Verbal threats, stealing money or possessions and inflicting bodily harm are all examples of intentional abuse. Indeed, abuse of

Table 1[7]

Types of Mistreatment and Possible Patient Signs and Symptoms of Abuse and/or Neglect

Physical Abuse	Sexual Abuse	Psychological/ Emotional Abuse	Financial/Material Abuse	Neglect

• Fractures
• Welts
• Lacerations
• Punctures
• Burns
  Unusual location, type, or shape similar to an object (ie Iron, cigarette burn)
• Bruises
  Presence of old and new
  Shape similar to an object (ie beltmarks, fingers)
  Bilateral on upper arms (from holding or shaking)
  Clustered on trunk (from repeated striking)
	• Torn, stained, bloody underclothing
	• Difficulty in walking or sitting
	• Pain, itching, bruising, or bleeding in genital area
	• Unexplained venereal disease or genital infections
		• Confusion
		• Excessive fears
		• Insomnia, sleep deprivation or need for excessive sleep
		• Change in appetite
		• Unusual weight gain or loss
		• Loss of interest in self, activities or environment
		• Ambivalence
		• Resignation
		• Withdrawal
		• Agitation
			• Inaccurate, confused, or no knowledge of finances
			• Unexplained or sudden inability to pay bills, purchase food or personal care items
			• Disparity between income/assets and lifestyle
			• Fear or anxiety when discussing finances
			• Unprecedented transfer of assets
			• Extraordinary interest by family member in older person's assets.
				• Dehydration
				• Malnutrition
				• Hypo/Hyperthermia
				• Excessive dirt or odour
				• Inadequate or inappropriate clothing
				• Absence of eyeglasses, hearing aids, dentures or protheses
				• Unexpected or unexplained deterioration of health
				• Decubitus ulcers ('bedsores')
				• Signs of excess drugging, lack of medication or other misuse (eg decreased alertness, responsiveness and orientation)

Adapted from Risa Breckman and Ron Adelman, *Strategies for Helping Victims of Elder Mistreatment*, a Sage Hieman Services Guide No 53, pp 35–41, copyright (c) 1988 by Sage Publications, Inc. Reprinted by permission of Sage Publications Inc.

the elderly encompasses a broad range of acts, often in the setting of complex family dynamics and stresses.

Barriers to 'Abuse'-Detection

The crucial intial step in the process of overcoming the problem of abuse of the elderly is detection of a situation which is frequently obscured by many barriers[9]. These barriers, listed in table 2 and described below, include resistance to disclosure by the victim, lack of training of professionals in the process of screening and assessment, isolation of the victim in the community, ageist attitudes of victims and resistance of health care providers to intervene.

Victim's feelings of embarrassment or guilt about the abuse is often a significant barrier to detection. The victim may also worry about retaliation or some form of punishment by the abuser as a consequence of exposing the situation. Moreover, the victim may fear institutionalisation (in the form of nursing home placement) as the only alternative solution to the problem. Although some victims may be willing to discuss their abusive situation with a health care provider, victims often minimize the seriousness of the abuse and display tremendous loyalty to their abuser.

Lack of training of professionals in appropriate methods to interview patients and family members can also result in significant underdetection of cases of abuse and neglect. Most health care providers have not had structured training in screening for abuse or in methods of conducting interviews with potential victims and abusers.

Isolation of the victim is another serious barrier to detection of abuse and neglect. Elderly victims may become secluded as abuse escalates, feeling uncomfortable having visitors in their homes or communicating with others about their problems. Abusers often isolate elderly victims by denying them access to friends and the telephone and escorting the victim when outside contacts are made in order to ensure secrecy. Some victims are functionally impaired and physically dependent on the abuser for access to the outside world.

A visit to the hospital or doctor may be the only contact the victim has with the outside world for several months or even years. Ageist attitudes of victims can also result in failure to

Table 2

Barriers to Detection of Abuse

Victim's Resistance to Disclose Abuse
Fear, shame, embarrassment about abuse by a family member or close friend often prevents the victim from reporting the abusive situation.

Lack of Training of Professionals
Lack of training in appropriate interviewing skills, screening techniques and assessment tools prevent health care workers from detecting abuse.

Isolation of Victims
Denial of victims access to communicate with the outside world, prevents disclosure.

Ageist Attitudes of Victims
Victim's view themselves as a burden to their caregivers, and thereby deserving of maltreatment.

Resistance of Health Care Providers to Intervene
Fear of interfering in a domestic problem, fear of litigation and a sense of inability to affect a positive change in the situation may prevent professionals from diagnosing abuse.

---

recognise an abusive situation. A victim may have the attitude that old people are a burden to their family and therefore deserving of neglect or even mistreatment.

Finally, a very significant barrier to detection may actually be resistance by the health care provider. For example, the doctor's response to an 80 year old man who tells him that his grandson is stealing his cheques is as follows: "*I know your grandson, he would never do that, maybe you forgot where you put your cheques!*". The health care professional may fear involvement with litigation, or may be hesitant to aggravate the present situation without feeling knowledgeable regarding alternative suggestions.

In summary, there are many complex and overlapping barriers to detection of abuse and neglect of the community-residing elderly, as there may be no one individual indicator of an abusive situation, and the health care provider may need to rely upon a clustering of signs and symptoms to make an appropriate decision.

Assessment

Specific risk factors for abuse and neglect by family members have been identified, including family member's psychopathology, transgenerational

---

violence, dependency, isolation, stress and living arrangements as described in table 3[7]. These can assist health care providers in identifying potential victims. Once there is suspicion of abuse, the next step in the process is assessment. Ideally, assessment is provided by a multi-disciplinary team, including a physician, nurse and social worker with different areas of expertise and training[10, 11]. Assessment is an ongoing process, which often requires several meetings to complete an initial evaluation. Table 4 outlines the areas that should reasonably be covered in an assessment of the potential victim by each member of a multi-disciplinary health care team. Although this outline categorises the different role of each team member, there is often overlap. In addition to comprehensive geriatric assessment which can help identify patients with risk factors and high potential for abuse or neglect, one can utilize a specific screening assessment tool to assess geriatric patients for mistreatment (table 5)[12]. It is critically important for health care providers to spend time alone interviewing the elderly patient.

Table 3

Risk Factors for Abuse & Neglect[8]

Family Member Psychopathology
Presence of mental illness, mental retardation, dementia, drug or alcohol abuse in the victim or abuser.

Transgenerational Violence
Family history of violence resulting in a pattern of inappropriate behaviour.

Dependency
Patient or family member dependent on the other for housing, finances, emotional support or caregiving related to activities of daily living due to medical or functional disabilities.

Isolation
Patient does not have the opportunity to relate to people or pursue activities and interests in a manner he or she chooses.

Stress
Stressful life events such as loss of a job, moving, death of a partner, physical illness, precipitate abuse and neglect of dependent family member.

Living Arrangements
Patient and family member live together.

Adapted from Risa Breckman and Ron Adelman, *Strategies for Helping Victims of Elder Mistreatment*, a Sage Hieman Services Guide No 53, pp 35–41, copyright (c) 1988 by Sage Publications, Inc. Reprinted by permission of Sage Publications Inc.

It is important to keep in mind that even a patient with cognitive deficits can communicate feelings about their situation.

In some situations, it may also be feasible and important to do a formal assessment of the potential abuser. This assessment would include an evaluation of living arrangements, finances and psychosocial stresses. Relevant information about the potential abuser might include drug or alcohol dependency and mental illness or disability. Financial dependency of the abuser on the victim for food and shelter may also adversely affect their relationship. On the other hand, dependency of the victim on the abuser may result in overwhelming caregiver stress. The abuser should be interviewed in a non-

Table 4

Multi-Disciplinary Team Assessment of the Victim

Medical Assessment
Comprehensive history (patterns of attaining medical care, consistency of history with medical observations).

Complete physical examination (including neurological examination, gait observation and inspection of the genitalia).

Cognitive assessment (assess ability to comprehend the risks and consequences of their actions).

Mood assessment (observe for signs of depression, withdrawal and fear without any clear signs of cause and effect).

Nursing Assessment
Functional assessment (activities of daily living, instrumental activities of daily living, assistive devices).

Nutritional assessment (24 hour dietary recall).

Skin assessment (turgor, traumatic lesions, ulcerations).

Medication compliance.

Social Work Assessment
Description of 'a typical day' (social contacts, adequate assistance for functional limitations).

Living situation (adequacy of food, clothing, shelter, phone accessibility, safety of the environment, lives alone or with others).

Financial assessment (income, expenses, resources, savings, power of attorney, dependants, homeowner, possession of lease).

Psychosocial assessment (stresses, job loss, death, divorce, substance abuse, family supports, living arrangements, isolation).

A GUIDE TO THE CARE OF THE ELDERLY

judgemental and timely fashion so as to avoid collusion with the victim in terms of co-ordinating responses to specific questions.

Intervention – Various Strategies

Once the assessment process has been initiated, one can begin to work on intervention in coping with situations of elder abuse or neglect. Intervention too, is often a multi-step, complex process involving a team of professionals[13, 14]. Options will be based on information obtained during the assessment. It is important to ascertain how the patient feels about the abuse and if any plans to cope with the situation have been formulated or implemented. Additionally, one needs to get a sense of over what period of time the abuse has been occurring, whether or not it is escalating in intensity or frequency, and whether the victim notes any precipitating factors for the abuse to occur. This information will help guide the planning of intervention strategies. For example, if the patient is in a life threatening situation, alternative living arrangements for the victim or abuser need to be explored. If the abuse is ongoing and chronic in nature, initial interventions may include education of the victim regarding emergency phone numbers for police, shelter, abuse hotlines and the establishment of safety plans. Table 6 is a comprehensive overview of possible interventional strategies, not all of which may be appropriate on an individual case basis. This table has been sub-divided into both short and long-range strategies for intervention. The main goal of short-range strategies is to prevent further injury or harm to an individual victim. For example, it is important for a health care provider to remain accessible to the victim who initially may reject offers for assistance, as victims frequently fluctuate between the stages of denial and acknowledgement of the abusive situation. This could be monitored by telephone or increased visits from the health care provider. The main goal of long-range strategies is prevention of situations that lend themselves to neglect and abuse of the elderly.

More intensive research and resources are needed to address this potentially devastating consequence of ageing so that we can better understand the problem and thereby develop effective programmes to serve victims and identify those at risk from mistreatment. In the meantime, screening for elderly abuse as part of yearly

Table 5

Elder Abuse/Neglect Screening Assessment Tool

Introductory comment
No matter how well people get along there are times when they disagree on major decisions, get annoyed about something the other person does, or just have arguments because they are in a bad mood or for some other reason. People also use many different ways of trying to settle their differences. I am going to read you some things that people do when they have arguments or problems, and ask you whether this has ever happened to you.

Ask patient directly:	Yes	No
1. Has anyone ever hurt you?	___	___
2. Has anyone ever touched you when you didn't want to be touched?	___	___
3. Has anyone forced you to do something against your will?	___	___
4. Has anyone ever taken anything that was yours, without permission?	___	___
5. Have you ever given anything away even though you really didn't want to?	___	___
6. Does anyone ever talk or yell at you in a way that makes you feel lousy or bad about yourself?	___	___
7. Are you afraid of anyone?	___	___
8. Has anyone ever threatened you?	___	___
9. Has anyone ever refused to help you take care of yourself when you needed help?	___	___
10. Has anyone ever used your money in a way you did not like?	___	___
11. Do you have ready access to a telephone?	___	___
12. Do you live with anyone or have any close family members who abuse drugs or alcohol, or have a psychiatric illness?	___	___
13. Do you feel that your basic needs for food, clothing, shelter and medications are adequately available to you all the time?	___	___
14. Are you able to go out of your house when you want?	___	___
15. Are you happy with how often you see your relatives and family?	___	___

If the answers to any of questions 1–11 is 'yes' or 12–15 is 'no' please explore further.

Table 5 cont.

Physical Assessment

Describe patient's general appearance (eg, inadequate or inappropriate clothing, dirty or odorous):
Check if any of the following are present and describe:

Bruises	_____
Fractures	_____
Burns	_____
Lacerations	_____
Abrasions	_____
Rashes	_____
Scars	_____
Welts	_____
Punctures	_____
Decubitus/Pressure sores	_____
Other	_____

Dating of Bruises:

0–2 days:	Swollen, Tender
0–5 days:	Red-Blue
5–7 days:	Green
7–10 days:	Yellow
10–14 days:	Brown
1–2 days:	Clear

Stages of Decubitus/Pressure Ulcer

I Redness not resolving after 20 minutes following pressure relief, epidermis intact.

II Break in skin involving the epidermis. May appear as a blister with erythema and/or induration.

III Skin break exposing sub-cutaneous tissue.

IV Skin break exposing muscle and bone.

Assistive Devices

If a patient needs and does not have devices, or patient has but does not use devices, this may be evidence of neglect.

Device	Needs	Has	Uses	Explanation
Dentures	_____	_____	_____	_____
Cane	_____	_____	_____	_____
Walker	_____	_____	_____	_____
Wheelchair	_____	_____	_____	_____
Hearing Aid	_____	_____	_____	_____
Other	_____	_____	_____	_____

Ask patient directly:
has anyone ever prevented you from obtaining or using aids?
*Yes   No
*If Yes, please explore further.

health assessment of patients over 75 by General Practitioners in the United Kingdom will be a step in the right direction. However, to do this effectively, there needs to be national and local guidelines on this very sensitive issue[15]. Most recently, in the United States, The American Medical Association has published a monograph on diagnostic and treatment guidelines for elderly abuse and neglect[16].

Table 6

Strategies for Intervention

(a) **Short Range Strategies**
– Written documentation (history, physical findings, inconsistent accounts of events).
– Education and support counselling (individual and group counselling of victims to overcome feelings of guilt, self-blame and low self-esteem; counselling of abusers, drug rehabilitation programmes).
– Community resource linkages (senior citizens centres, adult day care programmes, social services agencies, support groups, protective services for adults).
– Legal services (criminal court, family court, police, orders of protection, protection of income and assets).
– Alternative housing (for abuser or victim, shelters, respite care programmes, nursing homes).

(b) **Long Range Strategies**
– Training programmes for caregivers
– Education of health care providers
– Public awareness education programmes
– Governmental policies (voluntary and/or mandatory reporting, funding of educational programmes and services for the elderly
– Research initiatives (conferences, data collection, studies)

Elder Abuse and Neglect

Practical Points

1. Elder abuse is an increasing problem both in the USA and the UK – an estimated half a million elderly people in the United Kingdom are at risk for abuse and neglect.

2. Elder abuse and neglect are part and parcel of inadequate care of the elderly – the priority is to suspect it, followed by careful assessment and finally appropriate interventions.

3. Abuse and neglect can occur anywhere – in patients' own homes, residential homes of every type or in hospitals.

4. Elderly people with communication problems (ie those with strokes, Parkinson's disease and dementia) are at the greatest risk of being abused.

5. In keeping with the general ethos of the care of the elderly, management of elder abuse and neglect needs a multi-disciplinary approach.

6. Perhaps the most effective strategy to protect elderly people from abuse is legislation – in the USA, 48 states have legislation in place for this purpose.

7. Reserch on elder abuse and neglect is one area in the care of the elderly where the United Kingdom can learn from the USA. Happily, studies are underway in the UK.

References

1. Tomlin S (1989) *Abuse of elderly people: an unnecessary and preventable problem*. A public information report from The British Geriatric Society London.

2. Wolf RS (1988) *Elder abuse: ten years later*, Journal of the American Geriatrics Society, 36, 758–62.

3. *Abuse of Elderly People*. Care of the Elderly, 1989, 1:57.

4. Council of Scientific Affairs (1987) *Elder abuse and neglect*, Journal of the American Medical Association, 257, 966–71.

5. Bennett G (1990) *Action on elder abuse in the 90's: new definition will help*, Geriatric Medicine, 20, 53.

6. Lachs MS & Pillemer K (1995) *Abuse and neglect of elderly persons*, New England Journal of Medicine, 332, 437–443.

7. Breckman RS & Adelman RD (1988) *Strategies for helping victims of elder mistreatment*, Sage Publications, Newbury Park, 35–41.

8. The Mount Sinai/Victim Services Agency Elder Abuse Project (1988) *Elder mistreatment guidelines for Health Care Professionals; detection, assessment and intervention*, New York City: Mount Sinai Medical Center, 6.

9. Kosberg JL (1988) *Preventing elder abuse: identification of high risk factors prior to placement decisions*, The Gerontologist, 28, 43–50.

10. Bloom JS, Ansell P & Bloom MN (1989) *Detecting Elder Abuse: A guide for Physicians*, Geriatrics, 44, 40–4.

11. *Abuse of the elderly: aetiology, natural history and the doctor's role*. Geriatric Medicine. Meeting Report. November 1988, 18, 33.

12. Ansell P, Bloom J & Pillemer K. *Elder abuse/ neglect screening assessment tool*. Personal Communication.

13. Anetzberger GJ, Lachs MS, O'Brien JG, et al. (1993) *Elder mistreatment: a call for help*, Patient Care, 93–130.

14 Matlaw JR & Spence DM (1994) *The hospital elder assessment team: a protocol for suspected cases of elder abuse and neglect*,

Journal of Elder Abuse and Neglect, 6, 23–27.

15. Noone JF, Decalmer P & Glendenning F (1993) *The General Practitioner and Elder Abuse* in Mistreatment of Elderly People, 136–147, Sage Publications.

16. *American Medical Association Diagnostic and Treatment Guidelines on Elder Abuse and Neglect*. October 1992.

Acknowledgement

The author wishes to thank Pamela Ansell, MSW, for her proficiency and expertise in reviewing this chapter.

Acknowledgement

The editors acknowledge their gratitude to Sage Publications Inc. for their kind permission to reproduce the Tables 3.2 Page 39 (re. Possible Indicators of Physical Mistreatment); and Table on Risk Factors, Pages 35–36 from the book, *Strategies for Helping Victims of Elder Mistreatment,* by Risa S Breckman and Ronald D Adelman (A Sage Hieman Services Guide, No 53). Also Table 3.1 (re: Possible Indicators of Psychological mistreatment) on p 37 and Table 3.3 (Possible indications of Financial Mistreatments on p 41.

Section C

Some Important Specific Diseases

Chapter 26

Management of Hypertension in the Elderly

Prof J D Swales MA, MD, FRCP
Department of Medicine
University of Leicester
Clinical Sciences Building
Leicester Royal Infirmary
Leicester
LE2 7LX
UK

Dr R B Shukla MD, FRCPI
Consultant Physician
Dept of Medicine for the Elderly
North Manchester General Hospital
Manchester
M8 6RL
UK

Biosketch:

Professor J D Swales is Head of the Department of Medicine, at Leicester University Medical School. He is ex-president of the British Hypertension Society and has authored several books on hypertension, most recently the large multi-author 'Textbook of Hypertension' (Blackwells 1994). His interests include experimental hypertension and the management of high blood pressure in man. Professor Swales has been appointed new director of Research and Development at Department of Health from 1 January 1996.

Dr Raghu B Shukla – a General Practitioner turned Geriatrician – is Consultant Physician in Department of Medicine for the Elderly at North Manchester General Hospital. His interests include Hypertension, Cardiac failure, Osteoporosis and Falls, Housing and Prescribing in the elderly. He has travelled widely (USA, Canada, Saudi Arabia and Australia) professionally. He has several publications to his credit, including a book, Care of the Elderly (HMSO 1994).

Introduction

Elevated blood pressure is the most important risk factor for stroke, in addition to being a major risk factor for ischaemic heart disease, cardiac failure, peripheral vascular disease and renal failure. Recognition of hypertension is, therefore, of major relevance to medical care, particularly as we now know that some of these risks can be reversed by treatment.

Epidemiology

Systolic blood pressure rises throughout life. Diastolic blood pressure rises steadily until the 50s when it flattens out and begins to fall (figure 1). Hence elderly subjects as a group show increased pulse pressure reflecting the greater difference between systolic and diastolic pressure. This increase in pulse pressure is due to progressive rigidity in the aorta and large arteries, reducing their compliance. As a result, the arterial pulse wave produced by contraction of the left ventricle is not damped to the same extent as it is in the younger person and early reflection waves are increased.

Just as there is no discontinuity in the risk curve for blood pressure and cardiovascular disease, there is no discontinuity in the distribution of either systolic or diastolic blood pressure. Both conform to a smooth but skewed unimodal curve. As a result, we cannot separate out a discrete population of patients with 'hypertension' or a separate population of patients at increased risk.

Where we draw the line is quite arbitrary. Although the World Health Organisation suggested a dividing line of 160/95 mmHg, this has lost much of its usefulness with increasing trials and epidemiological data. This figure is often used to define patients who can be recruited to clinical trials but has no real meaning in everyday clinical practice.

Where we draw the line between normotension and hypertension makes an enormous difference to the apparent prevalence. Thus, if we use a diastolic blood pressure of 110 or more on a single reading, some population studies have revealed a prevalence of 2–3% for 'hypertension'. If we reduce our criterion to 90 mmHg, the figure will rise to over 15–25% (Figure 2). The other factor which makes an enormous difference

Figure 1a & b

Blood Pressure Trends with Age in Men and Women.

Note the fall in diastolic blood pressure in elderly subjects. Figures show upper and lower percentiles of blood pressure for age (systolic and diastolic).

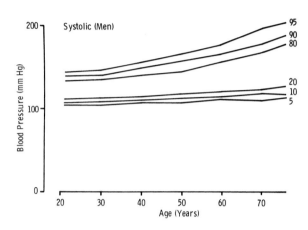

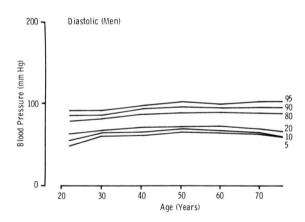

to the apparent prevalence of hypertension is the use of single or repeated readings of blood pressure. Thus, when blood pressure is measured repeatedly in populations, it shows a progressive fall as patients become habituated to the measurement. As a result, since the population blood pressure distribution is lower on the third measurement, the apparent prevalence of hypertension would also be lower when we use a single criterion. Indeed, the apparent prevalence of hypertension falls to a half or one-third on the second reading. This underlines the importance

Figure 2

Effect of Changing the Diagnosis Criterion on the Apparent Prevalence of Hypertension

Relatively few patients are defined using a criterion of 110 but the number increases enormously when a lower criterion is used.

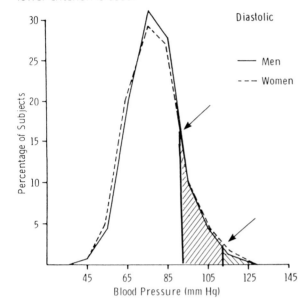

of repeated measurement of blood pressure before decisions are made about treatment.

Measurement of Blood Pressure

The mercury sphygmomanometer is still the most reliable means of measuring blood pressure in ordinary clinical practice. Aneroid sphyg-momanometers and electronic sphygmoman-ometers are useful where they have been carefully standardised against a mercury model, but they are more unreliable and if not properly stan-dardised can give rise to significant under-estimation or over-estimation of blood pressure. For conventional sphygmomanometery with a mercury containing instrument, the manometer should be upright and should read zero before the cuff is inflated. Valves should be clean and allow free rise and fall of the mercury column. The rubber occlusive cuff should cover at least 80% of the upper arm circumference. If it does not (as when an ordinary cuff is used in an obese patient) blood pressure is over-estimated. A large cuff should be available in every clinic therefore.

It is usual to measure blood pressure with the patient in the seated position. However, many elderly patients and particularly those receiving anti-hypertensive medication suffer from ortho-static hypotension and in these the blood pres-sure should also be measured in the standing position. The arm should be supported at the level of the heart and the cuff blown up to 30 mmHg or so above the systolic blood pressure level (established by palpating the radial pulse). The cuff should be gently deflated at a rate of 2 mmHg per second over the critical range. Sys-tolic blood pressure (Korotkoff phase I) is recorded as the point at which the sounds appear. Some clinicians use the point of muffling (Korotkoff Phase IV) as diastolic blood pressure. However, this is less reproducible and correlates less well with true diastolic blood pressure than the point at which the sounds disappear (Korotkoff Phase V). In some patients (particu-larly those on vasodilator therapy) the sounds may be heard down to zero and in this case Phase IV diastolic blood pressures have to be recorded, although a note should be made of this fact. Values for diastolic and systolic pressures should be rounded to the next even number (ie not the nearest five or ten). Blood pressures should always be compared in the two arms on first attendance. The higher of the two blood pressures should be taken as the true pressure and a note made that blood pressure should always be taken in that arm.

Some patients repeatedly show a pressor response when a doctor takes their blood pres-sure (white coat hypertension). This may be suf-ficient to raise their blood pressure to the moderate or even the severely hypertensive range. Undoubtedly, many patients have had unnecess-ary treatment as a result of white coat hyperten-sion. Possible indicators are the presence of high blood pressure levels in the absence of any clini-cal evidence of hypertension (ie fundal changes, left ventricular hypertrophy, electrocardiographic changes). The patient may often appear tense and have a tachycardia when blood pressure is measured. Under these circumstances the best plan is either referral to a Hypertension clinic for ambulatory monitoring or the loan of one of the small electronic devices for home blood pressure measurement.

Pseudohypertension

Elderly patients may have rigid brachial arteries which are calcified and not readily occluded by the sphygomanometer cuff. As a result, blood pressure may be over-estimated. This possibility is suggested by the presence of Osler's sign.

This is produced by inflating the blood pressure cuff above the systolic blood pressure. Although the radial pulse is non-pulsatile in this situation it can still be readily palpated indicating a thickened calcified anterior wall. Under these circumstances, diastolic blood pressure may be over-estimated by 10–50 mmHg[3].

Clinical Assessment of the Elderly Hypertensive

Apart from measuring blood pressure, clinical history and examination can give the doctor important information about future management. Clinical assessment has three aims. Firstly, is there evidence for cause of hypertension? Secondly, is there evidence of target organ damage and thirdly, is there information which may determine the form of treatment which the patient is given?

History

A history of sudden elevation of blood pressure (where it has been measured previously) often indicates a secondary cause and in the elderly patient should indicate the possibility of atheromatous renal artery stenosis.

Phaeochromocytoma is unusual in the elderly, but most of the clues are provided by the history, particularly in the form of palpitations, sweating, throbbing headache and paroxysmal hypertension. Primary aldosteronism is often associated with muscular weakness and cramps due to hypokalaemia. More common in the elderly, the ingestion of non-steroidal anti-inflammatory drugs causes slight elevation of blood pressure through sodium and fluid retention. These agents are frequently responsible for impaired blood pressure control in patients receiving anti-hypertensive drugs. Other possible drug causes are cough syrup containing sympathomimetic amines, monoamine oxidase inhibitors, carbenoxolone and oestrogens. Interestingly, oestrogens used in the treatment of post-menopausal symptoms do not seem to elevate blood pressure, although large doses used in treatment of carcinoma of the prostate can. All

patients should be asked about possible symptoms of target organ damage, ie cerebrovascular disease, ischaemic heart disease or peripheral vascular disease. Associated conditions may play an important role in determining treatment. Thus, beta-blockers would not be used in patients with obstructive airways disease or cardiac failure, whilst diuretics will not be used in patients with gout and preferably not used in patients with non-insulin dependent diabetes mellitus, although this is a relative rather than an absolute contra-indication.

Physical Examination

Secondary hypertension has few clinical signs. The patient with bilateral renal disease may show evidence of renal failure, although this will of course be fairly late. Abdominal bruits may be significant in renal artery stenosis, although they may originate in other vessels. Where they extend to the flank and where they occur both in systole and in diastole, they are more likely to be significant. Target organ damage is usually readily detectable on examination of the cardiovascular and peripheral vascular systems. Fundal examination is particularly important. Grade I and Grade II fundal changes are of no significance in the elderly. However, the presence of haemorrhages, cotton wood spots, hard exudates or papilloedema all indicate urgency of treatment. A high blood pressure in association with these advanced fundal changes is an indication for immediate drug therapy or admission to hospital. The term malignant hypertension, used to be reserved only for patients who showed papilloedema. It is now used for all cases with Grade 3 and 4 retinopathy. It is only occasionally seen in the elderly.

Investigations

Intensive investigation for a cause of hypertension is not indicated. Diseases such as primary aldosteronism and phaeochromocytoma are rare in the general population (well below 1%) and even rarer in the elderly. Renal disease (chronic pyelonephritis, atheromatous renal artery stenosis) is rather more common, but even where it is diagnosed, treatment is not usually altered in the elderly. The only indication for carrying out intensive renal investigations is progressive renal failure. Under these circumstances, intravenous urography or isotope renography should be carried out and, if abnormalities suggestive of renal artery stenosis are demonstrated, renal arteriography is performed. Bilateral renal atheroma or atheroma of the vessel to a single kidney may be responsible. Under these circumstances, it can often be corrected either by renal angioplasty or by a surgical revascularisation procedure. Where renal artery stenosis gives rise to hypertension without producing renal failure in this age group, treatment is usually medical and, therefore, intensive investigation is not indicated. Urinary catecholamine measurements (vanillyl mandelic acid, metadrenaline and normetadrenaline) should only be carried out where there is a clinical suspicion of phaeochromocytoma. Most patients will have uncomplicated essential hypertension (ie there is no single cause which can be detected). Under these circumstances, the optimal approach is probably to check renal function and electrolytes with a single measurement of serum urea, creatinine and electrolytes. A simple spot test of urine for protein is probably sufficient. Electrocardiography, however, is particularly valuable in assessing severity of hypertension. The presence of left ventricular hypertrophy or strain suggests severe hypertension, the treatment of which is a matter of urgency. Echocardiography probably offers the most valuable information of all since it is a much more sensitive measure of left ventricular hypertrophy. Thus, left ventricular hypertrophy is associated with a much worse prognosis. Indeed, echocardiographic left ventricular hypertrophy is a better predictor of cardiovascular risk than systolic blood pressure itself. The presence or absence of left ventricular hypertrophy is therefore extremely useful in excluding patients with either white coat hypertension or pseudo-hypertension (see above).

Management

Except in malignant hypertension or in acute hypertensive emergencies, drug treatment should only be initiated after careful assessment and repeated blood pressure measurements.

Impact of Treatment on Risk

Several multicentre trials have demonstrated that lowering the blood pressure in both severe to moderate and mild hypertension reduces the incidence of stroke[4]. The largest and most carefully conducted trials have studied the effects of treatment on mild hypertension (diastolic blood pressures 90–109 mmHg). Pooled analysis of these has shown a reduction in the incidence of stroke of approximately 40%. This sounds substantial. However, it has to be borne in mind that the populations studied were at relatively low risk. Elderly patients were excluded. Thus, in the MRC trial, the effect of treatment was to prevent one stroke in 850 patient years of treatment, ie 850 patients would have to be treated for one year to prevent one stroke, however mild[5].

A number of trials have been conducted on treatment in the elderly. The earliest were The European Working Party on Hypertension in the Elderly (EWPHE)[1] which recruited patients over 60 years of age, and the Hypertension in the Elderly in Primary Care Study of Coope and Warrender[2] which recruited patients over 65 years of age. Both showed a very similar reduction in strokes to that demonstrated in trials in younger subjects. However, the individual benefits were much higher. In the EWPHE Trial, for instance, treatment prevented 14 cardiovascular deaths per 1,000 years of treatment. The reason for this is simple. The cardiovascular risk is much greater in the elderly. A 40% reduction of this much higher risk therefore represents a much greater benefit.

The elderly therefore stand to gain much more from treatment of blood pressure than younger patients. Other more recent trials, ie the STOP trial, the MRC trial in the elderly and the SHEP trial have confirmed these results[10].

The effect of treatment on myocardial infarction is more confused. The majority of multicentre trials in younger patients failed to show any impact on the incidence of myocardial infarcts.

The EWPHE Trial showed a significant reduction in cardiac deaths[1], although the Coope and Warrender Study[2] showed no significant impact on myocardial infarction or cardiac deaths (14% reduction). Pooled analysis of all the controlled trials has shown a significant impact, but probably less than would have been predicted if the risk of myocardial infarction were completely reversible[4,5,7]. The reason for this is uncertain. It could be that atheromatous disease is already established at the time of treatment. It has also been suggested that metabolic effects of diuretics, which were used in most of these trials, are responsible for accelerated atherogenesis. This hypothesis has not been confirmed by examination of the changes in lipids or hypokalaemia in the relevant paper[4]. The impact of treatment on myocardial infarction in trials in the elderly has been, overall, rather greater than in younger subjects.

Who to Treat

For the reasons given above, treatment is not usually started on first presentation of the patient. On this occasion, clinical assessment and initiation of investigations is begun.

The only advice should be the general sort of advice which would be given to any patients. In particular, it is important to deter the patient from smoking. Usually a minimum of three measurements of blood pressure separated by one to four weeks should be carried out. Diastolic blood pressure consistently of 110 mmHg or above should be treated. Mild hypertension (ie diastolics of 90–109 mmHg) requires longer assessment for over three to four months measuring blood pressure perhaps each two to four weeks. The British Hypertension Society provided guidelines for treatment of this latter group of patients[6]. The suggestions were made slightly more conservative than those recommended in the United States. It was suggested that drug treatment should be confined to individuals whose diastolic blood pressure was 100 mmHg or more consistently. The second Working Party of the British Hypertension Society recommends therapeutic intervention in patients with a sustained systolic pressure of greater than 160 mmHg or a sustained diastolic pressure of greater than 90 mmHg or both in the presence of other cardiovascular risk factors[8]. In patients over 80 years of age or more in the EWPHE Trial, treatment seemed to carry no benefit and may even have been slightly deleterious. Numbers were however small and one has to be cautious about this conclusion. Below this age, the benefits of treatment are greater than those in younger patients.

As a part of 'whole patient' approach to ischaemic heart disease, it is important that other added risk factors, like left ventricular hypertrophy, hyperlipidaemia, glucose intolerance or persistent smoking, should be borne in mind while planning the drug treatment of a patient with hypertension.

Systolic Blood Pressure

The Systolic Hypertension in the Elderly Program (SHEP) Trial showed unequivocal benefit in the treatment of isolated systolic hypertension (BP>160 mmHg). Thus, strokes were reduced by 36% and myocardial infarcts by 27%[9]. This Trial used low dose diuretics as first line therapy, combined if necessary with a cardioselective beta-blocker. Systolic blood pressure is often more difficult to reduce to acceptable levels because of the development of diastolic hypotension and suboptimal control often has to be accepted. In general, currently, our goal should be to reduce systolic blood pressure to 140–150 mmHg and diastolic to 80–85 mmHg, although the level to which blood pressure should be reduced is still controversial[10].

Non-Pharmalogical Therapy

Advice to elderly patients may help to limit the amount of anti-hypertensive drugs which are used in their treatment. All overweight patients should be advised to reduce weight. Weight reduction of 7 kg will produce on average the same degree of blood pressure lowering as beta-blocker treatment.

Reduction in heavy alcohol intake to at most 2–3 glass of wine units a day (where one unit=half a pint of beer or one measure of spirits) will also have a useful impact on blood pressure. Physical training has recently, in several carefully conducted trials, been shown to lower blood pressure independently of any effect upon weight. Elderly patients whose disabilities do not prevent it, therefore, should be advised to take regular brisk walks. Salt restriction has been shown to lower blood pressure in patients with moderate hypertension and also patients receiving some classes of drugs, such as ACE inhibitors, beta-blockers and diuretics. It has a small effect on patients with mild hypertension. Where patients are prepared to undertake it, therefore, it is worth carrying out a therapeutic trial whereby salt intake is restricted. This can be achieved by the patient avoiding the addition of salt in cooking or at the table and avoiding heavily salted meats or processed foods, bread and cereals. With appropriate care, it is possible to reduce salt intake from the population average of about 150 mmols a day to 70–80 mmols a day. Other forms of dietary therapy have been advocated, but are so far unproven.

Probably the most promising of these are fish oils which have been very successful in some, but by no means all studies.

Which Drug to Use?

(Please see table below)

Where non-pharmacological management does not lower blood pressure below the threshold for treatment, drugs should be used. The elderly patient is more susceptible to adverse effects of drugs. A particular problem is postural hypotension.

Thus, cardiovascular reflexes become impaired in old age and blood pressure often cannot be sustained at adequate levels when the upright posture is assumed. Impaired cerebral blood flow as a result of vascular disease may make this situation worse. Diminished cardiac and renal reserve predispose the patient to cardiac failure when sympathetic drive to the heart is reduced by beta-blockers or to sodium and water depletion when potent diuretics are given. For this reason, careful, frequent monitoring of blood pressure is essential during the early phase of blood pressure control. Dose increments should be modest and an adequate interval between dose increments allowed. Thus, whilst in the younger patient, drug titration is often carried out at two weekly intervals, in older subjects it is wise to increase drug dosage not more frequently than four to six weekly.

The large trials of treatment in the elderly used diuretics and beta-blockers. Other classes of agent frequently used are the ACE inhibitors, calcium antagonists or alpha adrenergic blockers. Whilst short duration trials have shown that these are, in general, well tolerated and effective in elderly subjects, there have been no long-term trials to show whether they have a more favourable impact on strokes or myocardial infarction.

Doses and Common Side-Effects of some Drugs used in Treating Hypertension in the Elderly

Drug	Dosage	Side-Effects
Bendrofluazide	2.5 mg/d	• Hypokalaemia • Increased serum cholesterol • Hyperuricaemia • Insulin resistance • Sodium and water depletion • Impotence
Propanolol	40–160 mg BD	• Reduced effort tolerance • Bronchospasm
Atenolol	50–100 mg/d	• Exacerbation of cardiac failure • Cold extremities • Impotence
Celectol (Celiprolol)	200 mg/d	Cardioselective beta-blocker, with peripheral vasodilator action
Bisoprolol	5–10 mg/d	• Highly cardioselective beta blocker
Nifedipine (Retard preparation)	10–40 mg BD	• Vasodilator side-effects – Oedema
Amlodipine	5–10 mg/d	• Oedema (other vasodilator side-effects unusual)
Verapamil	80–240 mg BD	• Cardiac conduction disturbances • Constipation
Captopril	6.25–50 mg BD	• Chronic cough • Renal failure • Hypotension
Enalapril	2.5–40 mg/d	
Lisinopril	2.5–40 mg/d	
Doxazosin	1–16 mg/d	Hypotension
Terazosin	1–20 mg/d	
Cosartan	50–100 mg/d	• Hypotension, renal failure

d = daily; BD = Twice a day.

This is not to say that such benefits do not exist. Nevertheless, there is at present no strong evidence to depart from the British Hypertension Society Working Party suggestion that diuretics and beta-blockers should normally remain first-line therapy. The elderly are no exception in this respect, although the higher prevalence of cardiac disease and impairment mean that ACE inhibitors (in patients with left ventricular dysfunction) or peripherally acting calcium antagonists (such as Amlodipine, Nifedipine or Nicardipine) in patients with angina may be used more frequently.

Combination Therapy

When a single drug does not control the blood pressure, it is normal practice to add a second drug. The old stepped care regime in which initial therapy with a diuretic was supplemented by beta-blocker treatment and further supplemented with a vasodilator has now been rendered inappropriate by the wide variety of agents available. Nevertheless, certain combinations have proved particularly efficacious. These are:

a. diuretic/beta-blocker;
b. beta-blocker/calcium antagonist;
c. ACE inhibitor/thiazide diuretic;
d. triple therapy, eg thiazide diuretic/beta-blocker/calcium antagonist, may be necessary in a small minority of patients.

It is important to bear in mind that before combination therapy is instituted, optimal dosage of single agents should be used. In some cases, this requires careful dose titration up to the maximum in the recommended range. In the case of thiazide diuretics, regimens should be limited to a single low dose since anti-hypertensive efficacy does not appear to increase as dosage increases. During dose titration, particularly of calcium antagonists, adverse effects (such as vasodilator side-effects) may become apparent.

Under these circumstances, lower doses may have to be used and a second class of agent added. This underlies the fact that the second advantage of combination therapy is the ability to restrict dosage of primary agents.

Treating Hypertension after Stroke

In general, although about 80% of patients after stroke are noted to have hypertension on admission to hospital, only a third have a history of hypertension. Although there is no clear-cut guideline as to which patient with hypertension after stroke should be treated, it is prudent to withold treatment for 10 days as the raised blood pressure settles by itself within a few days. The exception to this general rule should be hypertensive encephalopathy and aortic dissection. Further work is needed on this aspect of treatment of hypertension[11].

Hypertension

Practical Points

1. Non-pharmacological measures like weight loss (where indicated), regular exercise, moderate salt intake, avoidance of cigarette smoking and reduction in alcohol consumption should be considered before starting drug therapy.

2. Blood pressure should be correctly measured and more than one blood pressure reading (usually 3) are pre-requisites before considering drug treatment.

3. Drug therapy should be individualised, ie side-effects of drugs, various pathologies and risk factors should be considered before initiating a particular drug.

4. Unless contra-indicated, thiazide diuretics and beta-blockers continue to be first-line drugs.

5. In view of generally poor response of ACE inhibitors and beta-blockers in Afro-Caribbean patients, diuretics and calcium antagonists should be preferred.

6. Not all patients with hypertension will need life-long treatment. In patients where hypertensive medication has been stopped, the blood pressure should be checked periodically for up to two years and then yearly.

References

1. Amery A, Birkenhager W, Brixko P et al. (1985) *Mortality and morbidity results from the European Working Party on High Blood Pressure in the Elderly Trial*, Lancet, i, 1349–1354.

2. Coope J & Warrender TS (1986) *Randomised trial of treatment of hypertension in elderly patients in primary care*, British Medical Journal, 293, 1146–1151.

3. Messerli FH, Ventura HO & Amoreo C (1985) *Osler's manoeuvre and pseudo-hypertension*, New England Journal of Medicine, 312, 1548–1551.

4. Collins R, Peto R, MacMahon S et al. (1990) *Blood pressure, stroke and coronary heart disease. Part II. Short-term reductions in blood pressure: overview of randomised drug trials in their epidemiological context*, Lancet, 827–838.

5. Medical Research Council Working Party (1985) *MRC trial of treatment of mild hypertension: principal results*, British Medical Journal, 291, 97–104.

6. British Hypertension Society Working Party (1989) *Treating hypertension agreement from the large trials*, British Medical Journal, 298, 694–698.

7. Reader R, Bauer GE, Doyle AE at al. (1980) *The Australian therapeutic trial in mild hypertension: report by the Management Committee*, Lancet, 1, 1261–1267.

8. British Hypertension Society (1993) *Management guidelines in essential hypertension: report of the Second Working Party of British Hypertension Society*. British Medical Journal, 306, 983–987.

9. SHEP co-operative Research Group (1991) *Prevention of stroke by anti-hypertensive drug treatment in older persons with isolated systolic hypertension*, JAMA, 265, 3255–3264.

10. Potter JF (1994) *Hypertension and the Elderly* in: Hypertension in Theory and Practice, British Medical Bulletin, Churchill Livingstone, 50, 408–449.

11. O'Connell JE & Gray CS (1994) *Editorial*, British Medical Journal, 308, 1523–1524.

Chapter 27

Rehabilitation of the Elderly – An Overview

Dr P J Reynolds BSc, MB, MRCP
Consultant Physician
Department of Medicine for the Elderly
Pembury Hospital
Pembury
Tunbridge Wells
Kent
TN2 4QJ

Dr S C Allen, BSC, MD, FRCP
Consultant Physician and Clinical Director
Department of Medicine for the Elderly
Royal Bournemouth Hospital
Castle Lane East
Bournemouth
BH7 7DW.

Biosketch:

Dr P J Reynolds, BSc, MB, MRCP is a Consultant Physician in Medicine for the Elderly in Tunbridge Wells. He has a special interest in diabetes in old age and in the myelodysplastic syndrome. He has published a number of papers in those fields.

Dr S C Allen, BSc, MD, FRCP is a Consultant Physician in General Medicine and Geriatric Medicine at the Royal Bournemouth Hospital. His special interests include health service management and respiratory disease in old age. His research interests are respiratory infection, management of asthma in old age, autonomic dysfunction and the outcome of various forms of stroke rehabilitation. His publications are mainly in the field of respiratory diseases in old age.

Introduction

The principles of rehabilitation form the core of geriatric medical practice.

There have been many definitions of the term rehabilitation, though a widely accepted one is 'the restoration of the individual to his (or her) fullest physical, mental and social capability'[1]; treating the whole patient, rather than focussing on pathological conditions. Although the ideal is to aim for the fullest recovery, this goal is often modified in reality, to a practical rather than an optimum level of improvement needed to restore the individual to independence.

There has been a change in the role of the Geriatrician from provider of custodial care to one of early assessment and active rehabilitation of all suitable aged patients. Besides, as Geriatricians successfully support very ill elderly patients through acute illnesses, a larger number of frail elderly patients survive longer and accumulate an unpredictable mix of pathological and degenerative conditions. This has led to a greater need for rehabilitation to increase the speed of their return to independence, and reduce both morbidity and mortality during this period[2].

The rehabilitation of patients with stroke is the subject of a separate chapter (chapter 28). In this chapter we give an overview of general rehabilitation in elderly patients (appendix 1), starting with some relevant definitions:

Impairment, Disability and Handicap

Disabling diseases and disorders become more common with advanced age. Disablement encompasses impairment, disability and handicap.

These terms have different meanings and are inextricably linked, as follows[3]:

Disease or Disorder

Impairment

Disability

Handicap

Impairment means an objective reduction from normality, in the physical or mental ability of the individual due to a disease or disorder, which may be temporary or permanent. This can be graded by severity using various scales, though the relation of a certain degree of impairment to loss of function is non-linear.

Disability means the apparent effect that impairment has upon daily function, when subjective differences in adaptation are balanced against normal expected activity.

Handicap means the perceived disadvantage within society that results directly from a particular impairment or disability.

Recovery

This means a partial or complete return to the premorbid condition. In rehabilitation this term should be restricted to natural recovery. For example, that seen spontaneously after an acute stroke. This must be separated from the *improvements* which can be obtained by retraining and adaptation.

Activities of Daily Living (ADL)

These are the functional abilities a person needs to be able to live with minimal dependence within the community. They include the ability to dress, wash, feed, mobilise and toilet oneself.

Multidisciplinary Team (Appendix 2)

The team should include, as a minimum, the clinician, the nurses, a physiotherapist and an occupational therapist. Ideally, it should also include a medical social worker, speech therapist, chiropodist, dietitian, continence advisor and, sometimes, tissue viability advisor.

The Setting for Rehabilitation

Rehabilitation is undertaken in a wide spectrum of settings[4], but increasingly takes place in specially designed units.

Dedicated Wards – With the increasing number of elderly people needing a rehabilitation service, the majority of health authorities have developed specially dedicated units.

Adequate space should be provided around beds and in the bathrooms for hoists and walking aids, both to encourage independence with mobility, and to facilitate nursing. Special beds, such as the Kings Fund Mark V, should be available to reduce complications from immobility.

Chairs and beds should be at the correct height to aid standing and there should be special showers and baths to aid washing, both for the assisted and independent patients. There should be some single bedrooms, a large dayroom allowing different activity areas and a secluded room for interviewing patients and relatives. The physiotherapy gym and occupational therapy department, including a kitchen and bedroom for ADL assessment, should be in close proximity. Ideally, there should be a level outside area, such as a garden or patio for use in good weather. The environment should be homely and not 'clinical', and so be less threatening for the patients.

Specialised Units – Most dedicated units are for general rehabilitation, but specialised units dealing with, for example, orthogeriatric rehabilitation, stroke rehabilitation or psychogeriatric problems have been established and work well. Orthogeriatric rehabilitation units have been shown to reduce the average length of stay[5,6]. More importantly, they allow specialisation of staff, particularly physiotherapists with orthopaedic skills, and encourage closer co-operation between orthopaedic surgeons and Geriatricians.

The Patients

Patient Casemix

The majority of the patients are over the age of 65 years, with a median on a typical unit of 80 years. There is a predominance of female over male patients, with a ratio of approximately 3:1, with the female patients being slightly older.

The majority of patients enter the rehabilitation unit after recovery from an acute illness or combination of illnesses, having already been under the care of a Geriatrician. The remainder are admitted, either as referrals from other medical or surgical specialities after acute admission, or are admitted directly to the unit after assessment in the out-patient clinic, or in the community by the Geriatrician or General Practitioner.

Patient Variability

Not only is there a variation between individuals in their capacity to benefit from rehabilitation, but there is also a variation in the ADL performance of an individual in different settings. For example, a patient who is independent in the hospital environment, may behave differently at home and apparently regress when interacting with their normal carers and family, even though the carer's demands are well within the patients capability. Conversely, an aged patient with mild cognitive impairment may appear unable to cope when assessed in strange hospital surroundings, but be independent and safe in their own home environment. This variation in performance, combined with factors associated with pathology, ageing, environment and personality, is one of the challenges of geriatric rehabilitation and must be taken into account when planning treatment, discharge and follow-up.

Patient Frailty

Some patients who are very frail as a consequence of being very aged and having multiple disabilities, often do less well in formal intensive rehabilitation settings. For this reason, a range of settings for rehabilitation is desirable and ideally will include a slower stream facility, where a greater degree of nursing support is possible. This often takes place in wards also used for continuing care or respite admissions.

Patient Selection

Patients do not all have the same potential for recovery or improvement. It is important that some form of assessment is made prior to entering a rehabilitation program, particularly in specialised units. For some patients, formal rehabilitation may be inappropriate or even impossible[7].

More stringent entry criteria are often necessary with specialised units, such as orthogeriatric units or stroke units, and such units often have very specific operational policies, including tightly defined selection criteria.

Diagnostic Framework

As the elderly have a higher incidence and prevalence of disease, and take more drugs, there is a greater potential for any given presenting illness to have multiple components. These may be pathological, psychological or social, and their interaction requires a careful assessment. This is important if some areas are not to be overlooked, and so that one particular problem does not attract excessive clinical importance. For example, the presence of ankle oedema in a patient presenting with cardiac failure may be the result of several causes, such as gravitational effects from sleeping in a chair, previous varicose venous disease, side-effects of drugs and low serum protein levels from poor nutrition, as well as a true manifestation of their cardiac failure. In this example, over-reliance on ankle oedema as the main marker of cardiac failure could cause excessive diuretic usage, with consequent side-effects such as postural hypotension and consequent delay in effective rehabilitation.

Management can be made easier by using a problem list once assessment has highlighted the factors that are likely to affect or respond to rehabilitation. This should include medical, social and functional problems, and can form the basis for discussion within the multidisciplinary team, and can constitute the rehabilitation plan. This can be achieved by the setting of particular goals which are to be met by the time of the next review, so catalysing individual efforts within the team. Such a problem-oriented approach can provide general guidance and help to focus the team's strategy.

Multidisciplinary Team

Nurses – The largest group in the team, nurses are responsible for most of the direct patient care and supervision. They serve as the natural day-to-day co-ordinators of the team at ward level. They have a wide range of tasks, from feeding, washing and toileting the patient, to implementing many of the treatments and procedures recommended by the doctor, physiotherapist, occupational therapist and speech therapist. The nurses also need to spend time talking to the patients and their relatives, and are often involved in more formal counselling of those who are distressed by their illness. Rehabilitation wards also provide a fertile training ground for student nurses.

Nurses play a key role in allowing a patient who needs help with a simple action like going to the toilet, but needs to be encouraged to improve their level of independence, to take a few 'calculated risks'. This requires patience, practical experience and knowledge of the illness and potential dangers. It is often a lot quicker, and safer, to take over and render the patient dependent. On the other hand, ignorance of technique or of a patient's particular illness, can lead to mistakes or accidents from taking too great a risk, and the consequent injuries can delay rehabilitation. A well staffed unit with a good skillmix allows effective supervised rehabilitation within the patient's limitations, as well as facilitating staff training.

Physiotherapist

The main aim of physiotherapy is an improvement in locomotor function. Physiotherapists are principally concerned with neurological and musculoskeletal impairment, though the perception of psychological as well as physical components is important so as to achieve a good level of patient motivation. In general rehabilitation, including that of patients with arthritis, certain key areas predominate, such as increasing muscle strength, stamina, neuromuscular co-ordination, joint stability and joint mobility. General improvement in cardio-pulmonary fitness is, of course, an extra bonus.

Physiotherapy essentially relies on manual techniques, utilising specialised equipment and facilities when necessary, and is performed with individual patients and with small groups. After assessment, an individual program is devised to concentrate on key factors which are limiting function. Progress is reviewed within the structure of the multidisciplinary team, with frequent references to the diagnostic, assessment and planning stages. Hydrotherapy can be particularly useful in patients with rheumatological or orthopaedic problems. There are also many physical treatments which help promote recovery by reducing inflammation and pain, and promote healing and muscle relaxation. These include short-wave diathermy, microwave dithermy, faradic stimulation, high frequency pulsed electromagnetic energy (eg, Megapulse), ultrasound and wax baths. Thus the physiotherapist has many tools to aid treatment but these need to be carefully selected for individual patients.

Physiotherapy is increasingly being carried into the community. There are two main ways of achieving this; firstly, by a patient attending the day hospital from home. This often allows continuity of treatment after an in-patient stay, and can be combined with medical review, occupational therapy and speech therapy. Secondly, by the physiotherapist visiting the patient's home, where treatment programs can be more accurately tailored to overcome particular environmental factors and can help to maintain improvements in function gained during in-patient treatment. Sufficient free space in a patient's home is a pre-requisite for successful domiciliary physiotherapy.

Occupational Therapist

The aim of the occupational therapist (OT) is to help the patient overcome physical or mental disability so as to reach the best level of independence possible and thereby minimise handicap. Each patient needs a tailor-made package of OT treatment. This must begin with assessment, with particular reference to activities of daily living. Manipulating the physical aspects of the home environment by performing adaptations or supplying aids, is another important function of the OT. They also have particular skills in dealing with impaired hand function, visuospatial perception, mobility from the viewpoint of access and wheelchairs, and social-skills training. When function is permanently impaired, the OT must have access to various mechanical aids to help maintain independence for ADL; these can often be individually adapted to suit a particular patient's needs. One of the most important contributions brought by OTs to the multidisciplinary team is information obtained from home visits: helping to ensure that not only the rehabilitation plan is appropriate and realistic but also that the suggested modifications are carried out.

Speech Therapist

The majority of patients needing speech therapy (ST) have cerebrovascular disease, dealt with in another chapter. However, there is opportunity for taking specialist ST advice in the case of patients with swallowing difficulties or problems with lip seal, for example, when patients with pre-existing neurological damage need general rehabilitation after an intercurrent illness.

Medical Social Worker

Especially since the Community Care Act came into force from 1st April 1993, the social services input in provision of various services in the community has become vitally important. They provide practical social, emotional and financial support to help patients return to the community.

One of their major skills is communication between agencies and individuals. As the hospital medical social workers have direct links with the community social services, they can help the patient obtain Home Care, Meals-on-Wheels, Sheltered Housing and Day Centre care. In addition, they provide advice about residential homes, both private and local authority funded, and can make arrangements for appropriate patients to enter these temporarily (including holiday relief admissions) and permanently.

Clinicians

The principal role of the physician in the rehabilitation setting is to identify pathological and ageing changes, which might impair the patient's ability to benefit from rehabilitation, and to treat these by pharmacological and non-pharmacological methods. The physician needs to ensure smooth functioning of the team and to take the overall responsibility for patient care and planning. This includes interviewing relatives where necessary.

Other Professions

Other staff provide valuable advice intermittently, such as the chiropodist, dietitian, surgical appliance officer and clinical psychologist. Continence advisors and nurses who specialise in pressure sore prevention and treatment are often involved in the broader rehabilitation team.

Optimising Medical Treatment

As outlined above, multiple interacting pathologies are common in the elderly. Cardiac, respiratory, neurological and joint complaints are particularly common, and their impact on the patient has to be minimised before the main aims of rehabilitation can be achieved. The responsibility for this lies with the doctor. Certain treatable conditions, in particular, should be sought. These include urinary tract infection, postural hypotension, depression, latent movement disorders, drug side-effects, earwax impaction and constipation. This list is by no means exhaustive.

Rationalising Medication

Poly-pharmacy is a particular problem in the elderly and is a consequence of multiple pathologies. Prescribing should therefore be frequently reviewed. A useful maxim is to prescribe only when one expects clear advantages. In short, the patient's review is not complete until the drug chart has been scrutinized.

One of the side-effects that prevents effective rehabilitation is postural hypotension, seen with a variety of classes of drugs (table 1). Sedative agents, such as benzodiazepines, can cause a chronic confusional state. Postural hypotension and sedation can be so severe that syncope with subsequent falls and fractures can occur. Exacerbating incontinence by excessive diuretic dosages in heart failure is common. One class of agents that have particularly serious side-effects are the Non-Steroidal Anti-Inflammatory drugs, which are often prescribed to control the pain from arthritis. These can sometimes be substituted by paracetamol and/or intra-articular corticosteroid injections, with physiotherapy. Where drugs are necessary they should be those which are well tolerated in the elderly whenever possible, and the dosage regime kept simple. The duration should be as short as possible and the need to continue the drug frequently reviewed.

Case Review and Problem Lists

Case management requires the regular review by the multi-disciplinary team of medical, functional and social factors. A problem-orientated approach, with goal setting, is particularly useful in this setting. A problem list, designed as the front sheet of the case-notes, can facilitate review and can be updated with subsequent progress.

Rehabilitation in Different Conditions

Arthritis (see chapter 20)

Stroke (see chapter 28)

Amputations

The majority of amputations of lower limbs occur in elderly men. Formal rehabilitation usually starts after the surgical post-operative management period has finished, though early attempts at standing and walking in the immediate post-operative period help retain baroreceptor function and balance, and improve morale. At the first stage of formal rehabilitation, temporary prostheses allow assessment and training to begin. Some patients will be unable to progress to independent walking and may remain in need of a wheelchair; this is particularly so when there are coexistent diseases such as heart failure, stroke, Parkinson's disease or blindness.

Phantom limb pain interferes with rehabilitation. Local causes should be excluded. Many treatments have been tried, with varying success, and include TCNS, nerve blocks, thalmic surgery, acupuncture, psychotherapy and drug therapy with antidepressants and anticonvulsants. A combination of approaches is often necessary.

Parkinson's Disease (see chapter 31)

Pulmonary Rehabilitation

Patients with chronic obstructive lung disease may benefit from a pulmonary rehabilitation program. The main emphasis should be on disease-education and exercise. These measures reduce

Table 1

Examples of Drugs That Can Effect Rehabilitation Adversely

Drug	Potential Adverse Effect on Rehabilitation
Benziodiazepines	drowsiness, falls, confusion, ataxia
Tricyclic Antidepressants	postural hypotension, falls, drowsiness, constipation
Diuretics	urinary urgency & incontinence
B Blockers	postural hypotension
Calcium Blockers	postural hypotension, ankle oedema
Prochlorperazine	parkinsonism, drowsiness
Neuroleptics	parkinsonism, drowsiness, postural hypotension

the patients' dependence and enhance their quality of life. In this context it is worth remembering that one shouldn't be unduly optimistic with this sort of rehabilitation as it won't alter the course of the disease[11].

Cardiac Rehabilitation

The value of cardiac rehabilitation – mainly after myocardial infarction and cardiac surgery – has been appreciated only recently. Important recommendations made in the British Cardiac Society's working party report on cardiac rehabilitation are as follows[10]:

a. need for a cardiac rehabilitation service in every major district;
b. programme tailored to individual needs of patients;
c. programme should be exercise-based and multidisciplinary;
d. need for research into social, psychological and physiological responses of rehabilitation.

It has to be stated, however, that cardiac rehabilitation means quite different things in the different countries of Europe (UK, Germany, Italy) and in the USA.

The Discharge (see checklist, appendix 3)

Planning for discharge should start at admission[8]. Preparations should be fine-tuned by regular case-review and after full discussion with the patient, carers, social services and district nurses. This prevents unnecessary re-admission and is of obvious benefit to the patient. However, some discharges are bound to fail because the patient or relatives insist on a discharge against professional advice and hence return to an environment unsuitable for the patients' limited degree of functional independence. The back-up of continued rehabilitation through facilities such as a Day Hospital or Community Services, leading to a 'cushioned' discharge, is particularly useful for frailer patients.

At the time of discharge, clear plans and clear methods of communication with the other agencies are essential. The best time for discharge has to be individually assessed. Discharge should be considered either when a functional plateau has been reached and further improvements are unlikely, or when functional targets have been reached, or when further rehabilitation can be undertaken in the community, either by community agencies or in the Day Hospital. Discharges into the community that are dependent on Community Services should preferably be avoided at weekends and Friday afternoons.

Communications

Information should go to those agencies who need to be aware of case details. This should include diagnosis, progress, medication, support services, follow-up and, of course, time and destination of discharge. This information should be relevant, concise and be provided promptly. When a discharge is thought to be precarious, contact by telephone often ensures that the community agencies, particularly the General Practitioner are aware, and can monitor progress without delay.

Follow-up

This should be considered when there are medical problems that need review, or if disability persists and there is a chance of further change after discharge. Hospital follow-up should not exclude the General Practitioner, but should encourage shared care, allowing the best possible balance of care after return to the community. When medical problems predominate, the best place for review is the out-patient clinic. If the problem is principally one of disability, but considered to require follow-up, the best location is a Day Hospital. This allows a more relaxed and protracted assessment, so the patient does not become too exhausted, and also allows further assessment by the rest of the multidisciplinary team.

While some patients will need hospital follow-up for a long time, the majority of them will need this for a limited period.

Day Hospitals

Finally, a brief mention of the value and function of a Day Hospital will be in order here. Day Hospitals allow provision of hospital-based services for patients living in the community who need further rehabilitation. Usually, the services include physiotherapy, occupational therapy, speech therapy and medical review. These services are not integrated in time or place in out-patient form, except in the Day Hospital. This enables the benefits of the multidisciplinary team approach to continue after return to the community.

The operational policy of a Day Hospital will depend on local needs and arrangements. For example, some are combined with other services such as psychogeriatric Day Hospital care. The value of Day Hospitals should not be under-estimated. Flexibility is achieved when the Day Hospital is utilised creatively alongside other hospital services. The usual categories of care provided include some[9], or all, of the following:

(i)   provision of assessment and treatment for those who are not acutely ill and do not require in-patient supervision, especially for disabling conditions requiring rehabilitation;

(ii) provision of facilities for those requiring special procedures and investigations who may be too frail to attend a conventional out-patient clinic;

(iii) provision of supervision after discharge from hospital for those requiring further physical therapeutic or nursing care;

(iv) to serve as a half-way house between hospital and home, providing reassurance to carers, relatives and patients in those cases when anxiety about the discharge exists (this is applicable to a minority of patients);

(v)   provision of a sufficient level of care to allow continued residence in the community for frail, old patients who might otherwise have to enter some form of residential care.

Lately, the functioning and indeed the continuing need for Day Hospitals has been under review. No doubt the findings of this review will be known in due course.

Appendix 1

Process of Rehabilitation

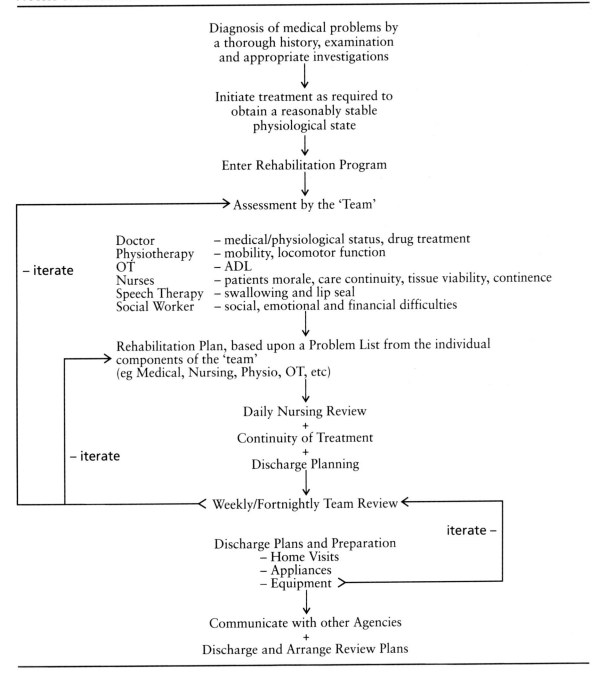

Diagnosis of medical problems by
a thorough history, examination
and appropriate investigations

Initiate treatment as required to
obtain a reasonably stable
physiological state

Enter Rehabilitation Program

Assessment by the 'Team'

– iterate

Doctor	– medical/physiological status, drug treatment
Physiotherapy	– mobility, locomotor function
OT	– ADL
Nurses	– patients morale, care continuity, tissue viability, continence
Speech Therapy	– swallowing and lip seal
Social Worker	– social, emotional and financial difficulties

Rehabilitation Plan, based upon a Problem List from the individual
components of the 'team'
(eg Medical, Nursing, Physio, OT, etc)

Daily Nursing Review
+
Continuity of Treatment
+
Discharge Planning

– iterate

Weekly/Fortnightly Team Review

iterate –

Discharge Plans and Preparation
– Home Visits
– Appliances
– Equipment

Communicate with other Agencies
+
Discharge and Arrange Review Plans

Appendix 2

The Multidisciplinary Team

The Caring Environment

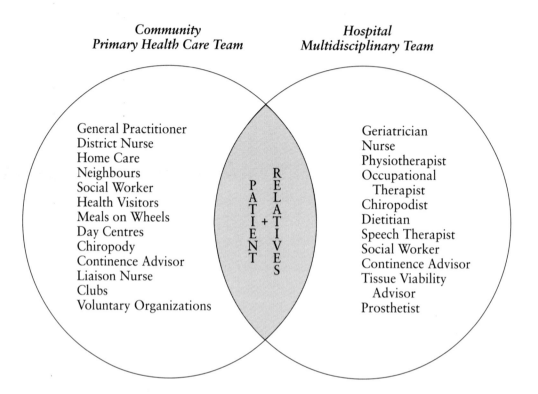

Community Primary Health Care Team

Hospital Multidisciplinary Team

General Practitioner
District Nurse
Home Care
Neighbours
Social Worker
Health Visitors
Meals on Wheels
Day Centres
Chiropody
Continence Advisor
Liaison Nurse
Clubs
Voluntary Organizations

PATIENT + RELATIVES

Geriatrician
Nurse
Physiotherapist
Occupational
   Therapist
Chiropodist
Dietitian
Speech Therapist
Social Worker
Continence Advisor
Tissue Viability
   Advisor
Prosthetist

Appendix 3

Discharge Checklist

Agency/Contact Informed	Yes/No	Date
Patient		
Relative		
Transport		
District Nurse		
Health Visitor		
Home Care		
Meals on Wheels		
Community Psychiatric Nurse		
Day Centre		
Day Hospital		
Out-patient Clinic		
Discharge letter to GP		
Solicitor		
Action Undertaken		
Home Access/Keys Secured		
Return of Property & Valuables		
Medication: ordered		
: and explained		

Rehabilitation of the Elderly

Practical Points

1. Rehabilitation is an essential part of the overall management of patients especially with stroke, arthritis, Parkinson's disease, cardiovascular problems (myocardial infarction and cardiac surgery) and amputation.

2. A careful assessment is essential to provide maximum benefit to the patients.

3. An adequate communication/liaison is essential between the various members of the multidisciplinary team on one hand and the patient and carers on the other.

4. General aspects of successful rehabilitation include a reasonably alert patient who has adequate nutrition and where possible, has good support from relatives and friends.

5. Needs of the immediate carers should not be forgotten. These include holiday relief admissions from time to time, nightsitters, and aids and appliances to help the patient in their activities of daily living.

6. Research and audit of various forms of rehabilitation in different conditions should be undertaken to assess their overall impact – physical, social and psychological – on the patient.

References

1. Mair A (1972) *Report of Subcommittee of the Standing Medical Advisory Committee, Scottish Health Service Council on Medical Rehabilitation*, HMSO, Edinburgh.

2. Applegate WB, Miller ST, Graney MJ, Elam JT, Burns R & Akins DE (1990) *A randomized, controlled trial of a geriatric assessment unit in a community rehabilitation hospital*, New Eng. Journ. of Medicine, 322, 1572–1578.

3. Wood P & Bradley E (1988) *The epidemiology of disablement*, in: Rehabilitation of the Physically Disable Adult. E Goodwill, CJ & Chamberlain MA (eds) Sheridan Medical & Croom Helm, 6–23.

4. Andrews K & Brocklehurst JC (1985) *A profile of geriatric rehabilitation units*, Journ. of the Royal Coll. of Physicians of London, 19, 240–242.

5. Murphy PJ, Rai GS, Lowy M & Bielawaska C. (1987). *The beneficial effects of joint orthopaedic-geriatric rehabilitation*. Age & Ageing, 16, 273–278.

6. Hempsall VJ, Robertson DRC, Campbell MJ & Briggs RS (1990) *Orthopaedic geriatric care – is it effective?* Journal of the Royal College of Physicians of London, 24, 1, 47–50.

7. Haas JF (1988) *Admission to rehabilitation centers: selection of patients*, Arch Phys Med Rehabil, 69, 329–33.

8. Gloag D. (1985) *Rehabilitation of the elderly*, Brit. Medical Journal, 290, 455–457.

9. Pathy MS (1969) *Day Hospital for Geriatric Patients*, Lancet, II, 533–535.

10. Horgan J, Bethall H, Carson P et al (1993) *British Cardiac Society Working Part Report on Cardiac Rehabilitation*. Journal of the Irish colleagues of Physicians and Surgeons, 22, 263–269.

11. Morgan MDL (1994) *Respiratory Seminar* in: Supplement to Hospital Update (March 1994).

Chapter 28

Stroke Rehabilitation

J. A. Barrett MD, MRCP
Consultant Physician in Geriatric Medicine
Clatterbridge Hospital
Wirral
Merseyside

Biosketch:

Dr James A Barrett is Consultant Physician in Geriatric Medicine and Rehabilitation working at Clatterbridge Hospital in the Wirral with a commitment to Acute Geriatric Medicine at Arrowe Park Hospital, Wirral and also part-time Clinical Lecturer in the University of Liverpool. In his clinical work his main interests are in rehabilitation when dealing with patients who suffer with one or more of the geriatric giants. Since his appointment in the Wirral six years ago he has been running a multi-disciplinary stroke rehabilitation unit as well as developing services for people with urinary and faecal incontinence.

Stroke can be defined as a focal neurological deficit which persists for over 24 hours. 30% of all stroke victims die in the acute phase of their illness, 70% of the survivors are left with some degree of permanent disability, 80% of all strokes are due to cerebral infarction of which three quarters are thrombotic and a quarter embolic in origin. The remainder are due to either cerebral haemorrhage (15%) or sub-arachnoid haemorrhage (5%).

Patients who are being considered for secondary prevention or who would be treated if they developed a deep venous thrombosis should all have a computerised tomographic (CT) brain scan within 14 days of the event to distinguish between cerebral haemorrhage and cerebral infarction as this is not possible clinically.

Acute Treatment of Stroke

There is no proven treatment that will limit the neuronal damage caused by stroke disease but a search should be made for the stroke risk factors and where indicated appropriate treatment given[1, 2].

Hypertension

Blood pressure is often raised early after stroke. Decisions on whether to commence anti-hypertensive treatment should therefore be delayed for 2–4 weeks as early reduction of blood pressure may interfere with cerebral auto-regulation, reduced cerebral blood flow and cause further cerebral infarction.

Prevention of Stroke

Low dose aspirin reduces the risk of stroke by 25% following a transient ischaemic attack (a focal neurological deficit lasting for less than 24 hours)[1].Cartoid endartectomy has been shown to reduce the risk of stroke in TIA patients with greater than 70% stenosis of the symtomatic carotid artery in spite of the peri-operative risk[2, 3].

Patients in atrial fibrillation with mitral valve disease should be anticoagulated as they have a high risk of stroke. However, in keeping with the findings of SPAF (stroke prevention in atrial fibrillation) II study, aspirin can be prescribed instead of anticoagulants (except in those at high risk, ie those with previous minor stroke), to patients having non-rheumatic atrial fibrillation, in view of aspirin's efficiency, safety, ease of administration and cost[4].

General Principles of Stroke Rehabilitation

Stroke patients should enter a multidisciplinary rehabilitation programme once their medical condition is stable to enable maximum recovery. At the end of their treatment, however, patients may be left with residual disability (loss of ability to carry out a task) but every effort should be made to prevent this becoming a handicap (restriction in lifestyle). The rehabilitation of older people is covered in more detail in chapter 16.

Medical Complications of Stroke

Sudden Death

This is due to the direct effect of the stroke and is the main cause of early death. Unconsciousness and bronchopneumonia are also associated with early mortality.

Dysphagia

Forty-five per cent of stroke patients experience dysphagia[5]. Approximately 90% of these completely recover their ability to swallow within 14 days. Swallowing assessment is made by observing patients attempting to drink 50 mls of water from a beaker whilst sitting upright. Inability to swallow or choking due to inhalation indicate the presence of significant dysphagia.

In these patients fluids should be avoided until water can be drunk without any choking. The ability to swallow solids/semi-solids, eg ice cream, yoghurt, returns before the ability to swallow fluids. These, therefore, can be reintroduced at an earlier stage than fluids. Use of a thickening agent in fluids may enable easier swallowing during the recovery phase. Whilst awaiting the return of swallowing, hydration must be maintained, preferably by administering intravenous fluids. Feeding via a nasogastric tube during this stage may increase the risk of aspiration pneumonia and delay the return of normal swallowing. Enteral feeding should, however, be considered in patients who survive for 2 weeks or more with continuing dysphagia, preferably via a feeding gastrostomy though many clinicians still use a fine bore naso-gastric tube.

Mental Status

Multi-infarct disease often presents with severe cognitive impairment. The prospects for successful rehabilitation in these patients tends to be poor and carer support is often the main aim.

Deep Venous Thrombosis (DVT)/Pulmonary Embolism

DVT is present in the legs of 50% of stroke patients. Most of these occur in the calf veins of the affected leg and do not require treatment. More extensive thrombosis however, do require treatment as they have a tendency to produce pulmonary emboli. Generally, elevation of stroke patient's legs to prevent or treat deep venous thrombosis should be discouraged as anti-spasticity positioning is impossible with the legs elevated. Pulmonary emboli are found in 50% of stroke patients who die, often as an incidental finding.

Avoidable Complication of Stroke

Painful Shoulder

The shoulder plays an important role in self care activities, balance, transfers and safe walking. Its stability depends upon the rotator cuff muscles holding the humeral head in the shallow glenoid cavity. These muscles are flaccid in hemiplegic arms which leads to subluxation of the shoulder but this is not painful unless there is superimposed capsular damage or tendonitis. These can be avoided by supporting the arm on pillows when the patient is sitting and never letting it hang unsupported. These patients should never be lifted using under the axilla techniques as this is probably the main cause of capsular damage. When the patient is standing or walking the arm should be supported by a nurse or phsyiotherapist until the patient regains sufficient control or his carer has been instructed in safe handling and transfer techniques.

Shoulder pain can also be caused by over enthusiastic movement of the shoulder. After the initial flaccid phase, muscle groups tend to become hypertonic. In shoulder elevation the scapula rotates around the thorax so that the glenoid faces upwards, this scapular movement is responsible for one third of full elevation. If the arm is forcefully elevated before the tone in the pectorals has been reduced by physiotherapy the unrotated head of the humerus will be pushed against the acromium trapping soft tissues and causing pain. Careful, passive, shoulder movements may be valuable in the early stages of stroke.

Spasticity

Spasticity is not inevitable even after a dense stroke. When it occurs it is often more disabling than weakness. It is made worse by pain, stress, cold, a full bladder, a loaded colon and inappropriate mobilisation. It may be prevented or reduced by eliminating pain and stress, sensory stimulation, appropriate antispasticity positioning and physiotherapy. Correct positioning of all stroke patients in the anti spasticity position is essential in the management of the stroke patient and should commence immediately after the stroke. The upper limb joints should be positioned in extension and the lower limb joints in flexion to counteract the positions that would otherwise be adopted with spasticity ie upper limb flexion and lower limb extension.

Treatment of spasticity is much less effective than prevention. If it occurs despite the above measures then physical treatments may help. Antispasticity drugs, eg Dantrolene, Baclofen, may be considered but there are serious potential side effects, eg liver damage with Dantrolene. Both drugs may also interfere with rehabilitation by reducing not only excessive tone in spastic limb(s) but also the normal tone in the other limbs.

Rehabilitation Topics

Successful rehabilitation requires that the patient's feet are comfortable. Measures must, therefore, be taken to prevent heel sores, excessively long toe nails should be cut and footwear must fit correctly. Clothing must fit correctly and be comfortable.

Balance

Nearly all stroke patients have some impairment in their mobility and/or balance. Recovery of these defaults tend to occur in a recognised sequence[6].

In stroke patients with severe impairment (neurological deficit) sitting balance tends to return before standing balance is achieved. The term static sitting balance is used when balance can be maintained in the sitting position but not when attempting tasks in the sitting position, eg dressing which requires dynamic sitting balance. Standing balance requires some degree of control over the position of the hip, knee and ankle joints. Joint instability, eg due to severe arthritis, interferes with regaining balance. Occasionally an orthosis may be required to correct this problem. Once balance has been regained the next goal is to restore mobility.

Physiotherapy Techniques

The principles described by Bobath are now widely employed in stroke rehabilitation[7]. A bilateral treatment approach is used to encourage the return of useful function rather than the old fashioned unilateral approach of strengthening the 'good' side, splinting the affected leg in a calliper and providing a tripod to aid mobility. Patients rehabilitated in this manner adopted a very abnormal pattern of walking sideways (crab walking) and mobility was usually not maintained for long. The aim of bilateral treatment is to integrate the affected side into all activities, the use of walking aids is discouraged unless found to be absolutely essential. Balance aids e.g. long pole are permissible.

Recovery, whether spontaneous or as the result of treatment, depends to a large extent on the degree of spasticity and the speed at which it develops. Spasticity is more likely to occur in patients in whom tone is already increased, especially if they use excessive effort as this tends to increase the tone on the affected side. This is usually due to an 'associated reaction' which is an increase in spasticity in an affected limb that is provoked by forceful tonic contraction of the muscles of unaffected limb(s). Excessive concentration on walking may therefore jeopardise arm function if introduced too early in the programme.

Wheelchair Use

Bobath principles suggest that the use of wheelchairs should be discouraged until it is evident that it is the only means by which some mobility can be restored[8]. Uncontrolled observations, however, suggest that morale is better when self propulsion in a wheelchair is permitted[9]. Patients who do not fully recover and require a wheelchair for long term use should be provided with either an attendant push or self propelled chair. The type will depend on the extent of the recovery, the ideal chair is one which a patients fits into snugly and can be seated on an appropriate cushion.

Occupational Therapy

The main input from occupational therapists in stroke rehabilitation is in the assessment of patient's ability to perform activities of daily living followed by appropriate practice, perceptual assessment and training, the assessment and provision of aids and appliances and pre-discharge assessment. In all activities, therapeutic or diversional, patients are encouraged to adopt a bilateral approach, thus reinforcing the 'Bobath' treatment.

Perceptual Neglect

Many stroke patients have perceptual abnormalities. Simple perceptual tests include, for example, asking the patient to 'draw a picture of yourself', 'copy this picture of a house', 'draw a clockface', and Albert's tests[10]. Most patients with perceptual neglect have a left hemiparesis and tend to ignore the left hand side of their body; they also typically ignore details on the left side of their drawings. These patients may also deny that their affected limbs actually belong to them[11]. Occasionally this form of denial can be very distressing especially when a patient finds an 'extra' arm in their bed which they are convinced belongs to someone else. These patients should not be wrongly labelled as confused.

Drawing Test

Although simple, correlate well with occupational therapist's observations during activities, eg dressing, and with more detailed assessments of parietal lobe function. There is also good correlation with eventual outcome as severe perceptual neglect is associated with a poor prognosis for recovery[12].

A GUIDE TO THE CARE OF THE ELDERLY

Dyspraxia

It is an individual's inability to sequence purposeful movements to carry out an act despite having normal primary motor skills, normal sensation and normal comprehension. They are often first detected by the occupational therapists during ADL practice, eg dressing.

Visual Problems after Stroke

The typical deficit after stroke is a homonymous hemianopia, contra lateral to the cerebral lesion. Although this may resolve, the deficit is frequently permanent.

A less common visual abnormality is visual neglect in which the visual fields may be normal when examined by confrontation but neglect of the visual field ipsilateral to the motor deficit becomes apparent when multiple images are presented. Patients with severe visual neglect often have an abnormal posture as they tend to sit with their head deviated away from the affected side. Neglect may also be demonstrated by asking the patient to read a few sentences from a book or even the headlines from a newspaper. Typically only words on the unaffected side will be seen and read. Provision of a visual cue, eg a brightly coloured marker down one side of the page, may help to overcome the problems. Patients with persistent visual neglect should be advised not to drive.

The ocular muscles may also be affected by stroke which may cause double vision. In severe cases this can inhibit rehabilitation. The above visual problems are all indications for an orthoptist's assessment as prisms attached to patient's spectacles may help to correct these problems. Covering one eye with an eye patch does not and should not be encouraged.

Communication Problems

Most communication problems in stroke patients are due to speech difficulties which include the dysphasis (expressive, receptive or mixed), dysarthria, dysphonia or speech dyspraxia. Deafness should also be considered as a possible cause. A speech and language therapist's assessment and treatment of these patients is invaluable; patient's family should also be included in some treatment sessions as communication is a two way interaction. Patients with severe communication problems often benefit by learning non-verbal communication skills when their verbal skills do not return. Use of gesture and sign language (eg Amerind) all have their place. Special gadgets, eg pencil and paper, Canon communicator or other devices with a digital display, are useful for a small minority of patients. Their success depends on the retention of language despite the absence of speech. Some treatment programmes initiated by a speech therapist may be very effectively continued by trained volunteers.

Psychological Problems

The psychological effects of having a stroke are clearly profound. Four main stages are recognised, ie grief, anger, adjustment and finally acceptance. Many patients experience depression following their stroke but most reach the stage of acceptance within 6 months. Severe depression and other psychological problems, eg emotional liability, and inappropriate mood responses, eg indifference, tend to prevent successful rehabilitation[13]. A clinical psychologist working as part of the rehabilitation team can help to identify and deal with these problems.

Urinary Incontinence

Urinary incontinence is discussed in chapter 18. Fifty-eight per cent of stroke patients are incontinent in the first 24 hours. The main cause being impaired consciousness[11]. Continence is an important prognostic factor for survival and recovery which is independent of conscious level. More than 80% of patients who are continent within 1 month of their stroke return home within the first 6 months. 74% of patients who walk between 1 and 6 months recover or almost fully recover bladder control in the first month[14].

Bowel Problems

Constipation is a common problem after stroke even in patients with previously normal bowel habit. This is mainly due to immobility leading to reduced colonic activity. It may respond to laxatives but use of a suppository or a microenema is often necessary to stimulate defecation.

Timescale of Expected Physical Recovery

Stroke patients generally achieve most of their recovery in the first 3 months after the event through many patients continue to improve, especially in communication skills, for up to 2 years or more after the stroke[15].

Finally a word about usefulness of stroke units. Although the issue is considered controversial, Longthorne *et al*, showed compelling evidence of reduced mortality in stroke units – the trials were geographically diverse, ie, these were carried out in the UK, Scandinavia and North America[16]. Furthermore, development of a stroke-service may not prove to be expensive and it does not matter what type of specialists run these units. The main emphasis, however, should be on organisation of a multidisciplinary team which co-ordinates patient's care. Understandably, patients with moderate stroke seem to benefit most in these units[17].

Appendix 1

Risk Factors for Stroke

1. Hypertension.
2. Atrial fibrillation.
3. Cardiac disease.
4. Diabetes mellitus.
5. Temporal arteritis.
6. Smoking.
7. Oral contraceptive pill.
8. Carotid bruit.
9. Peripheral Vascular Disease.

Appendix 2

Routine Investigations

1. Full blood count including platelets
2. Erythrocyte sedimentation rate (ESR)
3. Urea and electrolyte concentrations
4. Glucose concentration
5. Analysis of urine
6. Electrocardiography
7. Blood pressure measurement
8. Cholesterol concentration
9. Syphilis tests (where appropriate)
10. Sickling tests (where appropriate)

Stroke Rehabilitation

Practical Points

1. A stroke is a focal neurological deficit which persists for over 24 hours. One third die in the first 24 hours, two thirds of the survivors are left with some form of permanent disability.

2. Patients who are being considered for secondary prevention, or who would be treated if they developed a DVT should have a CT scan within 14 days to distinguish beetween cerebral haemorrhage and infarction.

3. Decisions about the need for hypotensive treatment should be delayed for 2–4 weeks as BP often rises following a stroke.

4. Post stroke patients should enter a multi-disciplinary rehabilitation programme once their condition is stable.

5. Nearly half of all stroke patients experience dysphagia but nearly all recover within 14 days.

6. Multi infarct disease is associated with severe cognitive impairment and poor prognosis.

7. Shoulder pain and spasticity can be prevented by good nursing/rehabilitation.

8. Rehabilitation may involve feet problems, balance, spasticity, communication, continence and psychological problems.

9. The assessment of dysphagia is made while observing the patient drinking 50 mls of water while sitting upright. Inability to swallow or choking indicates significant dysphagia.

References

1. Antiplatelet Trials Collaboration (1988) *Secondary prevention of vascular disease by prolonged antiplatelet treatment*, Br Med J., 296, 320–331.

2. European Carotid Surgery Trialists' Collaborative Group (1991) *MRC European Carotid Surgery Trial; interim results for symptomatic patients with severe stenosis (70–99%) or with mild (0–29%) carotid stenosis*, Lancet, 337, 1235–1243.

3. NASCET collaborators (1991) *North American symptomatic carotid andarterectomy trial first results*, N Engl J Med. 325, 445–453.

4. *Commentary: Aspirin or Warfarin for non-rheumatic and atrial fibrillation*, Lancet; 1994, 343: 683.

5. Gordon C, Langton Hewer R & Wade DT (1987) *Dysphagia in acute stroke*, Br Med J., 295, 411–414.

6. Partridge CJ, Johnston M & Edwards S (1987) *Recovery from physical disability after stroke: normal patterns as a basis for evaluation*, Lancet, i, 373–375.

7. Bobath B (1978) *Adult hemiplegia: evaluation and treatment*, 2nd Edition, Heinemann, London.

8. Ashburn A & Lynch M (1988) *Disadvantages of the early use of wheelchairs in the treatment of hemiplegia*, Clin Rehab, 2, 327–331.

9. Blower P (1988) *The advantages of the early use of wheelchairs in the treatment of hemiplegia*, Clin Rehab, 2, 323–325.

10. Fullerton KJ, McSherry D & Stout D (1986) *Albert's Test: a neglected test of perceptual neglect*, Lancet, i, 430–432.

11. Cutting J (1978) *Study of anosgnosia*, J Neurol Neurosurg Psych, 41, 5480555.

12. Fullerton KJ, Mackenzie G & Stout RW (1988) *Prognostic indices in stroke*, Quarterly J. Med, 250, 147–162.

13. House A (1987) *Depression after stroke*, Br Med J., 294, 76–78.

14. Barer D (1989) *Continence after stroke*, Age & Ageing, 18, 183–191.

15. Andrews K, Brocklehurst JC, Richards D & Laycock PJ (1981) *The rate of recovery from stroke and its measurement*, Int J Rehab Med, 3, 155–161.

16. Longhorne P, Williams BO, Gilchrist W & Howie K (1993) *Do stroke units save lives?*, Lancet, 342, 395–8.

17. Dennis M & Langhorne P (1994) *So stroke units save lives: where do we go from here?*, Br. Med. J., 309, 1273–7.

Chapter 29

Diabetes Mellitus

Dr T L Dornan DM FRCP
Consultant Physician and Honorary Clinical Senior Lecturer
Hope Hospital
Stott Lane
Salford
Manchester
M6 8HD

Biosketch:

Dr Dornan qualified from Oxford University with BM, BCh in 1975, had his
DM in 1982 and FRCP (UK) in 1992. He is currently Consultant Physician
with an interest in diabetes and endocrinology at Salford Royal Hospital NHS
Trust. He is also Honorary Clinical Senior Lecturer, University of Manchester
and Hospital Dean, Salford Sector, University of Manchester Medical School.
His research interests include diabetes and related topics. He has a host of publications to his credit, on diabetes and related topics.

Introduction

Diabetes deserves a prominent place in a text-book of elderly care for three main reasons: *first*, old age is the time of life when it is commonest; *second* it may be part of a complex pattern of multi-system disease and present a challenge to a physician who is not a specialist in diabetes; and *third*, injudicious treatment as well as the disease itself can cause serious ill health.

Definition and Prevalence

Nearly half of all people with diabetes are past retirement age. By age 70, the prevalence of known diabetes is over 5% and probably as many again have unrecognised glucose intolerance[1]. The WHO criteria for interpreting glucose tolerance tests[2] make no allowance for the fact that post-prandial blood glucose increases 0.5 mmol/l per decade after age 50 yrs in the 'normal' population and it is an unanswered question whether the otherwise well elderly who narrowly 'fail' a glucose tolerance test are diseased or not. True, the excess mortality associated with diabetes falls with age but even past 75 years of age there is evidence of increased mortality in patients with overt diabetes[3]. A sensible compromise is to avoid rigid criteria and think in terms of what can be achieved for each individual. An alert and well motivated 70 year-old with asymptomatic hyperglycaemia is a candidate for full preventive care including a 'prudent diet' (cardiovascular prevention) and periodic screening for diabetic complications. The same degree of hyperglycaemia in another individual with poor general health might be left untreated; it should not, however, be *forgotten* because it could worsen and become a threat to life or well-being in the future.

Morbidity and Mortality

While cardiovascular disease is the main cause of excess mortality in diabetic patients of all ages, there are also deaths due to infection, hypoglycaemia and hyperglycaemia. The metabolic causes of death are important, even if not frequent, because they are potentially avoidable. A survey in Nottingham found that the mortality from hyperglycaemic coma rose from <5% in young people to >40% in the elderly[4]. Delayed recognition contributed to the rising mortality with age; in particular, failure to recognise that elderly diabetic people were 'ill' and refer them to hospital meant that many were doomed by the time of their admission. Hypoglycaemia may also cause avoidable morbidity, particularly if it is due to over-zealous treatment or an inappropriate choice of regimen. Diabetic instability may signal the onset of dementia[5].

A community survey of elderly people with diabetes in Nottingham[6] found that cardiovascular disease was about twice as prevalent as in non-diabetic controls. Visual impairment was the single greatest cause of morbidity, more often due to cataract than retinopathy. Over three-quarters of patients had one or two complications, though few had more than two. One third of diabetic patients were on 3 or more prescription medications (excluding their hypoglycaemic therapy) and this 'polypharmacy' was twice as common as in controls. The diabetic patients consulted their GPs or were admitted to hospital more often and were more likely to be housebound than their non-diabetic peers. They perceived their health as much worse than controls. These observations suggest that the diabetic elderly are a group with high morbidity and great potential for health gain but who need a community-orientated approach to care.

Types and Causes

Between 10 and 20% of elderly diabetics are insulin-treated, some ketosis-prone but most 'tablet failures' with type 2 diabetes. An important point is that severely insulin-deficient diabetes may present in old age, albeit less commonly than in youth. In practice, rigid stereotypes of type 1 and type 2 diabetes are less helpful than a pragmatic approach which seeks the best treatment for each individual. Amongst causes of secondary diabetes, pancreatic carcinoma is worth bearing in mind when the degree of wasting and weight loss seem disproportionately great. Beta blockers and thiazide diuretics worsen glucose tolerance and may be responsible for deterioration in previously stable glycaemic control or the new presentation of diabetes.

Treatment

Provided simple rules are followed, the management of diabetes can be straightforward and rewarding. There is a simple hierarchy of treatments starting with diet and finishing with insulin; there is usually plenty of time for the patient and carer to find which works best. This approach can only be adopted, however, if the carer is alert to those situations where time is not on the patient's side.

Recognising the 'Ill' Diabetic Patient

A common difficulty, which may have disastrous consequences for the patient, is how to recognise the person who is 'ill' and needs specialist referral and/or insulin as a matter of urgency. Elderly people admitted with fatal ketoacidosis may have been non-specifically unwell for days or weeks with poor mobility, apathy, drowsiness, falls and vomiting, diarrhoea and incontinence. The diagnosis of severe hyperglycaemia can be hard to make in patients who are not known to be diabetic and can be missed even in those with known diabetes. Whether at presentation or in the course of diabetes, the following should be regarded as indications for urgent specialist attention (usually hospital admission):

- Persistent vomiting, diarrhoea and/or dehydration;
- Ketonuria;
- Symptomatic hyperglycaemia despite maximum oral hypoglycaemic therapy;
- Complications such as unstable angina or infection associated with symptomatic hyperglycaemia;
- Non-specific severe ill-health.

Over-reliance on blood glucose measurements to tell whether diabetes is out of control is a common mistake, though not usually a dangerous one since it favours over-referral rather than under-referral. Assessment should include a history, paying attention to the symptoms described above, a urine (or blood) test for ketones, an assessment of hydration, measurement of plasma urea and electrolytes and a thorough physical examination for causes or complications of hyperglycaemia (including urine culture, blood culture, ECG and chest X-ray). Uncontrolled diabetes or severe intercurrent illness in the diabetic elderly must be treated with insulin (even if the patient was previously non-insulin dependent) although some may be able to come off insulin after treatment of a precipitating infection or other disease.

Who Else Needs Insulin?

Another common mistake, though with less dramatic consequences, is failure to recognise the person who is chronically hyperglycaemic and needs insulin for their well-being.

Dependence on insulin may be intermittent; ketosis is easily recognised as an absolute indication for insulin but what of the person who is ketotic when they have a urinary tract infection and well controlled with tablets at other times? Unless there are strong practical difficulties with administering insulin, it is wise to keep such patients on it both to minimise ketosis if infection recurs and because the very fact of being on insulin alerts professionals to the possibility of decompensation. Other relative indications apply to the patient on full-dose oral hypoglycaemic agents and include:

- Underweight and/or continuing weight loss;
- Persistent hyperglycaemia (eg $HbA_{1c} > 8\%$);
- Pruritis vulvae and/or balanitis;
- Incontinence.

Even the most experienced diabetologist cannot predict confidently who will and who will not benefit; again, pragmatism is the best approach. Explaining to the patient that a change to insulin is not an irreversible step, that it means taking less tablets, that it is *not* a sign that their diabetes has 'worsened' and that they can change back to tablets if their well-being does not improve wins over all but the most hardened in their opposition. In my experience, the trial of insulin is usually successful and surprisingly few ask for their tablets back!

An Approach to the New Diabetic Patient

In general, diet should be the first treatment for all patients with non-insulin dependent diabetes although there is a case for giving patients with severe symptoms a short course of sulphonylurea to restore their well-being, provided the possibility that they may not need it long-term is remembered. Those who are underweight at presentation are likely to be severely insulin-deficient and need sulphonylurea or insulin in the long run but most people newly presenting with non-insulin-dependent diabetes are overweight; premature prescription of a sulphonylurea is likely to cause weight gain, (or, at least, minimise weight loss), and gives the misleading impression that it is the doctor's prescription rather than the patient's self-care which is the more important. Cutting sugar out of the diet can improve symptoms rapidly and may be the only treatment a patient needs. Whatever their age or circumstances, all diabetic patients should be seen by a dietitian at diagnosis and periodically thereafter. Dietetic services are often poorly provided in the community so many have to make do with second best, a diet sheet or advice from a non-expert. Sugar should be avoided as far as possible, calorie intake adjusted to attain and maintain as near ideal body weight as possible and meals spread through the day. Many elderly patients take great pride in following this advice. For others, particularly those in institutions, a 'diabetic diet' can too easily become monotonous and punitive. How rigidly the rules are applied needs judgement, remembering that blind pursuit of therapeutic targets may do more harm than good to the patient's overall well-being.

Only when diet has 'failed' should long-term oral hypoglycaemic therapy be initiated. The choice is between metformin and a sulphonylurea. Metformin is generally under-used; it has advantages over sulphonylureas in favouring weight *loss* rather than *gain* and is no less effective. About 25% of patients experience side-effects, including nausea, anorexia and a bad taste in the mouth. It is contra-indicated in patients with abnormal liver function tests, established renal impairment and active congestive cardiac failure but (contrary to popular belief) does *not* cause lactic acidosis if these cautions are observed[7]. It is best started at a dose of 500 mg daily increased in 500 mg increments at weekly intervals to a maximum dose of 1 gm tds, or until satisfactory blood glucose control is achieved or the patient experiences side effects. If control is still unsatisfactory, a sulphonylurea can be added. Choosing metformin as the first-line oral hypoglycaemic in overweight patients helps to minimise the morbidity of obesity in the diabetic elderly.

Patients who are underweight, intolerant of metformin or have contraindications to it should receive a sulphonylurea. Chlorpropamide and glibenclamide are relatively contraindicated in patients over the age of 70, particularly those who live alone, because they can cause severe, prolonged and potentially fatal hypoglycaemia. Glipizide, gliclazide or tolbutamide are suitable alternatives. Gliclazide and gliquidone are particularly suitable for patients with renal failure because they do not depend upon renal excretion.

Practicalities of Insulin Treatment

Whatever the indication for insulin, the regimen is likely to consist of one or two injections per day, usually of medium-acting insulin with or without soluble. Pork insulin might be chosen for the occasional person who complains of loss of hypoglycaemic warning but there is no reason not to use human insulin in those starting treatment *de novo*. Those patients who use combinations of short and medium acting insulin stand to gain little from drawing up the two types separately into the same syringe and there is now a wide range of pre-mixed combinations of soluble and isophane for both syringe and pen. The business of drawing up insulin may be harder than injecting it for those with poor manual dexterity so a pen injector with cartridged isophane or an isophane/soluble mixture is the treatment of choice for most elderly patients on insulin. If the patient or carer is able, it is best to opt for twice-daily insulin from the outset although some manage with a single injection (with obvious advantages if they depend on a district nurse).

Therapeutic Targets and Monitoring

Before discussing how diabetic control should be monitored, it is important to consider the range of possible therapeutic goals:

- Prevention of hyperglycaemic coma;
- Ability to maintain dignity and independence;
- Maximisation of energy and well-being;
- Avoidance of symptoms of hypo- and hyperglycaemia;
- Attainment of glycaemic targets;
- Attainment and maintenance of target weight.

In a patient who stubbornly insists on living alone despite dementia and disability, avoidance of severe hyperglycaemia may be all that can be hoped for. Just controlling symptoms may be the target for others, whilst patients with good health and motivation may strive successfully for normoglycaemia.

Weight should be monitored (at clinic visits) in all patients because it distinguishes over-eating from insulin deficiency as the cause of poor blood glucose control; weight loss may be the clearest pointer to the need for insulin. Those who are able should do some form of self-monitoring to alert them and their carers to deteriorating control. As a rule of thumb, ill health in the elderly cannot be due to hyperglycaemia if the urine is free of glucose. Only a minority of elderly people perform home blood glucose monitoring but some do so to very good effect. The extra precision of blood over urine glucose monitoring is valuable in adjusting doses of insulin and sulphonylureas so home blood glucose monitoring is best reserved for better motivated patients. Periodic clinic measurement of fasting blood glucose, HbA_{1c} or fructosamine is an important backup to self-monitoring because it is patient-independent and objective.

Complications

Controversy rages as to whether macrovascular complications are preventable and at least one important trial will be reported in the near future[8] but there is now clear evidence in young people with insulin-dependent diabetes that good control can prevent both the development and progression of microvascular complications[9]. These observations are of uncertain relevance to the elderly because life expectancy is shorter than in the patients in whom 'tight control' is proven effective; those who develop complications may already have them when their diabetes is diagnosed[10] and 'tight' control may be an unrealistic goal. It is reasonable to believe that good control may protect those who do not have complications from developing them but the greatest pay-off in preventing morbidity is likely to come from screening and early treatment of established complications.

Diabetic Eye Disease

Retinopathy and cataract are the two main causes of visual loss although glaucoma and macular degeneration are also prevalent in diabetes. 'Snowflake' cataract may develop very rapidly and is virtually pathognomonic of diabetes but is usually seen in younger patients. Cataract in diabetes is indistinguishable from cataract in the non-diabetic but occurs more frequently and at a younger age. The two forms of retinopathy which can cause visual loss are maculopathy and proliferative retinopathy. Several excellent colour atlases are available for the clinical features of diabetic eye disease[11, 12] although those taking a serious interest in the care of diabetes are advised to learn retinal examination in a specialist eye clinic. Two points should be appreciated: first, patients in general and the elderly in particular may have severe diabetic eye disease without complaining of visual symptoms. Proliferative retinopathy may cause no symptoms until vitreous haemorrhage occurs. Maculopathy, the form most likely to cause visual loss in the elderly, may develop slowly and be attributed to 'old age'. With either disease, early recognition is the key to preventing blindness. Retinal photocoagulation for maculopathy is ineffective once acuity has dropped below 6/36 and the patient may progress to advanced diabetic eye disease despite treatment once retinal new vessels have bled. Second, diabetic eye disease may be well established *at the time diabetes first presents*. the prevalance of retinopathy at presentation rises from <1% in patients below the age of 30 to 10% in those over 65, some of whom need urgent ophthalmic care. It follows from these general points that eye examination should be performed at diagnosis and at least yearly thereafter in all patients, irrespective how 'mild' their diabetes. This should include measurement of visual acuity (using a reading chart or Snellen chart) and fundoscopy through dilated pupils. 1% tropicamide causes mild discomfort when it is instilled and short-lived blurring of vision but is well tolerated and gives an adequate view of the fundus in most patients after about 30 minutes. It should be avoided in those with a history of angle closure glaucoma (because it may precipitate an attack) but is otherwise relatively free of side effects. The following are indications for ophthalmic referral:

- Definite or suspected new vessels;
- Significant background changes at or within one disc diameter of the macula;
- Pre-proliferative retinopathy;
- Unexplained loss of visual acuity.

Foot Disease

The rate of amputation is fifty-fold higher in diabetic subjects than controls[13]. Once ischaemic necrosis due to peripheral vascular disease is established, little can be done to prevent amputation. In sharp contrast, 80% of predominantly *neuropathic* ulcers can be healed provided presentation is early and treatment instituted promptly. In practice, several factors may contribute to an episode of foot ulveration:

Somatic Neuropathy	Feet insensitive Abnormal foot shape and pressure distribution
Autonomic Neuropathy	Skin dry and prone to crack

Ischaemia
Reduced Resistance to Infection
Poor Vision   Unable to see ulceration

The key to effective care is to *educate* patients about the risks; they must be informed that they may have insensitive feet and taught foot hygiene and the need for regular inspection of their feet. They should be regularly *screened* for neuropathy and peripheral vascular disease and instructed to *present immediately* if problems develop. Ideally, all diabetic patients should have preventive chiropody as well as immediate access to treatment. The service should include supply of appropriate orthotic appliances to take the weight off pressure point or ulcers. The treatment of established foot ulceration requires specialist hospital care which may be provided by a physician, vascular surgeon or orthopaedic surgeon working in conjunction with a chiropodist and diabetic foot nurse. The mainstays of treatment are early debridement, prolonged bed rest, early and appropriate antibiotic treatment continued until the ulcer is healed and regular dressings. Regular X-rays are important to detect osteomyelitis.

Ischaemic Heart Disease

Diabetic patients are 2–3 times more prone to cardiovascular disease than non-diabetics. This may present as angina, acute myocardial infarction or congestive cardiac failure. The general approach to management is the same as in non-diabetics. Intractable congestive cardiac failure due to a dilational ischaemic cardiomyopathy and associated with renal impairment is a particularly common problem in the diabetic elderly, requiring aggressive treatment with loop diuretics and synergistic agents such as metolazone. Another aspect of ischaemic heart disease relatively specific to diabetes is 'silent' myocardial infarction which may present with non-specific malaise, cardiac failure, vomiting or sudden loss of diabetic control. The hospital mortality of acute myocardial infarction is 2–3 times increased in diabetic patients. Fibrinolytic therapy is as effective in diabetic as in non-diabetic subjects and those with diabetes have, in absolute terms, much more to gain so an aggressive policy should be pursued. Too often diabetic patients are denied fibrinolysis on spurious grounds such as the presence of simple retinopathy.

Hypertension and Nephropathy

Second to ischaemic heart disease, renal failure is the most serious outcome of diabetes in younger subjects but has not generally been recognised for the major problem that it is in the elderly. Recently, many diabetic patients starting dialysis have been over the age of 65 and renal impairment has increasingly been recognised as a factor predisposing to cardiac failure (see above; best described as the diabetic 'cardiorenal syndrome'). Hypertension is especially prevalent in diabetes and may be a factor contributing both to cardiovascular risk and renal disease. ACE inhibitors appear to be particularly suitable for hypertension and early renal impairment in the diabetic elderly but must be used carefully because the diabetic elderly are at substantial risk of worsened renal function (due to occult renal artery stenosis) and/or potassium retention.

Self-Care and Structured Care

Diabetes has been described as the disease, par excellence, where the patient has to be 'his/her own doctor'. This is clearly seen in the insulin-treated executive who manages the complex task of balancing his treatment across time zones and through the hurly-burly of professional life but the same principles apply, albeit less glamorously, to elderly people with diabetes. Responsibility rests squarely on them to follow a diet, monitor their control, watch for early signs of complications, report problems and demand a high standard of care from the professionals looking after them. Many take up the challenge in retirement with a great deal more dedication than their younger counterparts, perhaps because a disciplined lifestyle comes easier to them in the later years of life. Those who cannot care for themselves depend on carers, often their spouse or family. There may be remarkable partnership between the elderly patient with diabetes and his/her spouse, with catastrophic results if the spouse dies or becomes disabled. It is important for professionals to encourage this sense of partnership by including family in discussions about management. Sensitive education of carers in the use of home blood glucose monitoring, glucagon and injection aids like the pen injector may make the difference between success and failure in getting an elderly person back out into the community. Traditional hospital diabetic clinics have a part to play in diagnosis, initiating treatment and sorting out coincidental or associated medical problems, but are most effective if they work in collaboration with community care. This is provided in many districts by diabetes specialist nurses who can liaise with district nurses, general practitioners and other professional groups and bring a very high degree of expertise out to the patient's home. General practice-based care is particularly well suited to the elderly, because it is nearer to the patient's home, more accessible, less daunting and better able to treat diabetes in a broad medical and social context, but must be backed up by good secondary care.

Best of all is a coordinated district-wide approach to diabetes care with mini-clinics in general practice, home visiting for patients who are housebound, ready access to specialist care both for specifically 'diabetic' problems and for the broader expertise of a hospital 'health care for the elderly' team. This sort of structure should be achievable in the British National Health Service and many districts are taking steps towards the ideal.

Diabetes and the Elderly

Practical points

1. Up to 10% of elderly people have symptomatic or asymptomatic diabetes; for every one with known diabetes there is another undiagnosed.

2. Even patients with asymptomatic diabetes may have severe complications when the diagnosis is first made.

3. Foot, eye and cardiovascular disease are the major tissue complications in this age group.

4. Diet is the first-line treatment; tablets should only be used if diet fails to achieve control; long-acting sulphonylureas such as glibenclamide and chlorpropamide are potentially lethal in the elderly.

5. 10% per annum of patients with 'non-insulin dependent diabetes' become uncontrolled on oral hypoglycaemics and need conversion to insulin; those caring for the diabetic elderly must be alert to this need.

6. Good blood glucose control can probably reduce complications in the elderly but must not be pursued at the expense of well-being and independence.

7. Provision of care is a multidisciplinary process which must be coordinated between the community and hospital; shared care following agreed protocols optimises care.

8. Diabetic patients and their carers should be active partners in the process of care and given the necessary education and support.

References

1. Neil HAW, Thompson AV, Thorogood M, Fowler GH & Mann JI (1989) *Diabetes in the elderly: the Oxford Community Diabetes Survey*, Diabetic Med, 6, 608–13.

2. WHO (1985) *Diabetes Mellitus*, World Health Organisation Technical Report Series, 727, Geneva.

3. Croxson SCM, Price DE, Burden M, Jagger C & Burden AC (1994) *The mortality of elderly people with diabetes*, Diabetic Med, 11, 250–2.

4. Gale EAM, Dornan TL & Tattersall RB (1981) *Severely uncontrolled diabetes in the over-fifties*, Diabetologia, 21, 25–8.

5. Griffith DNW & Yudkin JS (1989) *Brittle diabetes in the elderly*, Diabetic Medicine, 6, 440–3.

6. Dornan TL, Peck GM, Gow JDC & Tattersall RB (1992) *A Community Survey of Diabetes in the Elderly*, Diabetic Med, 9, 860–65.

7. Campbell IW (1984) *Metformin and Glibenclamide: comparative risks*, Br Med J, 289, 289.

8. UK Prospective Study Group (1991) *UK Prospective Study VIII. study design, progress and performance*, Diabetologia, 34, 877–90.

9. The Diabetes Control and Complications Research Group (1993) *The effect of intensive treatment of diabetes on the development and progression of long-term complications in insulin-dependent diabetes mellitus*, Engl J Med, 329, 97–86.

10. Soler NG, Fitzgerald MG, Malins JM & Summers ROC (1969) *Retinopathy at diagnosis of diabetes with special reference to patients under 40 years of age*, BR Med J, 3, 567–9.

11. Kritzinger EE & Taylor KG (1984) *Diabetic eye disease: an illustrated guide to diagnosis and management*, MTP Press, Lancaster.

12. Bloom A & Ireland J (1980) *A colour atlas of diabetes*, Wolfe Medical Atlases, London.

13. Waugh NR (1988) *Amputations in diabetic patients – a review of rates, relative risks and resource use*, Community Med, 10, 279–88.

Chapter 30

Gastrointestinal Malignancies

Dr Juanita Pascual MBBS, MRCP
Consultant Physician
University Hospital of Wales
Heath Park
Cardiff CF0 4XW
Wales

Professor Ken Woodhouse
Professor of Geriatric Medicine
University of Wales, 3rd Floor
College of Medicine Building
Llandough Hospital
Penlan Road, Penarth
South Glamorgan CS64 2FX
Wales

Biosketch:

Dr Pascual is a Consultant Physician in Geriatric Medicine based at the University Hospital of Wales in Cardiff. Her main areas of clinical and research interests include complications of surgical procedures in elderly patients and also the management of cardiovascular problems in the elderly. In addition, she has a strong interest in pharmacotherapeutics and has published several articles on drug prescribing in the elderly over a wide range of conditions.

Professor Ken Woodhouse qualified BM Honours, Southampton in 1977, and was awarded the Fellowship of the Royal College of Physicians (London) in 1990. His current position is that of Professor of Geriatric Medicine at the University of Wales College of Medicine in Cardiff, taking up his post in October 1990. He has experience in such areas as undergraduate and postgraduate education; clinical service provision; and NHS management and carries out various functions for national and international governmental and non-governmental agencies. His major research interests include drug metabolism and ageing; physiology and morphology of ageing; adverse drug reactions in ageing; analgesia in the elderly; trauma, orthogeriatrics and ageing.

Introduction

Gastrointestinal malignancy is common in the elderly, the incidence of most gastrointestinal malignancies increasing with advancing age. The elderly sometimes present differently to their younger counterparts and malignancy may be easily missed until a more advanced stage of the disease has been reached. It is important for physicians to be alert to these atypical presentations, as early detection and intervention will often influence morbidity and mortality. Age *per se* should not be a barrier to investigation and possible curative intervention. Each case needs to be judged on the probability of effecting a cure, the risks of treatment, the patient's frailty and coexisting illness, the presence or absence of metastatic disease. In addition, the patient's wishes for active intervention once they have been made aware of the likely risks and benefits should be paramount.

Even where a cure is not possible or desirable, there is much that can be done to palliate symptoms and improve quality of life (see chapter 24 Palliative Care). Patients need to be aware that choosing a non-aggressive option does not necessarily mean accepting an uncomfortable and painful death.

This chapter will concentrate on the more common gastrointestinal malignancies in the elderly, their presentation and diagnosis, and will explore the possible management options. (See chapter 24).

Carcinoma of the Oesophagus

The incidence of oesophageal carcinoma increases with age; most patients presenting over the age of 65. The main risk factors in Western Europe appear to be alcohol intake and cigarette smoking, being associated with 80–90% of patients with oesophageal cancer. However, patients with achalasia, long-standing reflux oesophagitis or Barret's oesophagus are all at risk and require careful endoscopic surveillance to detect early malignant change. The majority of carcinomas are squamous cell in origin and 80% are sited in the middle or lower third of the oesophagus.

Presentation and Diagnosis

Oesophageal carcinoma tends to present late, dysphagia being the most common presenting symptom. Dysphagia is usually initially for solids, but progresses over a few months to liquids. The oesophageal lumen is usually at least 60% stenosed at the time of presentation. Weight loss often occurs rapidly and pain on swallowing occurs in approximately 50% of patients. Other associated symptoms are regurgitation, especially when supine, and associated with cough and aspiration, and pain from local invasion of surrounding structures. Haematemesis may occur and may occasionally be massive if the aorta is eroded. Examination may reveal supraclavicular lymphadenopathy, a cervical mass or deviation of the trachea. Both superior vena cava obstruction or a Horner's syndrome may occur, while hepatomegaly should suggest metastatic spread.

Investigation should initially consist of barium studies which will indicate the size and position of the tumour. Subsequently, an endoscopy and biopsy are required to confirm the diagnosis. Further staging of the disease will require CT scanning of the upper abdomen and mediastinum to determine the extent of local involvement, and for lesions in the upper third of the oesophagus, bronchoscopy to determine tracheo-bronchial spread.

Management

For most patients, treatment is palliative with potentially curative resection being possible in only 20% of patients because of the late presentation of the disease.

In one large series, 60% of patients underwent surgery with 40% being resectable. Operative mortality was 13.7% in those aged over 70[1]. Long-term curative results are poor with 5 year survival rates ranging from 10–20%, although some centres have achieved much better results, but only with early disease[2]. Radiotherapy can also be used to treat patients with squamous cell carcinomas, especially in the upper third, but the 5 year survival rates are only between 5–20%. With palliative treatment alone, 5 year survival is in the order of 4%.

Options for Palliative Treatment

To relieve dysphagia, the oesophagus can be endoscopically intubated using an Atkinson tube. Celestin or Mousseau-Barbin tubes can also be inserted, but for these a laporotomy is required. All these tubes can become obstructed or displaced and can cause oesophageal perforation.

They may allow the patient to take a soft diet, but tend not to restore normal swallowing.

Laser therapy can be used to reduce tumour size and restore some oesophageal patency. However, it is a time-consuming procedure requiring multiple sessions of therapy and it is not yet widely available. Radiotherapy may provide useful palliation with reduction in tumour bulk, but occasionally can lead to a tracheo-oesophageal fistula. Intra-oesophageal radiotherapy is also attracting increasing attention and is becoming simpler and safer.

Carcinoma of the Stomach

Although the incidence of gastric carcinoma has fallen by approximately 55% in England and Wales over the past thirty years, as with other gastrointestinal malignancies there is an increased incidence with age. Chronic atrophic gastritis, adenomatous polyps, blood group A and previous gastric resection can all predispose to gastric carcinoma. However, epidemiology suggests a role for dietary and environmental factors, particularly dietary intake of nitrosamines, in the aetiology of the condition. Since atrophic gastritis is present in up to 90% of patients with gastric cancer, and it is believed to have pre-malignant potential, there has been increasing interest in the possible role of *Helicobacter pylori* in gastric carcinogenesis as it appears to be causally implicated in the development of chronic atrophic gastritis.

Presentation and Diagnosis

Gastric carcinoma tends to present in a vague and non-specific way with transient abdominal symptoms such as epigastric discomfort or 'bloating'. As such symptoms are common even in the normal elderly, these may pass unnoticed for a period of time and the majority of carcinomas present at an advanced stage. A high incidence of suspicion is, therefore, required, particularly in the presence of unexplained anorexia or weight loss, and should prompt early investigation by endoscopy. At present, it remains unclear whether screening by endoscopy of 'high risk' elderly, ie, those with known chronic atrophic gastritis, pernicious anaemia or a history of gastric surgery 15 or more years previously, is either beneficial or even practicable.

Endoscopy with direct visualisation, brush cytology and biopsy is the first choice in the diagnosis of gastric carcinoma. Ultrasound or CT scanning can be used to determine the extent of perigastric involvement and metastasis.

Treatment

Prognosis is related to the degree of penetration through the gastric wall: prognosis is worse if the tumour has penetrated through the muscularis propria and the serosa rather than being confined to the mucosa or submucosa.

Only 30–40% of patients have resectable tumours and the overall 5 year survival rate is only approximately 20%. Generally, massive upper abdominal resections are not to be recommended in frail elderly patients. In unresectable tumours, palliative surgery may sometimes be necessary, but such surgery should be kept to a minimum.

There is currently no evidence that either chemotherapy or radiotherapy are of benefit in unresectable tumours.

Post-gastrectomy problems which may occur are outlined in the table (appendix 1).

Other Gastric Malignancies

Gastric lymphoma is uncommon, accounting for about 5% of gastric malignancies. Presentation and appearance are as for gastric carcinoma, but the prognosis is much more favourable. Treatment is by total gastrectomy and subsequent chemotherapy. Gastric carcinoids are extremely rare in old age.

Hepatobiliary Malignancy

Helpatocellular Carcinoma

Primary hepatocellular carcinoma is rare in the UK and is usually associated with hepatic cirrhosis regardless of the underlying cause. It appears that the duration of an individual's cirrhosis is an important aetiological factor. More than 40% of those with hepatocellular carcinoma are over 70[3] at presentation.

Presentation and Diagnosis

Patients often present with the complications of cirrhosis – bleeding varices, ascites or jaundice and hepatic encephalopathy. A high index of suspicion, therefore, is required when an elderly patient presents with such a deterioration. Patients may also present with symptoms directly due to the tumour, ie, right upper quadrant pain and weight loss with bone pain from bony metastases. Prognosis is related to tumour size at detection and it is, therefore, recommended to screen all elderly patients with cirrhosis with a six monthly check on serum alpha-fetoprotein. Since this test is only 70% sensitive, some centres recommend regular liver ultrasound scans. Size, extent and number of tumours are assessed by hepatic CT scan, preferably with angiography and CT guided biopsy.

Survival time since presentation is poor, being often less than 6 months. small single lesions are sometimes resectable and ultrasound guided injection of ethanol appears moderately effective. Other treatments are currently under evaluation.

Biliary Malignancy

Carcinoma of the Gallbladder

Gallbladder malignancy is age-related and occurs most commonly at very advanced age. There is a slight increase in risk with gallstones, particularly if the gallbladder wall itself has calcified.

Presentation is usually late when the disease has advanced beyond the gallbladder itself. Typical presentation are upper abdominal pain, weight loss, a right upper quadrant mass and jaundice, and may be confused with other forms of biliary or liver disease. One year survival is less than 10%. Heroic surgery is rarely indicated because of its poor operative mortality and lack of improvement in 10 year survival figures. Treatment is, therefore, palliative, particularly the relief of biliary obstruction.

Cholangiocarcinoma

Bile duct carcinomas can arise at any point in the biliary tree. Usual presentation is with obstructive jaundice and pruritus. Weakness and weight loss may be prominent and epigastric discomfort and steatorrhoea may occur. Examination usually reveals jaundice and smooth hepatomegaly. Liver function tests show an obstructive picture.

Initial investigation with ultrasound usually reveals a dilated biliary tree down to the site of obstruction. ERCP, or if the lesion is within the liver, percutaenous transhepatic cholangiography (PTC), should be carried out to confirm the diagnosis and assess the extent of the lesion.

Prognosis and Treatment

The tumour is locally invasive, distant metastases being relatively rare. Prognosis even without treatment is in the order of one year. Surgical excision is rarely possible, but palliative stenting can be carried out endoscopically or transhepatically, depending on the site of the tumour. Mean survival is then of the order of 18 months with greatly improved quality of life due to decreased pruritus, weight gain and better general well-being.

Carcinoma of the Pancreas

The incidence of carcinoma of the pancreas is increasing and age itself is the most important known risk factor. In the UK, 80% of patients are aged over 60[4]. In the early stages, pancreatic cancer tends to be asymptomatic and is often detected only at an advanced stage.

Concequently, at presentation only 10–15% of tumours are resectable.

Presentation

Jaundice due to local invasion of the common bile duct by tumour is the most common presenting symptom of carcinoma of the head of the pancreas. Tumours of the body or tail usually present with pain; and jaundice occurs late. Regardless of the site, pain is a prominent feature. It is usually epigastric, radiating to the back and to the right or left hypochondrium. It is intense and persistent but is improved characteristically on bending forward. In the early stages this pain may be mistakenly diagnosed as arising from the dorsal spine. Anorexia and rapid weight loss are very common. Disturbed pancreatic function can lead to steatorrhoea, impaired glucose tolerance and frank diabetes.

Migratory thrombophlebitis has been described, but is rare. Examination may reveal wasting, jaundice and signs of scratching. In advanced stages, an epigastric mass may be felt and there is often severe pain on deep palpation of the epigastrium. Hepatomegaly may be present due to either metastases or cholestasis. Courvoisier's sign (palpable gallbladder) is found in 20–30% of cases of carcinoma of the head of the pancreas. Ascites and peripheral oedema occur in advanced disease.

Diagnosis

A good history is very important and the sudden appearance of jaundice or characteristic pain, especially when associated with anorexia or newly diagnosed diabetes, should alert the physician and prompt further investigation. Abdominal ultrasound is the first-line investigation and, in experienced hands, will detect around 85% of tumours. If a mass is demonstrated, further evaluation is by ultrasound guided needle-biopsy. If the diagnosis remains in doubt ERCP or CT scanning will usually establish the diagnosis. Pancreatic enzymes, eg, amylase, tend to be unhelpful as their levels can be widely variable. Elevation of liver enzymes can be due to biliary obstruction or to metastatic spread. Resectability is determined by the result of CT scanning plus angiography.

Treatment

Most patients die within 5–6 months of presentation.

Only tumours which are limited to the pancreas without evidence of vascular, lymphatic or metastatic involvement should be resected. Even with resectable tumours, 5 year survival is about 5 to 15%, although periampullary carcinomas have the best prognosis, and 30 to 55% 5 year survival has been reported[5]. For advanced tumours, only palliative therapy is indicated. Jaundice can be relieved by surgical biliary bypass or preferably by less invasive stenting by endoscopic or transhepatic routes. Chemotherapy and radiotherapy are largely ineffective. Palliation should concentrate on adequate pain relief, which can be difficult to achieve. When opiate analgesia is inadequate, relief may be obtained by coeliac plexus block or epidural anaesthesia. Diabetes, if it occurs, is treated with insulin; steatorrhoea with oral pancreatic enzymes.

Small Intestinal Malignancies

Malignant tumours of the small intestine are very uncommon in the elderly. Of those that do occur, carcinoid tumours are the most common type and their presentation, management and prognosis is no different in the elderly to that in younger patients.

Adenocarcinomas of the small intestine are rare, but tend to occur more frequently in the duodenum where they present with epigastric pain, vomiting and weight loss. They may present with iron deficiency anaemia secondary to occult blood loss, and jaundice occurs in about 30% of patients secondary to biliary obstruction (occasionally, they present with small intestinal obstruction).

Adenocarcinoma lower down the small bowel is extremely rare in the elderly. Tumours associated with Crohn's disease tend to arise earlier in life.

Small bowel lymphoma may occur in relation to pre-existing coeliac disease or de novo. It is important to remember that treatment of the condition with resection and subsequent radiotherapy may have excellent results even in very elderly individuals with large lymphomas.

Colorectal Malignancy

Carcinoma of the colon and rectum is the most common malignancy in old age, apart from carcinoma of the prostate in men and its incidence doubles with every decade of age over forty years[6].

Presentation and Diagnosis

Despite improvement during recent decades, delay in diagnosis remains an important problem. Presentation is often vague with lower abdominal discomfort, change in bowel habit, bleeding per-rectum or unexplained iron deficiency anaemia. Patients with such presentations require early investigation. Sixty per cent of rectal malignancies are digitally palpable and rectal examination is mandatory. Any older patient presenting with change in bowel habit, rectal bleeding or iron deficiency anaemia should have a sigmoidoscopy and double contrast barium enema performed. Barium contrast studies are also useful when a rectal tumour is found on sigmoidoscopy as the incidence of concomitant malignancy elsewhere in the colon is 6%.

Unfortunately, colorectal cancer can be missed by double contrast barium enema and colonoscopy is thought to be the best diagnostic tool in finding colorectal tumours. Colonoscopy is well tolerated in the elderly, but is not widely available. Elderly patients who have unexplained iron deficiency anaemia and a normal barium enema should have re-examination of the colon performed early, preferably by colonoscopy or by repeat barium emema. Risk factors for developing carcinoma are those with tubulovillous adenomas, ulcerative colitis, or a family history of bowel neoplasia.

Management

Pre-operative ultrasound of the abdomen is useful to determine the presence of hepatic metastases or ureteric obstruction. The presence of hepatic metastases should not be a contraindication to surgery as it can minimise subsequent anaemia, diarrhoea, tenesmus or bowel obstruction. Surgical excision is the only curative treatment and the prognosis following surgery is better than with malignancy at many other sites. Results of surgery in patients older then 70 years have recently been reported to be as good as in younger patients[7]. Five year survival figures for the various Dukes' stages are given in the table (appendix 2). Even if the tumour is unresectable some form of anastomosis may be undertaken to bypass the tumour. Chemotherapy has little part to play, but radiotherapy can be of value in reducing the size of a rectal tumour enabling its removal with less post-operative morbidity.

If a colostomy is to be fashioned then the implications need to be discussed with the patient and their carers. They should be seen by a stoma therapist as there may be particular problems, eg, poor vision, arthritic fingers, cognitive impairment, which may add difficulty to managing a colostomy.

Presentation with large bowel obstruction remains a problem, with emergency operations carrying twice the mortality of elective procedures and perforation carrying significant mortality and morbidity. Following adequate resuscitation, resection or bypass should be carried out as early as possible.

Gastrointestinal Malignancies

Practical Points

1. Most common gastrointestinal malignancies increase with advancing age. The majority tend to present at an advanced stage when curative treatment is no longer possible.

2. The key to improved prognosis is early diagnosis – there should be a high index of clinical suspicion which should prompt early investigation.

3. Colonic malignancy may be missed by barium enema X-ray – patients with unexplained iron deficiency anaemia should be re-examined early, preferably by colonoscopy or by repeat barium enema.

4. Gastrointestinal lymphoma responds well to treatment even in the elderly.

5. Carcinoma of the colon has a better prognosis than other forms of gastrointestinal malignancy and elective resection should be undertaken on all patients regardless of the stage of the disease.

6. Where curative surgery is possible, if co-morbidity is taken into account, elderly patients benefit as much as do their younger counterparts.

7. Palliative measures such as stenting for biliary malignancy or bypass anastomosis of colonic tumours can greatly improve quality of life.

References

1. Sugimachi K, Matsuzaki K, Matsuvra H, Kuwano H, Veo H & Inokuchi K (1985) *Evaluation of surgical treatment of carcinoma of the oesophagus in the elderly: 20 years' experience*, Br J Surg, 72, 28–30.

2. Shao L, Huang G, Zhjang D, Li Z, Wang G, Lui S, Wang L & Zhang F (1981) *Detection and surgical treatment of early oesophageal carcinoma*, in: Proceedings of the Beijing Symposim on Cardiothoracic Surgery, Beijing 20–24th September 1981, Brewer LA (ed), China Academic Publications/John Wiley, 168–71.

3. Cobden I, Bassendine MF & James OFW (1986) *Hepatocellular carcinoma in NE England. Importance of hepatitis B infection and ex-tropical military service*, Quarterly J Med, 60, 855–63.

4. Kairaluoma MI, Kiviniemi H & Stahlberg M (1987) *Pancreatic resection for carcinoma of the pancreas and peri-ampullary region in patients over 70 years of age*, Br J Surg, 74, 116–8.

5. Robertson JFR, Imrie CW, Hole DJ, Carter DC & Blumgart LH (1987) *Management of peri-ampullary carcinoma*, Br J Surg, 74, 816–9.

6. Cancer Research Campaign. (1988) *Facts on cancer mortality in the UK*, Cancer Research Campaign, London.

7. Irvin TT (1988) *Prognosis of colorectal cancer in the elderly*, Br J Surg, 75, 419–21.

Appendix 1

Problems Arising after Gastrectomy

Dumping Syndrome
Bile vomiting
Biliary gastritis/oesophagitis
Diminished stomach capacity – weight loss
Iron deficiency
B_{12} deficiency
Deficiency of fat solluble vitamins
Increased suseptibility to tuberculosis

Appendix 2

Five-year Survival Rates (crude and corrected) for Carcinoma of the Colon by Duke's Staging

Duke's category	Number of cases	Crude 5-year survival rate (%)	Corrected 5-year survival rate (%)
A	61	82.0	99.3
B	131	69.0	84.4
C	89	59.6	66.3
D	19	26.3	35.1

Fron Goligher JC. *Surgery of the Anus, Rectum and Colon, 4th ed*, 1981: 471. Reproduced with kind permission of the publishers, Bailliere Tindall Ltd.

Chapter 31

Parkinson's Disease

Dr V Khanna MBBS, MD, FRCP(Edin), MHSM, Cert MHS(MMU)
Consultant Physician, Department of Medicine for the Elderly and
Director, Parkinson's Disease clinic
North Manchester General Hospital
Delauneys Road
Crumpsall
Manchester M8 6RL

Miss Mary Baker
Director of Welfare Development
&
Bridget McCall
Information Officer
Parkinson's Disease Society
22 Upper Woburn Place
London WC1H 0RH

Biosketch:

Dr Khanna graduated from Banaras Hindu University, India in 1970. He pursued a career in General Medicine with an MD and MRCP(UK). After training in General Medicine he spent two years as Senior Registrar in Geriatric Medicine at the University of Manchester and a year in General Medicine before taking up the Consultant post at North Manchester General Hospital. His interest in Parkinson's Disease led him to develop Parkinson's Disease Clinic since 1987. His current interests are research into various types of Parkinsonism and measurement of disability in Parkinson's Disease.

Mary Baker is the Director of Welfare Development of the Parkinson's Disease Society of the United Kingdom, and since 1992, has been the first President of the European Parkinson's Disease Association. She is also Treasurer of Neuro-Concern (a consortium of 28 neurological charities) and serves as a member on a number of prestigious government advisory groups and health care organisations.

Bridget McCall has worked for the Parkinson's Disease Society for eight years, in the Welfare Department and for the last four years, as their Information Officer. She has written and produced many of the Society's publications for both lay people and health and social care professionals.

Introduction

This chapter has been dealt with in two sections:
1. In section 1, Parkinson's disease is dealt with by Dr V Khanna, Consultant Physician.
2. In Section 2, Mary Baker and Bridget McCall, from the Parkinson's Disease Society discuss the broad principles of management, entitled, 'What do People with Parkinson's Disease and their Carers want?'

Section 1
Parkinson's Disease
Dr Vaneet Khanna

Parkinson's disease was described in 1817 by a general practitioner who practised in the outskirts of London called James Parkinson. He called it 'The Shaking Palsy'.

In 1862 Charcoat and Vulpian named shaking palsy as Parkinson's Disease to eliminate the word palsy. What was described then was a combination of tremor, muscular rigidity, and hypokinesia. Charcoat remarked that the patient did not experience true paralysis but was imprisoned by rigidity.

Parkinsonism as we know it today can be subdivided into young onset and late onset Parkinsonism. There are other syndromes that carry features of Parkinsonism as well as special features of that particular syndrome. This category is called secondary Parkinsonism. Parkinson's Disease is becoming increasingly common with advancing age. The incidence increases to 2% over the age of 80 years. The prevalance is 200 per 100,000 population.

The pathophysiology lies in the Corpus striatum comprising of the caudate nucleus, Putamen, the globus pallidum, the substantia nigra and the Thalamus and the striato-nigral pathways make up the excitatory and inhibitory neurones. Lewy body inclusions in the Nigral cells were considered to be pathognomonic of Idiopathic Parkinson's Disease. Hornykiewicz in 1960 described the degeneration of Nigral cells and deficiency of striatal dopamine in their terminals as the cause of Parkinsonism. Modulation of tonic neuronal firing in the globus pallidus is a pre-requisite for spontaneous movement. The incidental finding of Lewy bodies in the brains of up to 10% of elderly people with symptoms or signs of Parkinson's disease may be taken as an indication of degenerative process.

Figure 1

Prevalence of Parkinson's Disease as a Function of Age. After Mutch *et al* (1986)[1]

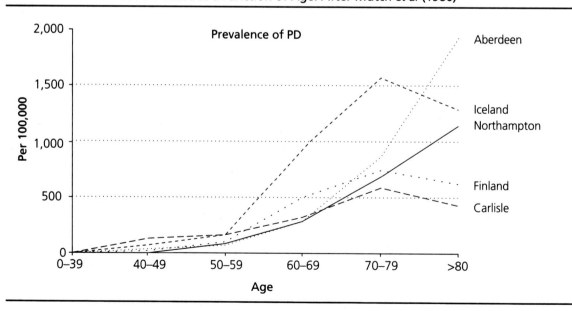

A GUIDE TO THE CARE OF THE ELDERLY

Etiology of Idiopathic Parkinson's disease has so far been unrewarding. Clinical features start to surface after loss of 80% striatal Dopamine. There is also a loss of dopamine in other dopaminergic pathways particularly in the hypothalamus and in the cortical and limbic areas of the brain. Selective nigral neuronal degeneration may be due to several factors one of which is the process of ageing itself. Decrease in complex I activity in the brain and in the platelets has been observed. Free radicals such as peroxide and superoxide not being mopped up may lead to damage of the nigro-striatal pathway. Manganese intoxication has been well known to produce a Parkinsonian state in Taiwan, Bombay and Chile. MPTP syndrome was caused by selective toxic damage by a neurotoxin MPP+ in drug addicts. In the Island of Guam a toxic plant Cycad is known to cause Parkinsonism. Failure to transmit the disease to primates and absence of antibodies would rule out viral etiology of Parkinson's Disease. Presymptomatic detection of Parkinsonism may be possible through test battery examining cognitive dysfunction, odour identification, visual and electrophysiological abnormalities, complex 1 deficiency, altered Cysteine to Sulphate ratio and changes in visual evoked potentials.

Clinical Features (Table 1)

The onset and progression of the disease may be extremely slow and variable. Patients and their relatives recall changes of a subtle kind that have occurred for several years before the diagnosis is made, such as falls, clumsiness, loss of interest, handwriting getting smaller and slowing down. This preclinical phase sometimes brings out the symptoms of Parkinsonism when patients are exposed to Phenothiazines and other dopamine blocking drugs or following head injury or trauma.

The cardinal features are pill-rolling tremor at rest, muscular rigidity and bradykinesia. Postural instability may exist to a variable degree. Some patients start with unilateral tremor progressing to bilateral tremor and then other features appearing over 3–5 year period. In others, stiffness and extrapyramidal rigidity dominate the clinical scene. The patients experience slowing down with disturbance of balance, falls, micrographia and hyphenated phonation. Loss of expression is usually noted by the family or friends. Gait is usually described as festinant. There is difficulty in initiating movement but once that is overcome patients progress from a walking pace to a running pace.

Musculoskeletal pain is a common early symptom or a early morning dystonia of the foot. The posture becomes fixed and arm swing is lost. Poverty of spontaneous movement and speech changes can often be detected by the experienced eye. The voice becomes quieter or slightly hoarse and develops a monotonous quality. Webster scale can be used for assessing progress and response to medication.

The disease often has an unremitting course. The young onset patients progress from impairment to severe disability over a 5–7 year period. They may develop Dyskinesias, Dystonias, Motor fluctuations, On-Off phenomenon, and End of Dose deterioration. Whether this is due to disease progression or toxic damage to nigrostriatal neurones of long term levodopa therapy is unknown.

The late onset Parkinsonism tends to run a more benign course. While some patients may become progressively disabled over 10–15 years, others may experience rapid deterioration showing impairment of motor function, cognition, emotional state, communication and autonomic function. Some 10–30% of patients develop coexistent dementia. Selective impairment of intellectual function occurs in many people with Parkinson's Disease which is not to be mistaken with dementia and is characterised by difficulty in switching attention from one topic to another.

A small number of late onset older patients do not respond to any drug therapy and their impairment progresses to gross disability. Concomitant cerebrovascular and Alzheimers pathology is usually associated in these subjects.

Table 1

Clinical Features of Parkinson's Disease	
Tremors	Rigidity
Bradykinesia	Facial immobility
Stoop	Micrographia
Festinant gait	Loss of arm swing
Reduced blinking	Slow response
Constipation	Detrusor instability
Cramps	Dysphagia
Drooling of saliva	Speech impediment
Postural hypotension	Intellectual impairment
Anxiety	Depression
Loss of righting reflex	

Differential Diagnosis (Table 2)

The characteristic Parkinsonian tremor occurs at rest and lessens or disappears on action whereas with essential tremor the reverse is true. In early stages there is no way clinically to distinguish Parkinson's disease as defined by presence of Lewy bodies from other degenerative disorders which may also produce features of Parkinsonism such as akinetic-rigid syndrome. The Multisystem Atrophy, Progressive Supranuclear Palsy, Corticobasal Degeneration and Normal Pressure hydrocephalus will declare themselves in time and are notably different because of their more rapid progression and by their failure to respond to levodopa therapy.

Table 2

Etiology of Secondary Parkinsonism

Drugs (stemetil, largactil, Melleril, Haloperiodol)
MPTP
Manganese
Carbon monoxide
Shy-Drager syndrome
Progressive supranuclear palsy
Cortico-basal degeneration
Striato-nigral degeneration
Olivo-ponto cerebellar atrophy
Diffuse Lewy body disease
Dopa responsive dystonias
Normal pressure hydrocephalus
Arteriosclerotic Parkinsonism

Investigations

Positron Emission Tomography (PET) and Single Photon Emission Computed Tomography (SPECT) are reliable tools to assess progression of nigral pathology. Flurodopa PET scan can help assess dopaminergic function in vivo. Magnetic Resonance Scanning is a useful tool for excluding causes of secondary Parkinsonism as is Computed Tomography.

Treatment (Table 3 and Figure 2)

Neuroprotection

Data for neuroprotection and modifying the progress of Parkinsonism is controversial. The view that oxidative stress from degradation of dopamine may contribute to neuronal loss led to the belief that selegiline (MAO-B blocker) may be neuroprotective. It has also been argued that mopping up free radicals like peroxide and super-oxide by high doses of Vitamin E may also be neuroprotective but results from the studies are equivocal. The early use of selegiline may delay the need for Levodopa and when given in younger patients allows them longer in employment. Levodopa and Peripheral decarboxylase inhibitor combinations response to Levodopa therapy is though to be diagnostic of Idiopathic Parkinson's Disease. Treatment strategy not based on Levodopa therapy comprising of Dopamine agonists monotherapy is now emerging to offset long term side effects of Levodopa treatment. It is felt that 90 percent of Parkinsonian patients tolerate Levodopa preparations but about 10 percent of patients do not tolerate L-Dopa. In these patients alternative drugs such as amantadine or dopamine agonists may be tried. Despite the effectiveness of L-Dopa patients experience increasing motor fluctuations and dyskinesias with time. After about 5 years of usage patients start to develop adverse side effects and end of dose deterioration and on-off phenomenon. Some elderly parkinsonian patients with slowly progressive Parkinson's disease may escape the side effects for 10 years or more.

Table 3

Preparations Available

Immediate release preparation

Sinimet LS	(L-Dopa 50 mg+12.5 mg Carbidopa)
Sinimet Plus	(L-Dopa 100 mg+25 mg Carbidopa)
Sinimet 110	(L-Dopa 100 mg+10 mg Carbidopa)
Sinimet 275	(L-Dopa 250 mg+25 mg Carbidopa)
Madopar 62.5	(L-Dopa 50 mg+Benserazide 12.5 mg
Madopar 125	(L-Dopa 100 mg+Benserazide 25 mg)
Madopar 250	(L-Dopa 200 mg+50 mg Benserazide)
Larodopa 500 mg	
Brocadopa	(Levodopa 125 mg, 250 mg and 500 mg)

Controlled release preparations

Sinimet ½ strength CR	(L-Dopa 100 mg+Carbidopa 25 mg)
Sinimet CR	(L-Dopa 200 mg+Carbidopa 50 mg)
Madopar Dispersible 62.5 and 125	
Madopar CR	(L-Dopa 100 mg+25 mg)

Figure 2

Principles of Dopaminergic Therapy

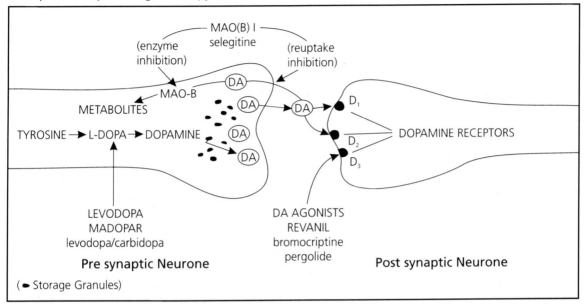

A small dose combination preparation in divided doses may be helpful in relieving symptoms. As disease advances dosage may have to be increased in amount and frequency to achieve optimal patient mobility and independence balanced by minimal side effects.

In about 50 percent of patients, immediate release preparations are beset with problems of 'On-Off' phenomenon. This phenomenon may be progressive leaving patient when ON period in a dyskinetic state and in the OFF period in the frozen akinetic state. They may also experience motor fluctuations and abnormal movement disorder. Controlled release preparations are helpful in these situations. They may also be successfully used in Peak dose dyskinesias, end of dose deterioration, and in improving sleep pattern. They help provide a more constant and sustained level of dopamine replacement. Although controlled release drugs are of benefit for day time symptoms they are best reserved for nocturnal akinesia or early morning akinesia and early morning dystonias. In patients with advancing disease and dysphagia, dispersible preparations of Levodopa do help because of rapid absorption. Dispersible preparations may also help in treating early morning bradykinesia.

Dopaminergic Agonists

Preparations

Bromocriptine (Parlodel) 1 mg and 2.5 mg
Pergolide (Celance) 0.05 mg, 0.25 mg and 1 mg
Lysuride Maleate (Revanil) 200 ug
Apomorphine Hydrochloride (Britaject) 10 mg/ml

These drugs are longer acting, produce less fluctuations, may be used as monotherapy early on in the disease to spare the use of Levodopa or as an add on therapy late in the disease when complications develop. Apomorphine is useful in selected patients for treatment of refractory motor oscillations and helping complicated advanced Parkinsonian patients to retain their mobility with subcutaneous infusion therapy. While apomorphine offers the prospect of reversing the off periods, it does little for dyskinesias.

Anticholinergics & Amantadine

Anticholinergics and Amantadine may be used in the early phase of the disease when impairment is mild. The effects are either minimal or too short lived and side effects profile make their usage

Figure 3

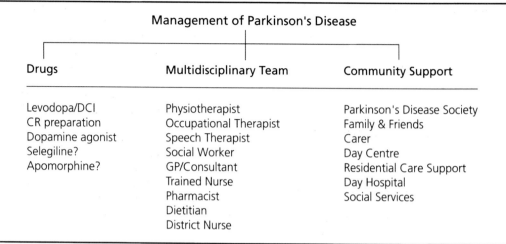

Figure 3

Management of Parkinson's Disease		
Drugs	**Multidisciplinary Team**	**Community Support**
Levodopa/DCI	Physiotherapist	Parkinson's Disease Society
CR preparation	Occupational Therapist	Family & Friends
Dopamine agonist	Speech Therapist	Carer
Selegiline?	Social Worker	Day Centre
Apomorphine?	GP/Consultant	Residential Care Support
	Trained Nurse	Day Hospital
	Pharmacist	Social Services
	Dietitian	
	District Nurse	

limited in the elderly (confusion, glaucoma, urinary retention, constipation).

Foetal or Adrenal Transplantation

Research into foetal mesencepahlic tissue transplantation into the putamen of the basal ganglia has taken place in a few centres but long term results have been disappointing. Short term benefit in terms of rigidity, tremor, and bradykinesia have been reported.

Resistance to Treatment (Table 4)

Disease progression leads to development of drug-resistant symptoms. Each resistant sympton has to be considered carefully and treated either by physiotherapists, laxatives, analgesia, speech therapists and psychologists.

Table 4

Drug responsive symptoms	Drug resistent symptoms
Bradykinesia	Imbalance
Bradyphrenia	Bladder dysfunction
Muscular rigidity	Constipation
Tremor	Pain
Gait	Dystonias
Mobility	Speech impediment
Turning in bed	Sexual dysfunction
	Psychological problems

Role of Multidisciplinary Team
(Please also see Section 2, below)

Physiotherapist, occupational therapist, and speech therapist have an important role to play in the management of a Parkinsonian patient. Physiotherapist can help with posture, gait, mobility. Occupational therapist can help with adaptations and tasks of daily living. Slow ejector chair, cutlery with aids, railing and extra bannisters all go to make life more comfortable in a patient with advancing impairment. Speech therapists help with phonation, communication, swallowing and feeding problems. Figure 3 illustrates the important role of the multidisciplinary team in the overall management.

Table 5

Therapeutic Goal Vs Treatments Under Consideration	
Prevention	P450 cytochrome genetic manipulation
	Environmental improvement
Slowing Disease Progression	? Selegiline
	Glutamase receptor antagonists
	? Dopamine agonists
	? Scavengers of free radicals
Symptomatic Improvement	New Dopaminetic drugs
	Glutamate
	Serotinin
	Neuropeptides
Transplantation Future Strategies	Dopamine synthesizing cells
	• COMT inhibitors
	• New MAO-B inhibitors
	• Levedopa prodrugs
	• NMDA antagonists

Social workers, Age concern, Voluntary organisations and Parkinson's Disease Society do help in allaying fear and anxiety and help provide essential domiciliary support or day care centre placement.

Finally, Table 5 summarises the future trends in management.

Section 2
What do People with Parkinson's Disease and their Carers Want?

Mary Baker and Bridget McCall

The only way to find out what people with Parkinson's disease and their carers really want, is to ask them, using an approach which allows them to give a good and honest response. They are the ones who have first hand knowledge of the disease.

The work that the Parkinson's Disease Society does is based on what we learn from listening to our members. Five principles have emerged as essential to the good management of Parkinson's disease. They are:
1. Referrals to a specialist with knowledge of their illness;
2. Early referral to a multi-disciplinary team;
3. A good telling of the diagnosis;
4. Continuity of care;
5. Involvment of the patient in the management of their care.

These principles are briefly discussed as follows:

1 Referral to a specialist with knowledge of their illness
There is no cure for Parkinson's disease. The treatment available, seeks to alleviate the symptoms, although the disease does continue to progress. There is no optimum drug treatment for Parkinson's disease and each person's regime (both in dose and timing) will be tailored to suit their individual needs. Long term use of the drugs can result in disabling side-effects such as the 'on-off' syndrome and dyskinesias, which can further complicate matters. The management of Parkinson's disease is complex and requires a highly individual approach and regular assessments/reviews to take account of the person's changing needs. It is important that people are referred to specialists who have a full understanding of Parkinson's disease and its treatment, and who perhaps have access to a full multi-disciplinary team.

The average GP will only see approximately three to four patients with Parkinson's disease on their personal list. It is not surprising, therefore, if they do not have the same level of knowledge about the range of treatments and care available as a consultant neurologist or geriatrician will have.

2, 3, & 4 Early Referral to a Multi-Disciplinary Team, the Telling of the Diagnosis and Continuity of Care
These 3 principles have been discussed together as they are inter-related.

Physiotherapy, speech therapy and occupational therapy have important roles to play in maintaining ability and facilitating activities of daily living for people with Parkinson's disease. Dieticians and chiropodists can also provide much needed advice and treatment. The value of all these professions is something which is not always recognised and, as a result, referrals are not always made. Early referral is recommended so that maximum levels of ability can be maintained for as long as possible and help with specific problems can be obtained as soon as they occur.

A multi-disciplinary approach to the management of Parkinson's disease has been advocated through the development of several models of good practice for the management of Parkinson's disease.

The Neuro-Care Team at Romford, initially funded by the Parkinson's Disease Society, uses a multi-disciplinary approach and has a particular approach to the telling of the diagnosis. The script has been written by people with Parkinson's disease.

The neurologist has an initial consultation with the patient and their carer, where he establishes what the person thinks they have, before giving the diagnosis. He then determines what they know about Parkinson's disease, so that he can correct any misconceptions and deal with any anxieties. At this consultation, he only gives a brief description of the condition, does not start treatment but makes a further appointment to see the person and their carer in a few weeks time.

A social worker/counsellor observes this initial consultation and afterwards, she discusses the diagnosis with the patient and carer. Most people do not absorb very much information when they are dealing with the shock of the diagnosis and it is important to check what they have taken in so misunderstandings can be corrected.

Before the second consultation, the members of the multi-disciplinary team assess the patient in their home environment so that the neurologist has a full picture of the patient's circumstances when he sees the patient again. At the second consultation, the neurologist spends much longer with the patient and carer, giving a much more detailed explanation of Parkinson's disease and the treatment and answering any questions they may have.

The approach of the neuro-care team also addresses the issue of continuity of care and the early involvement of therapists. A key worker for each patient is identified from the multi-disciplinary team, who then provides the link between the patient and the neuro-care team, making referrals where appropriate as problems arise. Although it might seem that this would mean increased demands, in reality this does not happen as the patients and carers feel much happier and reassured about their treatment.

An alternative way of ensuring continuity of care is through the employment of nurse practitioners/specialist nurses in Parkinson's disease, either attached to clinics or working in the community. The Parkinson's disease clinic at Barncoose Hospital in Cornwall involves a specialist nurse who is based in the hospital but who spends most of her time in the community. She is able to filter a lot of the work for the consultant, dealing with all the social and nursing queries and linking in with other members of the team as appropriate, referring back to the consultant as required.

A specialist nurse attached to the Apomorphine clinic at Middlesex Hospital in London has provided an invaluable service to patients receiving apomorphine treatment. The Parkinson's Disease Society has also set up a Nurse Practitioner project, involving a team of nurses who work in the community to support people with Parkinson's disease and their carers, linking them into the appropriate services as well as working with consultants in hospitals to set up specialist Parkinson's disease clinics.

Psychological factors associated with Parkinson's disease also need to be recognised and treated. Depression and problems with sexual dysfunction have been highlighted as specific areas of concern. Depression, a common experience of people with Parkinson's disease and their carers, often goes undiagnosed. Sexual dysfunction in Parkinson's disease can have a physical basis but psychological problems, such as low self-esteem and diminished self-worth, are frequent causes which need attention. Consultant psychiatrists and psychologists may, therefore, have a lot to contribute to the well being of people with Parkinson's disease and their carers as part of the multi-disciplinary team.

5 Involvement of the Person with Parkinson's Disease and their Carer in the Management of their Care and Identifying and Meeting their Needs

Each person's experience of Parkinson's disease will be different. Treatment and care needs to be person-centred and to take account of the fact that Parkinson's disease affects all areas of a person's life. The needs and expertise of the carer also needs to be recognised. They may require practical and emotional support and appropriate respite care facilities.

In 1990, the Parkinson's Disease Society produced a training video for professionals,

Table 6

Needs of Patients	Needs of Carers
1. To be treated as individuals	1. Recognition and acknowledgement
2. Dignity, respect and independence	2. Information
3. Access and early referral to all appropriate treatment and care	3. Honesty, reassurance and encouragement
4. Compassion, understanding, time and patience	4. To be valued and *listened to*
5. Quality of life	5. Practical and emotional help
6. Honesty, reassurance and encouragement	6. Access and early referral to all appropriate treatment and care
7. Information	7. A good night's sleep and time for themselves
8. To be involved and *listened to*	8. Understanding and loving respite care
9. A cure	9. Good health and financial help

which presented a 'personal view' of Parkinson's disease. The video gave people with Parkinson's disease and their carers the chance to talk about what having Parkinson's disease meant to them and the care they wanted from the professionals they were involved with. The needs they identified are summarised in Table 6.

These requirements highlight the importance of good communication and the need for positive attitudes amongst all professionals, which accord the person and carer respect and dignity. To fulfil them, both need to be valued as partners in care rather than simply as patients and carers. The patients need to be given encouragement to retain their independence and enjoy the best possible quality of life.

Parkinson's Disease

Practical Points

1. Parkinson's disease ranks third – after stroke and dementia – among the central nervous system diseases affecting the elderly.

2. The diagnosis is essentially clinical, the classical triad being tremor, rigidity and akinesia. Lewy's bodies are no longer considered to be pathognomic of the disease.

3. Management includes referral to a specialist, to a rehabilitation team, continuity of care and explanation of the disease to patient and the carer. A shared-care approach should also be explored.

4. L-dopa is the sheet-anchor of treatment in an established case. Neurosurgery has a limited role in the elderly patient.

5. Drug-toxicity, presence of other pathologies including cognitive dysfunction in the later stage of the disease, are helpful parameters in planning mangement and forecasting prognosis.

6. In common with other disabling neuro-degenerative diseases like dementia and motor neurone disease, advances are taking place in preventive aspect of Parkinson's disease.

Reference

1. Mutch WJ, Dingwall-Fordyce I, Downie AW, Paterson JG, Roy SK (1986) *Parkinson's Disease in a Scottish city*, Br Med J, 292, 534–6

Further Reading

1. Biggins CA, Boyd JL, Harrop FM, et al. (1992) *A controlled longitudinal study of dementia in Parkinson's disease*, J Neurol, neirosurg, Psychiatry, 55, 566–71.

2. Yahr MD (1977) *Long term Levodopa in Parkinson's disease*, Lancet, i, 706–707.

3. Rinne UK. (1985) *Combined bromocriptine – levodopa therapy early in Parkinson's disease*, Neurology, 35, 1196–1198.

4. Shoulson I. Parkinson's study group. (1988) *Effect of deprenyl on the progression of disability in early Parkinson's disease*, N Eng J Med, 321, 1364–71.

5. Freed Cr, Breeze RE, Rosenberg NL, et al. (1990) *Transplantation of human foetal dopamine cells for Parkinson's disease*, Ach Neurol, 47, 505–12.

6. Goetz CG (1990) *Dopamine agonists in the treatment of Parkinson's disease*, Neurology, 46 (suppl 3), 50–57.

7. Barker R, Duncan J & Lees A (1989) *Subcutaneous apomorphine as a diagnostic test for dopaminergic responsiveness in parkinsonian syndromes*, Lancet, i, 675.

8. PDRG-UK. (1993) *Comparisons of therapeutic effects of levodopa, levodopa and selegiline, and bromocriptine in patients with early, mild parkinson's disease; three year interim report*, Br Med Jr, 307, 469–72.

9. Hughes AJ, Daniel SE, Kilford L & Lees AJ (1992) *Accuracy of clinical diagnosis of idiopathic Parkinson's disease: a clinicopathological study of 100 cases*, J Neurol, Neurosurg, Psychiatry, 55, 181–4.

10. Hornykiewicz O, Pifl C, Kish SJ, Shannak K, Schingnitz G (1989) *Biochemical changes in Idiopathic Parkinson's disease, ageing, and MPTP Parkinsonism: similarities and differences*, in: Parkinsonism and Ageing, Calne DB (ed), Raven Press, New York.

Chapter 32

Surgery in The Elderly

D J Sherlock MS FRCS
Consultant Surgeon
North Manchester General Hospital
Delaunay Road
Manchester

Biosketch:

Mr David J Sherlock is Consultant General Surgeon at North Manchester General Hospital, Manchester. His main interest is gastro-intestinal surgery, with a particular interest in hepato-pancreatico biliary surgery. Has written widely on general surgery and developed experience in this field with attachments to clinics in America, Paris and London. He has published widely on his work in hepato-pancreatico biliary surgery.

Introduction

The juxta positioning of the terms 'surgery' and 'elderly' is considered by many to be an anathema. However it is frequently the case that the increased risk of surgery in the elderly has to be balanced against the greater need of this group of clients. It is this dilemma of equating 'benefit' against 'loss' that makes surgery in the elderly such a challenge. There have been several recent developments that have increased the importance of this subject and promoted a reevaluation of previously accepted attitudes of management in the elderly. There have been substantial technological advances in both the fields of anaesthesia and surgery, particularly with the introduction of minimal invasive surgery, therapeutic endoscopy, interventional radiology (see chapter 36) and day surgery. These have dramatically increased the proportion of elderly patients seeking and being offered surgery. In addition, the considerable expansion of the proportion of the population that will be elderly, estimated to be 40% expansion in the 75 to 84 age range, will mean that surgery in the elderly will have an increasingly important role in the future. This will have two important objectives, not only to extend life but also to maintain the quality of survival with the wider variety of new surgical techniques at our disposal.

In general, the normal ageing process increases the risk of any surgical procedure needing general anaesthesia. Reduction in the cardiovascular and respiratory reserves compromises the ability of the body to respond appropriately to stress. There are some important pathophysiological changes that occur in the elderly that can lead to acute or chronic surgical conditions. The process of ligamental laxity and alteration in the distribution of body fat have a significant role in the development of abdominal wall herniae. The age related increase in peptic ulceration may be due to a progressive breakdown in the mucosal defence mechanisms with age. The resistance of the gallbladder to cholecystokinin, with the increased secretion of cholestrol by the liver, and the reduced bile acid synthesis predisposes to the development of gallstones. The colon shows an increase in both circular and longitudinal muscle layers and this hypertrophy of the muscle layers is associated with many of the large bowel complaints seen in the elderly. Diverticulosis is present in 40% of 60 year old and 60% of 80 years old and the slower transit time of the gastrointestinal tract may provoke the deterioration to acute diverticulitis. Alterations in colonic transit and absorption are also thought to have an influence on the development of colonic cancers that also increase with age.

Unfortunately, many of the risk factors for surgery such as diabetes, ischaemic heart disease and peripheral vascular disease are also increasingly common in the elderly population. As a result, the elderly need more precise evaluation of disease before surgery as they have not the functional reserve of young patients to cope with additional stresses such as inappropriately lengthy incisions or extensive unnecessary dissection. It can also be argued that earlier intervention in the elderly is more appropriate than in the younger population, as the complications of delayed treatment are less well tolerated. It is essential to consider not only the quality of life but the quality of death, and not infrequently elderly patients suffer an acute surgical emergency that could have been avoided by a more timely earlier intervention. The difference between the morbidity and mortality of elective and emergency surgical procedures is enormous and still the majority of major surgery in the elderly is done as an emergency procedure[1]. The mortality for elective surgery in the elderly is between 5% and 10% whilst for an emergency procedure it is between 20% and 40%; this later figure rising to between 60% and 80% in the over 75 year population.

The overall perioperative 30 day mortality in the over 75 age group undergoing elective major surgery is approximately 10%. Much of this is due to associated age-related medical conditions and certainly in the over 75 age group it is unusual not to have at least two co-existing problems. About a third of patients have pre-existing respiratory problems. In the elderly, as a result of a reduction in the elastin content of the lung and reduced compliance, the small basal bronchioles normally have to be kept open by periodic respiratory 'sighs'. These respiratory sighs are reduced post-operatively by the prolonged effects of sedating drugs, the reduced response of the elderly to hypoxia and hypercapnia leading to closure of these small airways with retention of secretions resulting in the clinical procedure of atelectasis. It is essential that sedation in the elderly is well controlled and frequent physiotherapy is performed post-operatively to encourage deep inspiration with basal airway opening.

Cardiovascular complications after surgery are less common but surgery should be avoided within 3 months from an acute myocardial infarction as the mortality is high. Surgery in patients in established heart failure also carries a prohibitory high risk and pre-operative control of the failure with regulation of arrhymias is essential. Cerebrovascular accidents occur in 1% of the over 65 population post-operatively, rising to 3% in the over 80s and are more likely to be related to intra operative hypotension rather than hypertension. It is essential that the surgery and anaesthesia is performed as smoothly as possible to prevent great cardio-respiratory fluctuations that may have severe consequences in the aged with restricted physiological reserve. Venous thrombosis also increases with age and appropriate prophylaxis should be taken with intra-operative calf pumps, subcutaneous heparin and graduated compression stockings.

The challenge for surgery in the elderly is not having to learn a new set of principles unused in younger patients, but rather to pay extra attention to the unique weaknesses of the elderly, so as to avoid the complications that elderly patients have little margin of reserve to cope with.

This chapter will discuss the common conditions seen in a general surgical service and is complementary to chapter 30 on Gastrointestinal Malignancies and chapter 36 on The Role of Interventional Radiology in the Elderly.

Skin Conditions

Infected sebaceous cysts, sebaceous horns and large skin papillomas often cause distressing symptoms and can easily be removed by local anaesthetic surgery. Rodent ulcers particularly of the face are common in the elderly and if diagnosed early can be adequately excised under local anaesthesia. Larger lesions may well be safely excised by the use of rotation flaps which are often very much easier to do in the elderly due to the skin laxity. Another common condition seen in the elderly is onchyrogyphosis that is frequently due to the patient's inability to trim their toe nails due to immobility. This can be treated under local anaesthesia by a Zadek's procedure although care must be taken that the patient does not have severe peripheral vascular disease or diabetes which might lead to post-operative gangrene.

Oesophageal and Gastroduodenal Disease

Symptoms of oesophagal dysfunction are particularly common in the elderly, a recent study revealing more than 15% of patients over 80 years to have swallowing abnormalities[2]. There is commonly a deterioration in oesophageal function characterised manometrically by frequent tertiary contractions and incomplete sphincter relaxation. This form of dysphagia presents with difficulty to swallow both fluids and solids in contrast to the obstructive dysphagia of oesophageal cancer. Gastroesophageal reflux in the elderly frequently presents very atypically and may be associated with wheezing. The majority can be managed with elevation of the head of the bed, weight loss, avoidance of alcohol and smoking. Drugs such as alginates, omeprazole and cisapride are all used and surgery is indicated only in patients failing to respond to these drugs. Patients with peptic strictures are treated by endoscopic oesophageal dilatation after a guide wire is placed through the track, but severe reflux in association with a stricture will need reconstructive surgery. Results of the Nissen fundoplication are highly successful in this age group[3] and can be performed by minimal invasive techniques.

Other conditions that might present unusually are Zenker's pharyngoesophageal diverticulum, scleroderma and achalasia. These are diagnosed by a combination of radiology, manometry and endoscopic techniques as malignancy can often masquerade as these conditions. Achalasia can now be successfully treated in 75% of cases by pneumatic balloon dilation. Only a small proportion of patients are submitted to surgical myotomy of the lower oesophageal sphincter, but this is also highly effective if required.

Oesophageal cancer is a common disease in the elderly and pre-operative evaluation is fraught with difficulties[4]. Resection of the oesophagus provides the best chance for cure and frequently offers the best form of palliation for adenocarcinoma, but good results have been reported with radiotherapy for squamous lesions. Careful selection of patients submitted to oesophagectomy in the elderly is essential as high mortalities have been reported. Most authorities agree that with proper patient selection and cardiopulmonary assessment, age alone should not be a contraindication for surgery[4]. Palliative treatment to maintain an adequate pathway for food can be performed with endoscopically introduced tubes, expanding stents and laser debulking (cf chapter 30 on Gastrointestinal Malignancy).

Upper gastroduodenal symptoms are increasingly common as we age and whilst nearly 60%

of these complaints are functional, all patients should be investigated carefully to prevent the transformation of a chronic condition, that could be dealt with electively, to an acute condition that needs risky emergency surgery. A large proportion of deaths in the elderly after emergency surgery are as a result of peptic ulceration – a proportion of which might have been preventable[5]. The incidence of peptic ulceration in the elderly is increasing probably due to a combination of factors but certainly linked to the widespread use of non steroidal anti-inflammatory drugs. The main complications of peptic ulceration are perforation, haemorrhage and gastric outflow obstruction and 50% of elderly patients present with these complications initially. Mortality rates for complications of peptic ulceration can be 100% higher in the elderly, so emergency surgery should be avoided if possible and co-morbid conditions optimised prior to surgery. Haemorrhage accounts for 60% of the fatalities in the elderly from peptic ulceration and an aggressive surgical approach is indicated in patients without prohibitive risk factors. More than 6 units of blood transfused, rebleeding during medical treatment, the endoscopic indicators of fresh blood in the ulcer crater or a visible vessel occluded by clot are generally accepted as warranting surgery in the over 60 age group. Surgery involves direct control of the bleeding vessel, complemented with a truncal vagotomy and pyloroplasty at a definitive procedure in the majority of cases. Patients manifesting severe disease with large ulcers and considerable duodenal stenosis and scarring need a gastrectomy. Gastric ulcers can be treated by local resection if small, but larger ulcers are best treated by a gastrectomy, particularly if cancer is suspected. The risk of perforation doubles after the age of 50 years and duodenal perforation is a common cause of mortality in the elderly, particularly if surgery is delayed beyond 12 hours. Treatment should take into account the patients' general condition but a history of over 3 months prodromal symptoms or a history of prior medical treatment warrants definitive treatment in addition to closure of the perforation[6]. Gastric outflow obstruction may be either acute or chronic and resolution occurs in most patients when medical treatment is commenced. Repeat attacks eventually lead to scarring, stenosis and gastric hypertrophy until complete obstruction leads to the syndrome of pyloric stenosis. In 10% to 15% of cases there is

an unsuspected antral carcinoma but if benign disease, a simple vagotomy and pyloroplasty may be all that is required.

Adenocarcinoma of the stomach is also more common with advancing years and carries a poor prognosis unless it is found at an early stage and can be radically resected. Such a policy in the elderly has produced acceptable results with a mortality after curative resection of around 10% and a 25% 5 year survival[7]. Palliative resection does have many proven advantages, if it is possible, removing the pain from the tumour primary and particularly by relieving the distressing dysphagia. If too advanced or the patient is not sufficiently fit for either curative or palliative surgery other techniques are available. Whilst endoscopic dilation, endoscopic intubation and endoscopic laser ablation all have their advocates in certain situations, the quality of the results of treatment are rarely as good as can be achieved by palliative surgery and the survivial is frequently only measured in weeks. Adequate pain control, antiemetics, laxatives and the use of a liquid diet are the mainstays of palliative care, permitting for the majority a dignified death.

Breast Disease

Benign breast disease in the elderly is uncommon but breast cancer is frequent. For women over 60 the incidence is 322 cases per 100,000 whereas below that age it is only 60 cases per 100,000 of the population. The tumour appears less aggressive in post menopausal women with a decreased frequency of high histological grades and lymphatic invasion. Mastectomy is no longer the standard treatment for breast cancer but because of the remaining uncertainty of the relative benefit of the available procedures, treatment is varied according to individual circumstances. Mastectomy is a safe and good treatment with a low risk of local recurrence and a low operative mortality including women over 75 years of age. If the tumour is large or involving the nipple region, a mastectomy is preferable but if the lesion is small and peripheral a local wedge excision with some complementary radiotherapy is just as successful. It appears that the local recurrence rate after this form of treatment in the elderly is less than in younger patients[8]. Axillary dissection to stage the disease was advocated in the past when node positive patients received adjuvant chemotherapy. The trend now is for node negative and positive women over 60 years of age to be treated identically with Tamoxifen. Axillary sampling is still necessary for younger women and axillary dissection of palpable nodes is better at obtaining local control than radiotherapy, that frequently is associated with significant lymph oedema. Tamoxifen has been advocated as primary therapy in women over 75 years of age and unfit for general anaesthesia. A response rate of about 50% can be expected[9] but compared to surgery local recurrence is higher, although survival is identical. However, for elderly patients with a reduced life span, Tamoxifen is a viable alternative. Tamoxifen as adjuvant or complementary therapy after surgery has now an established role and is the treatment of choice for all menopausal women regardless of receptor status or staging. Chemotherapy in the elderly is more contentious but in certain cases it can be administered safely in the elderly with benefit. Reconstructive surgery to the treated breast in the elderly can also be an important part of the complete treatment of breast cancer, just as in younger patients.

Vascular Disease

Arteriosclerosis is increasingly prevalent in the elderly community and, as the risks of treatment decrease and the benefits are more widely known, the role of surgery is set to expand. The most common consequences of arteriosclerosis are aortic aneurysms, carotid artery disease and limb threatening peripheral vascular disease.

The abdominal aorta below the origin of the renal vessels is the most common site for aneurysm formation and numerous studies have shown that untreated, death from rupture is inevitable. The most important predictor of risk is size and once the aneurysm has reached 6 cm the risk dramatically increases. The increasing safety of surgery has now lead to surgery being performed earlier as a significant number of aneurysm less than 6 cm do rupture (25%) and there is no such thing as a 'safe' aneurysm. Despite the poor prognosis for untreated aneurysms, there has been a considerable reluctance to refer elderly patients simply because of their age and this appears to be based on misconceptions over the operation's safety[10]. The operative mortality of abdominal aneurysm repair in the over 80 age group is about 8% and is tending to reduce. In contrast, the mortality for emergency surgery on ruptured aneurysm is not improving and probably never will and the mortality in the aged is more than 60%. There is also considerable evidence to show the advantages of elective surgery after correction of co-existent medical conditions. The major risks after surgery has been renal failure and cardiorespiratory dysfunction. Renal damage is now largely prevented by careful fluid balance and administration of renal stimulants and respiratory problems are considerably reduced by pre-operative preparation. Cardiac morbidity has also been reduced by the pre-operative revascularization of severe coronary artery disease and the liberal use of cardiac catheters to monitor intra-operative and post-operative haemodynamics. Long term follow up has shown that the 5 year survival after surgery is similar to the general population with maintenance of good quality of life. The evidence certainly exists that the decision to advise surgery should be based on aneurysm size and symptoms and the physiological age of the patient rather than chronological age. In the absence of other factors, aneurysms over 5 cm should be operated on electively to avoid the extreme pain, misery and almost certain death that occurs when the aneurysm inevitably ruptures.

It has been estimated that 60% of strokes occur as a result of arteriosclerosis at the carotid artery bifurcation, and as such are amenable to surgical treatment if diagnosed prematurely[11]. Not only are strokes commoner in the elderly but also the consequences in terms of survival and morbidity are also greatly reduced and the majority of elderly sufferers are institutionised as a result, causing an immense financial burden. It seems logical that a proportion of these patients might benefit from carotid endarterectomy, now that the risks from this procedure are recognised to be low at about 2%. Patients present with either an audible bruit, a transient ischaemic attack or a reversible ischaemic attack. The high risk asymptomatic group are patients with at least an 80% stenosis where strokes are more frequent and the risk is reduced by surgery[11]. In symptomatic patients the risk is far higher and now multicentre randomised trials have clearly shown that symptomatic patients with at least a 70% stenosis do better following surgery than medical treatment[12].

Further advances in Doppler ultrasonography have now eliminated the need for invasive carotid arteriography prior to surgery. There appears to be little difference in terms of survival and morbidity between patients under 75 or over 75 years of age and long term follow up of sufferers shows no difference in survival in patients over 80 to the general population of octogenarians. These results certainly suggest an increasing role for surgery in the elderly with tight stenoses and hemispheric symptoms and, with the publication of further studies on moderate stenosis, an even wider group of elderly patents may be suitable for treatment in the future.

Severe limb threatening peripheral ischaemia manifest by rest pain, non-healing ulcers or gangrene is increasingly apparent as the elderly population increases. Amputation is a last resort but is nevertheless often associated with high mortality and it is less likely that elderly will ever ambulate with a prosthesis, resulting in institutionization and loss of an independent existence. Revascularisation is an expensive option but there is evidence that the cost of successful reconstruction was considerably less than that of amputation when performed in a group of octogenarians[13].

The range of procedure available to the vascular surgeon is now increasing. In addition to the classical operations of aortobifemoral and femero popliteal grafts, tranluminal angioplasty and extra anatomical grafts can now be carried out. The judicious use of combinations of these different modalities of treatment has lead to improvement in benefit and reduced risk. Recent reports have shown dramatic improvement in limb salvage with aggressive revascularization. The long term results in octogenarians is comparable at 5 years to much younger patients with an acceptably low operative mortality of about 4%. There is a strong case for timely surgical intervention in properly selected patients to prevent the inevitable consequences of atherosclerosis and maintain both the quantity and the quality of life in elderly patients.

Venous disease is also prevalent in the elderly population, and varicose veins are frequently a cause for surgical referral. The most dramatic presentation is following rupture of a varicosity with often torrential bleeding, and deaths have been attributed to this. Ligation of the saphenofemoral junction with multiple avulsions of varicosities or injection sclerotherapy will control the majority of patients. Graduated supportive stockings are another important method of control and are widely used. Varicose eczema or varicose ulceration are generally accepted as

indicators of the need for surgery, but care needs to be exercised to exclude cases of deep venous thrombosis with post-phlebitic ulceration which is made worse by surgery. Judicious use of compression stockings, regular dressings, elevation of the leg and perhaps anabolic steroids have all been shown to have benefits.

Small Bowel

The most sinister small bowel disease in the elderly is acute mesenteric thrombosis as a result of superior mesenteric artery thrombosis or embolism. Whilst the mortality is high, benefits have been reported with revascularization and a second look procedure 24 hours after surgery. Chronic ischaemia is a rare disorder resulting in intestinal angina when the flow of blood is inadequate to meet the needs of the bowel after food ingestion; treatment is by vascular reconstruction but is less successful in diffuse disease. Small bowel tumours are infrequent but Crohn's disease in the elderly is increasingly being recognised although it is often more distal in distribution in contrast to young sufferers.

Small bowel obstruction is however a common disorder in the elderly and is caused by a variety of disorders both intrinsic and extrinsic to the bowel. In the past, abdominal wall hernias were responsible for over half the cases of obstruction but in more recent times adhesions following previous surgery is the most common primary disorder. In general, colonic and gynaecological procedures are responsible for the majority of post-operative adhesions and the time from initial surgery can vary enormously from 1 week to 65 years. Some adhesions can be the result of previous inflammatory conditions such as Tuberculosis or Diverticulosis. Treatment with nasogastric aspiration and intravenous fluids will allow resolution in the majority of partial obstructions, but complete obstruction with aspiration of faecally stained gastric contents will require formal surgical release in two thirds of cases. Strangulation is very difficult to predict clinically and 50% of older patients with small bowel obstruction will require small bowel resection. Metastatic obstructions are also common in the elderly and useful palliation can be achieved with bypass surgery after appropriate pre-operative preparation. Radiation induced obstruction is a difficult condition to manage and surgery should be avoided as far as is possible, as resection is associated with a high rate of leakage. Intra luminal obstructions are far commoner in the elderly than in the young and include bolus obstruction from a variety of indigestible food stuffs to gallstones ileus.

Herniae

Abdominal wall herniaes are extremely common and in the over 65 age group in men occur in 13 per 1,000 of the population, with women suffering a quarter of this rate. The increase in acquired herniae in the elderly has been attributed to any age related condition which tends to increase intra-abdominal pressure. These include chronic constipation, bladder outflow obstruction, chronic cough and kyphoscoliosis. In addition, the relaxation of ligaments and fascia with aging with the reduction in body fat pads has a direct causal influence on the development of herniae, particularly in the femoral region in elderly women. Inguinal hernias are the most common in both sexes, with femoral herniae commoner in women than men and ventral, umbilical and incisional herniae being less frequent in both sexes. Once the hernia is diagnosed, repair should be considered regardless of chronological age. Little benefit is to be gained with a truss and the symptoms, limitations in mobility and risks of incarceration are invariably greater than the risk of an elective procedure. All patients should have investigations for, and if possible undergo, correction of the precipitating cause. Routine sigmoidoscopy in the elderly hernia sufferers has a high pick-up of occult colonic malignancy and this should always be suspected even with the slightest change in bowel habit. The technique of anaesthesia used is important in elderly patients in whom cardiorespiratory reserves are often limited. Local anaesthesia is increasingly being used in association with day surgery units and appers to have a high rate of patient acceptance. Mortality after elective surgery is extremely low and in octogenarians with significant coexistent disease can be performed with no mortality. In contrast, emergency herniorrhaphy, frequently done for incarceration or strangulation, carries a far higher mortality ranging from 8% to 14%[14]. Clearly the majority of these emergency operations could have been avoided with a significant saving of life and morbidity. Examination of these patients reveals that the majority had known about the hernia for at least a year prior to their emergency operation and had shown the general practitioner but not been referred for elective repair. The mortality from inguinal hernias could be eliminated if the safety of elective surgical repair was more widely appreciated and acted upon.

Colorectal Disorders

Both benign and malignant colorectal disorders are increasing in the elderly population and it is often difficult to differentiate these conditions from the minor disturbances of bowel function that occurs. However persistence of symptoms for more than a week might represent the early presentation of conditions such as diverticulosis, appendicitis, inflammatory bowel disease, volvulus and carcinoma.

Diverticular disease occurs in at least 50% of the over 80 years population and can present either as torrential gastrointestinal bleeding, peritonitis due to perforation, a phlegmon mass with or without abscess formation or as a fistula to surround structures. Bleeding from diverticular disease is often self limiting but rarely resection may be required. It is often difficult to distinguish the source of blood loss from angiodyplasia of the right colon and angiography may be invaluable as may on-table colonscopy. Acute perforation with faecal peritonitis carries a high mortality approaching 50% and surgery involves resection of the diseased bowel and formation of an end colostomy – the Hartmann's procedure. Acute diverticulitis can be treated with antibiotics, with drainage of collections and established abscesses being performed percutaneously. Elective one stage resection and reconstruction can be performed with a low mortality and has high patient acceptance in contrast to a two or a three stage procedure involving formation of temporary colostomies. Increasingly, surgery is performed with the aim of maintaining gastrointestinal continuity, so reducing to a minimum the stomas fashioned. This has been as a result of the considerable technological advances achieved with anastomotic staple 'guns' which can now safely join bowel in the most inaccessible of positions and the preservation of normal bowel that can be risked with pre-operative radiotherapy. It is not unusual for reconstructive surgery to be requested by octogenarian patients who fail to accept a stoma done as an emergency procedure.

Appendicitis is increasingly recognised in the elderly community and a higher proportion presents late with a higher incidence of perforation and complications[15]. The reason for this is largely due to delay in presentation to a doctor but equally the involution of the appendix and reduction in its blood supply in the ageing process may promote earlier perforation and gangrene than in younger subjects.

Inflammatory bowel disease most frequently occurs in younger patients, these diseases have a second peak of distribution in the elderly often with an atypical presentation. Ulcerative colitis can be more difficult to get into remission, recur quicker and progress more rapidly to toxic dilatation than in the young. Occasionally it can be segmental with relative sparing of the rectum that makes diagnosis more difficult which might allow reconstruction and avoidance of an ileostomy. Crohn's disease in the elderly is concentrated in the seventh, eighth and ninth decades and is often difficult to differentiate from diverticular disease. It presents with abdominal pain, diarrhoea and bleeding and can rapidly progress to acute toxic manifestations. Medical treatment is only successful in half the patients and the remainder require surgery that inevitably involves creation of a stoma.

Volvulus occurs most frequently in the sigmoid colon and less commonly develops around the caecum, splenic flexure and transverse colon. Symptoms include abdominal distension, vomiting and alternating diarrhoea and constipation. Sigmoid volvulus is treated by resection if recurrent but the acute episode can usually be deflated by a judicious sigmoidoscopy.

Ischaemic colitis can present as a transient reversible event with gastrointestinal haemorrhage and variable abdominal pain, an acute irreversible event where gangrene progresses to perforation and peritonitis or as a chronic disease with minimal symptoms but the development of long strictures causing delayed obstructive symptoms. Most cases can be treated conservatively but perforation will necessitate a Hartmann's type procedure.

Rectal prolapse or procidentia can be either partial or complete depending on the severity. It is commoner in women than men and is due to either iatrogenic injury to the puborectalis sling during child birth, neurological disorders of the lower spine, chronic constipation or congenital defects of the pelvic floor musculature. Initial treatment should be to correct constipation and limit straining with the use of the pelvic floor exercises. Surgery for patients with persistent prolapse involves either an abdominal approach releasing the overstretched lateral and rectal ligaments and fixing the rectum to the sacrum or the perineal approach, resecting the redundant bowel as it prolapses through the anus. The abdominal approach is reserved for patients without coexistent disease whilst the perineal approach is used in the more infirm.

Malignant colorectal disease is the third commonest tumour in the elderly behind lung carcinoma and prostatic cancer in men and breast cancer in women. The presentation is often very atypical and countless incidences of unnecessary delay in diagnosis abound. Earlier diagnosis of cancer results in less advanced disease and more early disease being resected. Hence, screening of the elderly population will have an important role in treatment of this disease in the future[16]. It is essential in the elderly that any symptoms of a change in bowel habit or haematochezia are investigated with a digital examination of the rectum and either a rigid sigmoidoscopy and barium enaema or a colonscopy. As 75% of colorectal tumours lie within the rectosigmoid region there is no excuse for failure to diagnose once medical advice has been sought. Sadly, the majority of patients still conceal their symptoms and it is unlikely that further improvements in the survival of colorectal cancer will be made unless a nationwide campaign to improve patient awareness is performed.

Studies in the elderly have shown that elective colorectal resections have been performed safely for many years and recent technological advances in anastomotic stapling 'guns' have lead to a progressive drop in the use of perminent colostomies. Successful colorectal surgery in the elderly depends heavily on good pre-operative mechanical bowel preparation and broad spectrum intraoperative antibiotics after adequate prior control of coexistent premorbid conditions. Post-operatively fluid balance and thrombosis prophylaxis must be maintained until the patients gastrointestinal function and mobility return. Adjuvant radiotherapy has reduced local recurrence rates and permitted more conservative surgery by reducing resection margins; long term survival rates in octogenarians are no different from younger elderly patients[17]. Less invasive techniques for palliation of rectal carcinoma are also now available for the more infirm patients and include endoscopic transanal resection, transcoccygeal excision and colonoscopic laser ablation.

Haemorrhoids and other minor anal conditions are common in the elderly. The use of rubber band ligation has permitted the outpatient treatment of both internal and prolapsing haemorrhoids. Third degree piles still need formal haemorrhoidectomy but the number requiring this treatment in the elderly is far less than in the younger population.

Hepato Pancreatico Biliary Disorders

Hepatic resection for primary or secondary liver tumours is being performed with increasing frequency and in many centres the operative mortality is less than 1%. Morbidity and mortality are related to residual parenchymal function rather than chronological age and whilst the numbers of aged patients in series is small, the results appear no worse than in younger patients. Liver resections for colorectal primaries has become increasingly important as studies have shown significant survival advantages. Hepatocellular carcinomas are aggressive tumours that frequently occur in a cirrhotic liver. Resection is associated with a high recurrence rate, as is liver transplantation, and this has been abandoned in all cases apart from small tumours. Chemoembolisation has now been shown to significantly improve survival and in combination with resection is the best treatment[18]. Benign cysts in the liver frequently present in the elderly and fail to respond to simple percutaneous aspiration but respond well to marsupilasation. Hepatic abscesses can present indolently after an acute septic episode and can be treated percutaneously in most cases avoiding surgery.

Cholelithasis is one of the commonest reasons for abdominal surgery in the elderly and all the complications of gallstones are commoner in this age group. Although commoner in women, the incidence increases rapidly in the over 60 age group and over 30% of octogenarians have gallstones. Whilst in the younger patient asymptomatic stones might be expected to become symptomatic in 15% within 10 years, there is evidence that gallstone disease in the elderly is more virulent with a higher risk of the more severe complications of emphysematous cholecystitis, gallbladder perforation and choledocholithiasis. Delay in treatment in the elderly appears less advisable as, not infrequently, the elderly present with one of the major complications without antecedent symptoms of cholecystolithiasis. In common with most disease of the elderly, emergency surgical treatment has a much greater risk than elective procedures.

The most dramatic change in surgery in recent years has been the widespread introduction of laparoscopic cholecystectomy which in most centres has now practically replaced open cholecystectomy. This technique was introduced in 1988 and has resulted in a shorter hospital stay, more rapid recuperation, less patient discomfort and a greater patient acceptance. Although the risk of bile duct injury is higher than open surgery, it has established a place in the surgical armamentarium and has a valuable role in surgery of the elderly. The importance and use of other treatments such as gallstone dissolution and electroshock wave lithotripsy have practically disappeared overnight and now have a limited role only in treatment of gallstones.

Complications of gallstones commonly seen are acute cholecystitis, gallbladder perforation, choledocholithiasis and pancreatitis. Acute cholecystitis in the elderly is increasing and is a common reason for surgical admission. The symptoms and signs may be very atypical but frequently are associated with distant results of sepsis in the elderly. Initial treatment is with antibiotics combined with either early or delayed cholecystectomy depending on the clinical response to treatment. In severely septic patients percutaneous transhepatic cholecystostomy may have a role in controlling sepsis but the high incidence of gallbladder wall gangrene makes this technique more liable to failure in the elderly. Acute emphysematous cholecystitis is evident when gas is demonstrated in the gallbladder wall as a result of anaerobic organisms, and unless treated directly with open cholecystectomy rapidly progresses to gangrene and gallbladder perforation with its inevitable greater morbidity from biliary peritonitis. The incidence of stones in the biliary system in the elderly ranges from 20% to 54%. Pre-operative endoscopic retrograde choledochography with endoscopic sphincterotomy and stone extraction allows laparoscopic cholecystectomy to be peformed and avoids the open surgery previously indicated for this condition. In jaundiced patients, endoscopic biliary decompression reduces the risk of operating in jaundiced patients and, in the aged and infirm, the insertion of biliary stents can avoid the need for further surgery.

Carcinomas of the gallbladder and extrahepatic biliary tract (cholangiocarcinomas) are uncommon malignancies but tend to occur in the older patients. Surgical resection is the only possible of cure but is rarely feasible because of the spread of malignancy. Palliation is achieved with endoprosthesis either inserted radiologically, surgically or endoscopically and survival is rarely more than 9 months.

Pancreatic disease in the elderly is a major cause of morbidity and mortality. Acute pancreatitis is not more common in the elderly but is associated with a higher risk because of their limited ability to cope with profound shock. In patients older than 70 years, a mortality of 20% and a mean inpatient stay of 3 weeks is to be expected. ERCP has a role in relieving biliary gallstones, frequently found in elderly patients, resulting in reduced morbidity and time in hospital compared to those treated conventionally[19]. In the elderly, the most severe complications noted after an attack of pancreatitis are related to the poor toleration of the patient to the profound shock. Respiratory complications leading to hypoxaemia which leads to multiorgan failure are commonly the cause of death in the elderly. Development of a pancreatic phlegmon or the addition of sepsis leading to a pancreatic abscess have severe consequences and need urgent surgical debridement and drainage. Pseudocysts occur in only 5% to 10% of cases of pancreatitis and may ameliorate with avoidance of oral nutrition and total parental nutrition. If they persist over 6 weeks and are greater than 6 cm in diameter internal surgical drainage is highly successful.

Nearly three quarters of pancreatic cancer occurs in the over 60 age group and most commonly affects the pancreatic head. The majority of patients present with painless unremitting jaundice and can be easily diagnosed with ultrasound, CT scan and ERCP. The only hope for cure is pancreaticoduodenectomy and the mortality from this radical procedure has fallen to 5% or less. The mortality of this procedure is higher in the over 70 age group and surgery should probably be restricted to those patients under 70 or with no co-existent risk factors. Palliation is best achieved by endoscopic intubation that is far more successful than for biliary malignancy. Randomised trials have shown the benefit of endoscopic intubation over surgical biliary decompression in cases confirmed by CT to be inoperable[20]. However, gastroenterostomy is necessary in 13% of cases and it is wise to exclude this prior to ERCP as, if present, this will require open surgery anyway to be relieved. Pain remains the most frequent symptom and can be controlled with chemical splanchnicetomy, performed at either open surgery or percutaneously as a coeliac axis injection, in combination with subcutaneous administration of Morphine.

Conclusions

Most diseases in the elderly require early assessment and treatment. Both delay in diagnosis and the inappropriate use of 'a wait and see' policy can easily convert what could have been an elective procedure into a surgical emergency. Elderly patients tolerate emergency surgery with its associated shock very poorly and are always associated with a high mortality and morbidity. In sharp contrast, elective surgery can now be performed for most conditions in the elderly safely and lead to a good preservation of life and quality of life. The challenge in the elderly is to ensure that surgery is considered early and used appropriately to avoid the inevitable consequences of emergency last resort procedures.

Surgery in the Elderly

Practical Points

1. Most commonly met surgical conditions can be treated with minimum risk if surgery is performed electively.

2. Elderly patients tolerate emergency procedures poorly.

3. Delay in diagnosis can deny the benefits of elective surgery.

4. Accurate pre-operative assessment can reduce the stress of surgery by removing the need for unnecessary exploration.

5. A common cause of death after the emergency surgery is from perforation of peptic ulcers associated with non steroidal anti-inflammatory drugs.

6. Breast cancer in the elderly appears less agressive and can be treated more conservatively.

7. Aortic aneurysm greater than 5 cm should be considered for surgery regardless of age.

8. Colorectal cancer is 'epidemic' in the elderly and delay in diagnosis leads to discovery of more advanced disease and to less favourable results.

9. Over 50% of all colorectal cancers can be diagnosed by digital examination without need of any sophisticated tests.

10. Gallstones lead to more serious complications in the elderly, but can be dealt with by minimally invasive and endoscopic techniques.

11. No elderly patient with pancreatic cancer should be denied the benefits of surgery just on the basis of age.

12. Palliative care to achieve a dignified death is just as important as the latest curative techniques.

References

1. Dunsmuir, B (1993) *General surgery in the elderly*, Surgery, 11, 549.
2. Bloem Br Lagaay AM, Van Beck W et al. (1990) *Prevalence of subjective dysphasia in community residents aged over 80*, BMJ, 300, 721.
3. Allen R, Rappaprot W & Hixon L (1991) *Referral patterns and the results of antireflux operations in patients more than 60 years of age*, Surg Gynecol Obstet, 173, 359–362.
4. Rice TW & Kirby TJ (1992) *Assessment of patients undergoing oesophagectomy*, Seminars in Thoracic and Cardiovascular Surgery, 4, 263–269.
5. McEntee G, Ryan W, Peel ALG et al. (1988) *A district general hospital experience of surgical treatment of gastric and duodenal ulcer from 1970–1982*, Surg Gynecol Obstet, 167, 55.
6. Sherlock DJ & Holl-Allen RTJ (1984) *Duodenal ulcer perforation whilst on Cimetidine therapy*, Brit J Surg, 71, 586–588.
7. Edelman DS, Russin DJ & Wallack MK (1987) *Gastric cancer in the elderly*, AM Surg, 53, 170.
8. Veronesi U, Salvadori B, Luini A et al. (1990) *Conservative treatment of early breast cancer*, Ann Surg, 211, 250–259.
9. Gazet J, Markopoulos C & Ford H (1988) *Prospective randomised trial of Tamoxifen verses surger in elderly patients with breast cancer*, Lancet, 1, 679–681.
10. Petracek MR, Lawson JD, Rhea WG et al (1980) *Resection of abdominal aneurysm in the over 80 age group*, South Med J, 73, 579.
11. Gelabert HA & Moore WS (1991) *Carotid endarterectomy: current status*, Curr Probl Surg, 3, 187.
12. North American Symptomatic Carotid Endarterectomy Trial collaborators (1991) *Beneficial effects of carotid endarterectomy in symptomatic patients with high grade carotid stenosis*, N Engl J Med, 325, 445.
13. Mackey WC, McCullough JL, Conlon TP et al. (1986) *The cost of surgery for limb threatening ischaemia*, Surgery, 99, 26.
14. Allen PI, Zager M & Goldman M (1987) *Elective repair of groin hernias in the elderly*, Br J Surg, 74, 987.

15. Sherlock DJ (1985) *Appendicitis in the over sixty age group*, Brit J Surg, 72, 245–246.

16. Robinson MHE, Thomas WM & Hardcastle JD (1993) *Change towards earlier stage at presentation of colorectal cancer*, Brit J Surg, 80, 1610–12.

17. Hobler KE (1986) *Colonic surgery for cancer in the very elderly; cost and 3 year survival*, Ann Surg, 203, 129–131.

18. Bismuth H, Morino M, Sherlock DJ, Castaing D, Miglietta C, Cauquil P & Roche A (1992) *Primary treatment of Hepatocellular carcinomas by combined arterial chemotherapy and embolism; chemoembolisation*, Am J Surg, 163, 387–94.

19. Neoptolemos JP, Carr-Locke DL, London NJ et al. (1988) *Controlled trial of urgent endoscopic retrograde cholangiopancreatography and endoscopic sphincterotomy versus conservative treatment for acute pancreatitis due to gallstones*, Lancet, 2, 979.

20. Shepard HA, Royle G, Ross APR et al. (1988) *Endoscopic biliary endoprosthesis in the palliation of malignant obstruction of the distal common bile duct a randomised trial*, Br J Surg, 75, 1166.

Section D

Development and the Wider Picture

Chapter 33

Objective Setting in Care of the Elderly

Professor D Metcalfe OBE, FRGP, FFPAM
Emeritus Professor of General Practice
University of Manchester
Rusholme Health Centre
Walmer Street
Manchester
M14 5NP

Biosketch:

A General Practitioner for 35 years, Professor Metcalfe's practice and teaching developed towards patient-centered care and communication as essential components of high clinical skill. His research focused firstly on the development of better medical records for supporting such care, and later on the effects of extraneous factors, such as social class, housing and poverty, on the pattern of care provided by GPs.

Being Old and Being a Patient

. . . to have life, and have it more abundantly . . .

Psychological age correlates but poorly with physical age. Being old is a role which is either self induced or laid upon a person by family and friends. The perception of being old carries with it not only intimations of mortality but of an agenda to be worked through. Functions and capabilities previously unconsidered are now consciously valued and protected. They become a matter of health. They should, therefore, be of central concern in the medical care of people who are, or consider themselves to be, old.

Conventional medical education focuses sharply on disease and its treatment: on diagnosis which aims at identifying the pathophysiology which in turn determines the measures to combat it. This reflects the sort of learning experiences made available to students and doctors in the training grades, which are almost entirely in the in-patient environment and to do with acute conditions or the acute phase of chronic diseases. It is quintessentially a 'doctor centred' perception of the medical task. The recipients of medical care are seen as 'patients' (or worse, as 'cases'), and their role, particularly while in-patients, as largely passive.

In reality, persons who are ill are only really 'patients' when in direct contact with their doctors: the rest of the time they are people with perceived variation from normal feelings and functions. They experience 'illness' not disease. 'Illness' is the subjective experience of disease. Since subjective experience is affected both by intrinsic factors such as personality, and extrinsic factors such as social support, it follows that the same disease, that is the same pathology, will generate different illness experience in different people. Just as chronic airways disease will have a different impact on a manual labourer than on a desk bound executive, so will heart disease in the elderly affect a widower living alone differently from a man with his wife and family about him.

Just as illness has to be differentiated from disease, management of that illness has to be differentiated from treatment of the underlying disease. Treatment will be aimed primarily at the pathophysiology in order to reverse or ameliorate it. Management will have broader aims, directed at the maintenance or recovery of function, both physical and psychological, in order to allow the person to go back to work on his or her remaining 'life agenda'. Thus, in a patient with rheumatoid arthritis, *treatment* with anti-inflammatory drugs aims to reduce the ESR and control pain, but *management*, involving splinting, physio and occupational therapy, aims to maintain abilities such as knitting or model making, as well as the daily tasks of self care.

Managing Disease and Managing Illness

In the old the treatment of disease itself must have realistic objectives. Nearly all the diseases suffered by the old are chronic manifestations of degeneration, and are by definition incurable. The aim cannot realistically be more than to 'level off' the decline in health, and will usually be only to diminish the downward gradient. Unrealistic aims may be pursued, for example by 'heroic' measures, at real cost to the recipient either in terms of side effects or of limitations of function inherent in compliance with rigorous regimes. Such regimes, in frustrating the person's ability to pursue his or her life agenda could actually be seen as diminishing health even while controlling disease. This is not to say, *of course*, that provided the aims are realistic, old people should not get the best possible treatment. Not only should their age be no excuse for poor care, but it should be remembered that they have made their contribution to the wealth of the nation, material or cultural, and that therefore they deserve the most effective care practicable. In the *management* of illness on the other hand, there is less likelihood of over-ambitious activity, since it is directed at the patient's own perception of loss of health. Here the danger is of under-care, which may result from one of two factors. The first is the tendency of doctors, trained as they are, to concentrate on the disease and its treatment to the exclusion of the illness and its management. The second is the lack of 'health ambition' in people who perceive of themselves that they are old and so of low self worth. Old people often have low expectations of the effectiveness of care.

The Need for Realistic, Explicit and Negotiated Objectives

These considerations make it imperative that those responsible for the medical care of people who are old set explicit objectives and use them to monitor and evaluate the effectiveness of that care. Setting explicit objectives is unfamiliar in medicine, perhaps because in the care of acute illness, which after all dominated the medical task in Europe until comparatively recently (and still does in most of the developing world), the objectives are so obvious that they do not need to be stated. Now, however, that the medical task (in the developed world at least), is dominated by the care of chronic disease, the setting of objectives should become part of the professionalism of doctors as it already is of nurses and therapists. Without explicit objectives, treatment tends to be titrated against parameters chosen by the doctor, the ESR or the blood urea, or symptoms with which the doctors can empathise, like pain. Physical, social, and psychological function, being entirely idiosyncratic to the person with the illness, are difficult for a doctor to utilise as markers when adjusting the management, let alone the treatment, *unless this has been negotiated with the ill person.* The classic example of such negotiation is in high standard terminal care in which the doctor ascertains from the patient how he or she sees the remaining 'life agenda' that has to be worked through, and organises pain control and all other measures to enable as much of that agenda to be achieved as possible. When such negotiations have taken place the doctor can accept that the patient will choose to suffer a certain amount of pain in order to stay functionally effective. Without such negotiation the doctor is likely to titrate analgesia against pain and render the ill person incapable of completing his or her agenda. Long before an illness becomes terminal, however, such negotiation in setting objectives is both proper and effective.

When providing medical care for an old person the doctor should ask him or her 'what do you want out of life, and how is this illness stopping you getting it?' Of course the person's ambitions may be unrealistic, either in wanting more than could possibly be achieved (even by winning the pools!), but much more often in being prepared to put up with much poorer quality of life than could be achieved. The former may have to be gently appraised of reality, the latter encouraged to seek for better things: that is why 'negotiation' is required, rather than simple and perhaps superficial enquiry. The second part to the question also may prompt negotiation, for again the ill person may mis-perceive the effect of the illness

on his or her life in one of two ways. He or she may find it easier to blame an illness (which is not his or her fault) for failure to achieve in life what he or she would have liked to do; on the other hand a person with a low self image may attribute 'failure' to personal shortcomings which actually are due to illness.

Having negotiated with the ill old person a reasonable expectation of what life should hold, and gained and agreed a clear and realistic understanding of how the illness is hindering it, doctor and patient are well placed to agree on explicit objectives of the medical care.

It must be recognised and accepted that there will be some cases in which the doctor has to accept objectives which do not conform to his or her own values. Patients sometimes say that *'the treatment is worse than the illness'*, and infer that they would rather have a shorter life or worse symptoms than suffer the side effects of the *'ideal treatment'*. If they have not been given the chance of negotiating the management of their illness their only answer is non-compliance with consequent loss of rapport and trust between themselves and their doctors. For example, however strongly doctors feel about hypertension it is the patient's right to decide that he would rather risk a stroke than suffer the impotence generated by the treatment even for mild to moderate hypertension! If however, there has been no negotiation, the doctor will continue to prescribe the unwanted drugs rather than explore the possibility of other ways of managing the illness and the patient will continue to leave the drugs untaken, but deceive the doctor on his routine visits to the surgery! When the doctor finds out he or she will be justifiably peeved and the mutual trust, so necessary between doctor and patient, will be damaged.

Health Status, Impairment, Disability and Handicap

Objectives for medical care not only vary between diseases, but between different phases in the natural history of an individual disease. Obviously in an acute myocardial infarction the objective is survival, the prevention of shock and dysrhythmias. Subsequently management is aimed at controlling angina and heart failure sufficiently to allow as normal an exercise tolerance and therefore social function as possible. Even *CABG* (coronary artery by-pass surgery) is directed to these aims rather than extending life expectancy.

This is a two dimensional 'cellular' model of any population. There is no such thing as a population in which everyone is healthy. It could however be postulated that a population is healthy if every member of it is in the right 'cell'. Obviously in an elderly population there will be more people with the chronic diseases than in a younger population, but there will be some who are in perfect health. There are seven 'cells' representing different health status: healthy, minor illness, acute illness, three levels of chronic illness, and terminal illness. The three levels of chronic illness utilise the convention of 'impairment', 'disability' and 'handicap'. 'Impairment' is the presence of pathophysiology without effect on lifestyle; the loss of some functions, but not essential functions, constitutes 'disability'; and limitation of essential function constitutes 'handicap'. (See Chapter 27 – Rehabilitation of the Elderly).

This model has two uses in considering objective setting in the medical care of the elderly. Firstly, it lays on the doctor the responsibility of making sure that the old person is properly categorised; that is, he or she is in the right 'cell'. Secondly, it helps the doctor to make sure that the objectives of management are appropriate to the 'cell' concerned.

It might be thought that categorisation is no more than proper diagnosis: making the right diagnosis will ensure that the patient is put in the right 'cell'. Old people, however, often do not present a simple problem. An old person can at the same time be suffering from an acute infection, one or more chronic diseases, and the normal ageing process, each of which will generate subjective symptoms and objective signs. It might be that whereas their care is normally characteristic of that pertaining to one of the 'chronic disease cells', for the time being they must be dealt with in the 'acute illness cell'. Alternatively, their acute illness may be minor and self limiting and should not be allowed to detract from the care of a chronic disease. The objectives of care for people who are properly categorised in the 'acute illness cells' will be disease-centred and treatment orientated. Those categorised in the 'chronic disease cells' should have negotiated objectives which are illness centred and management orientated.

The arrows in figure 1 indicate the moves between cells that individual people can make,

and most of them are reversible. These indicate the proper objectives, the aim being always to move people into the 'healthiest' (ie most functionally effective) 'cell' possible. In the 'acute illness cells' the focus must be on the accurate diagnosis of the disease, and the choice of the most effective treatment that is practicable or acceptable; in old people that choice is affected by their lower tolerance of some drugs and their side effects, and by interaction with medication being taken for intercurrent illness. In the 'chronic illness cells' however, where the diagnosis was achieved long ago, the focus must be

Figure 1

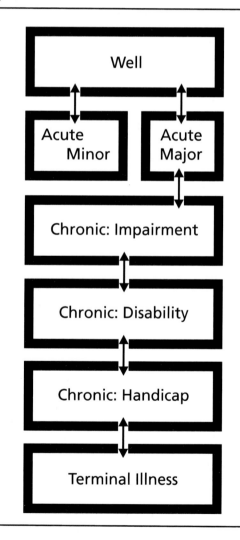

on function – physical, social and psychological. 'Function-directed' objectives aim to reduce handicap to disability, or disability to impairment. The former may be achieved by modifying the life of the subject so that their disability doesn't matter. This might be a question of changing jobs (from active to sedentary, for example) or it might involve making major environmental changes such as moving into a bungalow if the handicap was inability to get upstairs to the toilet. Sometimes the handicap centres on inability to pursue a much desired activity which is nevertheless not essential for worthwhile life, and here the objective might be to modify those desires, perhaps by counselling. A musician crippled by multiple sclerosis might become a teacher of her instrument, an actor a critic, and so on. The idea is to render the disability less important. For those in the 'disability cell' the aim is to restore function either by diminishing the effect of the underlying disease (for example better control of angina, or splinting in rheumatoid arthritis), or by deploying appliances which restore the lost function, or by-pass the necessity for it.

Objectives in the 'chronic disease cells' (and the 'terminal illness cell'), are, therefore, set primarily with reference to function; and since function has physical, social and psychological components, this can only be done by negotiation with the patient.

Changing Status

This cellular model of health has another implication. There is 'intracellular' activity, and 'intercellular' activity. Inside the cells the work is primarily done by the health professionals, with informed consent and co-operation from the patient. Here the patient is to some extent dependent, and dependence is always at some cost in autonomy (the more ill the patient the more dependent and the more dependent the less they can exercise autonomy: think of a patient in intensive care!). Within the 'cells' the patient is in a client role, albeit one which should respect his or her rights and preferences as a 'consumer'.

The intercellular work, on the other hand, is very different. This is concerned with transitions from one level of health status to another, the passage 'across the membranes' between cells, and that passage can only be achieved by negotiation. It cannot be assumed that patients would always want to move from handicap to disability for example: while most do, some enjoy 'secondary gains' from the dependency on family and friends, while others may be too tired and debilitated to be able to face a new approach to life. In the other direction acceptance of permanently reduced health and therefore functional integrity is not easy to accept and patients sometimes have to be persuaded to recognise severe limitations and not 'kick against the pricks' by operating denial or seeking after illusory treatments (bargaining) and thereby frustrating effective management.

Explicit objectives for the medical care of an old person, therefore, should be centred on the restoration or improvement in function in the broadest sense: the ability to work through a realistic life agenda. Implicit in such an objective or set of objectives is the proper diagnosis of the conditions which are reducing that capacity.

To set such objectives the ill person's expectations with regard to function and life agenda must be explored and, when inappropriate, negotiated, either 'up' or 'down'. Such objectives must be explicit, and that means not only fully and openly negotiated so that they are agreed, accepted and understood by the patient, the doctor, and sometimes other carers too, but written down in the medical record. This has three purposes: firstly to ward off criticism when the agreed care in some way differs from conventional standards; secondly to inform the other professionals involved so that care is 'seamless' and the patient is not exposed to conflict; and lastly, but perhaps most importantly, to ensure that management is titrated against them. If you have written '. . . and be able to type' or '. . . read the FT daily . . .' or '. . . hear his grandchildren properly . . .', you will be reminded to ask whether these functions have been maintained or restored whenever you see the patient.

Explicit objectives allow treatment and management to be titrated against the patient's perceived needs, and these may take precedence over more narrowly set medical goals. Old people who are ill have the right to settle for care which might be seen as medically suboptimal, in order to pursue better their remaining life agenda. This is only justifiable where that pattern of care is agreed on the basis of full appraisal and informed choices. The age and condition of the patient are never excuses for sub-optimal care in the absence of explicit negotiated objectives, but where there is evidence that such objectives have been negotiated, non-standard care can be justified.

Care of the elderly based on such principles demands skills and attitudes which are not commonly provided in conventional medical education. The setting of such explicit negotiated objectives in the medical care of old people requires skill in the elicitation and elucidation of the patient's self image, desires, and life agenda. It also requires willingness on the part of the doctor to relinquish power and pay real respect to the patient's vision of his or her life, without which 'negotiation' would be but a charade. Lastly, it requires some courage to pursue a patient-centred course of management for an illness which runs counter to conventional but essentially doctor-centred ideas of good care.

Objective Setting in Care of the Elderly

Practical Points

1. Psychosocial age correlates poorly with physical age.

2. Disease differs from illness as treatment differs from management.

3. Objectives need to be realistic, explicit and negotiated.

4. A good question when setting objectives is 'what do you want out of life and how do(es) this (these) illness(es) stop you from achieving it?'

5. Illness status can be changed.

Chapter 34

Audit in Geriatric Medicine

Dr J Catania MSC, MRCP(UK)
Consultant Physician in Geriatric Medicine
The Royal Oldham Hospital (NHS Trust)
Rochdale Road
Oldham
OL1 2JH

Dr P A O'Neill BSc(Hons), MB, ChB, MD, FRCP
Senior Lecturer/Honorary Consultant in Geriatric Medicine
University Hospital of South Manchester
Nell Lane
Manchester
M20 8LR

Biosketch:

Dr James Catania is a Consultant Physician in the Department of Adult Medicine at Royal Oldham Hospital, Oldham. His special interests are in Parkinson's Disease and rehabilitation of stroke patients.

Dr O'Neill qualified in Manchester in 1979 after intercalating in physiology and pharmacology (First Class). He was trained in general medicine in Manchester and Bristol and was awarded MD in 1985 for a thesis on Breathlessness. Appointed Lecturer in Geriatric Medicine 1986, subsequently promoted to Honorary Consultant and Senior Lecturer. His research interests are centred around stroke; from acute metabolic changes, through assessment and management of dysphagia to communication on a stroke rehabilitation unit and stroke prevention. He had a major role in medical undergraduate education in Manchester since being appointed Hospital Dean for Clinical Studies in 1991. From Sept 1994 he has been the Curriculum Facilitator for the undergraduate programme with a major remit to define and implement the core content of the medical curriculum. His major educational interests are small group/self directed learning and clinical skills acquisition. Outside medicine, his interests are family, sports and Bonsai trees.

Definition

Audit is derived from the Latin word auditare – a hearing. To many it implies an assessment involving a numerical review performed by an external monitoring body with the aim of preventing fraud. In medical practice, audit is interpreted as *"the sharing by a group of peers of information gained from personal experience and/or medical records in order to assess the care provided to their patients, to improve their own learning and to contribute to medical knowledge"*[1]. Although various terms have been used to describe this activity, 'clinical audit' has emerged as the more generally acceptable term as it embodies the spirit of a multidisciplinary approach to health care. The whole debate of audit activity in medical practice, therefore, focuses on maintenance of standards.

Why Clinical Audit?

Over the last few years there has been a sea of change in the perception of audit by the medical profession. This change has been provoked by pressures from three areas.

1. Political

In the United Kingdom, the government provides a comprehensive health service that is financed out of direct taxation. It is responsible for the appropriate use of resources and cost effectiveness in the delivery of care and views audit activity as a means of making the medical professional accountable.

2. Professional

Support for audit from the Royal Colleges and the other professional bodies such as the British Geriatrics Society, has been fuelled by:
a. The risk that without professional participation, managerial versions of audit, using inappropriate criteria, might well be imposed.
b. The knowledge that if the medical profession attempts to demonstrate proficiency, maintenance of professional independence is ensured.
c. The introduction of the more acceptable form of self-audit, on an informal basis which has an educational aim and relies on voluntary participation.

The Royal colleges have made the practice of self-audit a condition of approval for centres undertaking general and higher professional training.

3. The Public

People have become better informed through consumer organisations, formal education and communications technology. There has also been a discernable change throughout society towards an open accountable relationship between the provider and the customer. As financiers and consumers of the health care under NHS, the public require that the medical profession becomes more open in its endeavour to ensure high standards of care and is seen to check these standards. In other professions, agreed rules and codes of practice have already been developed which highlight the lack of continuous assessment for competence in the medical profession. For example, in aviation, on reaching the age of 40, a pilot on passenger flights has to pass two stringent medicals, a simulated flight and finally be examined by a senior captain!

The UK Government recently published the citizen's charter which outlines a commitment to making public services such as the National Health Service (NHS) more answerable to their users and to raising their overall quality[2]. The charter advocates the regular publication of performance of local health services to provide information to the public about the quality of the service, eg waiting times for all outpatients and for treatment.

How is Clinical Audit Performed?

The hallmark of effective clinical audit is a change in clinical behaviour that results in improvement of quality of care. This is more likely to be achieved in the setting of an active feedback process. The steps required for this can be considered as forming a cycle.

1. Choose a Topic and Set a Standard

a. Audit will usually be performed voluntarily by clinicians with the aim of improving their clinical practice. The topic chosen must therefore be perceived as a problem by the participants. This will ensure the interest and enthusiasm necessary for the audit exercise to be completed. The topic must deal with a common clinical activity (so that numbers accumulate rapidly), have a link with the outcome of care and finally be amenable to measurement and change. It is important to involve other professionals in the audit activity if it is envisaged that their co-operation would be required to meet the standard set. For example, the input of the nursing staff in the audit cycle would be essential if the topic selected is prevention of pressure sores or the quality of life on the long-stay wards.

b. There are various ways of setting standards of care to audit against. One of the participants may undertake a review of the subject and propose a set of medical expectations in the light of available resources. Recourse may be made to statements stemming from national or international consensus conferences. Recent examples include management of stroke[3]. Policy documents published by the various Royal Colleges provide norms for good practice, eg prescribing in the elderly[4], management of fractures of femur[5], the care of hospitalised elderly people[6], and ensuring equity and quality of care of elderly people[7]. Once the initial standards have been set these need to be discussed and amended according to local practice.

2 Observe Practice

Observation of practice may produce a true picture of current clinical management. Cases must be either selected randomly or include all occurences over a specified period of time. The practice can be audited prospectively or retrospectively. In prospective examination, the participants usually collect the data concurrently with the practice being monitored. For example, in an audit on discharge planning, the clinician would complete a form supplying details regarding Activities of Daily Living (ADL)/Home assessment, information given to patients, relatives and carers, the community services requested, and follow-up arrangements. This method, by heightening awareness of the problem under scrutiny, may cause a change in the clinical behaviour leading to a distorted image of the current practice. Retrospective analysis avoids this drawback but is

liable to inaccurate and incomplete information (see below).

The three main sources from which data can be collected are:

a. *Medical Records*
   It is widely recognised that medical records do not accurately reflect what actually occurs in practice. For the purpose of audit, medical notes based on a structured format will ensure more complete data that can subsequently easily be retrieved.

b. *Statistics*
   There are various statistics that are collected routinely in the NHS and offer a starting point for an audit exercise. Many are now contained in hospital computer systems. The patient administrative system (PAS) identifies each patient 'episode' and associated administrative details. Its main value is in providing lists of patients treated by a firm, ward or speciality or lists of deaths. The Hospital Activity Analysis (HAA) offers information of discharges by diagnosis. The Clinical Data Capture (CDC) includes diagnosis, operations and complications. Performance Indicators (PIs) are available in the form of a package from the Department of Health and offer information about how well NHS services are being provided in a particular locality by comparison with other districts. Lamentably, some of these sources can be up to 25% inaccurate.

c. *Ad hoc Surveys*
   Surveys based on questionnaires are particularly useful in assessing patients' satisfaction with the delivery of care and its outcome. We have also used this approach to evaluate the effectiveness of communication with local General Practitioners (GPs).

3. Comparison of Concurrent Practice with Standards of Care

There are two basic approaches. In the *explicit* method the observed practice is compared with a pre-set standard code of practice. This approach has the advantage of being objective, and therefore repeatable, and can be performed by non-medical personnel. For example, in an audit of medical records in a geriatric unit, one could draw a list of features that are considered essential to the proper assessment of an elderly patient. One would then assess each set of medical records against this predetermined list. In the *implicit* approach, the assessor uses his own subjective criteria as to whether a particular aspect of care has been deficient. As this method does not have pre-set criteria, it is more flexible but suffers from lack of objectivity. Although both methods may be effective, for the purpose of voluntary self audit, the explicit approach is to be preferred.

4. Implement Change

Usually, but not always, the conclusion of an audit cycle results in a change in the clinical behaviour of the participating clinicians. There are various means of achieving this.

a. *Education*

The most effective means to influence a doctor's knowledge and his clinical behaviour is the one that adopts an active participation of the doctor in learning together with corrective feedback.

b. *Concurrent review*

In this approach the actions of clinicians are compared to the established criteria concurrent to the action being taken. The advances in technology information and in its application to health care has made it possible to evolve computer systems that provide clinicians with an 'audit on line' service. Guidelines, check lists or logarithms can be used as a constant reminder to the participant of the standards to be achieved.

6. Re-observation of Practice

This is otherwise known as 'closing the feedback loop'[8]. Its function is to assess the impact of the changes implemented on the service provided and therefore on the quality of care. It is the litmus test of a successful audit exercise. If an audit activity does not result in change in clinical behaviour and improvement in outcome, then one must look critically at standards adopted and the method used. Standards may be unrealistically high and the audit cycle may prove deficient at one or more of the steps outlined above.

What to Audit

Health care delivery involves a process that is similar to any delivery of service. It has three main components: structure (representing resources), process (the way in which resources are applied) and outcome (the result of the intervention). As the overall aim of audit activity is to improve quality of care, audit should ideally focus on outcome. However, outcome measures in terms of quality of care are difficult to define, let alone measure. This is particularly relevant for geriatric medicine where patients often have more than one acute/chronic medical problem, of different degrees of severity, in association with complex social and functional problems. In contrast, outcome measures in surgery are more amenable to observation and value judgements. For example, in an audit of hernia repair operation, desirable outcome measures would include:

1. low incidence of post-operative infections;
2. low recurrence rate;
3. early return to work.

These represent well defined measurable end points.

The three main components of health care delivery will now be discussed.

Structure. This refers to the resources available. Its merit for audit is that these can be readily measured and the information is accessible. It is, however, a very indirect measure of outcome of treatment. One could look at facilities for provision of geriatric services at the local District level. The British Geriatrics Society has released various guidelines outlining the minimum recommended provisions to ensure good geriatric practice. Quality of care is also determined by the degree of accessibility to these resources. One could assess accessibility to endoscopy or coronary care units.

Process. This is how a particular problem is managed and gives information regarding how and whether things are done. The following are examples of topics that would be suitable for audit in Geriatric Medicine:

a. Communication:
   i) Medical records with particular reference to legibility, social and functional assessment, case conference outcome, ADL and home visits.
   ii) Discharge letters/summaries: relevance, conciseness, clear guidelines regarding after care, delay in despatch.
   iii) Outpatient appointments: review of general practitioners' referral letters with emphasis on appropriateness.

b. Drugs:
   Policy ie: on the prescription of antibiotics/laxatives/hypnotics, and monitoring for drug interactions, repeat prescription notes, re-assessment of medication.
c. Investigations:
   Review of indications and relevance (including indications for 'out of hours' tests), numbers performed, the action resulting from the report of the investigation.
d. Outpatients follow-up.
e. Trainee supervision/On-call Rota
f. Review of management of specific clinical situations, eg gastrointestinal bleeds, myocardial infarction (use of thrombolytic agents).

Outcome. Ideally an audit should identify differences between the outcome that is desired and that which actually occurs. In practice, both are hard to define and may occur so long after the initiation of treatment that many other factors will have intervened to confuse the issue.

Outcome in terms of the quality of care given can be determined by three elements:
a. *Effectiveness*: Defined as an improvement in outcome in terms of measured health status. This may be represented by two main end points: an improvement in life expectancy as reflected by reduction in mortality rates; and an improvement in the quality of life by reduction of disability and distress. Reduction in mortality rates is a crude but easily identifiable measure. Evaluation of physical disability and distress is more difficult but may, for example, be carried out using self-assessed patient questionnaires.
b. *Acceptability*: The increasing importance of this element is reflected in the title of the Government's white paper on the NHS, 'Working for Patients'[9]. The rights of the consumer have become increasingly recognised. Patients' satisfaction with standard of care could be monitored with questionnaires which, for example, may enquire about courtesy, waiting time, information given, fabric of life in continuing care wards.
c. *Efficiency*: This relates to improvement in outcome with reduced use of resources.

Although the three elements of delivery of care – structure, process and outcome have been described separately, some audit activities may require an evaluation of the three concurrently.

For example, in an audit focusing on pressure sores one would have to consider:
1. **Resources**: Nurse-staffing levels correlated with patients' dependency profile, availability and accessibility of pressure relieving apparatus.
2. **Process**: Assessment of vulnerability of patients. Minimisation of risks. Treatment of pressure sores (is there a common policy?).
3. **Outcome**: Reduction in the incidence of bed sores resulting in less risk of systemic infections, comfort and shorter length of stay in hospital.

Method of Audit

In America, audit has been part of the fabric of medical practice for over a decade. The primary motive for its introduction to medical practice was to limit the spiralling costs of health care. It was imposed by the Government and private medical insurance companies and is performed by non-medical personnel. Experience of this external regulatory form of audit has shown that it has poor educational value and consequently little impact on clinical behaviour.

The British Government recognises the principle that the quality of medical work can only be reviewed by a doctor's peers. The emphasis is therefore on voluntary participation of practitioners reviewing their own work in local groups. Audit activity is envisaged to be informal, with an educational aim and in most cases based on a topic chosen by local clinicians. Where appropriate, audit exercises may be initiated by the Royal Colleges or other professional bodies on a national basis. Such audit activity has proved successful in, for example, setting guidelines for pre-operative X-rays and reducing maternal deaths following confinement. In the recent NHS reforms, purchasers may request local audits.

The Government is also anxious to co-ordinate audit activity at district level. In the white paper, it proposed that each district (now Trusts) would have an audit advisory committee chaired by a senior clinician with representatives of the major medical specialities, including General practice. The committee would plan and monitor audit programmes, specifying methods to be used, and plan frequency of audit for each clinical team. This system would be overseen by a Regional Audit Committee. This was widely adopted and has to be altered to reflect the change in NHS practice.

Finally, one also has to consider to what extent patients should be involved in audit activity. It is argued that for clinical audit to work for patients (consumers), there is a need for the patients to be involved in the assessment of care and in the setting up of a professional standard. A consumer orientated independent audit agency is, however, likely to create antagonism in the medical profession. Currently, the community health councils have a 'Watchdog' role. In the future, it is envisaged that they will participate in audit activity by having representatives on the local Medical Audit Advisory Committee.

Thus, it is expected that all medical practitioners in the country will be involved in clinical audit in the future. In this chapter we have set out the compelling reasons for this, described the practical steps essential for this activity and shown how it can be applied to Geriatric medicine.

Audit in Geriatric Medicine

Practical Points

1. The hallmark of clinical audit is a change in clinical behaviour which results in an improvement in the quality of care.

2. The audit cycle involves choosing a topic, setting standards, observing practice, comparing practice with the standard, implementing change and re-observing practice.

3. The implementation of change involves intergrating the results of an audit exercise with education. This is most effective when it involves active participation and corrective feedback.

4. The three main components of health care delivery involve structure, process and outcome.

5. Outcome can be determined by three elements, effectiveness, acceptability and efficiency.

References

1. Committee of Inquiry set up for the Medical Profession in the United Kingdom (1976) *Competent to Practice*. (Alment Report) HMSO, London.

2. *The Citizen's Charter*, London: 1991 (cm 1599)

3. Consensus conference: *Treatment of Stroke*, BMJ 1988; 297: 126–128

4. *Medication for the elderly*, J Roy. Coll. Physicians (London), 1984, 18, 7–17.

5. *Fractured neck of femur: prevention and management*, J Roy Coll. Physicians, (London) 1989: 8–12.

6. *Improving Care of the elderly in Hospital.* British Geriatric Society/Royal College of Psychiatrist/Royal College of Nursing. Joint Publication.

7. *Ensuring equity and quality of care for elderly people*, R. Coll. Physicians, London 1994.

8. Smith T (1990) *Medical Audit*, BMJ, 300, 65

9. Secretaries of State for Health, Wales, Northern Ireland & Scotland (1989) *Working with Patients*, London, HMSO (Smnd 555).

Chapter 35

Research in Geriatrics – A Practical Guide

Dr P A O'Neill BSc(Hons), MB, ChB, MD, FRCP
Senior Lecturer/Honorary Consultant in Geriatric Medicine
University Hospital of South Manchester
Nell Lane
Manchester
M20 8LR

Biosketch:

Dr O'Neill qualified in Manchester 1979 after intercalating in physiology and pharmacology (First Class), was trained in general medicine in Manchester and Bristol. Awarded MD in 1985 for thesis on Breathlessness. Appointed Lecturer in Geriatric Medicine 1986, subsequently promoted to Honorary Consultant and Senior Lecturer. His research interests are centred around stroke; from acute metabolic changes, through assessment and management of dysphagia to communication on a stroke rehabilitation unit and stroke prevention. He has had a major role in medical undergraduate education in Manchester since being appointed Hospital Dean for Clinical Studes in 1991. From Sept 1994 he has been the Curriculum Facilitator for the undergraduate programme with a major remit to define and implement the core content of the medical curriulum. His major educational interests are small group/self directed learning and clinical skills acquisition. Outside medicine, his interests are family, sports and Bonsai trees.

Introduction

Busy clinicians need to have a grasp of research to enable them to:

1. understand how research applies to clinical practice;
2. use its tools to monitor clinical practice (audit) or to implement change;
3. identify and solve a problem which has particular local relevance.

Understanding and Criticising Research

Most readers, including the author, claim to have read an article when they have simply scanned the summary/abstract and glanced at the discussion. What is required for understanding and carrying out research is a more systematic approach, possibly by use of the following check list:

a. Hypothesis;
b. Design;
c. Subject selection;
d. Methods used;
e. Analysis;
f. Valid conclusions;
g. General application and relevance to the reader's practice;
h. Costs.

Each of the points on the check list will be discussed below in relations to a clinician setting up and carrying out a research project of his/her design.

Hypothesis

In medicine, clinicians feel comfortable with the dichotomy of disease and health but in geriatric medicine no such clear separation exists[1]. Fundamental design problems will occur unless a clear set of questions are formulated which can be tested. This can be illustrated by a common dilemma facing geriatricians: "*does treatment of hypertension benefit elderly people*"? This vague question could be reformulated with more clarity. "*Whether treatment of elderly male subjects aged 65–75 years and with a sustained systolic blood pressure of over 170 mmHg will reduce the risk of vascular death/myocardial infarction by more than 30% over two years*". This hypothetical study is obviously large-scale and costly but the same principles operate in a small study – the researcher must identify precise goals in a tightly defined domain.

Literature Search

In parallel with formulating a hypothesis a literature search must be undertaken. In general there is no point in repeating already published studies! Perusal of relevant publications will allow insight into the development of the proposed research field and where the unanswered problems lie.

There are a number of different means by which a literature search can be undertaken. A recent key paper can be used as the starting point. The references given in this can then be traced depending on whether they are of importance to the proposed study. This method starts at a single point and then ramifies backwards. The major drawback is that any paper is likely to be selective in the references that it quotes. The reason could be simply oversight or equally it could be that other key studies, not referred to, strongly refute the author's hypothesis and conclusions.

An alternative method is to initiate a search of a computer database reference system. There are a number of different ones, (eg Medline), each covering a slightly different set of journals and extending back a number of years. References prior to the inception of the database have to be traced manually. Some searches will give simply the journal reference, others will supply abstracts. The latter are of more use in selecting papers.

The search is initiated by deciding on a number of key words and how far back, in years, the search is to be carried out. Expert advice is needed here. If the clinician was interested in a study on the treatment of deep vein thrombosis (DVT) by heparin in elderly people, then a number of key words might be used. These are essential to define the scope of the search, if too narrow then few references will be traced, but if DVT alone was searched on, many thousands of publications would be indexed leaving the researcher no further forward.

A literature search can often be requested through hospital libraries and the librarian may help in this matter.

Design

Subjects

Many published studies give inadequate details of how the subjects participating were identified and selected. Protocols commonly require comparison between groups of individuals with a particular condition and those without. An important consideration is how should the control groups be selected to avoid being drawn from dissimilar populations with different characteristics. For example, if the study group is drawn from the acute assessment wards and the control group is from the Day Hospital, then unnecessary bias will be introduced.

In studies on changes with age, major flaws commonly exist. Firstly, what constitutes normal ageing? Is it the complete absence of disease or is it those criteria which define and contain 95% of the elderly population? The second flaw in design is that subjects are often compared using cross-sectioned groupings (ie 41–50 yrs, 51–60, 61–70 yrs). This is convenient but differences may not be due to the effects of ageing, they may affect other differences in the lives of the cohorts. One example would be the percentage loss of height with age which clearly depends on the absolute height obtained in young adulthood.

Longitudinal studies overcome this problem but they also have inherent difficulties: is it possible to study the subjects over a long period of time eg, 10–20 years? Many of those recruited subsequently drop out. This can be illustrated by the possible outcome of a study to determine the effect of smoking on the decline in forced expratory volume (FEV_1) which may show a change which is less than the true reduction because those with the greatest decline in FEV_1 will have an increased mortality rate over the period of study.

A further factor to be considered is whether sufficient numbers can be recruited into the different groups within the allocated time span. All of those involved in research are aware that once a common condition such as a gastrointestinal haemorrhage is chosen for study then it can be guaranteed that no such patients will be forthcoming for several months!

Measurement

The tools chosen for measurement depend on the end points selected. They range from semistructured interviews to detailed physiological methods. Whatever is decided upon, a number of items should be considered:
a. Is the method available to the clinician?
b. Is it acceptable to the patient and ethically justified?
c. Is any special expertise needed?
d. What is the variability of error of the assay/instrument?
e. How reproducible is the result (inter and intra-observer)?
f. How sensitive is it to change?
g. How will the results be stored and analysed?

Furthermore, it is imperative to select techniques which are capable of detecting any clinically significant change. The technique should also be widely accepted, many investigators design their own instruments which have not been validated.

Study Protocol

At times, the double blind randomised control trial may neither be possible to initiate or appropriate. It may be impossible to render a study even single blind if, for example, the side effects of one of the treatments is nausea. Interviews and questionnaires (postal or face-to-face) are appropriate for epidemiological studies.

Other than the validity of the instrument, the major problem is then one of sampling the population. What percentage should be taken, is stratification needed to ensure sufficient numbers in, for example, age or social class bands? How is the population to be identified? The electoral register or general practice age-sex register are both known to have a large element of inaccuracy. Furthermore, if no reply is forth-coming from a high percentage of the sample will these differ in any way from the responders?

If the research is to be a simple survey carried out in hospital, will the sample be biased even if randomised? This can be illustrated by a hypothetical study on the functional recovery from stroke. If one group, by chance, included a preponderance of patients with a left hemiparesis who were also elderly, it would bias the results.

When considering the number of subjects to recruit, most clinicians attempting research will probably design their study and propose a number to be studied that seems appropriate and sounds 'reasonable'. What is necessary, in place of guesswork, is to consider a pilot study. This is where, for example, a study questionnaire can be tested out, problems identified and procedure refined. It, by definition, only involves a small number of subjects. Not only does a pilot study allow design problems to be ironed out, it also helps in deciding the numbers of subjects required. From the results it is possible to work out the numbers required to detect the presence or absence of a clinically significant effect by use of appropriate statistical techniques. This is concerned with the 'power' of a study and is discussed below.

If a study is badly designed and the numbers involved are insufficient then the research is unlikely to be of value. It can be argued reasonably that it is unethical to recruit elderly people into such a study.

Analysis (Figure 1, Page 315)

It has been said that there are lies, damn lies and statistics. Most clinicians have an inadequate grasp of statistical techniques and put too much emphasis on the mythical $p<0.05$. It is strongly suggested that, if at all possible, a statistician is consulted at the initial stages of planning.

In the development of a project the ultimate analysis of the data must be considered. If the study is designed to determine whether an intervention has a useful clinical effect, such as a reduction in the length of stay in hospital, then a number of elements have to be given due weight. Firstly, there may be differences between a statistically and clinically significant change. It will be possible, given sufficient numbers, to detect a very small but statistically significant alteration in the length of stay. The second factor to be considered in analysing the results is the errors inherent in any statistical technique. The p value estimates the Type I error which is a probability of detecting an effect which has simply occurred by chance. At $p=0.05$ this would occur, on average, in 1 in 20 studies. The Type II error is the opposite of this, that is the probability of missing an effect when it is there.

One example of a Type II error is the research published on intravenous Streptokinase therapy. It is now widely accepted that such treatment will reduce the risk of death following an acute myocardial infarction by approximately 25%. However, it took a trial (ISIS 2) involving 17,000 patients to prove this. Prior to ISIS 2 a meta analysis was carried out, which involved an overview of all the published (and where possible, unpublished) studies. A number of these did not find a statistically significant effect though one was almost certainly there. Thus, these studies probably had a Type II error. On the other hand, a mischeaviour analysis of the ISIS 2 data showed greater benefits for certain astronomical star signs (a type I error?)!

By use of either the results of a pilot study or by setting out in the initial hypothesis the magnitude of change which would be considered to be clinically significant, then it is possible to calculate the number of subjects required to reduce the Type II error to an acceptable level.

The next point regarding analysis is to consider the nature of the data which will be collected. In the initial planning stages it should be clear whether the data are parametric (obtained from ordinal (ordered) interval measurements of a continuous variable). Parametric data are either normally distributed or can be transformed to such a distribution. It can then be analysed using techniques such as Students 't' test.

Non-parametric data could be categorical (nominal) data such as the presence or absence of urinary incontinence or it could be ordinal but not interval data. An example of the latter would be the rating of pain into absent, mild, moderate and severe. These categories, although they imply a ranking order, do not contain any statement of the magnitude of change in moving from one category to another. Particular techniques are used in analysing non-parametric data such as the Wilcoxon signed rank test. Many of the measurements used in geriatric medicine, such as activities of daily living scales, produce non-parametric data.

The next step in planning the analysis, having decided on the type of data, the numbers needed and the confounding variables (any factor which might modify an effect – such as concurrent prescription of the tricyclic antidepressants in a trial of blood pressure reduction) is to determine the recording and storage of the data. Standardised forms should be designed and the method of storage decided upon.

Computer databases can be constructed to hold the data and the forms should facilitate numerical codes. Once the data are stored then analysis can take place. It is now possible to use much more refined and powerful statistical techniques using personal computers compared with the pen, paper and calculator method. The danger in using computer programmes to analyse the data without expert advice must be recognised. Programmes will generate p values, confidence intervals etc, without difficulty, but they may be entirely inappropriate leading to rejection of the paper at a later stage, or damning criticism at a scientific meeting.

Ethical Committee Approval

Hospitals in the UK have an ethical committee whose remit is to examine any proposed research proposal. The clinician should clarify with them what is required to obtain approval.

Funding

At an early planning stage the full cost of the study should be estimated, which should include the use of any of the hospital's NHS facilities. Costings also need to take into account any payment to subjects and their travel expenses. It is then possible to approach a funding body with a submission for financial aid. All of this takes time and together with seeking ethical committee approval will necessarily delay the start of the project. The journals can be scanned for any possible source of finance, and local bodies may also have limited funds. The same advice as given above applies, namely, find out the requirements necessary for a submission.

Presentation of Data

Once the data is analysed then inferences need to be drawn on whether any significant change has been observed. This is termed rejecting the Null hypothesis and accepting the Alternative hypothesis. It is not satisfactory to simply state this in terms of $p<0.05$. Statistical computer packages give exact p values and in a small trial, if the p value was actually 0.06 rather than 0.40 this would convey much more meaning as to possible inferences from the study. Confidence intervals are a development of this theme giving a measure of the weight that can be assigned to a particular result. It conveys the range in which it is 95% (or any percentage value) probable that the population mean or the difference in means lie. The smaller the range and the further away from zero (in a test of the difference in mean) the confidence interval lies, the more certain it is that the effect is a true one.

Presentation and Publication of the Study

An effective means of communicating the results from a piece of work is to present it to one's own colleagues, which could be at a local meeting. The research could subsequently be presented to a learned society. The British Geriatrics Society is the most obvious choice of a platform for presentation of research in geriatric medicine in the UK. It holds meetings twice a year and invites submissions of abstracts for consideration. The initial hurdle, therefore, is to have the abstract accepted.

All societies have very strict rules of submission regarding abstract forms to be used, type face (font), order of authors etc. These *must* be absolutely adhered to, failure to do so will result in rejection of the abstract without consideration. The abstract should be written as a 'mini paper' with a *short* introduction, methods, results and conclusions.

If the research is accepted then careful thought and attention should be given to its presentation. If it is a poster, the presenter needs to know whether any formal verbal presentation is also required. If possible, the Department of Medical Illustration should be involved early in the preparation.

The aim of any presentation is to communicate a concise summary of the results with any conclusions, which must be understandable to the non-specialist. Poster display should not contain masses of text which are unreadable from more than 1 metre away, any diagrams should be self-explanatory and the general lay-out has to be simple. The object is to invite those interested to read the poster and discuss your work informally.

A similar approach should be adopted for a platform presentation. Consider what is the essential message of the work and build around it. Concentrate on presenting the study rather than a complete review of the literature. Draw only valid, sustainable conclusions and do not be drawn into generalities. One of the biggest failures of verbal presentations is that they involve too many slides which are not legible from all parts of the auditorium. A good method of preparing for presentation is to practice in front of one's colleagues. Check the time and adhere strictly to that allotted. Consider the faults in the study and any potentially damaging questions. It is better to be prepared than to ignore them. Once the conference/meeting is finished many societies publish abstracts as a supplement to their journal. These can be referred to in a Curriculum Vitae but it must be clear that these are not full research papers.

A large number of the above considerations also apply to submitting a paper based on the research to a journal. Each journal will have their own special interests and requirements. There is no point in submitting a piece of work on clinical geriatric medicine to a journal which only accepts papers on pure biological ageing research.

One of the major errors to be avoided in writing a research paper is lack of detail in the methods such that these cannot be assessed or that the study cannot be reproduced elsewhere. Failure to give details of statistical methods (or use of inappropriate one) and poor presentation of results are other common faults. In the discussion, many authors generalise and draw sweeping conclusions which cannot be justified. It is strongly recommended to consult one of the references given at the end of this chapter relating to the submission of research for publication.

Conclusions

A broad and superficial outline of research in geriatric medicine has been presented. An interested clinician of whatever grade should be able to criticise the published literature and have some insight into how a research project might be carried out avoiding major pitfalls. Two rules should be used as a guidance.
1. Only attempt what is possible. A research project should develop out of local practice and availability of resources.
2. Obtain as much expert advice as possible in the planning stage.

Figure 1

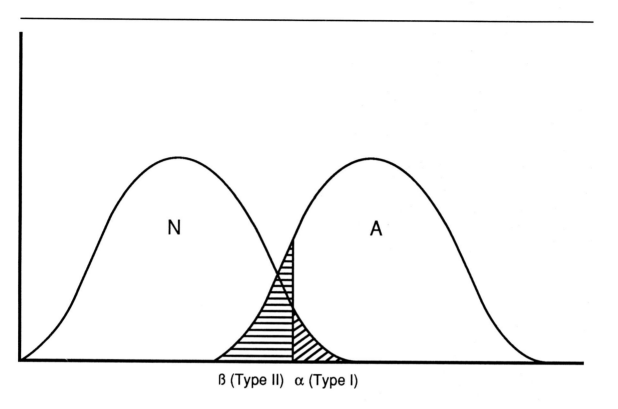

β (Type II) α (Type I)

Research in Geriatrics

Practical Points

1. Research hypotheses must be framed in such a way that they are capable of being tested.

2. A recent key review paper is a useful source of relevant references. A computer search is more comprehensive but can produce too many.

3. The design of a study is critical and should be discussed with experienced workers.

4. A statistician should be consulted during the design of the study so that analysis is considered before data is collected.

References

1. Grimley Evans J (1988) *Ageing and disease. Research and the ageing population.* Wiley, Chichester, Ciba Foundations Symposium, 134, 38–57.

Suggested Reading

1. Journal Club (1989) *Let's audit*, Lancet, *i*, 594.

2. Bland M (1987) *An introduction to medical statisics*, Oxford University Press.

3. Gardner MJ & Altman DG (1989) *Statistics with confidences*, British Medical Journal Publications, London.

Chapter 36

The Role of Interventional Radiology in the Elderly

Dr A N Khan, MBBS, LRCP (Lond), MRCS (Eng), FRCP (Edin), DMRD, FRCR, MHSM Cert
Consultant Radiologist
North Manchester General Hospital
Crumpsall
Manchester M8 6RL

Biosketch:

Dr A N Khan is a Consultant Radiologist at North Manchester Healthcare Trust/Lecturer Part-time University of Manchester Medical school. Author of 3 books, 183 publications, chapters, abstracts and post graduate lectures (Local, National and International). United Nations Visiting Professor to Pakistan 1992. Visiting Professor to the Soviet Union, Russia, Uzbekistan, Kazakistan, and Kirghizia 1991, 1992, 1993, 1994, and 1995. On the United Nations 'Talent Pool' for transfer of knowledge through expatriate nationals. Chaired five international scientific conferences. English editor 'Lymphology' (A CIS Journal). Several research interests in nuclear medicine, ultrasound and vascular intervention.

Introduction

Radiologists' first venture into intervention started when they began to look at blood vessels using crude instruments, home made guide wires and catheters and using crude contrast materials. This was in the forties and fifties. Techniques, instruments and contrast materials have improved constantly. Methods of imaging have also made great strides with improved image quality. In 1953, Seldinger[19] described his technique of catherterising arteries percutaneously. This technique forms the basis of most interventional radiology procedures. The equipment required to accomplish this technique consists of a needle, a guide and a catheter compatible with each other so that the guide wire fits into the needle, and the catheter can be threaded over the guide wire. The needle used in the Seldinger method has two parts: (1) an outer blunt cannula and (2) an inner pointed trocar. The Seldinger method involves introducing the needle into the blood vessel, withdrawing the trocar, pulling back the cannula until there is free flow of blood. A guide wire is then introduced into the blood vessel via the trocar, the trocar then withdrawn, leaving the flexible guide wire *in situ*. A catheter of appropriate size is then threaded over the guide wire introducing it into the blood vessel. The guide wire is then pulled out, thus providing ready access into the lumen of the vessel for introducing radiographic contrast media, medication, fluids and embolic/occlusive materials. This technique is not only employed for angiography, but also for blocking and unblocking blood vessel and treating blockages in the biliary, gastrointestinal and urinary tracts.

Radiologists soon ventured into what was once considered tiger territory, biopsying masses in the thorax, abdomen, pelvis and the skeleton guided by fluoroscopy, ultrasound computed tomography or MRI, making exploratory laparotomy and thoracotomy a thing of the past.

Radiologists drain cysts, abscesses, effusions, empyemas, obstructed biliary tree, obstructed kidneys etc and are venturing into percutaneous gastrostomy and cholecystostomy. Most of these developments have occurred over the past 10–15 years.

Most of these procedures are carried out under the influence of local anaesthetic, light sedation and analgesia if required. The therapy is minimally invasive, needs little pre-operative and post-operative preparation and care. In fact, interventional radiology represents 'key hole' surgery *par excellence*. When doing vascular intervention, the radiologist has access to the whole vascular tree, both arterial and venous, via the groin, the exception being the portal venous system which needs direct puncture when portal intervention is required.

Interventional radiological procedures are especially suited to the elderly because they are minimally invasive and do not involve general anaesthetic. Image guided biopsy procedures may avoid major surgery and give the clinician vital information on management and prognosis. Limb salvage intervention in critical ischaemia may at best save limbs and at worse result in less drastic amputation. Biliary surgery has major implication for the elderly; some, if not most, can be avoided by radiological techniques.

Biopsy Techniques

Biopsy techniques are the simplest form of radiological intervention. Biopsies are usually taken percutaneously under a local anaesthetic, using a fine needle for target-specific cytological study or trucut or similar needle for histological examination. Most intrathoracic, intra-abdominal, skeletal or superficial non-vascular masses can be biopsied in this way. Complications from the procedure are minor and few. The techniques save on more involved surgical procedures which have a significant morbidity and mortality and cost implications. Biopsies are a short cut to diagnoses in the appropriate clinical setting and provide invaluable information on patient management. While carrying out recanalization techniques in the biliary or urinary tract, cells for cytological examination may be obtained via a brush biopsy.

Abscess and Cyst Drainage Techniques

Abscesses, empyemas, cysts and other intra-thoracic or intra-abdominal fluid collections can be tapped for diagnostic purposes using ultrasound guided fine needles or drained therapeutically using catheters. Sclerosants can be introduced to prevent re-accumulation of fluid in cysts of renal or hepatic origin. These cysts are only drained if they are symptomatic. Large pig tail catheters can be utilised to drain abscesses containing thick pus. Pancreatic pseudocysts may be drained through the stomach and pelvic abscesses through the vagina in female patients. Most fluid collections are drained using a Seldinger technique, which may also be extended to drain more superficial fluid collections.

Revascularization Techniques

The technique of dilating vascular stenosis percutaneously was first described by Dottor and Judkins[20] in 1964. The technique was poorly accepted because they used a co-axial system of catheters of large diameter to achieve a dilation. In 1974, Gruntzig and Hopff[21] developed the double lumen polyvinyl balloon catheter. The first encouraging results of the use of the balloon in lower limb occlusive vascular disease were reported in 1976. Since then the treatment of peripheral vascular disease by percutaneous angioplasty has become common place and more aggressive (figure 1). The hope being that a significant reduction in open surgery and extremity amputation may be achieved.

The secret of success in performing a successful angioplasty is a safe crossing of a stenosed or occluded vessel by a guide wire. If a guide wire crossing cannot be achieved in an occluded vessel, it cannot be recanalised. To achieve a passage of a guide wire across an occlusion several other techniques have been explored. One way of achieving this is to use laser probes to initially

form a tract through the occlusion with a subsequent passage of a guide wire. Other devices that are used in the treatment of peripheral vascular disease are atherectomy catheters. These devices have a rotating retractable blade at the leading end of the catheter which cuts across atheroma, which is subsequently sucked out. Self-expanding endovascular stents are now available to be placed in long occlusion. These devices reduce recurrence rates of vascular occlusion. These stents are also used for recanalisation of major veins such as the subclavion veins and superior vena cava. Catheters are used for removal of clots from the pulmonary artery. Two types of such catheters are available: (1) catheters that achieve fragmentation and recirculation of thrombus and (2) catheters that cause fragmentation with subsequent aspiration of the thrombus.

Thrombolytic drugs can be delivered to the site of an acute arterial or venous thrombosis via catheters. Acute variceal haemorrhage remains a difficult clinical problem in patients with portal hypertension. Several excellent surgical techniques are presently available to construct a porto-caval shunt, but these are a major undertaking in patients that are already severely ill and are moreover associated with a high incidence of accelerated hepatic failure and encephalopathy. In 1969 Rosch *et al*[1] created a percutaneous transhepatic portosystemic shunt in experimental dogs. It was not until 1982 that Colapinto *et al*[2] applied the technique of transjugular intrahepatic portosystemic shunt (TIPS) to humans with life

Figure 1

(a) shows a 2 cm occlusion of the proximal popliteal artery (arrow), (b) and (c) following balloon angioplasty patency has been achieved.

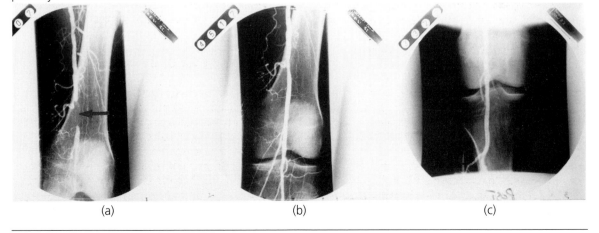

(a) (b) (c)

threatening variceal haemorrhage. In 1983[2] the same authors reported on a larger series of patients on whom a TIPS procedure was performed. Very few of these shunts remained patent at six months. The advent of metal stents renewed interest in TIPS. The use of the first metal stents in TIPS were reported by Richter *et al* in 1990[3]. These shunts controlled variceal bleeding in all patients and remain patent for up to 9 months.

The incidence of encephalopathy following a TIPS procedure appears to be considerably lower than after standard surgical procedures. The technique involves advancing a long curved needle via the internal jugular vein through a catheter into a hepatic vein; the needle is then introduced into a portal vein branch through the hepatic parenchyma. The tract thus created between the hepatic and portal veins is dilated with placement of a metallic stent across it. A portosystemic shunt is thus created inside the liver.

Transcatheter Vessel Occlusion

Vascular malformations in most body parts are amenable to embolotherapy using various embolic material, absolute alcohol or plastic polymers via specifically designed catheter systems. Tumours in the kidney may be embolized as a definitive procedure in the elderly (figure 2) especially if they are the cause of symptoms such as haemturia. The techniques can be used to achieve a superselective embolization of the tumour itself rather than sacrificing the whole kidney. Renal embolization can be used as an alternative to nephrectomy in other conditions in the elderly unfit patient. Alcohol ablation is usually painful; the patient may, therefore, need strong analgesia during the procedure and a few hours after the procedure. Embolization techniques can be extended to the bladder to control haematuria from bladder lesions. The indications for transcatheter embolization of the kidney tumours in the elderly include haemodynamic

Figure 2

Superselective embolization of a lower pole hypernephroma of the right kidney

(a) before embolization, (b) after ablation of the tumour with absolute alcohol (arrows).

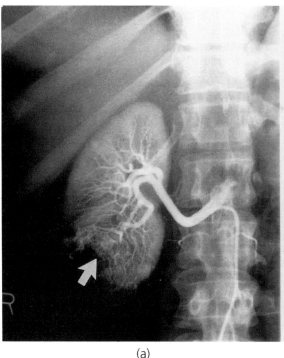

(a)

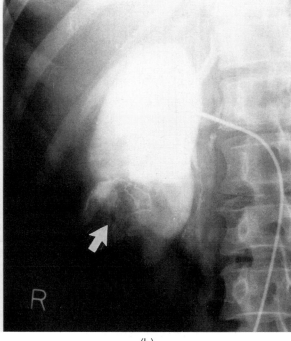

(b)

A GUIDE TO THE CARE OF THE ELDERLY

abnormalities such as haematuria, heart failure from arterio-venous shunting, hypertension from an ischaemic kidney, polycythemia and to provide definitive therapy[4].

Life threatening haemoptysis such as occurs in tuberculosis, bronchiectosis and mycetomas can be successfuly controlled by embolization of the bronchial arteries.

An alternative approach to treatment of metastases from islet cell tumours of the pancreas and hepatomas is transcatheter embolization.

In the past, life threatening pulmonary emboli from the legs used to be treated by surgical plication of the IVC. The operation was performed in critically ill patients with significant mortality and morbidity. This operation has now been largely replaced by the placement of inferior vena caval filter[5] by a percutaneous approach via catheters (figure 3).

Figure 3

An umbrella placed in the IVC as prophylaxis against pulmonary emboli (arrow).

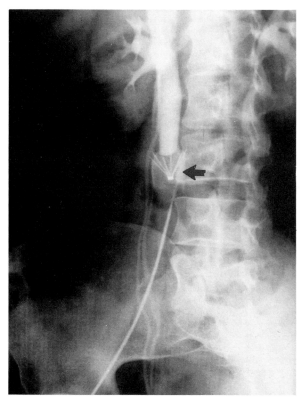

Following any form of embolization technique, most patients suffer from a post-embolization syndrome, manifested by nausea, vomiting, pain and fever. The symptoms settle with supportive measures.

Transcatheter embolization of the spleen is an alternative to surgical splenectomy. Serious complications were reported initially after total embolization. Although experience is still limited, complication rate is less with fractionated embolization carried out in stages as advocated by Spigos et al[6] and Owman et al[7].

Non-vascular Intervention in the Liver and Biliary Tree

Direct Ablation of Solid Tumours

Ablation therapy can be delivered directly by percutaneous approach into hepatomas, cholaniocarcinomas and liver metastases. The use of ethanol injection directly into solid liver tumours such as hepatomas, cholagiocarcinomas, lymphoma, adenomatous hyperplastic nodules and metastases was first reported by Sugiure et al[8] in 1983. This form of therapy has achieved wide acceptance. Histopathological studies of treated tumours show complete destruction of malignant tissues in the majority of patients. The technique has achieved remarkable survival rates. The procedure involves the injection of absolute ethanol percutaneously via a 20 or 21 gauge needle under ultrasound guidance. Because the spread of alcohol is limited, this treatment is usually limited to tumours 5 cm or less in diameter. Patients with gross uncontrollable ascites or bleeding diathesis cannot normally have this form of treatment.

Percutaneous Cholecystostomy

Surgical cholecystostomy which is used as a compromise procedure in the elderly or high risk patients carries a postoperative mortality of 6–20% and a high morbidity. Experience with percutaneous cholecystostomy (PC)[9] so far has demonstrated a complication rate less than 3%. Like surgical cholecystostomy, PC is used as a stop gap to tide patients over the acute phase before definitive surgical treatment is instituted. However, PC has been used as a definitive treatment in acalculus cholecystitis. Indications for PC include acute calculus and acalculus cholecystitis empyema or pericholecystic abscess in patients unsuitable for definitive surgical treatment. The technique involves transhepatic insertion of a catheter into the gall bladder using a Seldinger technique. It is possible to extract stones via the PC catheter after they have been shattered or alternatively dissolution therapy can be applied directly to cholesterol calculi using methyltetrabutyl ether.

Percutaneous Biliary Drainage

The prototype of percutaneous biliary drainage (PBD)[10], the combined internal/external drain is an alternative to surgical biliary decompression. The standard technique of PBD involves the placement of catheter into the biliary tree. The catheter has multiple side holes which are usually placed above and below the site of the biliary stricture thus allowing drainage of bile. The technique is used for palliation of advanced malignant obstruction, sepsis-cholangitis, failed biliary-enteric anastomoses, stone dissolution or extraction. A similar technique is involved for placement of ednoprosthesis, basket extraction, chemical dissolution of bile/duct calculi, balloon

dilatation of benign or malignant biliary strictures and placement of self-expanding metal stents across bile duct strictures.

Pre-operative biliary decompression reduces post-operative complications but does not affect the overall mortality. Contraindications to the procedure include uncontrollable bleeding diathesis, massive replacement of the liver by metastatic disease and hepatic cirrhosis.

Endoscopic Retrograde Cholangiopancreatography (ERCP)

ERCP is performed using a flexible fiberoptic side viewing duodenoscope. The procedure is a team effort employing the expertise of an endoscopist and radiologist. However, more and more radiologists are taking up endoscopy and ERCP. The indications for ERCP can be divided into diagnostic and therepeutic. Cannulation of both the common bile duct (CBD) and pancreatic ducts are undertaken via the endoscope and a diagnostic cholangio-pancreaticogram obtained. Endoscopic sphinterotomy may benefit several types of patient including those with CBD calculi (figure 4), sphincter of Oddi dysfunction, papillary tumours and gall stone pancreatitis. Internal

Figure 4

Endoscopic Retrograde Cholangiopancreatography

(a) showing a large calculus lower CBD (arrow), (b) following papillotomy the calculus has been released into the bowel with a subsequent reduction in the size of the CBD.

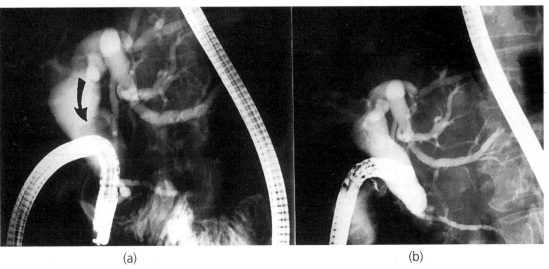

(a)　　　　　　　　　　　　　　　(b)

transpapillary stents may be placed via ERCP and since the tip of these stents protrude into the duodenum they can easily be replaced endoscopically. Biliary strictures can be dilated using balloon catheters, brush biopsies taken from the bile or pancreatic ducts and fluid aspirated for cytological examination. ERCP may also aid by placing nasobiliary catheter, allowing bile ducts to be perfused by antibiotics or calculi to be dissolved by direct dissolution therapy. Complications of ERCP include pancreatitis, drug reactions, instrumental injury and cholangitis. Haemorrhage may follow sphinterotomy. Contrindication to sphinterotomy include bleeding diathesis, acute pancreatitis and calculi over 2.5 cm.

Non-vascular Intervention in Urology

Percutaneous Nephrostomy (PCN)

Antegrade placement of catheters[11] in the renal pelvis under local anaesthetic is one of the most frequently performed techniques in uroradiology. The indications for the procedure in the elderly are: (1) obstructive uropathy; (2) urinary diversion; and (3) as a prelude to stricture dilatation, calculus removal or stent placement. The complication rate for a simple PCN is low and include arterio-venous fistulae, extravasation of urine and occasional puncture of extra-renal organs. Uncontrolled bleeding diathesis and untreated urinary tract infection are regarded as contraindications.

Percutaneous Treatment of Ureteral Fistuals[12]

A uretal fistula may develop as a result of trauma, calculi, inflammation or neoplasm. The standard treatment for ureteral fistulas is considered surgical with immediate drainage of urinomas and repair of the ureteral fistulas. However, recent advances in percutaneous uroradiological intervention makes it possible to manage ureteral fistulas by percutaneous technique. Urinomas can be drained percutaneously under ultrasound guidance and urinary diversion created via PCN. Ureteric stents are placed using the PCN route to eliminate flow through the fistula and thus giving it time to self-repair.

Percutaneous Suprapubic Cystostomy (PSC)[13]

This technique is the counterpart of PCN in the upper urinary tract. Like PCN a suprapubic cystostomy can be used as a simple drainage procedure or as part of a more involved uroradiological procedure such as bladder calculus removal or balloon dilatation of urethral strictures. Complications from the procedure are rare and not usually serious contrary to what Hippocrates wrote 15 centuries ago: *"cuy vesica persecta . . . lethal"* which translated means 'to cut through the urinary bladder is lethal'.

Radiological Intervention in the Male Urethra

Recently retrograde prostatic urethroplasty with a balloon catheter (Castaneda *et al*[14]) has been performed with variable results and long term trials are awaited. The urethra remains patent for up to 9 months in the majority of patients with minimal after-micturition dribbling.

Surgical prostatectomy has been the mainstay of therapy for symptomatic benign prostatic hypertrophy (BPH). The majority of patients undergo transurethral resection. Improvement in patients' symptoms have been reported in 75–90% of patients for up to 5 years, but there is a re-operation rate in up to 80% at 5 years. In addition, there is significant morbidity and mortality associated with surgery. Recently, there has been renewed interest in minimally invasive treatment for BPH. This particularly applies to the elderly unfit patients in whom a variety of temporary and permanent endourethral stents have been tried. The permanent stent, although expensive, may prove an alternative to surgery.

Radiological Intervention in the Oesophagus[15]

Benign strictures are usally dilated by balloon catheters. Endoscopic intubation of both benign and malignant strictures is widely practiced by gastroenteroligists. With the development of hydrophillic guide wires, most strictures of the oesophagus, no matter how tight, can be traversed and their dilation undertaken. Although endoscopic intubation is simple and cheap, it is painful and carries a risk of perforation. Furthermore, dysphagia may recur with further complications of tube dysfunction and tube migration.

A self-expanding metal stent placed endoscopically may prove to be a better alternative with long term patency and little risk of migration.

Percutaneous Gastrostomy and Cystogastrostomy

Surgical feeding gastrostomy performed in the malnurished and debilitated patient carries a high morbidity and mortality. In 1980, Gaudeser and Pansky[16] introduced percutaneous gastrostomy. This technique is now practiced by many radiologists using the Seldinger technique[17]. The procedure is minimally invasive with considerable reduction in morbidity and mortality over the surgical procedure.

Pancreatic pseudocysts have traditionally been drained surgically into the stomach, duodenum or jejunum. One prerequisite for such a procedure is that the pseudocyst should be 'mature' with well defined walls on imaging. This normally takes 4–6 weeks. Surgical intervention may be called for earlier with a complicated pseudocyst, in this instance, an external drainage may be performed which causes a high morbidity and mortality. Percutaneous aspiration of pseudocyst may be carried out at any time. Many pseudocysts lie posterior to the stomach. This has led to a percutaneous transgastric approach of draining pseudocysts leading to lower incidence of fistula formation. The procedure is straightforward and a cheap way of treating pseudocysts and may be performed without waiting for maturation of the cyst.

Coeliac Plexus and Splanchnic Nerve Block[18]

Sensory nerve fibres carrying the sensation of pain from the abdominal viscera are relayed in the coeliac plexus while other nerves travel via the splanchnic and vagus nerve to the CNS. The pathway can be interrupted by coeliac plexus and splanchnic nerve block with alcohol or phenol providing a significant long term relief from visceral pain, both acute and chronic. The procedure is particularly helpful in carcinoma and chronic pancreatitis. Approach to coeliac plexus is made percutaneously via the anterior or posterior abdomen while the splanchnic nerve is approached from the back around D12. Most authorities perform a test block with local anaesthetic before injecting alcohol and phenol – patients whose symptoms are not relieved by the local anaesthetic are not submitted to risks involved (neurological complications such as paraphegia has occurred in 1% of patients in whom alcohol or phenol is used) with a permanent block. The needles are guided into place using fluoroscopy or computed tomography.

The Role of Interventional Radiology in the Elderly

Practical Points

1. Interventional radiology is minimally invasive and represents 'key hole surgery' *par excellence.*

2. The treatment is simple, quick, cheap, usually performed under local anaesthetic, and causes minimal discomfort to the patient and, therefore, ideally suited to the elderly and critically ill.

3. Little pre-operative preparation is required and post-operative care is minimal.

4. May be an effective alternative to conventional surgery.

5. Some treatment is stop gap and a prelude to definitive surgery, so a planned surgical procedure is carried out, reducing the risks involved with emergency surgery.

References

1. Rosch J, Hanajee W & Snow H (1969) *Transjugular portal venography and radiologic portocaval shunt: an experimental study*, Radiology, 92, 1112–1114.

2. Colapinto RF, Stronel RD, Gildiner M, et al. (1983) *Formation of intrahepatic portosystemic shunts using a balloon dilatation catheter. Preliminary clinical experience*, AJR, 140, 709–714.

3. Richter GM, Noeldge G, Palmaz JC et al. (1990) *Transjugular introhepatic portocaval stent shunt: preliminary clinical results*, Radiology, 174, 1027–1030.

4. Wallace S, Charnsangares C, Carrasco CH & Swanson A (1990) *Embolization of malignant tumours*, in: Clinical Urography. Pollack HM (ed) W B Saunders, Philadelphia, 3003–3017.

5. Cho KJ, Proctor MC & Greenfield LJ (1994) *Efficacy and problems associated with inferior vena cava filters*, in: Current Techniques in Interventional Radiology, Cope C, 8, 1–8, 17.

6. Spigos DG, Tan WS, Mozez MF, et al. (1980) *Splenic embolization*. Cardiovasc. Interven. Radiol., 3, 282.

7. Owman T, Lunderquist A, Alwmark A, et al. (1979) *Embolization of the spleen for treatment of splenomegaly and hypersplenism in patients with portal hypertension*, Invest. Radiol., 14, 457.

8. Sugiura N, Takara K, Ohto M, et al. (1983) *Percutaneous intratumoral injection of ethanol under ultrasound imaging for treatment of small hepatocellular carcinoma*, Acta Hepatol Jpn., 24, 920.

9. Lindemann SR, Tung G, Silverman SG & Mueller PR (1988) *Percutaneous cholecystostomy. A review*, Semin. Intervent. Radiol., 5, 179–184.

10. Ferruci JT, Meuller PR & van Sonnenberg E (1983) *Transhepatic interventions*. In: Radiology of the gallbladder and bile ducts. Diagnosis and intervention, W B Saunders, Philadelphia, 432–491.

11. Pfister RC (1990) *Interventional Uroradiography*, in: Clinical Urography, Pollack MC (ed), W B Saunders, Philadelphia, 2701–2703.

12. Lang EK (1987) *Non-surgical treatment of ureteral fistules*, Semin. Intervent. Radiol., 4, 53–69.

13. Snyder JA & Smith AD (1987) *Endourologic management of lower urinary-tract disorders*, Semin. Intervent. Radiol., 4, 94–98.

14. Castaneda F, Reddy PK, Hulbert JC, et al. (1987) *Retrograde prostatic urethroplasty with balloon catheters*, Semin. Intervent. Radiol., 4, 115–121.

15. Neuhaus H (1991) *Metal oesophageal stents*, Semin. Intervent. Radiol., 8, 305–210.

16. Gauderer MWL, Ponsky JL & Izont RJ (1980) *Gastrostomy without laparotomy: a percutaneous endoscopic technique*, J. Pediatr. Surg., 15, 872–875.

17. Halkiev B, McCloughlin MJ & Ho CS (1988) *Percutaneous gastrostomy and cystogastrostomy*, Semin. Intervent. Radiol., 5, 223–229.

18. Lieberman RP, Liberman SL, Cuka DJ & Lund GB (1988) *Coeliac plexus and splanchnic nerve block*, Semin. Intervent. Radiol., 5, 213–221.

19. Seldinger SI: 1953 *Catheter replacement of the needle in percutaneous arteriography*, Acta Radiol [Diagn], 39, 368–376.

20. Dotler CT & Judkins MP (1964) *Transterminal treatment of arteriosclerotic obstruction: description of a new technique and preliminary report of its application*, Circulation, 30, 654–670.

21. Grüntzig A, Hopff H (1974) *Perkutane rekanalisation chronischer arterieller verschlüsse mit einem neuen dilatationskalheter: Modifikation der Dotler-technik*, Dtsch Med Wochenschr, 99, 2502–2505.

Chapter 37

Law, Ethics and the Elderly:
Worthless Treatment or Worthless Lives?

Dr John Keown DPhil (Oxon)
Barrister, Lecturer in the Law
and Ethics of Medicine, University of Cambridge
Fellow, Queens' College, Cambridge, CB3 9ET

Biosketch:

Dr John Keown graduated in law from Cambridge before proceeding to take a doctorate at Oxford. He teaches the law and ethics of medicine in the Faculty of Law at Cambridge and has written widely on the subject. He is the author of *Abortion, Doctors and the Law*, published by Cambridge University Press in 1988, and editor of *Euthanasia Examined: Ethical, Legal and Clinical Perspectives*, to be published in 1995 by Cambridge University Press.

Introduction

This short paper has three simple aims.

It seeks first, to outline the principle of the 'sanctity of life', a principle which has traditionally guided medical decision-making but which is currently widely misunderstood and under increasing attack, with grave implications for all patients, not least the elderly.

It then seeks to show how the decision of the House of Lords in the Tony Bland Case ([1993] 1 All England Law Reports 821) is subversive of that principle and may pose a real threat to the care and treatment of the elderly.

Thirdly, it argues that the recent report of the House of Lords Select Committee on Medical Ethics (HL Paper 21 – I of 1993–94) has done little to diminish that threat.

The paper concludes that there is an urgent need to rediscover and reassert the principle of the 'sanctity of life', and the traditional ethical distinction between judgements about the worthwhileness of a treatment – which are ethically proper – and those about the 'worthwhileness' of a patient's life – which are not – and to reassert the equality-in-dignity of all patients regardless of condition or age.

The 'Sanctity of Life'

Few ethical concepts are more widely understood – by medical practitioners, lawyers and the general public – than the principle of the 'sanctity of life'. Many think it means that human life must be preserved at all costs and either crazily embrace it or lazily dismiss it. But this misunderstanding of the principle is simply a gross caricature.

The idea that life must be preserved at all costs has nothing to do with the principle of the 'sanctity of life'. It is, rather, 'vitalism', an idea which is not only ethically untenable but whose implementation is physically impossible. The 'sanctity of life' is not vitalistic. It holds, rather, that all human beings share an inherent, inalienable dignity or worth, regardless of differences such as race, sex or age, and that it is, therefore, wrong intentionally to kill any human being. Intentional killing denies inalienable worth, for it assumes that life is only an instrumental rather than a basic good, a good only in so far as it serves as a means to an end, whether that end be conceived of as the good of the race, or the state, or of another, or the living of a life of a certain minimum 'quality'.

The inalienable worth posited by the principle of the sanctity of life derives not from any developed abilities a person may be able to exercise, such as reading books or playing snooker, but simply from his or her humanity. It is shared equally by the great composer and the profoundly deaf; by the poet and the illiterate; by the infant and the senile. That worth is, moreover, inalienable: it cannot be given away, as by selling oneself into slavery, nor can it be taken away, as by being sold into slavery.

This principle has long enjoyed widespread acceptance and still continues to do so. The notion of an inalienable dignity in virtue of one's humanity is, for example, implicit in the Universal Declaration of Human Rights, whose Preamble states: "*Whereas recognition of the inherent dignity and of the equal and inalienable rights of all members of the human family is the foundation of freedom, justice and peace in the world . . .*".

Article 1 states: "*All human beings are born free and equally in dignity and rights . . .*"

and Article 2 affirms that "*Everyone is entitled to all the rights and freedoms set forth in this Declaration, without distinction of any kind, such as race, colour, sex, language, religion, political or other opinion, national or social origin, property, birth or status . . .*".

Article 3 provides that "*Everyone has the right to life, liberty and security of the person*";

Article 6 that "*Everyone has the right to recognition everywhere as a person before the law*"

and Article 7 that "*All are equal before the law and are entitled without any discrimination to equal protection of the law . . .*".

However, the notion that all human beings enjoy an equality-in-dignity, simply in virtue of their humanity, and the principle that it is wrong intentionally to kill any human being (except unjust aggressors and capitally-convicted criminals) has never enjoyed universal acceptance. It is now under sustained attack by a number of prominent medical ethicists who adopt an 'end justifies the means' approach to ethics and who openly advocate a division between patients who (like competent adults) qualify as 'persons' and those who (like those with advanced senile dementia) do not, and between those with 'worthwhile' lives and those who would be 'better off dead'. Such an approach is clearly inconsistent with the principle of the sanctity of life and, indeed, with the concept of fundamental human rights, but it is surprisingly influential both inside and outside the medical profession.

The implications of the principle of the sanctity of life for medical practice are clear: all decision-making must be predicated on the inalienable worth of each patient. And, given that all patients enjoy an inalienable worth simply in virtue of their humanity, there is no room for judgments based on the supposed 'worthlessness' of the patient's life. In arriving at decisions about treatment the doctor must focus on the worth-whileness of the treatment, not on the supposed 'worthwhileness' of the patient's life, and he or she must never aim to shorten life. The patient, however sick, however dependent, is never a means to some end but is an end in himself and must, even if he has lost sight of his inalienable worth, be respected as such.

The principle has played a crucial formative role in the development of medical ethics. Indeed, it long predates the emergence of the modern medical profession in the last century. However, the principle has, to a considerable extent, been abandoned by many practitioners. The most dramatic breach was effected by legislation permitting abortion, now practised in the UK with a frequency and for reasons which would surely have staggered many of those who voted for it. Further, the practice of sedating and starving to death infants with disabilities who are rejected by their parents is, as the trial of Dr Leonard Arthur revealed, far from unknown.

Where does this erosion of the principle leave those patients whose vulnerability lies not in their youth but in their advanced age? The recent decision of the House of Lords in the Tony Bland case has done little to guarantee their inalienable human right not to be intentionally killed.

The Tony Bland Case

Tony Bland was a victim of the Hillsborough football stadium disaster, from which he never regained consciousness. The medical evidence indicated that he was in a 'persistent vegetative state' and that he had irreversibly lost consciousness. He was fed by nasogastric tube. His doctor and parents wished to discontinue his tube-feeding and the hospital trust sought a declaration from the courts that it would be lawful to do so. The House of Lords upheld the granting of the declaration.

Counsel for the Official Solicitor, representing Bland, opposed the withdrawal on the ground that it would amount to murder. In English law, a person commits murder when he causes the death of another with intent to kill (or to cause really serious harm) either by an act (such as giving a baby poisoned food) or by an omission where he is under a duty to act (as by starving his baby to death). Counsel argued that stopping Bland's feeding would be just as much murder as cutting the air-pipe of a deep sea diver.

The majority of the Law Lords clearly accepted that the doctor's intention in stopping the tube-feeding would be to kill Bland. But all the Lordships nevertheless held that it would not amount to murder because stopping feeding would be an omission, not an act.

But was not feeding, albeit by tube, part of the basic care which the doctor was duty-bound to provide for the patient? No, held the Law Lords. Tube feeding was 'medical treatment' and an omission to provide medical treatment was lawful provided the doctor was of the opinion that stopping the treatment was in the patient's 'best interests' and provided his opinion coincided with that of a 'responsible body' of medical opinion. As Bland's doctor was of the opinion that withdrawal was in Tony Bland's best interests and as this opinion was supported by a 'responsible' body of doctors on the ground that life in Bland's condition was of 'no benefit' to him, the removal of the tube-feeding would be lawful – even if carried out with intent to kill.

This decision is, with respect, wrong. It invites a number of serious criticisms, such as the categorisation of tube-feeding as 'treatment' (what, it might be asked, is it supposed to be treating?) and the effective delegation to 'responsible' medical opinion of the decision whether the patient is 'worth' preserving. Most important, however, is the fact that their Lordships' reasoning is inconsistent with the principle of the sanctity of life. This principle has long informed the criminal law no less than medical ethics and accounts for the blanket prohibition, as murder, of the intentional killing of any human being by an act or by failing to care for a person in one's charge.

Unfortunately, the principle was misunderstood by the Law Lords (and by counsel for the Official Solicitor) who confused the sanctity of life with 'vitalism' and overlooked the crucial distinction between assessing the worthwhileness of the treatment and the 'worthwhileness' of Bland's life.

The sanctity of life is not, as noted above, 'vitalistic'. It does not require the preservation of life at all costs and permits the withdrawal of treatment which is not worthwhile. It will not be worthwhile (and will, to use alternative terminology, be 'extraordinary' or 'disproportionate') where it offers no reasonable hope of benefit or where it is too burdensome as, for example, where it would impose excessive pain or expense on the patient. In such cases, it may properly be withheld or withdrawn, even if the hastening of the patient's death is foreseen as a side-effect of the decision. Such decisions involve a judgment that the treatment is no longer worthwhile, not that the *patient* is no longer worthwhile.

Of course, in assessing the worthwhileness of the treatment, the doctor should have regard to the condition of the patient. If the patient is near to death from cancer, a course of distressing chemotherapy is more likely to be judged disproportionate than in a patient who has just been diagnosed and who has a good chance of recovery. But although the patient's condition (or, less happily, 'quality of life') is properly taken into account, it is taken into account in assessing the worthwhileness of the treatment, not the patient's life. The reasoning is 'Given the patient's "quality of life", this treatment is not worthwhile', not 'Given this patient's quality of life he would be better off dead'.

The Law Lords endorsed a competing principle, antipathetic to the sanctity of life, that it is permissible to withdraw treatment on the ground that the patient's life is of no benefit. They did reaffirm the absolute legal prohibition on intentional killing by an act, but this serves only to highlight what one Law Lord referred to as the 'morally and intellectually misshapen' state in which the decision leaves the law: one may never kill by an act but one may do so by omission, provided it is in the 'best interests' of the patient. But if it is in the 'best interests' of the patient to die, why may a doctor starve him to death but not despatch him immediately with a shot of potassium chloride? The decision leaves the law of murder laughing at itself.

The decision is, moreover, not only difficult to defend in principle, it also threatens in practice to expose patients to fatal omissions on the basis of a judgment by their doctors that their lives are no longer 'worth living'. The reasoning underlying the Law Lords' decision can surely in principle, and may well in practice, be applied to patients other than those in persistent vegetative state (PVS). Indeed, one Law Lord asked, without answering, what the position would be if the patient were not in PVS but had glimmerings of awareness. Indeed, once one has accepted the principle that there is such a thing as a life which is 'not worth living', there is little reason to suppose that it could, or should, be confined to those in PVS. What of those with advanced dementia or the frail elderly?

The House of Lords Select Committee on Medical Ethics

In the speeches of the Law Lords in the Bland Case, calls were made for Parliament to investigate the issues it raised. Consequently, in 1993 the Government appointed a Select Committee of the House of Lords whose terms of reference were to consider the *"ethical, legal and clinical implications of a person's right to withhold consent to life-prolonging treatment, and the position of persons who are no longer able to give or withhold consent; and to consider whether and in what circumstances actions that have as their intention or a likely consequence the shortening of another person's life may be justified on the grounds that they accord with that person's wishes or with that person's best interests . . .".*

The Select Committee reported in February 1994. It recommended that the law should not be amended to accommodate active euthanasia. Reaffirming the prohibition on intentional killing, the Committee said:

"That prohibition is the cornerstone of law and of social relationships. It protects each one of us impartially, embodying the belief that all are equal. We do not wish that protection to be diminished and we therefore recommend that there should be no change in the law to permit euthanasia. We acknowlege that there are individual cases in which euthanasia may be seen by some to be appropriate. But individual cases cannot reasonably establish the foundation of a policy which would have such serious and widespread repercussions. Moreover, dying is not only a personal and individual affair. The death of a person affects the lives of others, often in ways and to an extent which cannot be foreseen. We believe that the issue of euthanasia is one in which the interests of the individual cannot be separated from the interests of society as a whole" (HL Paper 21–I of 1993–'94; paragraph 237)

This may seem at first sight to be a comprehensive reaffirmation of the principle of the 'sanctity of life'. It is not. For the Committee defined 'euthanasia' as a 'deliberate *intervention* to end a life to relieve intractable suffering (paragraph 20. Emphasis added.) In other words, it did not include as euthanasia the intentional killing of a patient by *omission*.

Moreover, the Committee was divided on the question of withdrawing tube-feeding from those in PVS. It was unanimous, however, that the question need not, and should not, arise since in a case like Bland's, "*it might well have been decided long before application was made to the court that treatment with antibiotics was inappropriate, given that recovery from the inevitable complications of infection could add nothing to his well-being as a person*" (paragraph 257)

But what is meant by 'his well-being as a person'? It is far from clear that the Committee is ruling out a judgment based on the supposed 'worthwhileness' of the patient's life.

In short, the report of the committee contains a welcome and timely reaffirmation of the prohibition on active intentional killing and rightly locates its rationale in the fundamental equality of all patients. Yet the Report oddly fails to condemn intentional killing by the withdrawal of treatment or tube-feeding. Its endorsement of the principle of the sanctity of life only goes, therefore, half way and the Report is, no less than the law of homicide after Bland, a victim of its own inconsistency. If intentional killing of patients is wrong, it is surely wrong whether the doctor decides to carry out his intention by an act or by an omission.

Lords and how the Select Committee missed an opportunity to recover the situation. The principle, affirming the innate worth of every patient, is the only sure safeguard of the elderly, not least in view of increasing pressures on social and medical resources.

It is now far from uncommon to hear the ageist accusation that the elderly are 'unproductive' and a 'financial drain on society', an accusation which would not be tolerated in relation to other groups in society such as the unemployed. Those professionally involved in the care and treatment of the elderly have a vital role to play in reasserting, both in the political forum and in their everyday practice, the inalienable worth of each of their patients and the need for adequate resources to fund as high a level of care and treatment as society can reasonably afford. It is often said, surely rightly, that a society should be judged on how it treats its vulnerable members.

The sanctity of life principle does not pretend to answer all the many difficult questions relating to care and treatment which arise in everyday practice. But it establishes the framework of good, ethical care, requiring that the inherent dignity of each patient be respected and, in particular, that his or her life never be intentionally shortened, by act or omission. Within that framework, treatment and non-treatment decisions should be made by the patient in consultation with the doctor in the light of the promised benefits of the treatment and its likely burdens to the patient.

Conclusion

The reasoning of the Law Lords in the Bland case and the Report of the House of Lords Select Committee on Medical Ethics have profound implications for the profession of medicine as a whole and, in particular, for those caring for patients vulnerable to the accusation that they would be 'better off dead' on the ground that their lives lack worth or dignity. There can be few more vulnerable than the dependent elderly.

It is important for those dedicated to the treatment and care of the elderly to grasp the extent to which the principle of the sanctity of life has been misunderstood and eroded by the Law

Law, Ethics and the Elderly

Practical Points

1. All medical professionals and carers should respect the inalienable worth of each patient and never intentionally shorten a patient's life by act or omission.

2. In making treatment decisions in consultation with a competent patient or in relation to an incompetent patient, assess the 'worthwhileness' of the treatment rather than trying to assess the 'worthwhileness' of the patient's life.

3. In assessing the 'worthwhileness' of the treatment, consider whether, in the light of the patient's condition, the proposed treatment offers a reasonable hope of benefit and, if so, whether any benefit will be outweighed by any excessive burdens, such as excessive pain or expense.

Chapter 38

Prescribing and Therapeutic Strategies

Dr R B Shukla MD, FRCPI, CertMHS, MHSM
Consultant Physician
North Manchester General Hospital
Department of Medicine for the Elderly
Delaunays Road
Manchester M8 6RL

Dr S Arya, MBBS, MRCP(UK), Medical Registrar
Victoria Hospital, Blackpool
Whinney Heys Road
Blackpool
Lancs FY3 8NR

Biosketch:

Dr R B Shukla qualified in Medicine from Prince of Wales Medical College, Patna (Patna University), India, in 1962 and passed MD in General Medicine in 1966. He came to the UK in 1969 and has served in the National Health Service ever since. A General Practitioner turned Geriatrician, he has been a Consultant Physician in Medicine for the Elderly at North Manchester General Hospital since 1982. His clinical responsibilities include general care of the elderly and Rehabilitation, including orthopaedic-geriatric rehabilitation. His interests are Hypertension, Cardiac failure, Osteoporosis and falls in the elderly, Drug treatment in the elderly, Housing for the elderly and Retirement. A Fellow of Royal College of Physicians of Ireland (FRCP) since 1990, Dr Shukla has several publications to his credit. He has been involved in Policy issues, eg with NHS Health Advisory Service and with North Western Regional Mental Strategy.

Dr Sanjay Arya graduated from Nalanda Medical College, Patna, India in 1988. He obtained the MRCP, UK in 1994. He is currently on a Registrar rotation in Cardiology between Victoria Hospital in Blackpool and Wythenshaw Hospital in Manchester. He is involved in all aspects of invasive and non-invasive cardiology. He has a special interest in heart failure and coronary revascularization in the elderly.

This short chapter takes a much wider view of prescribing. Although several general points, including audit and research are touched upon, the main emphasis has been given to the following points:

a. Introduction – size of the problem.
b. Consultation pattern of elderly patients.
c. Advances in drug therapy of several clinical conditions.
d. General guidance on prescribing, with special reference to the full assessment of the patient. This forms the main theme of this chapter.
e. The value of good record-keeping, especially the computerised clinical data system within this country and in wider Europe.
f. Concluding remarks.

Introduction

Keeping abreast of advances in drug treatment of different diseases is a major challenge for a Clinician. Hence, prescribing of a drug should be considered both as a science and an art. The prescribing doctor should have the patient's full confidence. This becomes all the more important when we are reminded of the classical cynicism of Voltaire – which he uttered well over two and a quarter centuries ago – defining medical treatment as the art of pouring drugs of which one knew nothing into a patient whom one knew less[1, 7]. It is essential, therefore, that we prescribe drugs most appropriately, ie taking into account both the patient's overall condition (physical, mental and to some extent social) and the drug's profile, ie its effectiveness, side-effects and the cost. It is also important that a patient's choice is considered.

Consultation Pattern of Elderly Patients

In the primary care set-up with 34,000 General Practitioners in the UK, altogether 250 million consultations take place. A large chunk of these consultations relate to elderly patients. In this context, a few important facts need to be kept in mind:

i) Increased prescription rate does not parallel the increased consultation rate. It is true, though, that elderly patients consult their doctors more often than younger patients.
ii) Elderly women visit their doctors more than elderly men and they are on more medication than men.

iii) An important factor in drug side-effects in the elderly may be due to the fact that elderly patients may have their prescriptions checked less often than their younger counterparts[2]. Over 2000 patient user leaflets are approved by the Medical Control Agency. These could be distributed to patients when drugs are being dispensed[3].

Advances in Drug Therapy

During the last 15 years, great strides have been made in the treatment of several diseases, mainly of the cardiovascular and central nervous systems. This has clearly improved the quality of life of the patients. Listed in table 1 are the names of the newer drugs in some important diseases.

General Guidelines/Precautions while Prescribing

It is not possible to list all the guidelines and precautions in this short article. Only the main points are innumerated below:

1. Whether a drug is indicated at all, should be the first thought in the prescriber's mind[5]. One must, therefore, try to get the diagnosis right, as a wrong diagnosis is a harbinger of *wrong* treatment. In an elderly patient, it pays to find the cause of the patient's problem by his/her full assessment. One of us, (RBS), vividly remembers a 75 year old patient a while ago, who was being treated for uncontrolled atrial fibrillation with increasing doses of Digoxin (0.25 mg TDS, in fact) and Valium. Not surprisingly, the patient had become confused, drowsy and immobile. She turned out to be thyrotoxic after full assessment and thyroid function tests and did extremely well after radio-iodine treatment.
2. Occasionally one may not be sure of the possible side-effects of the drug being prescribed. If in doubt, MIMS or British National Formulary should be consulted. A stitch in time saves nine.
3. Whether a patient is allergic to a particular medication is likely to be missed in a multiple-partner practice. Drug allergy, therefore, should be clearly mentioned at a strategic place in the patient's notes.

Table 1

Name of the disease	Developments in drug therapy
Hypertension	– Calcium channel blockers and Angiotension-converting enzyme inhibitors – Recently introduced drug: Angiotensin II antagonist (losartan Potassium: cozaar)
Myocardial Infarction	– Thrombolysis therapy – Use of ACE inhibitors – Aspirin
Cardiac Failure	– Use of ACE inhibitors
Atrial Fibrillation	– Anti-coagulants (to reduce the risk of stroke)
Alzheimer's Dementia	– Tetrahydroamino acridine (THA) eg Tacrine. Liver function tests should be carefully monitored during therapy. (Not available on Prescription in UK, yet).
Depression	– 5HT re-uptake inhibitors, eg Fluvoxamine (Faverin), Sertraline (Lustral), Fluoxetine (Prozac) and Paroxetine (Seroxat). This group of drugs is a useful alternative; also Reversible MAO-A inhibitor, eg Moclobemide (Manerix)
Epilepsy	– Advances have taken place in the last decade in the treatment of epilepsy. Newer drugs are Vigabatrin, Gabapentin and *Lamotrigine* (Please see note below) – Side-effects need monitoring. – Not used as mono-therapy yet but useful as add-on therapy. More new drugs are in the pipeline.
Peptic Ulcer	– Treatment of H-pylori. Its eradication is indicated when a person with peptic ulcer disease is shown to have H-pylori[4]. Several Protocols are available and many more are in the pipeline.
Osteoporosis	– (a) Hormone replacement therapy in post-menopausal osteoporosis has been used for some time – (b) Cyclical Etidronate: didronel PMO in young elderly (65–75 years). – (c) Calcium and Vitamin D, eg. Calcichew D3 to old elderly (in house-bound, aged 80 and over).
Benign Prostatic Hyperplasia	– Selective 5-alpha reductase inhibitor, eg Proscar and the alpha blockers, eg Terazosin, Indoramin and Prazosin. (Initial response with proscar is promising)
Anti-Viral Agents	– eg Valaciclovir (Valtrex) indicated in treating shingles (Herpes zoster)

Note: Lamotrigine is now being used also as monotherapy for partial, primary and secondarily generalised tonic-clonic seizures (source: MIMS, Oct. 1995)

4. Patients must be clearly advised that a particular drug (hypnotics, anti-histamines, for example) may make them sleepy and their ability to drive may become impaired.

5. Elderly patients, in general, are more prone to have drug side-effects. The drugs acting on the nervous system should be prescribed with greatest caution, ie anti-Parkinson's and opiates.

6. Prescribing drugs for age-related symptoms is not only unnecessary but positively harmful, eg prescribing Prochlorperazine for giddiness is an example par-excellence.

7. Regular review of medications is a must. The best example is that of hypnotics and diuretics, especially if the latter has been prescribed for postural oedema. The dangers of repeat prescriptions are well-known.

8. Poor drug compliance could be due to our poor advice – patients must be properly advised what to do when the medicine runs out!

9. Patients should be warned that they should keep the drugs out of the reach of children.

10. It is important that patients are advised as to when to take the drugs in relation to meals, ie before, after or with food, or indeed when to avoid alcohol.

11. There are clinical situations where the lean body-weight of a patient needs to be considered while prescribing, for example, Digoxin.

12. Formularies are now available, both in Hospitals and General Practitioners' surgeries. These should be consulted, as and when necessary.

13. It is encouraging to note that audit on drug prescribing is taking place not only in the Hospitals but also in the community. Prescribing doctors should take note of the recommendations of such audits.

14. Protocols for treating various diseases (such as angina, peptic ulcer, H-pylori infection and osteoporosis) are now available both in Hospitals and General Practitioners' surgeries. These should be consulted, if necessary, when prescribing.

15. Prescribing of a drug by its generic name is preferable to its brand name because it is not only economical but also it provides the Pharmacist choice of brand names.

16. Finally, even if the diagnosis and drug doses are right, occasional problems do crop up in view of the prescriber's bad handwriting! This mistake may be avoided by printing the drug's name.

17. Looking at both national and international publications, it is welcoming to note that more studies/trials are being performed on elderly patients. This trend must continue, as the extrapolation of results of drug trials from younger patients to elderly patients may be positively harmful.

The Value of Good Clinical Records and the European Dimension

About a quarter of Europe's population is of pensionable age and most countries of Europe now have specialist Geriatric facilities[6]. When a doctor is planning a patient's management, he has to rely on the patient's clinical data to formulate a suitable drug-regime. Clearly, this task will be made easier if the clinical data – past or present – is quickly available. To improve the care of our patients, one should, therefore, take advantage of information technology, both in this country and across Europe.

It is now generally agreed, that the computerised clinical data system or electronic patient records which allow automatic searching and summarising of specific items, has the potential to overcome the inherent problems associated with conventional medical records[7]. We feel that elderly patients, many of them with multiple pathologies, will benefit from this data system as this would

a. help sensible prescribing; and

b. help reduce polypharmacy in patients who are already on medications. After all, reducing polypharmacy should be one of the main aims of sensible prescribing.

Efforts are already underway to have computerised health records across Europe. It is hoped that the ultimate European health records will be comprehensive yet simple to use (automatically translated between languages) and medico-legally acceptable[8].

Again, there is going to be a welcome change in the working of the provision of medicines in the United Kingdom. The European Medicines Evaluation Agency (EMEA) has been established from 1 January 1995 (up until now, the Medicines Act of September 1971 has provided the legal basis for controlling the manufacture, sale, supply and marketing of Medicines in the United Kingdom). EMEA, which is based in London, will act as a co-ordinating centre, housing and servicing the Committee for Proprietary Medicinal Products (CPMP). This body will be equivalent to our Committee on Safety of Medicines (CSM). This new arrangement will ensure uniform arrangement for licensing drugs throughout the European Union. The whole process is likely to be completed by 1998. UK Medicines Control Agency, concerned with the marketing of drugs in only the UK will, of course, continue to function beyond 1998[9].

All in all, there is a need to get involved in shaping both medical gerontology and primary care across European countries now that we are part and parcel of expanded Europe. Only then can we provide adequate care to our elderly patients on a wider scale.

Concluding Remarks

Drugs, whether old or new, are not silver bullets. While they can benefit patients from minor ailments to life-threatening diseases, they themselves can cause serious adverse drug-reactions. Apart from medical, it is doctor's legal and ethical responsibility to inform patients about the proper use and adverse side-effects of prescribed drugs[3]. Experience shows that when in doubt, patients do not come to harm if their medications are stopped, unless, of course, the drugs happen to be very specific, ie a steroid in Addison's disease and Insulin/oral anti-diabetic drugs.

In summary, then, a prescriber should have four aims: (i) to maximise effectiveness; (ii) to minimise risks; (iii) to minimise costs and, (iv) to have due consideration for the patient's choice[10].

Prescribing and Therapeutic Strategies

Practical Points

1. **Full assessment of a patient's condition** is the first requisite of sensible prescribing.

2. **Before prescribing**, it should also be decided whether the drug being prescribed is for cure, (eg pneumonia), prevention (eg osteoporosis), or palliation (eg pain in patients with advanced cancer)

3. **Before prescribing**, we should consider the efficacy, the side-effects and the cost-effectiveness of a drug.

4. **Adequate communication with the patient** re duration of treatment and important side-effects of prescribed drugs is essential.

5. **Regular supervision of prescribed drugs** is necessary as drugs may need to be discontinued, their doses reduced, side-effects, if any, observed *or* even drugs changed altogether.

6. **Improving compliance** could be done by doctors (by prescribing a drug in suspension form – if possible – if tablets cannot be swallowed; and advising what to do when the drug runs out), District Nurses (by supervising confused patients), pharmaceutical industry (suitable packaging) and Pharmacists (supplementing doctor's advice).

7. **Good record keeping** should be considered as part and parcel of sensible prescribing.

8. **In order to keep pace with drug developments**, there is a need for continuing education for both hospital doctors and General Practitioners.

References

1. Dunlop, D (1976) *Principles of treatment*, in: Current Medical Treatment, Harvard CWH (ed), John Wright and Sons Ltd, 1–15.

2. Allan SC, Fairweather DS & Brocklehurst JC (1987) *Prescribing for old people*, in: Case Studies in Medicine for the Elderly, M&P Press, 163–171.

3. George FC (1994) *What do patients need to know about prescribed drugs?*, Prescriber's Journal, 34, page 10.

4. *Eradication of Helicobacter pylori should be pivotal in managing peptic ulceration*, BMJ (1994); 309, 1570–72.

5. *Prescribing for the Elderly*. British National Formulary, 25, (1993), 14.

6. Dall JLC (1994) *The greying of Europe* (in Series, Medicine in Europe), BMJ, 309, 1282–1285

7. Wyatt JC (1994) *Clinical Data System, Part I: data and medical records*, Lancet, 34, 1543–1547.

8. Kalra D (1994) *Electronic health records: The European Scene*, BMJ, 309, 1358–61.

9. Drug and Therapeutic Bulletin December 1994, 32, 89–90.

10. Barber N (1995) *What Constitutes good prescribing*, BMJ, 310, 923–5.

Further Reading

1. Freely J (ed) (1994) *New Drugs* 3rd edition. BMA.

2. BMA/Royal Pharmaceutical Society (1994) *British National Formulary No 28*.

3. Grimley Evans J & Franklin Williams T (1992) *Oxford Text Book of Geriatric Medicine*, Oxford University Press.

4. *Medicine in Europe* – Intermittent series of articles looking at medical issues in Europe, published in BMJ (1994–95).

5. *Prescriber's Journal* (HMSO). Published 6 times a year.

6. Tyrer PJ (1982) *Drugs in psychiatric practice*, Butterworth.

Chapter 39

Complementary Medicine

Dr Andrew Demetriou
MB, ChB, DRCOG, DCH, MRCGP, MFHom.
Family Doctor and Homeopathic Physician

&

Sister Myra Coyle SRN, SCM, HEd Cert.
Huntley Mount Medical Centre
Huntley Mount Road
Bury
Lancs
BL9 6JA

Biosketch:

Andrew Demetriou works in NHS and private practice as a General Practitioner and Homoeopath providing a holistic approach to family medicine. He is a trainer and member of the Bury MAAG. Publications and research interests involve prevention of CHD, audit, quality of care and complementary medicine involving the team approach in primary care.

Myra Coyle is a Nurse, Midwife, Look After Your Heart Tutor and Counsellor working in primary care with two General Practitioners who also practice Homoeopathy and Acupuncture. She has special interests in Prevention, Stress Management and Homoeopathy. The ethos of approach to all aspects of her work is one of 'the whole person'.

Introduction

'First, do no harm'
         Hippocrates

As the name suggests, the various therapies under the umbrella of complementary medicine are practised alongside the conventional orthodox medicine. There are around 160 complementary therapies in existence worldwide and several of them are still to be evaluated scientifically. The three major complementary therapies presently in use are, homoeopathy, acupuncture and osteopathy, all of which have a place in treating the elderly.

At present, we are experiencing a breaking down of barriers in the West and a prime example is the acceptance of acupuncture as a respectable form of alternative pain relief.

Trials in a conventional setting have shown the value of this therapy in treating acute and chronic conditions. The discovery of endorphins has given a better understanding of the biochemical nature of pain and has, therefore, given scientific credibility to acupuncture.

Acupuncture and homeopathy are both ideally suited to General Practice. Once full postgraduate training and qualification are achieved in the complementary specialty chosen, there are many opportunities to combine both orthodox and complementary medicine. Because complementary therapies relatively cost less, they are particularly suited to many countries that can ill afford expensive technological medicine. Modern day Doctors see themselves as part of a wider team. Having a complementary practitioner as a member of the team can provide enhanced and positive benefits to patient care.

Complementary Therapies

Acupuncture

This is an ancient Chinese system of medicine involving the use of needles. Acupuncturists maintain that regular sessions perhaps at the change of seasons, keep the body 'healthy' by 'tuning' up the systems promoting health and energy, and helping to alleviate diseases of ageing. It is now more accessible and has proven effective over the past decade[1].

Alexander Technique

This is a method of re-training the body's movements and positions in order to improve posture and relieve conditions such as neck pain, back pain and headaches. It can relieve stress and promotes harmony between mind and body. This technique is very popular amongst musicians.

Aromatherapy

This is the fine art of using plant oils to stimulate the 'body rhythms'. It is most useful in the elderly where the metabolism is naturally slower; using various essential oils to restore the balance is thought to delay the ageing process of the skin and help the regeneration of tissue cells thus promoting better health.

Biorhythms

A method of using a chart system to gauge good and bad days. The physical, emotional and intellectual fluctuations charted are useful in the elderly to work out which days are suitable for which activity, thus conserving energy and preserving mind and body for a longer and more rewarding life.

Biochemics

Biochemics is simply a replacement therapy of the natural mineral salts which are essential for normal body function, and are reduced in the elderly due to a combination of natural ageing, bad diet and lack of exercise. Replacing these tissue salts restores the natural balance, particularly after an illness, helping the body to combat disease and prolong active life. For example, KALI PHOS, KALI MUR, SILICA are some tissue salts used in this kind of treatment.

Chiropractic

This is primarily a pain relief procedure involving manipulation which also combines the use of modern technology, such as X-rays and similar diagnostic procedures. Most patients attend with musculo-skeletal pain especially the lower back and neck. This is very popular in America.

Colour Therapy

This is a natural therapy from light. The human body is thought to need colour to re-generate cells to sustain life. Red light has been used to stimulate circulation and raise blood pressure, while Blue light has a calming effect. Colour has been found to affect mood and helps heighten concentration. People react to colourful environments in a much more positive way, lifting the spirits of the elderly which in turn reflects on the quality of their life.

Faith Healing

This speaks for itself. Through an individual's faith in himself or herself or religious belief, which encourages a positive approach to illness, stress and suffering is relieved. This is particularly true in elderly people whose religion has sustained them through their life allowing the body's natural defences to operate without fear and anxiety. The companionship of that faith allows the problems of ageing to be shared.

Herbal Medicine

Phytotherapy or herbal remedies use only natural plants and herbs. This form of treatment has stood the test of time with few side effects, but as with any medicine, care has to be taken with prescribing. The remedies are fairly cheap and easily obtainable over the counter. Herbal remedies can be used as part of the daily diet; garlic, for example has been shown to be effective in the prevention of coronary heart disease. Infusions of herbal tea can be beneficial in many disorders.

BACH remedies are a form of herbal medicine, but use a slightly different principle. A mixture of herb or plant with springwater infused with sunlight produces the dew principle. Altogether, there are thirty eight BACH remedies. They are useful in self-treatment. The remedies are proven to be very safe and are becoming increasingly popular.

Homoeopathy

This is the only complementary therapy fully integrated in the National Health Service (NHS). There are five centres of treatment in the NHS where General Practitioners can refer patients. These centres are based in London, and other places (appendix 1). In-patient facilities are also available but by far, most of the work is based on an out-patient basis. The Faculty of Homoeopathy at the Royal London Homoeopathic Hospital was founded by an Act of Parliament in 1950, two years after the NHS Act.

Homoeopathy is derived from the Greek meaning 'like suffering'.

In Latin, the phrase 'similia similibus curentur' also describes the main principle of 'let like, cure like'. Remedies are derived either from plant, animal, mineral or diseased tissue, whereby the extract is diluted and succussed (shaken) to such a degree that at high dilutions none of the original molecules of the substance remain in the diluent. The physical changes imparted to the diluent by this process is thought to give it an activity, which in turn when taken as a medicine sublingually, stimulates a patient's immune system to facilitate a cure or to alleviate symptoms[2]. This is in contrast to conventional medicine where psychological emotions are suppressed with sedatives and anxiolytics, pain with analgestics, infection with antibiotics, all suppressing the body's reaction to these situations. Homoeopathic remedies, then, stimulate the body's immune system enhancing its healing properties to overcome such conditions as infection, inflammation, rheumatological conditions and psychological disorders, enabling the body to recover.

In life threatening conditions there is a place for conventional and homoeopathic treatment being used together. As Hahnemann said in the 18th century, 'there are no diseases, only sick people', referring to the symptom-complex pertaining to an individual patient rather than a disease label. Repertoirising involves matching the patient's symptoms-complex as closely as possible to a similar remedy symptom-complex, thus facilitating the choices of remedy in homoeopathic prescribing.

Research using double blind placebo controlled trials have shown the positive aspects of some treatments in homoeopathy, thus demonstrating the therapeutic potential of homoeopathy[3, 4]. On cost alone the Data Research Unit at Bristol Homoeopathic Hospital has shown that the average expenditure per patient of homoeopathic remedies was five fold less than the average cost of conventional prescribing in general practice. Integrating homoeopathic and conventional medicine systems could have great economic and therapeutic benefits. A survey of family Doctors in the UK who offer both homoeopathic and conventional treatment, found that one quarter of prescriptions were for homoeopathic remedies, and that they prescribed 12% fewer drugs than the national average[5]. The figures compare favourably with France where 10% of the total prescribing is for homoeopathic remedies.

Practical Examples

For the elderly, homoeopathy offers a system of treatment free from side-effects. Homoeopathic remedies often used in musculo-skeletal disorders are: Rhus toxicodendron, Ruta gravis, Rhododendron, Causticum and Bryonia. Homoeopathic remedies such as Apis can relieve congestive cardiac failure more gently and 'naturally' than diuretics, alleviating the shortness of breath in mild heart failure without inflicting the frequency of micturition which so often leads to urinary incontinence. Night cramps can be relieved by the use of Cuprum metallicum on an intermittent basis, rather than the perpetual prescription of Quinine sulphate.

Pre and post-operative recovery, rehabilitation after a stroke and the post-trauma pain can all be helped with a few doses of Arnica. Depression, insomnia and other psychological problems, including the physical complaints of terminal care, can be alleviated with homoeopathy.

Respiratory infections, upper and lower, can be treated with such remedies. In pneumonia, however, some homoeopaths would consider using antibiotics as well as homoeopathy. Vertigo, skin complaints, any infective process including cellulitis, will respond to homoeopathic treatment. Indeed, virtually any complaint can be treated with homoeopathy. All remedies are given sublingually; thus a patient with gastroenteritis, for example, or other stomach complaint, will tolerate this route much better than conventional drugs which may possibly cause upper gastrointestinal side-effects.

Hydrotherapy

This is one of the most neglected forms of therapies. It is also one of the most relaxing and invigorating therapies, guaranteed to encourage healing, and is particularly beneficial for ageing joints and muscles. Just watching or listening to the flow of water has relaxing powers. It can be used as a spray, mineral compress or bath and in the pool or the sea. The most important factor is the temperature. Water flotation is a fairly new phenomenon in Britain but is currently gathering momentum.

An anti-gravity effect is created by a dense solution of Epsom Salts which eliminates the body's specific gravity and imparts a feeling of total weightlessness. This method has many benefits for the problems of ageing and can also be used in relieving stress and anxiety.

Hypnotherapy

In Greek, Hypnos means sleep. This method of treatment has been around since 1843. Hypnotherapy is now practised more and more by the medical profession and psychologists, as a valuable form of complementary medicine. This technique has been used successfully for relief of pain, emotional problems, phobias and even for smoking cessation, to name but a few conditions. It must only be practised by an experienced therapist.

Naturopathy

Naturopathy is a process of simply giving the body a helping hand to cure itself. Here, positive thinking helps measures like a balanced diet, exercise, massage, relaxation and breathing techniques to produce good effect. Basically, it encourages all things natural to promote good health and a longer life. This is suitable for all age groups.

Osteopathy

This is probably the most well known complementary therapy. The art of manipulation, particularly of the spine and neck should only be carried out by fully trained, approved Practitioners. The work of the osteopath is well documented and used widely in the treatment of musculo-skeletal conditions in the elderly.

Reflexology

(A form of ancient chinese medicine) Foot massage is a gentle method of stimulating specific reflex areas in the foot. Reflex stimulation is thought to help in certain areas of the body, relieving stress, anxiety and physical conditions. Having reflexology treatment at intervals can work in a preventative way, it can do little harm and is very relaxing. Back pain, heart and circulatory conditions and migraine are among several conditions where reflexology has proved beneficial[6].

Yoga

Yoga is a comprehensive system of spiritual, mental and physical training which encourages mind over body. Most areas have yoga teachers. This technique combines relaxation with gentle physical exercise and is fairly popular, more so with women. Once learned, the technique could be used alone or in groups.

Discussion

Undoubtedly, there is a real need for the same high standard practised in orthodox medicine to be applied to complementary therapies. True complementary medicine can, then, be practised utilising all modern medical knowledge to arrive at a diagnosis by history taking, examination and investigation. Once a diagnosis is arrived at, the place of complementary medicine is then to offer safe treatment with minimal side-effects. Many therapies rely on the body's own healing processes, drawing on the 'natural healing' propensity to aid recovery to health. Here, too, the psychological, physical and social factors are taken into account. Counselling is often appropriate in both complementary and allopathic medicine. Lifestyle plays a major role in many medical conditions presenting to the Doctor, and just as an orthodox Doctor would give appropriate advice on alcohol, smoking, diet, weight control, exercise and relaxation to relieve stress, so would a complementary practitioner. Thus, the holistic approach provides a detailed profile and treatment of the whole person.

At least 10% of hospital admissions are due to iatrogenic diseases. Using complementary medicine wisely may well reduce that in the elderly. It is the possibility of drug side-effects which most often lead the elderly patient in search of alternatives. It would be unethical to give unrealistically high expectations of therapies and the limitations of both complementary and allopathic forms of treatment must always be explained, especially in relation to the ageing process.

For the elderly patients seeking complementary therapies, there is difficulty in obtaining any information from the NHS. The current Health Service structure makes it difficult for patients to have any real informed choice to have a particular course of treatment. Many patients seeking alternative therapies, therefore, have to rely on private treatment. Where family Doctors are trained in complementary therapies, this gives them the ideal opportunity to offer care on a day to day basis with on-going treatment and continuity of care. The individual tailoring of treatment is then possible by offering these complementary options to the patient.

The Way Forward

So what needs to be done now that more patients are turning towards complementary therapies? We would like to make the following suggestions:

1. Planned research is needed in important branches of various complementary therapies.
2. Both medical and non-medical Practitioners undertaking the various forms of complementary therapies need adequate training, for which Governmental funding will be necessary.
3. In the wider contexts, now that we are part and parcel of the EU (European Union), there should be a regulatory body at the EU level to oversee important branches of complementary therapies. The above measure, it is hoped, would not only improve the overall image of complementary therapies, but, more importantly, will make these therapies more acceptable and indeed beneficial to the growing number of patients of all ages, especially the elderly.

'Length of days is not what makes age honourable, nor number of years the true measure of life; understanding, this is man's grey hairs, untarnished life, this is ripe old age.'
The Book of Wisdom 4.8–9.

Complementary Medicine

Practical Points

1. There is now a growing interest in various forms of complementary therapies.

2. The three major complementary therapies currently in use are homoeopathy, acupuncture and osteopathy and all have a place in treating the elderly.

3. Complementary and orthodox medicine can be practised together.

4. The benefits include fewer side-effects and less iatrogenic disease, economy of care and a holistic approach to patient's problems.

5. Both medical and non-medical Practitioners in complementary therapies should have adequate training.

6. Planned research is needed in various forms of alternative therapy.

7. Closer liaison should be established and maintained with those countries – like India and China – where the various forms of complementary therapies are well established.

References

1. Dundee JW & McMillan CM (1990) *Clinical uses of P6 acupuncture antiemesis*. Acupunct. Electrother. Res., 15 (3–4), *211–215*.

2. Turner P (1959) *Is there a bridge between homoeopathy and conventional medicine?*, Homoeopathy, 39, *146–158*.

3. Fisher P, Greenwood A, Huskinson EC et al. (1989) *Effect of homoeopathic treatment of fibrositis (primary fibromyalgia)*, British Medical Journal, 299, *365–366*.

4. Reilly D, Taylor M, McShany C et al. (1986) *Is homoeopathy a placebo response?* Controlled trial of homoeopathic potency, with pollen in hayfever as model, Lancet, 2, *881–885*.

5. Swayne J (1989) *Survey of the use of homoeopathic medicine in the UK Health System*, Journal of the Royal College of General Practitioners, 39, *100–106*.

6. Hall NM (ed) (1994) *Reflexology – a way to better health*. Gateway Books, Bath 1991 (Reprinted 1994), *123–155*.

Bibliography

1. British Medical Association, (1993) *Complementary Medicine; new approaches to good practice*, Oxford University Press.

2. Boyd H (1981) *Introduction to homoeopathic medicine*, Beaconsfield.

3. Demetriou A (1990) *Homoeopathy in practice*, in: Members reference book, The Royal College of General Practitioners, Sterling Publications, 415–416.

4. Pietroni P (ed) (1991) *Readers Digest Family Guide to Alternative Medicine*, Readers Digest.

Appendix 1 – Homoeopathy's Centres of Treatment in U.K.

London

The Royal London Homoeopathic Hospital
Great Ormond Street
London WC1N 3HR
Tel: 0171–837–8833
(Out-patients: 0171–837–7821)

Glasgow

Glasgow Homoeopathic Hospital
1000 Great Western Road
Glasgow G12 0NR
Tel: 0141–339–2786

Out-patient Clinic for Adults and Children
Buchanan Street
Balliston
Glasgow G69 6DY
Tel: 0141–771–7396/7397

Liverpool

The Department of Homoeopathic Medicine
Mossley Hill Hospital
Park Avenue
Liverpool L18 8BU
Tel: 0151–250–3000 Ext 278

Bristol

The Bristol Homoeopathic Hospital
Cotham Road
Cotham
Bristol BS6 6JU
Tel: 01179–731231

Tunbridge Wells

Tunbridge Wells Homoeopathic Hospital
Church Road
Tunbridge Wells
Kent TN1 1JU
Tel: 01892–542977

Manchester (Non-NHS)

Manchester Homoeopathic Clinic
Brunswick Street
Manchester M13 9ST
Tel: 0161–273–2446

Further Reading List

1. Evans JG & Williams F (1992) *Oxford Textbook of Geriatric Medicine*, Oxford University Press, ISBN 261590-40.

2. Andrews K (1987) *Rehabilitation of the older adult*, Edward Arnold London, ISBN 0-7131-4524-2.

3. Age Concern (1986) *The Law and vulnerable elderly people*.

4. Bennett GJ & Ebrahim S (1992), *The essentials of health care of the elderly*. Edward Arnold London. ISBN 0-34-0545593.

5. Coni, Davison & Webster (1993) *Lecture notes on geriatrics*. 4th Edition; Blackwell Scientific Publications.

6. Lowry S (1991) *Housing and health*. British Medical Journal.

7. Jacques A (1992) *Understanding dementia*, 2nd Edition, Churchill Livingstone.

8. Marinker M (ed) (1990) *Medical audit and general practice*. British Medical Journal, for MSD Foundation.

9. Baker R & Presley P (eds) (1990) *The Practice Audit Plan*. Severn Faculty RCGP, ISBN 85084-1461, £3.50.

10. Thompson K (1990) *Commonsense geriatrics*. Clinical Press, ISBN 1-85457-007-2.

11. Elkrington A R & Khaw P T (1988) *ABC of Eyes*, British Medical Journal, £11.95, ISBN 0-7279-0240-7.

12. Pendleton D et al (1984) *The consultation: an approach to learning and teaching.* Oxford University Press, ISBN 0-19-261349-9.

13. Freeling P & Harri C (1984) The doctor-patient relationship. Churchill Livingstone, £5.95, ISBN 0-443-02375-1.

14. Roland M & Coulter A (1992) *Hospital referrals*. Oxford University Press, £18.50, ISBN 0-19-262174-2.

15. Williams EI (1995) *Caring for older people in the community*. Radcliffe Medical Press.

16. *Technology foresight – progress through partnership: health and life sciences*, HMSO. This is a new government report. Price £15.00.

17. Action on Elder Abuse (1995) *Everybody's business – taking action on elder abuse.* London.

Books which may be recommended to patients and carers

(From the 'Caring in a Crisis' Series published by Age Concern, 1268 London Road, London, SW16 4ER, 1994)

1. M Lewycka. *What to do and Who to turn to.*

2. M Lewycka. *Finding and paying for Residential and Nursing Home Care.*

3. S. White. *Going Home from Hospital.*

4. P Mares. *Caring for Someone who is Dying.*

General Index

Author Index

Wormals RP 138
Wrenn K 103
Wyatt JC 334, 336
Yemm R 132, 133
Yemmin RJ 133
Yen SSC 173
Young V 124
Yudkin JS 252
Zager M 285
Zhang F 260
Zhjang D 260
Zilkha E 190
Zimmerrn P 174

Printed in the United Kingdom for HMSO
Dd300763 1/96 C8 G559 10170